W9-CSS-571

Also by Anna Thomas

The Vegetarian Epicure (1972)

This is a Borzoi Book, published in New York by Alfred A. Knopf

the vegetarian epicure
book two

the vegetarian epicure book two

by anna thomas

illustrations by julie maas

alfred a. knopf   new york   1978

THIS IS A BORZOI BOOK PUBLISHED BY ALFRED A. KNOPF, INC.

Copyright © 1978 by Anna Thomas
Illustrations ©1978 by Julie Maas

Library of Congress Cataloging in Publication Data
Thomas, Anna.
    The vegetarian epicure, book two.

    Includes index.
    1.   Vegetarian cookery.   I.   Title.
TX837.T462   1978   641.6′5   77-16685
ISBN 0-394-41363-6
ISBN 0-394-73415-7 pbk.

Manufactured in the United States of America

Published April 24, 1978
Second Printing, April 1978

For my husband, Greg

acknowledgments

I would like to gratefully acknowledge my friend Gail Hand, for her cheerful and efficient help in preparing countless recipes; Judith Jones, for all her clear-headed and tactful editing and advice; and Gregory Nava, for running to the store so many times.

contents

Introduction   3

Menus   7

Breads   23

Soups   55

Sauces and Salad Dressings   93

Eggs, Soufflés, Omelets   111

Salads and Cold Vegetables   133

Stews, Casseroles, Hot Vegetable Dishes   163

Croquettes, Pâtés, Cheeses   191

Savory Pastries: Quiches, Pizzas, Pierogi   211

Crêpes   223

Italian Pastas, Vegetables, and Frittatas   235

Spanish Specialties, Including Tapas and Tortillas   261

Mexican Dishes   279

Indian Foods: Curries, Raitas, Pilaus, etc.   299

Desserts   323

Preserves and Relishes   361

Tiny Open-faced Sandwiches   379

Index   385

the vegetarian epicure
book two

introduction

Why a second book? Because we always itch to expand horizons. Book Two is not just a continuation of the first volume but an exploration of rich new lodes. The first book came out of my own past, and from the tremendous need for a collection of really good vegetarian recipes. This second volume is the result of new adventures: It broadens the scope of the gourmet vegetarian kitchen with forays into entirely different cuisines and cultures. It is a record of culinary discoveries that I'm eager to share, and a notebook of travels.

The writing of this book came about in a most enjoyable way. I spent the last four years traveling, eating, reading, taking notes, cooking, and writing. Work and whim took me through large parts of Europe—Portugal, Spain, Italy, France, Greece, Austria, Hungary, Poland—as well as to England, on a brief sally into the Middle East, and on a jaunt through Mexico. Everywhere I went, I was delighted by the food, by the rewards of being eager to sample the new and unfamiliar.

I thought of each meal as a little adventure (and some turned out to be big ones). When I was lucky enough to be staying with relatives or friends, I followed them into the kitchen and pestered them for their best recipes. If, while touring, I discovered a particularly wonderful restaurant, I didn't mind staying a day or two longer in that city to do it justice.

Many people, I found, were curious how a vegetarian could survive, and even eat splendidly, while traveling abroad. The answer is, easily.

Nearly everywhere I went, I discovered that the emphasis on meat was much less overwhelming than it is here in the United States, for economic reasons as well as from long-standing tradition. Most restaurant menus commonly include some enticing dishes made of fresh vegetables or fruits, eggs, cheeses, or grains. In all the *tavernas, trattorias, kellars, cafés,* and *ristorantes* I visited, the choices offered me ranged from adequate to exciting.

In Italy, of course, the antipasto and pasta were a constant temptation; in France we discovered omelets anew and ate dozens of cheeses that we had never tried before. In Madrid and Segovia, every restaurant offered an array of vegetable dishes, along with the eggy Spanish *tortillas*, which appeared in endless variation. And in England, that bastion of roast beef, the most sophisticated vegetarian cuisine was everywhere available, in a phenomenal number of Indian restaurants.

In Poland and Hungary we found marvelous fruit soups, pancakes in wonderful new roles, subtle and cooling salads made of cooked vegetables, and a whole repertoire of tasty ways with simple, fresh cheeses. I also recall evenings in Greece, sitting by the Aegean at sunset, munching grape leaves stuffed with rice and dill and washing them down with ouzo. And during the long, hot summer days in Cairo, when we weren't devouring the sweet, juicy watermelons, we were sampling *tahini* and *baba ghanouj* and hotly spiced bean cakes.

The list goes on; really, the only problem was not to overdo the pleasures of the table so much that a new wardrobe would become necessary en route!

In hotel rooms and on long train rides, my husband and I would reminisce and fill notebooks with descriptions of wonderful dishes we had eaten, along with the new ideas that cropped up constantly alongside these discoveries. Dining cars were best for this. Rumbling past slowly changing landscapes and thousands of telegraph poles, we detailed the high points of a culinary odyssey.

Whenever we returned home, the serious cooking would shortly begin. Great eating became even better as favorite friends joined us at the table. I would experiment with re-creating memorable dishes from our travels and adapting foreign ideas to my own style.

Friends and family were often gathered in our little dining room, under the mirrored globe, to sample the new fare. I would gauge their responses, make more notes, and cook or bake things again if necessary—until it was all absolutely right.

Of course, not every recipe in this book is the fruit of travel. Often my friends share their particular specialties with me. Sometimes I feel the need of a little celebration, or I have a house guest to pamper, and then I like to devise something new, and usually write it down. But it is just a matter of doing something I enjoy, and that's just how I hope this book will be used by others.

In the course of all this testing and trying, my feelings about the main "secret" of good cooking were constantly reaffirmed. The one piece of advice I invariably repeat when people ask me how one should go about cooking well is this: Use good ingredients. Always, always start with the best possible ingredients—the freshest butter and milk and cream, the nicest vegetables, the finest pasta, the loveliest rice, vine- or tree-ripened fruit, aged cheeses, good wines. You won't be sorry. With high quality at the outset, you have a fair chance of achieving superior results. Yes, it's possible to destroy even the best ingredients if you don't know what you're doing, but at least you can be confident that they won't destroy you! So procure the best you can, don't be shy in the kitchen, and good things will follow.

As in the first *Vegetarian Epicure*, the good things in this book are meatless, but it is not a book for vegetarians only. It is for anyone who can enjoy foods like fettucine alfredo, pea soup with dumplings, fondue, pimiento and olive quiche, tomatoes filled with hearts of palm, Liptauer cheese, wild mushroom soufflé, Caesar salad, and frozen strawberry mousse. It is true, however, that a great many people today are eating less meat, for reasons of health, economy, or simply personal preference, and I am convinced that these new styles in dining, far from being dreary, can be infinitely varied and inspired. For those who want to expand their repertoire because they are eating less meat than they used to, and for those who, like myself, prefer not to eat meat at all but don't intend to compromise on the satisfactions of really delicious food, I hope this book provides a bonanza of pleasureable eating.

Arranging all this new material in a manner that made sense was an interesting task, so I'd like to say something about the way we finally did it. Several chapters are devoted to the foods of specific countries; most of the recipes, however, are grouped by type rather than by place of origin. With such an arrangement, there are bound to be a few things which fit into more than one category, so a bit of cross-referencing has been done. Gazpacho, for example, is included with the soups, but there is a note about it at the end of the section on Spanish foods.

I hope, finally, that this book will be as enjoyable for you as it has been for me. The most important thing about food, after all, is enjoyment, and what a grand thing it is that eating is such a renewable pleasure: We always do get hungry again! Preparing those delectable meals should be a pleasure as well. It's an act of creation that is all the more charming because it is so ephemeral. There's something pleasing about the fact that a great meal is not a lasting thing; that, rather, all the thought and work are enjoyed by one small group of people, for one brief and delightful while, then vanish, to linger in memory only.

We all eat, and it would be a sad waste of opportunity to eat badly. It's true that the meals we consume in a lifetime number in the tens of thousands, but the number is finite; each one should be as nice as it can be, for it can never be regained.

So, have a good time, and *buon gusto!*

menus

A good menu is like a good story. It must have the proper balance of dramatic elements, sorted out and arranged in such an order that each new course fulfills the promise of the one that came before while setting the scene for the one to follow, and everything must be resolved in the end, for unlike some stories, all meals should have happy endings.

Before plunging on to the ways in which this is accomplished, I should say a word or two about vegetarian menus versus traditional ones. It makes sense that a pattern that works for meals designed primarily around meat won't work so well for a varied assortment of nonmeat dishes. I won't say that vegetarian cooking has no "main courses" because there clearly are meals which do have such a central dish. However, that is just one part of a flexible range of possibilities, and more often than not, a fine meatless menu will consist of two or three complementary courses of equal importance.

This is no new idea, nor is it particular to vegetarian cooking. The *primero* and *secundo* of an Italian meal are an example of this style of eating. Spain has a similar tradition: The typical restaurant menu there shows no special categories for soup, salad, or entrée; rather, foods are listed in three groups, the last being the most substantial, both in weight and in price, and dinners are composed from these groups according to the diner's own preference.

This sort of attractive flexibility should be kept in mind when planning a meatless menu. It allows for a real variety of satisfying meals, any of which can make delicious culinary sense on its own terms. As long as one doesn't try to force vegetarian cooking into a narrow form which does not suit it, then ideas can be found everywhere, and tasty meals devised according to a few basic rules.

Contrast, as a good storyteller knows, is an invaluable tool in creating effect. The simpler the dish preceding your pièce de résistance, the more wonderful the latter will seem. Surprise, too, is a dramatist's stock in trade. But the most effective surprise is the one that, once sprung, is quickly followed by the sense that it was inevitable. Of course, you should consider always the tastes of the diners, the time of year, the time of day, and the setting. A candlelit dinner in a formal dining room on a nice, crisp, evening in November is quite a different story from a picnic in August or a family meal in the kitchen.

Practically speaking, the question is, with every meal, where exactly to begin? The best way is with a blaze of inspiration, but lacking that (and we all have our off days), start with one good, solid idea. It might be a particular dish, a type of dish, or even a certain ethnic flavor for which you've developed a sudden craving. Then consider what is in season. There's nothing like seven or eight months' deprivation to whet the appetite for crisp stalks of asparagus in the spring or ripe, golden pumpkins and roasted chestnuts in autumn. Whatever your idea, seasonal planning is a surefire way to proceed. Having considered the possibilities, give a thought to the limitations as well. If it's going to be a buffet for twenty, then you'll want to concentrate on dishes that can be prepared ahead of time, will keep well, and are served with a minimum of fuss. And for any kind of meal, try not to plan more than one or two dishes which will require your last-minute attention, unless you thrive on the edge of hysteria.

When preliminaries are decided, think in terms of balancing sweet dishes with tart ones, hearty with light, and creamy food with something that will afford a crisp, satisfying crunch. If it's pasta that you're hankering for, then you'll want to start with tangy marinated vegetables or salad with a vinaigrette dressing, and the dessert should be light. If it's a birthday, and cake will be required after dinner, avoid starchy or overly heavy dishes. One rich and saucy course is generally all the sauce a meal will want, and the same is true, as a rule, of foods sautéed in decadent amounts of butter or olive oil.

All these suggestions, though, are merely suggestions, and not law. If an unusual combination of foods strikes you as being perfectly appetizing, go ahead and try it! If you know that the group for whom you are cooking develops a prodigious capacity for sweets at Christmastime, indulge it and serve three desserts at your gala dinner. Or, if you're longing to do something that is deliberately out of season and are able to procure ingredients of high quality, by all means have fresh strawberries or melons (flown halfway around the world) in the middle of December. Taste and circumstance will guide you, after all, but imagination will set you free.

There is only one rule that must never, under any circumstances, be broken: Don't try to prepare something if you can't, for any reason, procure the highest quality ingredients for it. However good your idea, no dish is better than what goes into it, and the best planned menu won't save it.

When it comes time to cook, make everything as lovely to look at as you can, arranging colors and shapes with as much care as you do seasonings; keep your sense of humor; and enjoy yourself.

One final note. Even the best story needs the proper telling to bring it off, and so we come to the idea of timing. A meal should be served as thoughtfully as it is planned and prepared. Now, I'm not suggesting that you should starve anyone to ensure the proper reception for your food, but a little bit of a wait among pleasant company can be quite enjoyable and serves to heighten not only the appetite but the drama as well.

In the case of the omelet or the soufflé, the fresh, hot crêpes, or pasta *al dente*, the timing is nothing short of critical, and it is far better for the diner to wait awhile for the soufflé than the other way around. But any time at all that food is being served in courses, hurrying from one to the next is not recommended. Remember the value of suspense! Allow enough time to savor each dish with the proper, leisurely absorption and to deliciously anticipate the following one.*

In Florence, in restaurants like Che' Ce' Ce' and Fagioli, the antipasto is generally the heart and soul of a meal or even the whole of it. There, the antipasto is not some insignificant tray of celery sticks and olives brought to your table by a waiter. No, indeed. The magnificent sight of it grips your attention from the moment you enter and dominates it thereafter. A table of awe-inspiring size is laden with an abundant assortment of raw and cooked salads, marinated dishes, pickles and olives and peppers of all sorts, mild and sharp concoctions, heavy and light ones. Once, at Che' Ce' Ce', we tried counting—and lost track somewhere around forty.

You probably don't have the facilities or the inclination to set out an antipasto of quite such wealth at home, but it's not too much trouble, really, to toss together a selection of four or five dishes, augmented by some good, vinegary things from jars or from a delicatessen. Then serve a great pasta, not overdone and not too saucy, and a light or fruity dessert.

The ornaments on either side of a recipe indicate that it is included in this book.

The two meals that follow are reminiscent, in a scaled-down way, of the way we ate in Florence.

ᴥ antipasto ᴥ
pickled peppers, lima bean salad,
peperonata, tomatoes with vinaigrette dressing,
cured olives, sliced provolone cheese

ᴥ penne al cardinale ᴥ

ᴥ pasta with creamy tomato sauce ᴥ

ᴥ melons in vermouth ᴥ
almond cookies or torrone

espresso

ᴥ antipasto ᴥ
marinated mushrooms, garbanzo bean salad,
fresh mozzarella salad, frittata of zucchini,
pickled peppers, cured olives,
sliced tomatoes and cucumbers, green onions

ᴥ penne al boccalone ᴥ

ᴥ pasta with spicy herb sauce ᴥ

ᴥ cherry and amaretto soufflé ᴥ

espresso

A lovely and festive dinner, with a high amusement quotient, this is designed for a small group—four to six, ideally—sitting at a round table. The salads can be prepared well ahead of time and likewise the fabulous dessert. Only the fondue wants some last-minute stirring in the kitchen.

I like to put each antipasto in individual oblong bowls or dishes and ring them around the chafing dish or fondue pot in the middle of the table. If you have a lazy Susan large enough to carry this entire operation, then you're really in business. Pass a large basket of cubed bread first so that all can take as much as they like onto their plates, and pour the wine. Bring the fondue out, adjust the flame under it, and the job is done. The idea is to nibble on bites of salads in between scoops of fondue.

ᴥ gnocchi salad, white bean salad ᴥ
ᴥ eggplant caviar, peperonata, ᴥ
pickled peppers, cured olives

ᴥ italian fondue ᴥ
cubes of french or italian bread

ᴥ spumoni cake ᴥ

espresso

Here is another kind of Italian dinner.

The dish which needs your real attention at the last moment is the Spaghetti e Cipolla, of course. Don't let the pasta cook a moment too long. Drain it as soon as it is *al dente*, have the onion sauce ready and steaming hot, toss them together, and serve instantly—on warmed plates. Don't make the portions too large, though, or the delicious stuffed eggplant (which can wait in the oven an extra five minutes with no harm done) could be too much.

After a filling meal, fruit is the best. In this case, oranges and tangerines would be welcome, or melons of any kind.

☙ insalatone ❧
(a marinade of cooked vegetables)

☙ spaghetti e cipolle ❧
(spaghetti and onions)

☙ melanzana al forno ❧
(baked eggplant)

assorted fresh fruit

espresso

In Spain, *tapas* belong to *tapa* bars. They are, by definition, those snacks that are eaten, in small individual portions, to accompany a glass of wine while one is standing at the bar. I ate many fine dinners in Madrid by roaming through several good bars of this type and having a little of this here and a little of that there, with many glasses of red wine. Once back in California, I sorely missed the *tapa* bars, so I'd prepare a little selection of my own tapas and serve them buffet-style to my friends— with Spanish wine, of course, or *sangría* in the summertime.

☙ tortilla española ❧

☙ ensaladilla russa ❧

☙ champiñónes a la plancha ❧
(steamed mushrooms)

☙ barcelona white bean salad ❧

☙ roasted eggplant and peppers in oil ❧

cured olives

cheeses

crusty bread or rolls

hearty red spanish wine

For cold days and hearty appetites, Spanish Cocido is really a whole meal: The cooking broth combined with vermicelli makes a light soup, to be followed by the assorted stewed vegetables, garbanzo beans, and dumplings, then a light salad to clear the palate before dessert.

∕∞ cocido ∞
with crusty rolls or garlic bread

tossed green salad

∕∞ flan ∞
(caramel custard)

coffee

In Mexico tortillas often appear in every course. In this simple but interesting meal the popular appetizer Guacamole is served with tortilla chips, followed by an unusual tortilla soup, and then Enchiladas, which are simply stuffed and sauced tortillas.

∞ guacamole ∞
(a spicy avocado dip)

∞ tortilla soup tlaxcalteca ∞

∞ enchiladas salsa verde ∞
∞ mexican rice ∞

fresh fruit

Croquettes, or _croquetas_, are a big favorite in the _tapa_ bars of Madrid, and the Menestra de Verduras, a hearty and interesting assortment of stewed vegetables, is equally popular in the restaurants. Although this is a very Spanish meal, I find that a bit of tomato-apple chutney or even some cranberry relish goes very well with the rich, mild croquettes.

∞ tossed salad with herb dressing ∞

∞ egg croquettes ∞

∞ menestra de verduras ∞
(spanish steamed vegetables)

∞ apple tart ∞

With this Mexican dinner you can be very flexible. If you don't care for beer or tequila, the Cantaloupe Water, a very cooling drink, can be served at the start of the meal and sipped throughout. It makes a pleasant foil for the hot sauce that accompanies everything. Or it can be served at the end as a very light sort of fruit dessert.

∞ avocado tacos ∞
∞ bean and potato tacos ∞
∞ hot sauce ∞

∞ rajas con queso ∞
(peppers with cheese)
∞ fresh, hot corn tortillas ∞

∞ cantaloupe water ∞

The little *tortitas* that make the first course of this meal should be freshly made and warm, but you can shape the shells of corn dough, or *masa*, ahead of time and just do the actual baking and filling, which doesn't take long, at the last minute. *Tortitas* are one of the best accompaniments to a good margarita I've ever tasted, so have your glasses salted and a cold pitcher of margaritas ready when the shells come out of the oven. The rest of the meal is simple enough to prepare and serve if you only keep in mind that refried beans should be cooked for a long time and enchiladas only long enough so that they are piping hot all through.

margaritas
tortitas con queso

spinach enchiladas suizas
spicy refried beans

strawberry water

The salad is satisfying but not heavy, and the Cheese Soup elevates it to a perfectly pleasant warm-weather meal. What's more, the order can be reversed. If it's *very* hot, start with salad and, once refreshed, move on to Cheese Soup and bread, with a cold, crisp-flavored white wine.

cheese soup
with garlic toast

watercress and green bean salad

any fruit tart

coffee

This is one of the best of simple meals—quiche and soup. And so easy to serve the two either together or one after the other (remember quiche is just as good at room temperature). A delightful lunch or dinner to have in warm weather outdoors with a good, dry wine. Be sure to indulge in great, generous portions of whatever wonderful berries are at peak season.

pimiento and olive quiche

eggplant soup

green salad with vinaigrette dressing

fresh berries with cream

coffee

There are no courses in an Indian meal. So, although these two Indian menus are relatively simple, they will have the appearance of a banquet when everything is served, all at once.

To make your Indian dinner into an exotic event, find a bright-colored tablecloth and arrange the table in such a way that there is ample room in the center for six or seven attractive serving dishes. If you have some nice-looking shallow copper pots or gratin dishes, polish them up and put them to use. Set each place with a large plate and, for the soupy *dal* or the cold *raita*, an additional little bowl. Then bring on the feast.

The *pakoras* are a snack or appetizer and must be served hot, so plan on frying them at the last minute. They can be served first, by themselves, to nibble while sipping a gin and tonic or Pimm's and soda; both of these drinks, I've found, are excellent, cooling accompaniments to the spicy flavors of Indian cooking. Another fine choice is a good pale ale. If you'd rather forgo alcoholic beverages, a spicy hot tea with milk will do very nicely.

After the *pakoras*, everything but the sweet should be placed on the table at once, together with little dishes of nuts, raisins, spicy pickles, and whatever other garnishes you desire.

✍ pakoras ✍ (hot vegetable fritters)	✍ smothered potatoes ✍
✍ green curry ✍	✍ purée of scorched tomatoes ✍
✍ curried garbanzo beans ✍	✍ dal ✍
✍ saffron rice ✍	✍ plain pilau ✍
✍ banana and coconut raita ✍	✍ eggplant raita ✍
✍ cachumber ✍	fresh fruit
✍ chutneys ✍	✍ chutneys ✍
✍ puris or chapatis ✍	✍ puris or chapatis ✍
tea	tea
any fresh fruit dessert	

When you're feeling dramatic, have this dinner. It starts quietly but deliciously with the Artichoke Puff, which can be served cool but is really more wonderful hot out of the oven. The rich soup version of Pasta i Fagioli, an Italian combination of pasta and beans, is also modestly served, but the Caesar Salad is a performance, prepared and tossed at the table. Then, instead of bowing out with something simple, serve crêpes for dessert! They can be made ahead of time and reheated when you're ready for them; the lemon juice and powdered sugar are passed separately and added to taste, so it's really much easier than it sounds.

artichoke and cheese puff

pasta e fagioli
french or italian bread

caesar salad

fresh lemon dessert crêpes

This is a good fall or winter menu, with hearty dishes made of leeks, potatoes, and cabbage, though you could also enjoy it in the spring. But if you had a garden in the summer and froze vegetables when they were abundant, it's fun to bring out some tender green peas in the middle of winter and treat yourself to this most delicate, fresh-tasting soup.

Drink a dry, somewhat spicy white wine with this meal, or an excellent Pilsner beer.

marinated leeks

creamed fresh pea soup with dumplings

mushrooms and potatoes in wine sauce
red cabbage with apples

fresh fruit
cheese

The Cheese Pastries can be made early in the day, or even the day before, and chilled, then baked at the last minute and served hot. While everyone is nibbling, start the rice; then serve the Broccoli Mousse with no delay, and the rice should be just right when you are ready to serve the second course.

cheese pastries

cold broccoli mousse

mushroom stew
with steamed rice

pumpkin pie with whipped cream

coffee

In Warsaw, where some of the best restaurants are Hungarian, I ate stuffed pancakes of this type many times, and they were always a delight—but so filling! Consequently, I've found that a light touch is needed in the rest of the menu.

Have a Gewurz Traminer with this. The dry, slightly spicy flavor of the wine will bring out the best in the food. And one word of warning: It takes too long to make the large potato pancakes at the last minute if you are serving more than two people (unless you have more than two hands), so make them a few hours before dinner. Just before filling and serving them, reheat them quickly on both sides in a very lightly oiled pan.

chilled ukrainian stewed eggplant
with dark rye bread

stuffed potato pancakes, hungarian style
with hot paprika sauce

coffee mousse

espresso

Here's a meal that keeps topping itself, with one exotic delicacy after another. It takes an investment of advance preparation but is well worth it.

The *bibbelkäse* is fairly simple and might well be made a day or two ahead. The hearts of palm are an expensive but wonderful treat: They can marinate in their dressing all day, if it's convenient, before being spooned into the tomatoes. Some last-minute work must be done for the soufflé and its rich sauce, though. Mousseline sauce is hollandaise based, so it must be made very carefully and can't be kept warm too long, but what a special sauce it is.

Many desserts would be anticlimactic after such an array, but Wenia's Mazurek, an elaborate torte, is splendid enough for any occasion. Make it the day before if you can—it will keep perfectly.

bibbelkäse
(spiced white cheese)

tomatoes stuffed with hearts of palm

wild mushroom and dill soufflé
with spicy mousseline sauce

Wenia's mazurek

coffee or tea

A soup to celebrate the cherry season, a frankly baroque crêpe cake, which can be constructed ahead and baked at the last, and a salad to be tossed at the table. Only the elegant dessert must be assembled just before serving.

❧ cold cherry soup ❧

❧ wild mushroom crêpe cake ❧

❧ salad torcoloti ❧

❧ crème à la Irena ❧

espresso

To enjoy the last of the zucchini and the first cold days, here's a hearty and interesting combination. The stuffed zucchini make a salad that is at once assertive and delicate, with its subtle taste of cilantro. It will wake up the palate before you go on to more solid fare.

The Sauerkraut Soup, obviously, is at the heart of this plan—rich and satisfying, redolent of tomatoes, onions, and hot paprika, it is a perfect foil for the *pierogi* with their cases of soft yeast dough wrapped around fillings of cheese, black mushrooms, or buttery cabbage and egg. The meal ends with a light touch: Apricots in Brandy.

❧ avocado-stuffed zucchini ❧

❧ assorted pierogi ❧
(cheese filled, mushroom filled, cabbage filled)
❧ sauerkraut soup ❧

❧ whole apricots in brandy ❧

coffee or tea

The croquettes are hot and a little bit spicy, a nice accompaniment to the cool, refreshing soup. The giant stuffed mushrooms are necessarily a rare dish, as it isn't every day that you can find mushrooms impressive enough in size to fit this bill. For the dessert, prepare the batter and the apples in advance. Then, when you take the mushrooms out of the oven, put the pudding in, and it will be ready at the perfect moment. No wine with the soup, but a nice, light red wine or a full-bodied white will go well with the mushrooms.

❧ garbanzo bean croquettes ❧
❧ cold buttermilk soup ❧

❧ giant mushrooms stuffed with eggplant
on a bed of
spinach and dill rice ❧

❧ apple pudding ❧

coffee or tea

For autumn or winter, a meal that is easier to prepare than it seems and worthy of any occasion. The salad should be prepared a few days before, so that it can develop flavor. The Spinach Soup is uncomplicated, as is the dessert. Only the soufflé needs careful timing. Put it in the oven just before you sit down to eat, then take your time with the salad and soup. Just remember to heat the sauce five minutes before the soufflé is finished. Afterward, enjoy cool, soft apples, juicy and slightly sweet, with a lick of cream.

beet and pineapple salad
with dark bread and sweet butter

spinach soup

spicy cheese and potato soufflé
with dill sauce

baked apples with cold fresh cream

coffee or tea

This is a meal to celebrate spring and indulge spring fever, a meal of subtle textures and fresh, delicate flavors. Drink Asti Spumante with it, or another fruity Italian white wine, and really celebrate.

butter lettuce with vinaigrette dressing
baked stuffed tomatoes,
with eggplant and zucchini filling

asparagus crêpes
cucumber-avocado sauce

fresh strawberries
butter cookies

coffee

As many Cheese Pastries as you care to serve is exactly the number that will be devoured, so be forewarned and don't make so many that appetites for the later courses will suffer! The Sweet Potato Soup is not very heavy at all; instead, quite delicate—but the roulade with its sauce is delightfully rich.

cheese pastries
celery root salad

sweet potato soup

zucchini and eggplant roulade
with mornay sauce

rum baba

coffee

This dinner, largely Viennese in flavor, with some influence from other parts of Eastern Europe, is elegant but still hearty. Allow two or three hours for this meal. First there are salads to sample and Liptauer Cheese to taste, and this should be an unhurried activity. After the velvety carrot soup, allow a little break, so the chattering which accompanied the appetizers can resume while a new bottle of wine is opened and glasses filled. Then the cabbage rolls; by now spirits are high, and plenty of time must be allowed, not only to eat, but to finish the wine and the arguments. By the time the fresh berries and melons are served, everyone has pushed his or her chair back a little and sighed with contentment to see a light and refreshing dessert. Afterward, linger over fresh, hot coffee or espresso.

❧ assorted cold appetizers ☙
(paprikasalat, potato salad,
liptauer cheese, black bread, pickles)

❧ cream of carrot soup ☙

❧ mushroom and barley stuffed cabbage rolls ☙

❧ fresh strawberries and melons in brandy
with whipped cream ☙

coffee or espresso

For a special dinner on a warm summer night, I suggest a menu that includes only one hot dish—the stuffed crêpes. Everything else has been chilled.

Set the table with linen and shining crystal, open the windows to the garden, and chill an excellent white wine. The pâtés are a beautiful way to begin. It feels so luxurious to have an assortment and enjoy the variety of flavors, but cut them in thin, thin slices because this course must tease the appetite, not sate it. Next, one of the world's great salads, which is really a soup: the sharp, icy cold gazpacho of southern Spain. Then the palate is ready for something warm, mild, and a bit rich. The stuffed crêpes, sautéed in butter to a golden brown just before serving, are perfect. For dessert, Frozen Strawberry Mousse, cool, light, and ambrosial.

❧ appetizers ☙
(mushroom pâté, white bean pâté,
egg and olive mold, thin-sliced french bread)

❧ gazpacho ☙

❧ crêpes with feta cheese ☙
garnish: thin wedges of cantaloupe

❧ frozen strawberry mousse ☙

coffee or espresso

There are times when a light, simple, and quickly prepared meal is in order; something more than a snack but less than a serious dinner. Late suppers, planned for after the movies or theater, hot-weather lunches, or other things of that sort, have their own requirements. Either the food must be something that can be largely prepared ahead of time or it must be very easy and quick to make—but just because a meal is not elaborate is no reason for it to be dull. Six menus follow which bear this out. They range from the unusual and sophisticated to the simple and unadorned.

The dessert must be prepared in advance and the sauce for the Fettucine Alfredo can be as well, so that leaves tossing and dressing a salad and boiling the noodles—no great task. Have a nice, chilled white wine, a Soave, for example, with the fettucine, and this simple meal will be very agreeable indeed.

tossed green salad with herb dressing

fettucine alfredo

oranges in wine

espresso
amaretto

A Cold Omelet Salad is no snap to prepare, but it can be finished up to six or seven hours in advance without suffering and then just brought out on your fanciest silver tray. The Cheese-Filled Bread, of course, is done ahead, and so are the Baked Apples. The result is a light, pleasant meal that needs, by way of last-minute work, only to be carried out and served, yet is quite elegant.

cold omelet salad
cheese-filled bread

baked apples

tea or coffee

Have some cold soup ready—it could be the Cold Avocado Soup or a gazpacho—and you can be eating this very tasty meal in about twenty minutes' time. The Potato and Zucchini Omelets are also an ideal choice for brunch; serve with any assortment of fresh fruit, some hot muffins or toast, and fresh-brewed coffee.

cold avocado soup

potato and zucchini omelets

fresh fruit and cheese
biscuits

coffee or tea

Start with Ensaladilla Russa, the simple and tasty Spanish version of a Russian vegetable salad—it is the right preliminary to Garlic Soup, which must be eaten only among good, garlic-loving friends. Garlic Soup is made moments before it is served, but takes only five or ten minutes to prepare (and packs a real punch for such a quickie). After this soup, fresh fruit is the obvious choice, but something a bit sweeter and richer might be wanted a little later, so serve another Spanish winter favorite, the thick hot chocolate, instead of coffee.

ensaladilla russa

garlic soup

fresh fruit and cheese

castillian hot chocolate

Although the mushrooms must be cooked just before serving, they take so little time that this does not present a problem. I've suggested the Paprika-Cucumber Salad here because it must be done ahead and keeps nicely, but almost any salad would do.

paprika-cucumber salad

mushrooms on toast

custard or pudding

coffee or tea

Sometimes the absolutely simplest fare is the best, more suited to the mood and appetite than anything sophisticated or rich.

This menu was inspired by memories of my stay in England during the cold, dark month of November. There, late one night, in front of a bright, hot fire, I first feasted on William Bryan's pungent, spicy pickled onions and a good old English cheese, along with a crusty bread and an excellent bitter beer.

The preparation for this meal, except for the tart, is all in procuring a fine cheese and the very tastiest pickled onions. The best thing to do is to open a jar of the onions you pickled yourself (with the recipe on page 375), six or eight weeks before. But in the event that you neglected to do that, you must shop around until you find the right ones, plump and spicy (not the little white cocktail onions).

pickled onions

sharp cheddar cheese

crusty rolls and butter

dark beer or ale

apple tart

coffee

breads

All the fickleness of my nature emerges on the subject of bread. There are at least a dozen different kinds that I could call my favorite without batting an eye. I can't help loving the light, long French *baguettes*, however many times I'm reminded that white flour is not as nutritious as whole wheat. On the other hand, my fondness for the dark, dense, shiny-surfaced ryes and pumpernickels of northern and Eastern Europe remains undiminished. I could and often do make a meal of a thick, moist slice of Rye Bread with Fruit, or Beer Bread.

On another day, my favorite is corn bread, yellow and buttery and hot; a classic corn bread recipe is given in the first *Vegetarian Epicure*, but now I have new variations on that tasty theme—Pumpkin Corn Bread, which marries two compatible and uniquely American flavors, and Corn and Rye Muffins. Then, when nothing will do but a chewy oatmeal bread, I dicker between filling Oatmeal-Rye Bread and the slightly sweet Oatmeal Raisin Bread.

Rich-textured whole wheat bread is certainly one of my continuing favorites, and I've added two excellent versions to my repertoire here: Whole Wheat Anadama Bread is an early American variety, a little heavier than others for the addition of some corn meal; and Whole Wheat Egg Bread, rich and mild, can also be made into a fine cinnamon loaf with practically no extra trouble.

Flat breads and fried breads, like the easy-to-make Indian *puris* and *chapatis*; beautiful, egg-varnished brioches or braided Vienna Bread; quick soda breads, served warm—like the addictive Cranberry Bread; and elegantly coiled Sweet Coffee Bread, on its way to becoming cake, opulent with egg yolks, butter, raisins, and lemon rind—they're all my favorites, and that without taking anything away from biscuits, rolls, muffins, and rusks. What's more, I'm always ready to be tempted by some new discovery.

As everyone seems to be noticing these days, making bread at home can be relaxing, enjoyable, and gratifying in many ways. Most of us do little enough with our hands now and find that the chore of kneading, once we get the knack, is a pleasantly sensual experience (at least until the phone rings when both hands are immersed to the wrists in dough). Furthermore, baking bread is not nearly as complicated or time-consuming as many believe. The actual working time is usually no longer than half an hour; for the rest of it, the hours of rising and baking, the bread takes care of itself. Those hours can be arranged very conveniently, too, since you can always retard the rising of your dough by putting it in the refrigerator if you get the yen to go to a movie, for instance.

The whole bread process, from kneading to shaping to baking, is progressively more delightful as you go along. But finally, whatever may be said about the joy of kneading and the mouth-watering aroma of baking bread, the real payoff in making our own bread is in the last step, the ever-renewable joy of eating.

MAKING BREAD

With a little practice, you will find making a yeast dough and forming loaves the easiest things in the world—they become practically second nature. The basic techniques are uncomplicated, and only a few rules have to be kept in mind.

Remember, first of all, that yeast is a living organism and is affected by temperature. Active dry yeast should be dissolved in lukewarm water. Hot water will kill it, and cold water will not activate it, so test the water on your hand or wrist: It should feel just comfortably warm.

When the yeast is dissolved, the liquids and flours can be combined with it immediately to make the dough, or else a soft "sponge" can be made first and allowed to rise for a while before the rest of the flour is added. For this second method, the dissolved yeast is combined with enough warm liquid and flour to make a rather thick batter, which is left in a warm place for an hour or longer. During that time, it bubbles and expands very impressively, until it looks exactly like a big, soft sponge. The remaining flour and other ingredients are then stirred into the sponge, and a normal, stiff dough is formed that is kneaded and left to rise as usual. Breads made with the sponge method take a little longer but seem to have a wonderful flavor and texture.

The questions of exactly how much flour to mix into your bread dough and how long to knead cannot be answered except by the practiced touch of your hands, once you've made a few loaves. However, the techniques can be described, and applying them should lead you to a recognizably good dough.

First, flour is added to the liquid mixture in the bowl until it is too stiff to be stirred. The dough is then turned out onto a large, well-floured board and sprinkled with more flour. It is important, at this stage, to keep the entire surface of the dough, top and bottom, well coated with flour, as it can be very annoying to get your hands stuck in it when it is still in a soft, gluelike state. (That's when the phone rings.)

Keeping it well dredged in flour, press the dough down with the heels of your hands, then fold it over. Press down again, pushing it out a bit, and fold over from the other side. That's all there is to kneading. The dough, which starts out soft and a little lumpy, gradually becomes more elastic, smoother, and less sticky as it is kneaded and the necessary flour is worked in. After about ten or fifteen minutes, it should be quite springy, very smooth, and no longer sticky.

Now you pat the dough into a ball and place it in an oiled or buttered bowl to rise. Turn the dough over once or twice so that all of its surface is coated with the butter or oil—this will prevent its drying out. Cover the bowl with a tea towel or plastic wrap and leave it in a warm, draft-free place. The temperature of the dough during the rising is important. Left in a cozy place at about 75 to 85 degrees, the dough will rise quite speedily, perhaps in an hour or so, though the kind of flour used will affect rising time, too. If it's a bit chilly in the spot where the dough is left, it may take several hours, though the dough is not at all harmed by this. If it's cold, you can wait till the world looks level, and nothing will happen.

When the dough has doubled in size, it must be punched down. Just make a fist and plunge it into the dough. It will sigh and collapse softly around your hand. At this point the dough should be ready to be formed into loaves.

Making a simple loaf is just a matter of rolling out and rolling up. Roll the dough out into an oblong shape about ¾ inch thick with a rolling pin, making it just a little wider at one end of the oblong. Starting at the narrower end, roll it up tightly into a cylinder. Pinch the seam, pull the ends over, and pinch the end seams. Or if you prefer, just pat the dough into a loaf shape with your hands, pull it together along one side, and pinch the seam securely. Put the formed loaf into a pan, seam side down, and there you are. Round loaves can be made by gathering the dough into a ball and pulling the ends together in one spot, where they can be firmly pinched together. The ball is then placed on a prepared baking sheet, pinched side down.

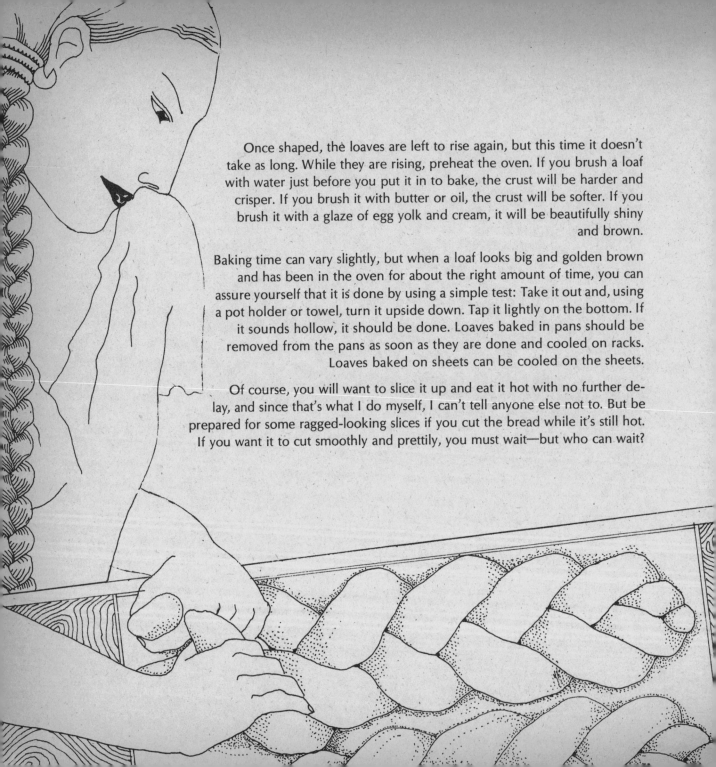

Once shaped, the loaves are left to rise again, but this time it doesn't take as long. While they are rising, preheat the oven. If you brush a loaf with water just before you put it in to bake, the crust will be harder and crisper. If you brush it with butter or oil, the crust will be softer. If you brush it with a glaze of egg yolk and cream, it will be beautifully shiny and brown.

Baking time can vary slightly, but when a loaf looks big and golden brown and has been in the oven for about the right amount of time, you can assure yourself that it is done by using a simple test: Take it out and, using a pot holder or towel, turn it upside down. Tap it lightly on the bottom. If it sounds hollow, it should be done. Loaves baked in pans should be removed from the pans as soon as they are done and cooled on racks. Loaves baked on sheets can be cooled on the sheets.

Of course, you will want to slice it up and eat it hot with no further delay, and since that's what I do myself, I can't tell anyone else not to. But be prepared for some ragged-looking slices if you cut the bread while it's still hot. If you want it to cut smoothly and prettily, you must wait—but who can wait?

braided whole wheat egg bread

2 packages (2 Tbs.) dry yeast
⅓ cup warm water
2 cups milk
3 Tbs. butter
2 Tbs. sugar
7 to 7½ cups whole wheat flour
1 Tbs. salt
1 whole egg
4 egg yolks
1 tsp. cream
sesame seeds

Dissolve the yeast in the warm water. Scald the milk and stir the butter and sugar into it. Pour the hot milk mixture into a large mixing bowl, and when lukewarm, stir in the yeast.

Mix together the flour and the salt. Add about 2 cups of flour to the milk and beat with an electric beater until the mixture is smooth.

Beat the egg and the yolks together lightly. Reserve about 2 tablespoons of the beaten egg mixture and add the rest to the batter. Beat again until smooth.

Gradually stir in enough flour to make a stiff dough. When the dough is too stiff to be stirred with a spoon, turn it out onto a well-floured board and knead about 10 to 15 minutes, adding more flour as necessary, until the dough is smooth and elastic.

Form the dough into a ball and put it in a large, buttered bowl, turning it over once so that it is coated on all sides. Cover the bowl with a towel and leave it in a warm, draft-free place for about 1½ hours, or until the dough has doubled in size.

Punch the dough down and cut it into 2 pieces. Pat each piece into a smooth oblong, about 14 inches long and 6 inches wide. Slice the oblongs into 3 even strips, leaving them connected at one end. Starting at the connected end, form a thick braid, tucking under the last bit and pinching it to the others.

Place the braids in 2 buttered medium-sized loaf pans, cover them with a towel, and let rise for about ½ hour, or until half again as large.

Stir about 1 teaspoon of cream into the reserved egg and brush the tops of the loaves with it. Sprinkle the loaves with sesame seeds and bake them in a preheated oven at 375 degrees for 45 to 50 minutes.

Makes 2 large loaves.

vienna bread

2   packages (2 Tbs.) dry yeast
1   cup warm water
2   Tbs. sugar
5½ to 6½ cups white flour
1   cup milk
1   Tbs. salt
3   Tbs. butter, melted

glaze

1   egg yolk
1   Tbs. milk

Dissolve the yeast in the warm water and stir in 1 tablespoon of the sugar and 1¾ to 2 cups flour, enough to make a soft, spongy dough. Cover the bowl with a towel and put the sponge aside in a warm place to rise for about 45 minutes, or until it is puffed and soft.

Add the milk, the remaining sugar, the salt, and the melted butter, and stir the sponge down well. Work in as much of the remaining flour as is needed to make a fairly stiff dough. Turn the dough out onto a heavily floured board, sprinkle a little more flour over it, and knead it for 10 to 15 minutes, or until it is smooth and elastic; add flour as needed to keep the dough from sticking.

Form the dough into a ball and put it in a large, buttered bowl, turning it over once so that it is coated with butter on all sides. Cover the bowl with a light towel and put it in a warm, draft-free place for about 45 minutes to 1 hour, or until the dough has doubled in size.

Punch down the dough and form it into 2 oblong loaves or large braids. Put the loaves on buttered baking sheets, cover them with a light towel, and leave them in a warm place to rise for about ½ hour, or until they have nearly doubled in size.

Beat together the egg yolk and the tablespoon of milk and brush the loaves delicately with the glaze. Put them in a preheated 425 degree oven and after 5 minutes lower the heat to 375 degrees. Bake the loaves for 35 to 40 minutes more, until they are golden brown.

Cool the loaves on racks before slicing.

Makes 2 medium-sized loaves.

whole wheat anadama bread

1 package (1 Tbs.) dry yeast
1⅔ cups warm water
1 Tbs. sugar
3 Tbs. molasses
3 cups whole wheat flour
1 cup white flour
1 cup yellow corn meal
1 Tbs. salt
2 Tbs. butter, melted

Dissolve the yeast in the warm water with the sugar and molasses. Mix together the flours, corn meal, and salt and add about 1½ cups of the dry mixture to the liquid. Stir vigorously until smooth and put this sponge in a warm place to rise for about 1 hour.

Stir down the sponge, add the melted butter, and gradually stir in as much of the flour mixture as you can. When the dough is too stiff to be stirred, sprinkle the remaining flour mixture on a large board, turn the dough out onto it, turn it over, and begin gently kneading. Knead the dough until it is even-textured and elastic, working in as much of the flour as necessary to keep it from sticking, but no more.

Form the dough into a ball, put it in a buttered bowl, turn it over once or twice, and then cover the bowl with a towel and leave the dough to rise, in a warm, draft-free place, until it is double in size. Punch it down, knead it a couple more times, and form it into a high, round loaf, pinching the seams together on the bottom. Place the loaf on a baking sheet that has been buttered and coated with corn meal, and leave it to rise until it has almost doubled in size.

Cut a shallow cross in the top of the loaf with a sharp knife, and brush the loaf with cold water. Bake in a preheated oven at 400 degrees for about 45 minutes.

Makes 1 large loaf.

brioches

½ cup plus 1 Tbs. warm milk
1 package (1 Tbs.) dry yeast
2 tsp. sugar
2½ cups flour
½ cup soft butter
1 tsp. salt
3 eggs

glaze

1 Tbs. milk
1 egg yolk

There are two methods of making brioches: the hard way, which involves plenty of energetic beating by hand, and the delightfully easy way, with a food processor. Here's the hard way first.

Blend the warm milk, the yeast, and the sugar, stirring until the yeast is dissolved. Beat in 1 cup of the flour. Add the soft butter and the salt and continue beating, either with a heavy-duty electric mixer or by hand, until the mixture is perfectly smooth.

Add the 3 eggs, one at a time, beating again after each. Then gradually add the remaining flour and beat vigorously until the dough is glossy and elastic. If you are using a wooden spoon, or your hand, the best method is to slap the dough hard against the side of a large bowl, pulling it up high each time and flinging it back down. The dough is ready when it starts to blister and pull away from your hand or the side of the bowl.

Place the dough in a large, buttered bowl, cover it with a towel, and let it rise in a warm place until it has doubled in bulk, about 2½ to 3½ hours.

Stir the dough down, cover the bowl with plastic wrap, and chill the dough in the refrigerator at least 6 hours or overnight.

Butter two 7½-inch brioche pans.

Divide the dough into 2 equal parts, and leave 1 in the refrigerator. Take the other part and, on a lightly floured board, form it into 2 smooth balls, 1 large one and the other about ⅕ its size. To shape the balls, flour your hands and pull the dough down gently to a point at the bottom of the ball, pinching the ends together there securely.

Place the large ball of dough in one of the brioche molds, pinched side down, and cut a small cross in the top of it with a sharp, pointed knife. With floured fingers, pull the dough apart slightly where it has been cut, forming a hole almost large enough to hold the small ball of dough. Place the small ball of dough into that hole, nesting it gently inside. It should be about half-hidden.

Shape the remaining half of the dough the same way, and put the brioches in a warm place, covered with a light towel, to rise for 2½ to 3 hours, or until nearly doubled in bulk.

Beat the egg yolk and milk together for the glaze and gently brush the brioches with it. Bake them for 45 to 50 minutes in a preheated 350 degree oven. Unmold and serve warm. Or allow to cool first on a wire rack.

Brioches must be eaten fresh!

food processor method

Dissolve the yeast in the milk and stir in the sugar and 1 cup flour. Put the steel blade in the food processor and pour the yeast-flour mixture into the container. Process for 15 to 20 seconds, or until smooth.

Add the soft butter and the salt and process for another 20 seconds. Add the 3 eggs and process again for about 20 seconds.

Add the remaining flour and process for about 3 minutes, stopping occasionally to scrape down the sides of the container. The dough should be velvety smooth, glossy, and elastic. Proceed exactly as above in allowing the dough to rise, chilling it, shaping it, letting the brioches rise once more, and baking them.

Makes 2 medium-sized brioches.

oatmeal-rye bread

2   packages (2 Tbs.) dry yeast
3   cups warm water
¼   cup molasses
2   cups white flour
2   cups whole wheat flour
1   Tbs. salt
2   cups dark rye flour
2   cups rolled oats
more white flour as needed (1 to 1½ cups)

Stir the yeast into the warm water in a large bowl. Add the molasses and stir until it is dissolved. Add the white flour and the whole wheat flour, about 1 cup at a time, stirring well after each addition. When all 4 cups of flour have been stirred in, beat the mixture vigorously with a wooden spoon for about 10 minutes. It should be smooth and very soft.

Cover the bowl with a dry tea towel and put it in a warm, draft-free place for 45 minutes to 1 hour. The yeast sponge should rise considerably and be rather bubbly at the end of this time.

Now sprinkle the salt over the sponge and fold it in. Add the rye flour and the oats, a little at a time, and fold them in. The dough should be quite thick. If it is not thick enough to handle, add a little more white flour. As soon as the dough is manageable enough to be removed from the bowl in more or less one piece, turn it out onto a floured board and begin kneading. Knead in only as much additional flour as is necessary to form a reasonably nonsticky dough. When the dough is smooth and elastic (about 20 minutes of kneading), form it into a ball and put it in a large, buttered bowl, turning over once so that it is coated with butter on top as well.

Cover the bowl with a tea towel and put it aside for about 1 hour to rise. The dough should be doubled in size.

Punch the dough down and divide it into 2 parts, forming each into a loaf. Put the loaves in buttered, medium-sized loaf pans, cover them with tea towels, and put them aside to rise for about 50 minutes. Bake the bread in a preheated oven at 350 degrees for 1 hour. When it is done, remove the loaves from the pans and allow them to cool on a rack.

Makes 2 loaves.

rye bread with fruit

This is a dense, rich bread, meant to be cut in thin slices. It is very good buttered, excellent with a mild cheese, and keeps well for a couple of weeks.

1 cup warm potato water*
2 packages (2 Tbs.) dry yeast
2 cups warm mashed potatoes
½ cup molasses
approximately 4 cups whole wheat flour
2½ cups dark rye flour
2 tsp. salt
½ cup wheat germ
⅔ cup chopped prunes
⅔ cup golden raisins
⅔ cup currants
⅔ cup chopped walnuts

glaze

1 egg yolk
2 Tbs. water

Dissolve the yeast in the warm potato water and stir it into the mashed potatoes in a large bowl. Add the molasses and 2 cups of the whole wheat flour and blend well. Cover the

*Just the water in which you've cooked the potatoes.

bowl with a light towel and put it away in a warm, draft-free place for 1½ hours to let the sponge rise.

Stir down the sponge. Mix together the rye flour and the salt, and stir them in, along with the wheat germ, fruit, and nuts.

Turn the dough out onto a heavily floured surface and knead in as much more of the whole wheat flour as is necessary to make a manageable dough. Continue kneading the dough until it feels elastic and springs back when pushed down.

Form the dough into a ball and put it in a large, lightly buttered bowl, turn it over once, cover the bowl with a towel, and put it aside in a warm place for 1½ hours, or until the dough has risen to about twice its former size. Punch the dough down, form a ball again, and let the dough rise again for about 45 minutes.

Divide the dough into 2 parts and shape each into a ball. Place the balls, smooth side up, on buttered baking sheets. Cover them with a light towel and let them rise for 45 minutes. Brush the loaves with the glaze and bake them in a preheated oven at 375 degrees for 1 hour.

Allow the loaves to cool before slicing.

Makes 2 large loaves.

raisin-rye bread

2   packages (2 Tbs.) dry yeast
1½ cups lukewarm water
1   tsp. sugar
1⅓ cups raisins
1   cup milk
¼   cup brown sugar
grated rind of 2 oranges
½   tsp. fennel seeds, crushed
4½ cups rye flour
3   Tbs. butter, melted
1   Tbs. salt
2½ cups white flour
corn meal

In a small bowl, dissolve yeast in ½ cup of the lukewarm water and stir in 1 tsp. sugar. Leave the yeast to proof for about 10 minutes.

Pour boiling water over the raisins and let them plump up in it for 10 minutes, then drain.

Combine the cup of milk with the remaining cup of water and heat the liquid until it is lukewarm. In a large bowl, stir together the milk and water, the yeast mixture, brown sugar, raisins, orange rind, fennel seed, and 2 cups of rye flour. Beat this mixture with a wooden spoon until there are no lumps of flour left, then stir in the melted butter and salt.

Beat in the remaining 2½ cups of rye flour, ½ cup at a time, plus 1 cup of the white flour. The dough should now be getting a bit too stiff to be beaten with a spoon. If not, add a little more of the white flour until it is.

Sprinkle 1 cup of white flour over a large, flat wooden or marble surface and dump the dough out on top of it. Sprinkle the remaining white flour on top of the dough. Carefully start kneading, keeping the dough well coated with flour at first, as it will be sticky. Knead in as much flour as is necessary to make a smooth, elastic dough. The kneading should take about 15 to 20 minutes.

Form the dough into a ball and put it in a large, buttered bowl. Turn the dough over once or twice so that it is completely coated with butter. Cover the bowl with a tea towel and leave the dough to rise in a warm, draft-free place for 1 hour, or until it has doubled in size.

Punch the dough down, knead it a few times, and cut it in half. Form each half into a smooth ball, pinching it together firmly at the seams.

an easy herb bread

Put the loaves, seam side down, on buttered baking sheets that have been sprinkled with corn meal. With a sharp, serrated knife, cut a large X in the top of each loaf. Cover the loaves with a tea towel and leave them to rise again for another hour, or until almost doubled in bulk.

Brush the loaves with water and bake them in a preheated oven at 375 degrees for 1 hour, or a little longer, until they sound hollow when tapped on the bottom.

Cool the loaves on racks.

Makes 2 medium-sized loaves.

This is a yeast bread, but it doesn't take as long to make as most of them and is wonderful to serve warm with dinner.

1   cup water
1   cup milk
¼   cup sugar
2   packages (2 Tbs.) dry yeast
¼   cup vegetable oil
1   clove garlic, finely minced
3   Tbs. minced onion
approximately 5 cups whole wheat flour
1¼   tsp. salt
½   tsp. dried basil, crushed
½   tsp. dried oregano, crushed
¼   tsp. dried thyme, crushed
1   egg

Heat together the water and milk until lukewarm, then stir in the sugar and the yeast.

Heat the oil in a small skillet and sauté the garlic and onions in it until they just begin to color.

In a large bowl, combine the yeast mixture with about 1½ cups of the flour and beat with an electric mixer until smooth. Add the salt, the herbs, the oil mixture, and the egg and beat again. Gradually add approximately

an easy herb bread (continued)

another 1½ cups of flour and beat for 5 minutes. The dough should be soft and smooth.

Stir in another cup of flour, then turn the dough out onto a floured board and knead it for 5 minutes, working in as much of the remaining flour as is necessary to keep it from sticking. The dough should be smooth and elastic and still quite soft. Form it into a ball and put it in an oiled bowl, turning it over once so that it is evenly coated with the oil. Cover the bowl with a towel and leave it in a warm place for 45 minutes, or until the dough has nearly doubled in size.

Punch down the dough and form it into 3 small loaves. Place them in small, oiled loaf pans, cover them with a towel, and leave them to rise again for about ½ hour. Bake the loaves in a preheated oven at 375 degrees for 35 minutes, or until they sound hollow when tapped on the bottom.

Makes 3 small loaves.

beer bread

If you like hard-crusted, coarse-textured breads, go no further. This is the bread for you. It has a beautiful dark color, a rich flavor, and a combination of chewiness and crunch that few loaves can claim. However, you must give it ample time to rise before baking, or it will come out of the oven like a regular little brick.

½ cup whole wheat berries
3 cups water
1 cup dark beer, warmed
2 packages (2 Tbs.) dry yeast
¼ cup molasses
1½ cups white flour
1 Tbs. salt
½ tsp. fennel seeds, finely crushed in a
    mortar
2¾ to 3 cups stone-ground dark rye flour

Put the wheat berries and the water in a medium-sized, heavy-bottomed saucepan, bring the water to a boil, then lower the heat and leave the wheat berries to simmer very gently for about 2 or 3 hours, or until they are very tender and bursting open.

In a large bowl, combine the warm beer, the yeast, and 1 tablespoon of the molasses, and leave it for about 10 minutes, or until it foams up.

When the yeast mixture foams, stir in the remaining molasses and the white flour and beat vigorously with a wooden spoon until the mixture is smooth. Cover the bowl with a tea towel and leave it in a warm place for about 40 minutes to let this sponge rise. It should be bubbly and doubled in size.

Stir down the sponge and mix in the salt and fennel seeds. Gradually add the rye flour, stirring it in until the dough is too stiff to mix with a spoon. Sprinkle some of the rye flour onto a large, flat wooden surface and turn the dough out onto it. Sprinkle more rye flour over the dough and begin kneading. Knead the dough for at least 10 minutes, working in as much of the flour as necessary to keep it from sticking. When the dough is elastic, form it into a ball and put it in a buttered bowl, turning it over once so that it is coated with butter all over. Cover the bowl with a towel and leave it in a warm, draft-free place for 1 hour, or until the dough has doubled in size.

Punch down the dough, turn it out onto the floured board, and flatten it slightly. Drain the cooked wheat berries thoroughly, spread some of them on the flattened dough, fold the dough over, and start kneading them in. Continue flattening the dough, adding more wheat berries and kneading until they are all incorporated into the dough.

Form the dough into a smooth, round ball, pinching the seams together securely, and place it, seam side down, on a buttered baking sheet. Brush the loaf lightly with butter, cut a shallow cross in the top with a sharp knife, cover it with a tea towel, and leave it in a warm, draft-free place to rise until it has nearly doubled in size.

Bake the loaf in a preheated oven at 425 degrees for 10 minutes, then reduce the heat to 375 degrees and bake it for another 55 minutes to 1 hour, or until it sounds hollow when tapped on the bottom.

Brush the hot loaf again with butter, and let it cool. Slice the bread with a very sharp, serrated knife.

Makes 1 large loaf.

oatmeal-raisin bread

2 cups rolled oats
5 cups water
⅓ cup honey
2 Tbs. salt
⅔ cup wheat germ
2 packages (2 Tbs.) dry yeast
6 cups whole wheat flour
1 cup raisins
2 cups white flour

Cook the oats in 4 cups boiling water until they are just soft (5 to 10 minutes). Stir in the honey, salt, and wheat germ and let the mixture cool to lukewarm.

Dissolve the yeast in 1 cup warm water and stir it into the oats along with 3 cups of the whole wheat flour. Beat the sponge with a wooden spoon for a few minutes, then cover the bowl with a tea towel and let the sponge rise in a warm, draft-free place for about 1 hour, or until it has doubled its volume.

Stir down the sponge and stir in the raisins and the remaining 3 cups whole wheat flour. Sprinkle 1 cup of the white flour over a flat wooden or marble surface and turn the dough out onto it. Sprinkle the second cup of white flour on top of the dough and carefully begin kneading.

Knead the dough for about 10 minutes, or until it is smooth and elastic. Form it into a ball, and put it in a large, buttered bowl, turning it over so that it is evenly buttered. Cover the bowl with a tea towel and put the dough away to rise for 1 hour, or until it has doubled in size.

Punch down the dough, cut it into 4 even parts, and form each part into a loaf. Place the loaves in 4 buttered medium-sized pans, cover them with a tea towel, and let them rise for about ½ hour. Bake the loaves in a preheated oven at 400 degrees for 15 minutes, then turn the heat down to 350 degrees and bake them for another 30 to 40 minutes.

Makes 4 loaves.

variation: cinnamon bread

Prepare the bread dough as described above. When you are ready to form the loaves, take each portion of the dough and roll it out in an oval shape until it is about ½ inch thick. Brush it with melted butter, evenly sprinkle about 1 teaspoon cinnamon over it, then sprinkle about 2 Tbs. sugar over the cinnamon. Starting at one of the narrow ends of the oval, roll it up into a loaf and pinch together the bottom. Place in buttered pans and bake as described above.

Makes 4 loaves.

cheese-filled bread

dough

1   package (1 Tbs.) dry yeast
¼   cup lukewarm water
2   Tbs. plus 2 tsp. sugar
1   cup milk, scalded
1½ tsp. salt
4½ to 5½ cups flour
2   eggs
½   cup butter, melted

filling

1½ lbs. Munster cheese, grated
2 to 3 oz. Roquefort or blue cheese
2   Tbs. butter, melted
2   eggs

glaze

1   egg
1   Tbs. cream

Dissolve the yeast in the water and stir in 2 teaspoons of the sugar. Combine the scalded milk in a large bowl with the remaining 2 tablespoons sugar and the salt, and allow it to cool to lukewarm. Stir in the yeast and 2 cups of the flour, and beat the mixture vigorously with a wooden spoon for about 10 minutes.

Beat the eggs lightly and add them to the dough. Beat with a wooden spoon again until the eggs are completely incorporated, and then stir in the butter. Continue beating, slapping the dough up against the sides of the bowl, until it blisters. Gradually beat in 2 more cups of flour.

Sprinkle a large board with the remaining flour, turn the dough out onto it, and knead it gently until it is perfectly smooth, elastic, and no longer sticky. Form the dough into a ball, put it in a large, buttered bowl, turning it once so that it is coated with butter. Cover the bowl with a tea towel and put the dough in a warm,

cheese-filled bread (continued)

draft-free place to rise for about 1½ hours or until it has doubled in bulk.

While the dough is rising, prepare the filling. Put the grated Munster cheese in a medium-sized bowl. Mash the Roquefort cheese with a fork until it is a soft paste, and stir in the melted butter. Beat the eggs lightly, beat in the Roquefort-butter mixture, then pour it over the grated Munster and stir the whole thing up thoroughly.

When the dough has risen, punch it down and turn it out onto a lightly floured board. Roll it out into a circle about 24 inches across, dust it lightly with flour, and transfer it carefully onto a buttered 9- or 10-inch cake pan. Press the dough evenly into the pan, leaving the edge hanging over the sides.

Spread the filling over the dough in the pan and fold the sides of the dough up over it, pleating it as you bring it in to the center. Gather the edges up to the center and twist them together, forming a little knob on top of the loaf.

Let the loaf rise for about ½ hour. Make a glaze by beating an egg with 1 tablespoon cream and brush the loaf with it. Bake the loaf in a preheated oven at 350 degrees for about 1½ hours. Serve the bread warm, cut into wedges.

Makes 1 large loaf.

another way

To make smaller, less spectacular but more manageable loaves, cut the dough in half. Roll out 1 portion into a rectangle about ½ inch thick. Spread half the filling over the dough, leaving an inch-wide border around the sides and the near end, and a 2-inch border at the far end. Roll the dough up over the filling, finishing at the end with the wider border. Tuck under the ends, moisten the edge lightly with water, and pinch the seams together securely. Fill and shape the second portion of the dough the same way.

Place the loaves, seam side down, on buttered cookie sheets and let them rise in a warm, draft-free place for about ½ hour. Brush them with egg glaze and, just before putting them into the oven, make a very shallow slash, with a sharp knife, lengthwise down the center of each loaf. Bake in a preheated oven at 350 degrees for about 1 hour and 15 minutes.

Makes 2 medium-sized loaves.

sweet coffee bread

Not quite a coffee cake, but a delicious, sweet bread to have with tea or coffee.

dough

1	package (1 Tbs.) dry yeast
½	cup lukewarm water
6	Tbs. sugar
3	cups white flour
1	cup whole wheat pastry flour
1	tsp. salt
1	cup raisins
3	whole eggs
2	egg yolks
⅓	cup milk
½	cup soft butter

filling

1½	cups pot cheese or cottage cheese
6	Tbs. sugar
2	egg yolks
2	tsp. finely grated, fresh lemon rind
3	Tbs. flour
melted butter	
confectioners' sugar	

Dissolve the yeast in the lukewarm water, add 2 tablespoons of the sugar and ¾ cup of the white flour, and stir well. Put this sponge aside in a warm place for ½ hour, or until it begins to puff and bubble.

In a large mixing bowl, sift together 2 cups of the white flour, the whole wheat flour, the remaining sugar, and the salt. Add the raisins. In another bowl, beat together the eggs, egg yolks, and milk. Stir this mixture into the dry ingredients, along with the yeast sponge, and then begin working in the soft butter.

When all the butter has been incorporated, beat the dough vigorously with a wooden spoon, slapping it up against the sides of the bowl, until it becomes glossy and starts to blister. It should come away from the sides of the bowl pretty easily at this point.

Cover the bowl with a towel and put it in a warm, draft-free place for about 1½ hours, or until the dough has doubled in size. Punch the dough down and turn it out onto a well-floured board. Sprinkle the dough with the remainder of the white flour and knead it gently a few times, just until it is smooth enough to handle.

Sieve the cheese by forcing it through a strainer to make smooth or spin it in a food processor.

Make the filling by combining the sieved cheese, sugar, egg yolks, lemon rind, and

sweet coffee bread (continued)

flour. Stir well until the mixture is completely blended and free from lumps. It should be thick enough to hold a shape.

On a floured board, roll the dough out into a rectangle about 20 inches long and 12 inches wide. Spread the cheese filling over it, leaving a 2-inch border at the ends and along one side, and a 3- to 4-inch border along the other side.

Roll the dough up lengthwise over the filling, toward the side with the wide border. When it is almost completely rolled up, pull up the wide-bordered edge and stretch it slightly over the top of the roll. Moisten the edge with a bit of water and pinch the seam together securely. Turn the ends up and pinch them as well.

Turn the roll over carefully so that the seam is on the bottom. Transfer it carefully to a buttered baking sheet and shape it into a circle or a nearly closed horseshoe. Cover it with a tea towel and set it aside in a warm place to rise for about 45 minutes, or until it has nearly doubled in size. Brush the top with melted butter and bake it in a preheated oven at 350 degrees for 1 hour and 10 minutes. Check it once, about 20 minutes before it is done, and if the top is getting very dark, cover it with a loose sheet of aluminum foil.

Allow the bread to cool and dust the top with confectioners' sugar.

Makes 1 large loaf.

soft dinner rolls

1   package (1 Tbs.) dry yeast
¼   cup warm water
1¼ cups warm milk
1   egg, lightly beaten
4   cups unbleached white flour
¼   cup sugar
¼   cup butter, melted
1   tsp. salt
melted butter for brushing rolls

Dissolve the yeast in the warm water and combine it in a large, warm bowl with the milk, egg, and a scant 2 cups of the flour. Beat by hand or with an electric mixer until all the lumps of flour are gone and the mixture is perfectly smooth. Add the sugar, melted butter, and salt and beat with a mixer again until smooth and glossy.

Stir in another cup of flour. The dough should now be getting stiff enough to hold together. Sprinkle half the remaining flour onto a large board, turn the dough out onto it, and sprinkle the rest of the flour over the dough. Gently begin kneading the dough, keeping it coated with flour at all times to prevent sticking. Knead in as much of the flour as is needed to make a dough that is manageable but still soft.

When it is smooth and elastic, form the dough into a ball and put it in a warm, buttered bowl, turning it over once so that it is coated with butter on all sides. Cover the bowl with a towel and leave the dough to rise in a warm, draft-free place for about 1 hour, or until it has doubled in volume.

Punch the dough down, place it on a lightly floured board, and roll it out into a rectangle about 18 inches by 9 inches. Cut the rectangle in half lengthwise, and then cut each half into 1-inch-wide strips, crosswise. To form a roll, pick up one of the strips, stretch it out slightly, twist it around a few turns, then tie it in one loose knot, and a second one next to it. Put the roll down on a buttered baking sheet, tucking the ends underneath.

These rolls will have an uneven oval shape. Of course, the rolls can be shaped any way that you prefer, and they'll be just as tasty—this is just my way of forming rolls, preferred because it is so fast and simple.

When all the dough is shaped into rolls and arranged several inches apart on buttered baking sheets, cover the rolls with light towels and leave them in a warm place to rise for about 25 minutes, or until nearly doubled in size. Brush the rolls lightly with melted butter and bake them in a preheated oven at 425 degrees for 10 minutes, just until they begin to turn golden brown. Don't let them get too dark!

Serve hot or cool. Makes about 3 dozen rolls.

buttermilk dinner rolls

1 package (1 Tbs.) dry yeast
1 cup warm buttermilk
1 Tbs. brown sugar
¼ tsp. baking soda
1½ cups whole wheat flour
1 cup white flour
1 tsp. baking powder
1 tsp. salt
3 Tbs. butter, melted

Dissolve the yeast in the warm buttermilk and stir in the brown sugar and baking soda. Put this mixture aside for a few minutes, until it starts to foam and bubble.

Sift together the whole wheat flour, white flour, baking powder, and salt. Stir about 1 cup of this into the yeast mixture, then stir in the melted butter, and beat with a wooden spoon for a few minutes. Gradually add as much of the remaining flour as you can stir in, then sprinkle the rest onto a large board. Turn the dough out onto it and begin kneading. Knead the dough until it is smooth and elastic, working in only as much flour as is necessary to keep it from sticking. Form the dough into a ball and put it in a buttered bowl, turning it over once.

Cover the bowl with a tea towel and leave it in a warm place to rise until the dough has doubled in size. Punch it down and turn it out onto a lightly floured board.

Roll the dough out to a thick rectangle about 14 to 15 inches long and 6 to 8 inches wide. Cut it crosswise in inch-wide strips. Take a strip, twist the ends around in opposite directions a couple of times, then tie it in a simple knot and loosely tuck under the ends. Form all the rolls this way (or any way you like if you have a preference!) and arrange them several inches apart on a buttered baking sheet.

Cover them lightly with a tea towel and leave them to rise in a warm place for about 45 minutes, or until they have nearly doubled in size. Bake the rolls for 15 to 20 minutes in a preheated oven at 425 degrees.

Makes about 15 rolls.

pumpkin corn bread

Despite the amount of sugar, this bread is not too sweet or cakey to eat with dinner.

1½ cups whole wheat flour
5   tsp. baking powder
¾   tsp. cinnamon
¼   tsp. allspice
½   tsp. salt
1   cup yellow corn meal
½   cup soft butter
⅔   cup brown sugar
3   eggs
3   Tbs. lemon juice
1½ cups puréed cooked pumpkin
1   cup milk

Sift together the flour, baking powder, cinnamon, allspice, and salt. Stir in the corn meal.

Cream the soft butter until it is smooth. Beat in the sugar and continue beating until the mixture is fluffy. Add the eggs and lemon juice and beat again until smooth. Finally, thoroughly mix in the pumpkin purée.

Continue to beat as you alternately add the flour mixture and the milk, until everything is combined.

Spoon the batter into 2 buttered medium-sized loaf pans and bake in a preheated oven at 350 degrees for about 1 hour and 20 minutes, or until a knife inserted in the center comes out clean and dry.

Let the loaves cool in their pans for 5 minutes, then carefully remove them and let them finish cooling on racks.

Makes 2 loaves.

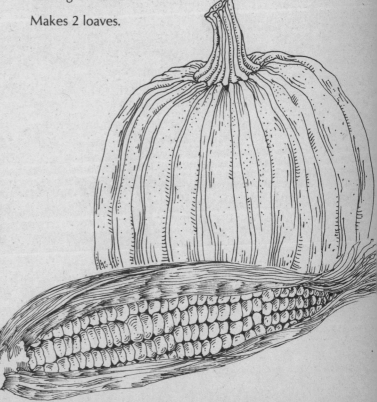

cranberry bread

1   cup white flour
1   cup whole wheat flour
¾   cup sugar
1½   tsp. baking powder
¾   tsp. salt
½   tsp. baking soda
¼   tsp. cinnamon
¼   tsp. ground cloves
grated rind of 1 orange
¾   cup orange juice
1   large egg
¼   cup butter, melted
1   cup firm, fresh cranberries
½   cup chopped walnuts

Sift together the flours, sugar, baking powder, salt, baking soda, and spices. Lightly beat together the orange rind, orange juice, egg, and melted butter. Stir the wet ingredients into the dry ingredients.

Coarsely chop the cranberries and add them to the batter along with the chopped nuts. Mix everything together thoroughly and pour the batter into a buttered medium-sized loaf pan.

Bake the bread in a preheated 350 degree oven for 1 hour, or until a toothpick inserted near the center comes out clean and dry. Cool on a rack and wrap tightly to store.

Makes 1 loaf.

orange-date bread

1½   cups whole wheat flour
1   cup white flour
½   tsp. salt
2   tsp. baking powder
4   Tbs. soft butter
¾   cup sugar
1   egg
1   cup fresh orange juice
2   Tbs. fresh-grated orange rind
½   cup chopped dates
½   cup rolled oats

Sift together the whole wheat flour, white flour, salt, and baking powder. Cream together the butter and sugar, then beat in the egg. Alternately add the flour mixture and the orange juice, beating after each addition, until you've used all but 2 tablespoons of the flour (use all of the juice). Add the grated orange rind.

Sprinkle the chopped dates with the reserved flour and roll them around in it, separating the bits from each other until they are no longer sticking together in clumps. Add the coated dates and the oats to the batter and stir well.

Spoon the batter into 1 large buttered loaf pan or 2 small ones, and bake in a preheated oven at 350 degrees for 1 hour, or until a toothpick inserted near the center of a loaf comes out clean. Serve warm or cool with cream cheese.

Makes 1 large loaf or 2 small ones.

cheese pastries

These pastries, served warm, are a wonderful accompaniment for a soup, a cold vegetable mousse, or any salad.

1   cup flour
½   tsp. salt
½   tsp. paprika
a bit of fresh-ground black pepper
½   cup butter
⅓   cup grated Parmesan cheese
4   oz. Cheddar cheese, grated
2   Tbs. heavy cream, well chilled
1   egg beaten with 1 Tbs. cold water

Stir the flour together with the salt, paprika, and some fresh-ground black pepper. Cut the butter in with a pastry cutter or spin briefly in a food processor until the mixture resembles coarse meal. Toss it together with the grated cheeses, then sprinkle the cream over it, and work the mixture with your hands until you have a smooth dough. Chill it for about 1 hour.

Roll the dough out on a lightly floured board to a thickness of a little less than ¼ inch. Cut it into strips ½ inch wide and 1½ inches long. Brush the strips with the beaten egg, arrange them on ungreased cookie sheets, and bake them in a preheated oven at 325 degrees for 12 to 14 minutes, or until they are slightly puffed and beginning to brown on top.

Makes several dozen, enough for 6 to 8 to have as an accompaniment to a first course.

chapatis

These are the simple breads which accompany almost every Indian meal. Their delicious flavor and chewy, soft texture depend on their freshness, and ideally the *chapatis* should be served hot off the griddle, like tortillas. They can, however, be made an hour or two before dinner and reheated.

2   cups whole wheat flour
½   tsp. salt
2   Tbs. vegetable oil
½   cup water
ghee (clarified butter; see page 301) for
      brushing *chapatis*

Mix together the flour and salt, then add the vegetable oil and rub it into the flour with your fingers until the mixture is fairly homogeneous. Quickly stir in the water and start working the dough with your hand, in the bowl, until it holds together easily. If the dough continues to crumble, add a bit more water, 1 tablespoon at a time, adding just enough to allow the dough to hold together.

Take the dough out of the bowl and knead it energetically on a lightly floured surface until it is smooth and elastic, about 5 to 10 minutes.

Divide the dough into 12 equal-sized pieces and form each piece into a ball. Roll the balls out as evenly as possible into thin circles about 7 inches across. Stack them and keep them covered to prevent them from drying out.

Heat a cast-iron frying pan and have a little bowl of *ghee* and a pastry brush handy. Do not butter or oil the pan. Cook the *chapatis*, one at a time, for a minute or so on each side. If they puff up, just press them down gently with a spatula. The *chapatis* are done when brown spots show evenly over both sides.

As the *chapatis* are finished, stack them on a plate, brushing each one lightly with *ghee*. If it is necessary to reheat the *chapatis*, place them in a very hot pan for a few seconds on each side, or wrap them tightly in foil and put them in a hot oven just until they are warmed through.

Makes 12 *chapatis*, enough to serve 6 people.

puris

Puris are made of the same type of dough that is used for *chapatis*, but these little Indian breads are deep-fried in hot oil and puff up like balloons. They should be eaten almost immediately.

1   cup whole wheat flour
¼   tsp. salt
1   generous Tbs. vegetable oil
¼   cup water
vegetable oil for deep frying

Sift together the flour and the salt, then add the vegetable oil and rub it into the flour with your fingers until the mixture is fairly homogeneous. Quickly stir in the water and start working the dough with your hand, in the bowl, until it holds together easily.

Take the dough out of the bowl and knead it vigorously on a lightly floured board for 5 to 10 minutes, or until it is smooth and elastic. Add a bit more flour or a few drops more water as necessary if the dough seems either too sticky or too dry to hold together well.

Divide the dough into 10 or 12 equal-sized pieces and roll each piece into a smooth ball. Roll the balls out into circles about 4 inches across, stacking them on a plate and keeping them covered to prevent drying out.

Heat about 2 cups of vegetable oil in a wok or heavy, deep skillet, and when it is very hot, slide in one of the dough circles. It should bubble up to the surface almost immediately and start to inflate like a balloon. Very gentle pressure with a flat spatula on top of the *puri* will help it inflate evenly.

Turn the *puri* over gently, using a slotted spoon or spatula, and cook it until both sides are golden brown—this will take only a few minutes. Lift out the *puri*, letting the oil from it drip back into the wok for a few seconds, and put it down on a plate lined with paper towels.

Continue frying the *puris* in this manner until all of them are done, then serve immediately. The *puris* can be kept warm in a low oven for a short time.

To make small *puris* such as are used in Potato Chat Puris (page 320), divide the dough into about 18 small pieces, roughly the size of little walnuts. Roll them out into circles approximately 2 to 2½ inches across, and continue as above. With the small *puris*, several can easily be fried at one time.

Makes 10 to 12 large *puris*, enough to serve 4 to 6 people.

biscuits

2   cups white flour
4   tsp. baking powder
¾   tsp. salt
½   cup butter
½ to ⅔ cup cold milk

Sift together the flour, baking powder, and salt.
Slice the butter while it is very cold, add it to the
dry ingredients, and cut it in with a pastry
blender or two knives until it is in bits the size
of split peas. The texture of this mixture should
be a little more coarse than that of a short-crust
mixture before the liquid is added. This could
be done in a food processor but blend for only
a few seconds.

Sprinkle ½ cup of cold milk over the flour and
butter, and stir it in quickly with a fork. Add
only as much more of the milk as is necessary to
make the dough hold together.

Gather the dough up into a ball, working it
together with your hands very briefly, and then
roll it out ½ inch thick on a floured board. Cut
out small rounds and place them on ungreased
baking sheets. If you aren't going to put them
in the oven immediately, chill them in the
refrigerator until ready to bake.

Bake the biscuits in a preheated oven at 450
degrees for 10 to 12 minutes, or until puffed
and lightly browned on top. Serve them hot
with butter.

Makes about 20 biscuits.

sweet finnish rusks

½   cup soft butter
⅔   cup sugar
grated rind of 1 orange
2   eggs
2½ cups white flour
1½ tsp. baking powder

Cream the butter with the sugar and orange rind until it is fluffy, then beat in the eggs. Sift 2 cups of the flour with the baking powder, and add this mixture gradually to the butter mixture, beating it in till smooth.

Sprinkle the remaining flour over a large board or other smooth surface and turn the dough out onto it. Knead the dough for several minutes, incorporating the remaining flour; the dough should be smooth and easily manageable.

Break off pieces of dough the size of very large walnuts and roll them into smooth balls. Flatten the balls with a spatula until they are about ¾ inch thick. They will have the shape of miniature English muffins.

Arrange them 1 inch apart on lightly greased baking sheets and bake in a preheated oven at 400 degrees for 10 minutes, just until they are beginning to turn golden brown and are puffing up a bit.

Take the rusks out of the oven, let them cool for a couple of minutes—just until you can handle them. While they are still warm, slice them in half with a sharp, serrated knife. Arrange them on baking sheets, cut side up, and put them back into the oven, reducing the heat to 350 degrees. Bake them for another 8 to 10 minutes, or until they are dried and golden but not brown.

Serve the rusks with coffee or tea. Makes about 24 to 30 rusks.

corn and rye muffins

1 cup whole wheat flour
¾ cup yellow corn meal
¼ cup dark rye flour
1 tsp. baking powder
¾ tsp. baking soda
½ tsp. salt
1½ cups buttermilk
1 egg
¼ cup vegetable oil
¼ cup honey

Sift together the dry ingredients. Beat together the wet ingredients.

Stir the two mixtures together just until they are well combined, then spoon the batter into buttered muffin tins.

Bake the muffins in a preheated oven at 400 degrees for about 20 minutes, or until a toothpick inserted in the center of one comes out clean and dry. Serve warm.

Makes 12 medium-sized muffins.

four-grain muffins

¾ cup whole wheat flour
¾ cup yellow corn meal
½ cup dark rye flour
2 tsp. baking powder
½ tsp. salt
½ cup rolled oats
1½ cups milk
1 egg
¼ cup vegetable oil
¼ cup honey

Sift together the wheat flour, corn meal, rye flour, baking powder, and salt. Stir in the rolled oats.

In another bowl, beat together the milk, egg, oil, and honey. Stir the two mixtures together vigorously just until they are well combined. Then spoon the batter into buttered muffin tins.

Bake the muffins in a preheated oven at 400 degrees for 20 minutes. Serve warm.

Makes 12 muffins.

oatmeal muffins

1½ cups whole wheat flour
2   tsp. baking powder
½   tsp. salt
¾   cup rolled oats
¼   cup ground filberts (optional)
1   cup milk
1   egg
3   Tbs. butter, melted
2   Tbs. molasses
½   cup currants

Sift together the flour, baking powder, and salt. Mix in the rolled oats and ground nuts.

In another bowl, beat together the milk, egg, melted butter, and molasses. Add the currants and stir the two mixtures together just until they are well combined; then spoon the batter into buttered muffin tins.

Bake the muffins in a preheated oven at 400 degrees for about 20 minutes. Serve warm.

Makes 12 muffins.

soups

Anything so sensible and versatile as soup should not be too difficult to prepare, and for once things are as they should be. The great majority of soups are so little trouble to make and so economical that there is hardly any excuse at all for canned soups. But the flavor, the tantalizing aroma, the downright goodness of a good homemade soup would be a bargain at twice the exertion or twice the price.

The idea that a homemade soup must take hours of time should be laid to rest right now. Garlic Soup (Sopa de Ajo), for instance, is a marvel of convenience (for garlic lovers only, though). It is ready in about twice the time it takes to poach an egg, costs pennies, can easily be prepared just one serving at a time, and makes a nourishing, warming meal. In Madrid and Segovia, where winters are bitter, Sopa de Ajo takes its place on all the menus when gazpacho is taken off till the next summer, and we used to eat it nearly every day. One might think that something so practical would have no right to be delicious as well, but there you are; it's just one of those things.

Soups based on stocks, or broths, will never be as quick as that, but the actual work time required for most of them is not great. All the ingredients for a good broth can be put together in a quarter of an hour, and after that it doesn't bother anyone for a long while as it simmers. Once it's finished, just a little extra attention can transform it into one of any number of delicacies, simple or fancy. In Mexico I found out about Tortilla Soup, made of a lightly creamed, tomato-flavored broth with crisp-fried strips of corn tortillas, chunks of hot, half-melted cheese, and morsels of onion and chili. It was such a simple soup to make, when I set about doing it in my own kitchen, and has a wonderfully intriguing, slightly exotic flavor.

Some of my other long-time favorites are the soups that make a meal and satisfy a big hunger, like the Pistou, with its combination of beans and big chunks of fresh vegetables, all flavored with that incomparable paste of olive oil, basil, pine nuts, garlic, and Parmesan cheese. Another one to satisfy body and soul is Sauerkraut Soup. It was devised one chilly evening for a friend who had a stubborn craving for sauerkraut; we went down to the kitchen and got right to work, with whatever supplies were on hand. The result was wonderful. Others of that type are Garlic Soup, Pasta e Fagioli (both), Cheese Soup, Dutch Cheese and Potato Soup, Beer and Onion Soup, Split Pea Soup, and Green Chili and Cheese Soup. No matter what the season of the year, and no matter what you may have on hand, chances are that a very palatable dish of soup can be concocted from it. Inventive cooks are in their element with soup, and for the novice who wants to experiment, this is the place to begin. If only you know a few basics of proportion and technique, which are quickly learned with the first few pots, it's hard to go wrong.

But right along with all this practicality, soups can still rise to the most elegant occasion. Nothing suits me as well for the start of an elaborate meal as a delicate Clear Beet Borscht, with slivers of wild mushroom, or the Creamed Avocado Soup, which is still unusual enough to be a nice surprise. And in the summertime, I like to serve the most ambrosial cold soup of them all, one that is well worth a little extra effort—the Cold Cherry-Lemon Soup. It's a show stopper, and wonderful with champagne.

Since almost every imaginable food can find its way into a soup, there should be something for everyone, and I can't imagine the person who doesn't like soup at all. In my own enthusiasm for all these delicious hot and cold liquids, I've compiled here no less than thirty-six new soup recipes, and I think of it as just a nice sampler of what's possible.

vegetable broth I

This and the other broths that follow are pleasant just as they are, served in a cup. However, they are tremendously useful as stocks in the making of other soups, sauces, etc. They will keep well in the refrigerator for 2 to 3 days and can be frozen.

5   qts. water
4   medium-sized stalks celery, thickly sliced
2   medium-sized onions, peeled and halved, stuck with 2 cloves
2   medium-sized potatoes, scrubbed and thickly sliced
2   turnips, scrubbed and cut in 1-inch dice
5 to 6 large carrots, scraped and thickly sliced
several large sprigs parsley
2   bay leaves
8 to 10 peppercorns
4 to 5 cloves garlic, peeled
salt

Combine all the ingredients in a large kettle, bring the water to a boil, lower the heat, and simmer uncovered for 3 to 4 hours. Strain the broth in a colander or large sieve and taste it. If it is weak, return it to the pot and continue simmering until it is reduced to the proper strength of flavor. Season to taste with salt.

Makes 5 to 6 cups broth.

vegetable broth II

Serve the broth with dumplings, or use it as a base for other soups.

½   oz. dried wild mushrooms
3   medium-sized leeks
about ½ medium-sized head cabbage
2   large stalks celery
3   large carrots
1   turnip
1   large potato
several sprigs parsley
10   medium-sized cloves garlic
3   qts. water
2   bay leaves
10 to 12 peppercorns
large pinch of thyme
dash of Tabasco sauce
2   Tbs. olive oil
juice of ½ lemon
1   Tbs. salt

Pour a small amount of hot water over the dried mushrooms and let them soak in it while you prepare the other vegetables.

Trim the green parts off of the leeks, cut them in half lengthwise, just to the base, and wash them carefully. Cut the cabbage into wedges. Thickly slice the celery. Scrape and thickly slice

vegetable broth II (continued)

the carrots. Peel and slice the turnip. Scrub and cube the potato. Separate the garlic cloves, but do not peel them.

As soon as the dried mushrooms are somewhat softened, wash them very carefully, one by one, to get rid of all the sand and grit.

Put all the vegetables and garlic in a large kettle with the water. Add the bay leaves, peppercorns, thyme, Tabasco sauce, olive oil, lemon juice, and salt and bring the water to a boil.

Reduce the heat until the liquid is just simmering and allow it to simmer, uncovered, for 1½ hours or slightly longer; the broth is ready when the flavor is full and strong.

Strain the broth through a colander and again through a fine sieve, and correct the seasoning if necessary.

Serves 6.

potato peel broth
garlic broth

Potato Peel Broth and Garlic Broth, those fragrant liquids with the amusing names, are such good, basic stocks for soups and sauces that I couldn't leave them out. Both recipes are repeated here essentially as they appeared in the original *Vegetarian Epicure*, with a few slight alterations that I developed in my repeated use of these broths and that strike me as improvements.

The Potato Peel Broth is a bit richer in flavor by the addition of some herbs and oil which I had formerly added only to the sweeter Garlic Broth. And, monosodium glutomate, about which we know too little but enough to scare us, has been deleted. To make Garlic Broth, it is only necessary to add a full head of garlic, split into cloves, to the Potato Peel Broth recipe.

So, back by popular demand, here is:

potato peel broth

peels from 6 to 7 large, healthy brown-skinned
    potatoes
1   large onion
2   carrots
1   medium-sized stalk celery
2   qts. water

1 large sprig parsley
1½ Tbs. olive or mild vegetable oil
½ to 1 bay leaf
¼ tsp. dried whole thyme
pinch of sage
salt and pepper to taste
1 clove garlic (optional)
dash of Tabasco (optional)
dash of lemon juice (optional)

First scrub the potatoes very thoroughly and cut away any blemishes, then peel them, cutting off strips at least ¼ inch thick. Reserve the peeled potatoes for another use. Peel the onion and quarter it. Wash the carrots and celery and slice them.

Combine all the ingredients but the Tabasco and the lemon juice in a large pot and simmer for about 1½ hours, or until all the vegetables are very soft. If too much water evaporates during the cooking, add enough to keep all the vegetables covered with liquid. When the broth is done, there should be about 6 cups of it, but this may vary slightly. The most important thing is to taste it, smell it, look at it. If it is light brown, fragrant, and delicious, it's ready; if it seems weak, simmer it a bit longer and reduce it; if it seems too strong, add a bit of water.

For a clear broth, just strain out all the vegetables through a sieve and correct the seasoning if necessary. For a soup with the consistency of a thin purée, first fish out the celery, garlic, and bay leaf, then press everything through a fine sieve until only a rather dry pulp is left.

Finally, for giving both Potato Peel Broth and Garlic Broth that final touch of seasoning, I've found that a delightful flavor is brought out by the addition of a few drops of Tabasco or a few drops of lemon juice—or both.

garlic broth

Proceed exactly as for Potato Peel Broth, only add a full, large head of garlic rather than just one puny clove, and be sure to use olive oil. Break the head of garlic up into separate cloves and peel them if you wish, though they can also be used unpeeled—a method that many people feel yields richer flavor. Simmer the broth gently for a long time—1½ to 2 hours— and then strain everything out through a sieve for a fine, clear, and delicate broth.

Each method yields about 6 cups of broth.

dumplings for soup

These dumplings are good with any broth, and they are a must with Creamed Fresh Pea Soup (page 83).

6 Tbs. soft butter
2 eggs
1½ cups flour
⅓ cup milk
½ tsp. salt
⅛ tsp. nutmeg
⅛ tsp. cayenne pepper

Cream the butter in a deep bowl and beat in the eggs. Add the flour and milk alternately, beating after each addition, until all the flour and milk are incorporated. Beat in the salt, nutmeg, and cayenne. The mixture should be smooth and creamy but fairly stiff.

Bring a large pot of heavily salted water to a boil and drop the dough in by ½ teaspoonfuls. Boil the dumplings, covered, for about 15 minutes and transfer them to the soup with a slotted spoon.

The dumplings can also be boiled in a broth.

Makes 6 to 8 servings.

a very simple noodle soup

6 cups Vegetable Broth I or II (page 57)
3 cups broth from cooking lima, kidney, or garbanzo beans
2 Tbs. butter
1 tsp. paprika
dash of cayenne
salt and pepper
2 to 3 oz. fettucine or other noodles

Heat the broths together in a pot, and when they are simmering, stir in the butter, paprika, cayenne, and salt and pepper to taste. Raise the heat and add the noodles, breaking them up to whatever length you prefer. Simmer for about 20 minutes, or until the noodles are perfectly tender.

Serves 6 to 8.

vegetable soup I

This was put together by clearing out all the odds and ends left in the vegetable bins, after a busy couple of days of cooking. It is the simplest kind of soup to make and a delicious, hearty supper dish for a cold evening. You can invent your own versions easily by rummaging through the kitchen and putting together whatever you think will make a pleasing combination. The proportions I've given here are flexible.

kernels from 1 ear of corn
½ medium-sized eggplant (½ lb.), cubed in 1-inch pieces
1 large pale-skinned potato, washed and cubed
1 large red bell pepper, seeded and cut in 1-inch pieces
2 medium-sized zucchini, thickly sliced
1 yellow onion, peeled and cut in 1-inch squares
5 or 6 mushrooms, sliced
4 cloves garlic, peeled and thinly sliced
3 green onions, coarsely chopped
1 cup shredded cabbage
1 dill pickle, very thinly sliced
1½ cups chopped fresh spinach
2 tomatoes, cut in thin wedges

approximately 3 qts. water
salt
black pepper
2 Tbs. olive oil
2 Tbs. red wine vinegar
ground cumin
cayenne pepper
oregano

To prepare the soup, just wash and trim the vegetables as required, chop or slice them, and put them all together in a very large kettle with the water. Salt and pepper to taste and season with the olive oil, vinegar, and spices to taste. Simmer the soup for at least ½ hour and serve piping hot with bread and cheese.

Serves 6 to 8.

vegetable soup II

1   ear of corn
½   medium-sized eggplant (about ½ lb.)
2   medium-sized carrots
1   stalk celery
1   large pale-skinned potato
1   fresh red pimiento pepper
2   medium-sized zucchini
1   yellow onion
5 or 6 medium-sized mushrooms
¼   head cabbage
1   small dill pickle
4   cloves garlic
2   Tbs. olive oil
3   green onions
1½ cups shredded fresh spinach
2   tomatoes
salt
fresh-ground black pepper
cumin seeds, crushed
cayenne pepper
oregano
red wine vinegar

optional garnish: croutons

Wash the corn and scrape the kernels off the ear. Cube the eggplant, scrape and slice the carrots, slice the celery, and scrub and cube the potato. Remove the ribs and seeds from the pimiento and cut it into medium-sized squares or strips. Wash and slice the zucchini and peel and very coarsely chop the onion. Wash the mushrooms thoroughly and slice them. Shred the cabbage, and thinly slice the pickle.

Put all these vegetables in a large pot and add enough water to cover them amply. Simmer the soup over a medium flame.

Peel and mince the garlic and sauté it in the olive oil. Slice the green onions, including the tops, and add them to the garlic and oil. When the onions are quite soft and the garlic golden, add this mixture to the soup.

When the other vegetables are about half-cooked, add the shredded spinach and the tomatoes, cut in thin wedges. Let it all cook together for a few minutes, stirring often; then season to taste with salt, pepper, crushed cumin seeds, cayenne, oregano, and a teaspoon or two of red wine vinegar. Continue cooking until all the vegetables are tender, adding more water if necessary.

Serve steaming hot, with croutons if desired.

Serves 6 to 8.

spinach soup

This is such a light and refreshing soup that it makes a perfect foil for a hearty or especially rich dish—like stuffed crêpes or filled potato pancakes.

2   qts. water
1   lb. fresh spinach (2 bunches)
2   medium-large potatoes
¾   cup sliced green onions
salt and pepper to taste
½   cup sour cream
2   Tbs. fresh lemon juice

garnish

sour cream (optional)

Heat the water in a large pot. Wash the spinach leaves carefully and remove the stems. Peel the potatoes and cut them in ½-inch dice. Add the spinach leaves, the potatoes, and half the green onions to the water with a little salt and pepper, and simmer the soup very gently for about 1 hour, stirring occasionally.

Add the remaining green onions and ladle out about a cup of the hot broth into the sour cream. Whisk the sour cream and broth together and stir it back into the soup. Add 1½ tablespoons of the lemon juice and let the soup simmer for another hour. Taste, add more salt and pepper as needed, and the remainder of the lemon juice if the soup is not tart enough for your taste.

Serve this soup hot or cold, with additional sour cream if desired.

Serves 6.

garlic-tomato soup

2½ Tbs. olive oil
3   cloves garlic, pressed or minced
2   Tbs. paprika
4½ cups Garlic Broth or Potato Peel Broth
      (page 58)
4   cups puréed fresh tomatoes, strained
salt to taste
Tabasco sauce to taste
butter to taste
6   slices French bread
Parmesan cheese, grated

Heat the olive oil in a large, heavy skillet and sauté the garlic in it for a minute or two. Remove the skillet from direct heat and stir the paprika into the oil. Return to low heat and continue stirring the paprika and oil for another moment. The instant it begins to sizzle, add the broth and the puréed tomatoes. (If it's winter and you can't get good, fresh tomatoes, canned tomatoes can be substituted: Purée them in a blender or food processor with all their juice, and strain through a sieve to get rid of the seeds.)

Simmer the soup for 10 to 15 minutes, taste it, and season with salt and a little Tabasco.

Butter 6 slices of French bread and sprinkle them generously with grated Parmesan cheese. Rub the cheese lightly into the butter with a knife. Bake these croutons in a hot oven for about 10 minutes, or put them under the broiler for 2 to 3 minutes. They should be lightly browned around the edges. Put 1 in each of 6 bowls, pour the hot soup over the croutons, and serve immediately.

Serves 6.

clear beet borscht with mushrooms

1   oz. of the best dried wild mushrooms*
3   qts. plus 1½ cups water
2   medium-sized potatoes, scrubbed and
     sliced
2   medium stalks celery, sliced
2 to 3 cloves garlic, peeled
1   large turnip, peeled and sliced
4   medium-sized carrots, scraped and sliced
1 or 2 bay leaves
1   Tbs. salt
8 or 9 peppercorns
1½ lbs. beets
3   Tbs. lemon juice
1   Tbs. sugar

garnish

sour cream

Soak the dried mushrooms in 1½ cups water for about 2 hours or overnight.

In a large kettle, combine 3 quarts water, the potatoes, celery, garlic, turnip, carrots, bay leaves, salt, and peppercorns. Simmer gently for about 1 to 2 hours. The broth should be subtle but flavorful.

Strain the broth and discard the cooked vegetables.

Drain the mushrooms and reserve the liquid in which they have been soaked. Wash the mushrooms carefully, one by one, and slice them in julienne strips.

Strain the mushroom liquid through several layers of muslin or through a paper coffee filter. Add the strained liquid and the mushrooms to the broth.

Peel the beets and cut them in julienne strips. Add the beets to the broth, as well as the lemon juice and sugar.

Simmer the soup for another 20 to 25 minutes, or until the beets are quite tender; then taste, correct the seasoning, and serve, garnishing each bowl with a spoonful of sour cream.

Serves 12.

*Mushrooms from Italy or from Eastern Europe are very good, but the dried Japanese forest mushrooms are also excellent.

tortilla soup tlaxcalteca

6   cups Garlic Broth (page 58)
5   corn tortillas
vegetable oil for frying
10 oz. panella or fresh mozzarella cheese
½   red onion
1½ cups puréed fresh tomatoes
½   cup light cream
paprika
fresh chili sauce

While the Garlic Broth is cooking, cut up the tortillas in strips about ½ inch wide and 1½ inches long, and fry them in hot oil until they are crisp. Drain them well on paper towels and put them aside.

Cut the panella or fresh mozzarella into ¼- to ½-inch cubes. Peel and slice the red onion and cut the slices into 1-inch lengths.

Add the puréed fresh tomatoes and the cream to the hot Garlic Broth, as well as the onion slices. Cook over a low flame for about 15 minutes, stirring occasionally. Season the soup to taste with paprika and fresh chili sauce. The soup should not be too terribly hot with chili, but its flavor should be subtly present.

About a minute before the soup is to be served, stir in the fried tortilla strips and the cubes of panella cheese. Stir gently and then ladle the soup into warmed bowls or small casseroles, and serve steaming hot.

Serves 6.

sweet potato soup

1¼ lbs. sweet potatoes
3   small carrots
1   large stalk celery
1   bay leaf
6   cups water
1½ tsp. salt

2   Tbs. lemon juice
1   tsp. paprika
1½ Tbs. butter
½   cup heavy cream

Peel the sweet potatoes and cut them in small dice. Scrape and thinly slice the carrots. Slice the celery. Put all the vegetables and the bay leaf in a pot with the water. Bring the water to a boil, then lower the heat and let the soup simmer for about 1 hour, stirring occasionally.

Add the remaining ingredients and simmer the soup for another 10 minutes or so.

Serves 5 to 6.

cheese soup

Be sure to use good, properly aged cheeses for this soup. A cheese that is too "green," or young, will curdle and turn rubbery when heated, but a mature cheese will melt beautifully as long as it is not boiled.

6   Tbs. butter
5   Tbs. flour
4½ cups hot milk
1   cup cream
9   oz. Gouda cheese, grated
4½ oz. smoked Edam cheese, grated
2   Tbs. Worcestershire sauce*
1   tsp. paprika
dash of Tabasco or cayenne pepper
salt and pepper to taste
garlic toast (optional)

*Several readers of my earlier book have expressed concern about the use of Worcestershire sauce, pointing out that it contains a trace of anchovies. *Alanna* brand Worcestershire sauce, manufactured by Goodalls of Ireland and available in health food stores, contains no anchovies.

Melt the butter in a large saucepan and stir in the flour. Cook this roux over very low heat for a few minutes, stirring. Add the hot milk and stir with a whisk over medium heat until the mixture is thickened and perfectly smooth.

Add the cream. Adjust the flame so that the soup stays hot but does not boil. Gradually add the grated cheeses, stirring constantly with a wooden spoon.

When all the cheese is melted and the soup has a smooth, velvety consistency, add the Worcestershire sauce, paprika, Tabasco, and salt and pepper.

Serve hot with garlic toast.

Makes 6 servings.

pasta e fagioli I
(pasta with beans)

1½ cups dried red kidney beans, washed
2   qts. water
2   large carrots, scraped and chopped
1   large onion, chopped
1   large stalk celery, thinly sliced
1   bay leaf
large pinch of basil
pinch of rosemary, crushed
4   cloves garlic, thinly sliced
1   Tbs. olive oil
4   Tbs. tomato paste
salt and pepper
6   oz. fettucine noodles

garnish

grated Parmesan cheese
fresh-ground black pepper
olive oil

Boil the washed beans in lightly salted water for ½ hour. Add the carrots, onions, celery, herbs, and olive oil. Simmer for at least another ½ hour, or until the beans are tender.

Ladle half the beans and vegetables into a blender or food processor with some of the broth, and blend to a purée. Return the purée to the soup and stir in the tomato paste. Season to taste with salt and pepper.

Twenty minutes before serving, add the fettucine noodles, as well as a little boiling water if the soup should seem too thick. Cook until the noodles are *al dente*—tender but still firm—and serve very hot.

Pass grated Parmesan cheese, a pepper mill, and a pitcher of very good olive oil to garnish the soup.

Serves 6 to 8.

pasta e fagioli II

1½ cups dried red kidney beans, washed
12 cups water
1½ tsp. salt, and more to taste
2 small carrots, scraped and finely diced
4½ Tbs. olive oil
1 small onion, peeled and chopped
2 small cloves garlic, minced
½ tsp. rosemary, crushed
4 oz. thin fettucine noodles
⅓ to ½ cup grated Parmesan cheese
fresh-ground black pepper

Put the beans in a pot with 9 cups of the water and 1½ teaspoons salt. Bring the water to a boil, then lower the heat and simmer the beans for 1 hour. Add the diced carrots and simmer another 10 minutes.

Heat the olive oil in a pan and sauté the onions and garlic in it until they begin to color. Add them to the soup, along with the crushed rosemary, and let it continue cooking for 10 minutes more. By this time the kidney beans should be tender, and the liquid should be becoming quite thick.

Add the remaining 3 cups water, bring the soup back to an easy boil, and add the noodles. Cook them for 12 to 15 minutes, or until they are tender, then stir in the Parmesan cheese, season to taste with more salt and more fresh-ground black pepper, and serve.

Serves 6 to 8.

garlic soup *(sopa de ajo)*

per serving

4 small cloves garlic
1 Tbs. olive oil
1 tsp. paprika
½ tsp. salt
1½ to 2 cups hot water

dash of Tabasco sauce (optional)
dash of Worcestershire sauce (optional)
approximately 1½-inch-thick slice dry French
   bread
1 egg

Peel the cloves of garlic and slice them thinly. Heat the olive oil in a saucepan or an earthen-

garlic soup (continued)

ware casserole and sauté the garlic in it until it is just beginning to turn golden. Add the paprika and salt and stir quickly for about ½ minute, then add the hot water. Simmer the broth for a few minutes, taste, and add a dash of Tabasco and a dash of Worcestershire if you like.

Break the bread up into chunks, or if it is still soft enough, cut it in paper-thin slices. Add the bread to the broth. When the bread is quite soft and the broth is simmering again, break in the egg and ladle some broth over it. Turn down the flame and continue to simmer the soup until the egg is poached to your taste.

split pea soup

1   lb. green split peas
3   qts. water
1½ tsp. salt
2½ Tbs. butter
1½ cups finely chopped carrots
1   cup finely chopped sweet potato
1   cup finely chopped onions
½   cup finely chopped celery
½ to ¾ tsp. ground marjoram
1   tsp. dried basil
1 to 2 cloves garlic, crushed or minced
½ to ¾ tsp. ground cumin
½   cup dry white wine
fresh-ground black pepper to taste

optional garnish

croutons

Put the split peas in a large pot with the water and salt, bring the water to a boil, then lower the heat and simmer for about 1 hour. Skim off the foam from the top and discard it.

Sauté the finely chopped or minced carrots, sweet potato, onions, and celery in the butter for about 10 minutes, stirring almost constantly. Add the herbs, and cook the vegetables for another 5 minutes, then add them to the soup. Simmer the soup, stirring occasionally, for another 45 minutes to 1 hour.

Ladle out approximately ½ the soup and purée it in a blender or force it through a sieve. Return the purée to the pot, add the wine and pepper, stir, and bring the soup back to a simmer. Serve hot, alone or with croutons.

Serves 6 to 8.

dutch cheese and potato soup

5 to 6 russet potatoes
5 Tbs. butter
2 large yellow onions
2 bay leaves
1 tsp. dill seeds, crushed in a mortar
2 Tbs. flour
2 cups milk
6 oz. Gouda cheese, grated
1 Tbs. paprika
1 Tbs. Worcestershire sauce (see page 67)
salt
fresh-ground black pepper

Peel the potatoes and cut them into small cubes. Boil them in just enough lightly salted water to cover until they are tender. Do not discard the cooking water.

Meanwhile, melt 3 tablespoons of the butter in a large, deep skillet or pot. Cut the onions in half crosswise and slice them thinly. Sauté the sliced onions in the melted butter along with the bay leaves, stirring often, until the onions just start to turn golden. Add the crushed dill seeds and stir a minute more, then add the cooked potatoes along with their water.

Melt the remaining 2 tablespoons butter in a heavy-bottomed skillet, stir in 2 tablespoons flour, and cook a minute or two over low heat. In a separate saucepan heat the milk, and then stir it into the roux. Stir constantly with a whisk until the sauce has thickened and is completely smooth. Add it to the soup.

Bit by bit, add the grated cheese, stirring slowly all the while. Then add the paprika, Worcestershire sauce, and salt and pepper to taste. Keep the soup barely simmering on a low flame, stirring often, for about 15 minutes more. Serve hot.

Serves 6.

beer and onion soup

3   lbs. onions (8 to 10 medium sized)
2 to 3 cloves garlic, minced
¾   cup butter
2   cups Vegetable Broth I or II (page 57)
2½ cups dark beer or stout
1¼ cups cream
2   tsp. salt
2   tsp. paprika
dash of Tabasco sauce
fresh-ground black pepper to taste
2 to 4 tsp. sugar (depending on the bitter-
      ness of the beer used)
2   tsp. cider vinegar
4   egg yolks

optional garnish

hot paprika
toasted croutons and grated Parmesan cheese

Peel the onions, halve them crosswise, and slice them. Cook them slowly with the garlic in the butter until all the onions are transparent and soft—about 1 hour. Add the vegetable broth and, in batches of 2 or 3 cups, purée the mixture in a blender or food processor.

Pour the purée into a large pot together with the beer and cream. Add the salt, paprika, Tabasco, pepper, sugar, and vinegar, and simmer the mixture, stirring often, for about 20 minutes.

Beat the egg yolks with a whisk. Continue to beat them as you add a small amount of the hot soup, then pour the egg yolk mixture into the pot with the rest of the soup and whisk it all together quickly. Cook the soup a few minutes more over very low heat, stirring constantly. It should be slightly thickened.

Serve the soup very hot and sprinkle a little hot paprika on top if you like, or garnish it with the croutons and the Parmesan cheese.

Serves 6 to 8.

sauerkraut soup

4   Tbs. olive oil
4   Tbs. butter
3   large onions, coarsely chopped
3   cloves garlic, peeled and minced
2   Tbs. sweet paprika
¼   tsp. hot paprika
2   lbs. sauerkraut
6   cups water (more if needed)
1   stalk celery, sliced
1   carrot, peeled and sliced
3   cups sliced peeled tomatoes, with their
      juice
1   tsp. caraway seeds
2 to 3 oz. dried black mushrooms
3   tsp. sugar
½   cup red wine
1   tsp. dill weed
1½ tsp. salt, or more to taste
pepper to taste

Heat the olive oil and butter in a large, heavy-bottomed skillet. Add the chopped onions and garlic, and sauté them until they begin to turn golden. Add the 2 paprikas, stir for a moment, then add the sauerkraut, water, celery, carrot, and tomatoes.

Pound the caraway seeds lightly in a mortar and add them to the soup. Soak the black mushrooms in water for a few minutes. Drain them, discarding the water, and wash each one very carefully. Then cut them into thin strips and add them to the soup.

Season the soup with sugar, red wine, dill weed, and salt and pepper. Let the soup simmer gently for at least 1 hour, longer if possible. Add a little more water if the soup becomes too thick.

Serves 6 to 8.

pistou

2½ qts. water
1½ cups scrubbed, diced potatoes
1½ cups peeled, sliced carrots
1¾ cups cleaned, sliced leeks (white parts)
2 tsp. salt
1 cup sliced zucchini
1 small red bell pepper, diced or cut in strips
2 cups cut green beans
1½ cups cooked kidney beans
¼ cup dry bread crumbs
⅛ tsp. saffron

pistou sauce

2½ oz. Parmesan cheese, grated (about ½ cup)
3 oz. tomato paste
⅓ cup pine nuts
1½ Tbs. dried basil or ¼ cup chopped fresh
4 to 5 cloves garlic
⅓ cup olive oil
fresh-ground black pepper

In a large pot, combine the water, potatoes, carrots, leeks, and salt and simmer for 40 minutes.

Add the zucchini, red pepper, green beans, kidney beans, bread crumbs, and saffron. Simmer the soup for another 20 minutes.

Meanwhile, prepare the Pistou Sauce: Grate the Parmesan cheese and stir it into the tomato paste. Grind the pine nuts finely and add them to the tomato-cheese paste, along with the basil. Crush the garlic and stir it in. Finally, add the olive oil and process the sauce in a blender at high speed until it is perfectly smooth and homogeneous. Lacking a blender, pound all but the olive oil with a pestle or a wooden spoon until you have a smooth paste, then gradually beat in the oil. Season with pepper to taste.

Ladle out about a cup of hot broth from the soup and stir it into the pistou sauce. Now add the mixture to the soup, stir, and serve.

Serves 8 to 10.

green chili and cheese soup

1½ Tbs. butter
1½ Tbs. olive oil
1½ medium-sized yellow onions
4 to 5 cloves garlic
2   tsp. paprika
3½ cups water or Vegetable Broth I (page 57)
1½ lbs. fresh, ripe tomatoes
4   oz. green chilis, seeded and skinned
2   small white-skinned potatoes
¼   tsp. ground cumin
1   Tbs. chopped fresh cilantro (coriander leaves)
1   tsp. salt, plus more to taste
4   oz. Monterey Jack cheese

Melt the butter in a large pot and add the oil. Peel the onions and cut them into 1-inch chunks. Peel and chop or thinly slice the garlic. Add the onions and garlic to the butter and oil and sauté for several minutes. Then add the paprika and sauté 1 or 2 minutes more, stirring constantly.

Add the water or broth. Cut the tomatoes into wedges and spin them briefly in a blender or food processor. They should be partly puréed and partly chopped. Cut the chilis into small strips or coarsely chop them. Scrub the pota-

toes and cut them into ½-inch cubes. Add the tomatoes, chilis, potatoes, ground cumin, and chopped cilantro to the soup and simmer until the potatoes are tender, about ½ hour.

Season to taste with salt.

Cut the cheese into small chunks and divide it among 4 large soup bowls. Ladle the soup, bubbling hot, over the cheese in the bowls. Serve immediately.

Serves 4.

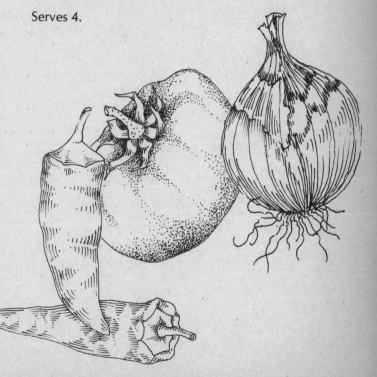

spiced lentil soup

2½ cups lentils
3½ qts. water
1½ tsp. salt, and more to taste
¼ cup olive oil
2 onions, peeled and chopped
4 to 5 large cloves garlic, peeled and sliced
2 large bay leaves
½ tsp. cinnamon
½ tsp. ground cloves
½ tsp. ginger
1½ tsp. ground cumin
2½ Tbs. minced green chilis
2 to 3 Tbs. chopped fresh cilantro (coriander leaves)
¼ cup chopped fresh parsley
2 to 3 Tbs. butter
lots of fresh-ground black pepper

optional garnish

paprika
sprigs of cilantro

Put the lentils in a large pot with 3½ quarts water and the salt, bring the water to a boil, then lower the heat and simmer the soup for 1 hour.

Heat the olive oil in a skillet, add the onions, garlic, and bay leaves and sauté them, stirring often, until the onions begin to color. Add the cinnamon, cloves, ginger, and cumin to the onions and stir over low heat for about 2 minutes. Stir the onions and spices into the soup, along with the chilis, cilantro, and parsley. Let the soup simmer for another hour, stirring it occasionally.

When all the lentils are completely soft, purée at least half the soup in a blender, in batches of 2 or 3 cups, or force it through a sieve. Return the puréed soup to the pot and stir in the butter. Grate in a generous amount of black pepper, stir, taste, and add more salt or pepper as needed.

Serve the soup hot and, if you like, sprinkle a little paprika on it just before serving, or garnish each bowl with sprigs of cilantro.

Serves 6 to 8.

cream of carrot soup

3 cups scraped, sliced carrots
1 large yellow onion, peeled and chopped
½ cup butter
1 tsp. sugar
1 tsp. salt, and more to taste
1 medium-sized potato, peeled and diced
½ cup water
1½ cups light cream
4 Tbs. flour
4½ cups milk
fresh-ground black pepper
paprika
cayenne pepper
1 clove garlic, minced (optional)
brandy

garnish

croutons or chopped parsley

Sauté the carrots and onions in a large skillet or soup pot in 4 tablespoons of the butter for a few minutes. Add the sugar, 1 tsp. salt, the diced potato, and the water. Cover tightly and simmer until the vegetables are just tender.

Purée the vegetables in a blender with the cream.

Melt the remaining 4 tablespoons butter in a skillet and stir in the flour. Cook the roux until it is golden. Heat the milk and stir it into the roux with a whisk. Cook the white sauce over a very small flame, stirring often, until it is thickened.

Combine the carrot purée and the white sauce in a large pot. Grate in some pepper and add paprika and cayenne to taste, as well as a little minced garlic if you like. Add a little brandy and salt to taste.

Simmer the soup gently for another 10 or 15 minutes, stirring occasionally. Serve hot, garnished with croutons or chopped parsley.

Serves 8.

eggplant soup

3   lbs. eggplant
2½ tsp. salt
2 . Tbs. olive oil
4   cloves garlic, minced
1   Tbs. paprika
¾   tsp. ground cumin
2½ cups hot water
¾   cup finely chopped celery
1   cup finely chopped onions
3   Tbs. butter
½   cup cream
2   cups milk
pinch of hot paprika

garnish

fresh-grated Parmesan cheese and croutons

Prick the eggplants in several places with a fork and bake them in a 375 degree oven for 40 to 50 minutes, depending on their size. The skins should be wrinkled and the eggplants soft. As soon as they are cool enough to handle, cut them open and scrape all the eggplant out of the skins. Purée the eggplant with 2 teaspoons of the salt in a blender and put it aside.

Heat the olive oil in a large pot and add the minced garlic. Cook the garlic, stirring often, until it is golden, and then stir in the paprika, cumin, and the remaining ½ teaspoon salt. Heat the spices in the oil for about ½ minute, then add the hot water and simmer the broth gently for several minutes.

Sauté the finely chopped celery and onion in the butter until the onion is golden and beginning to brown. Combine these vegetables with the eggplant purée and stir all of it into the hot garlic-paprika broth.

Add the cream, milk, and a little pinch of hot paprika. Simmer the soup for another 10 to 15 minutes, stirring occasionally, then taste it and correct the seasoning if necessary.

Serve the soup hot with croutons and grated Parmesan cheese.

Serves 6 to 8.

carrot-yogurt soup

4   Tbs. butter
1   onion, peeled and chopped
1 to 2 cloves garlic, minced
½   tsp. mustard seeds
½   tsp. tumeric
½   tsp. ginger
¼   tsp. cayenne pepper, and more to
        taste
½   tsp. salt, and more to taste
½   tsp. ground cumin
¼   tsp. cinnamon
1   lb. carrots, scraped and sliced
1   Tbs. lemon juice
3½ cups water
2   cups yogurt
1   Tbs. honey
black pepper to taste

garnish

chopped fresh cilantro (coriander leaves)

Melt the butter in a skillet and sauté the onions and garlic until they are golden. Add the spices and cook for several minutes, stirring constantly. Add the carrots and lemon juice. Continue cooking for several more minutes, stirring often, then add 2 cups of the water, cover tightly, and simmer for at least ½ hour, or until the carrots are tender.

Purée the spiced carrots in a blender with the remaining 1½ cups water. Return the purée to the skillet and whisk in the yogurt and the honey. Heat the soup, but do not allow it to boil.

Taste, correct the seasoning with black pepper and more cayenne and salt as desired, and serve hot, with chopped cilantro sprinkled on top.

Serves 4 to 5.

creamed avocado soup

4   Tbs. butter
2   Tbs. flour
3   cups hot Potato Peel Broth (page 58)
1   lb. ripe avocados (about 2 medium sized)
1½ cups light cream
½   cup yogurt
6   Tbs. fresh lemon juice
½   tsp salt, and more to taste
½   tsp sugar
fresh-ground black pepper to taste

garnish

fried corn tortilla strips
any good hot chili sauce (optional)

Melt the butter in a medium-sized, heavy-bottomed saucepan and stir in the flour. Cook the roux over low heat for several minutes, stirring constantly, until it begins to turn golden brown. Pour in the hot broth and continue stirring until the mixture is slightly thickened and smooth.

Peel and remove pits of the avocados and purée them in a blender or food processor with the cream, yogurt, and lemon juice. Combine the broth and the avocado mixture in an enameled pot and stir in the salt, sugar, and pepper. Heat the soup just to the simmering point, but don't let it come to a boil. Taste and correct the seasoning if necessary.

Serve the soup hot, putting a few crisp-fried tortilla strips in each bowl. Hot sauce can be passed separately and added as desired.

Serves 6.

Note: I don't recommend making this soup too far in advance, keeping it hot for a long time, or reheating it more than once. Avocados can be a little bit fussy once they are removed from their skin and pit.

watercress soup

A lovely soup for a big party, but the proportions can easily be cut in half.

½ cup butter
1⅓ cups chopped onions
6 Tbs. flour
9½ cups hot Potato Peel Broth (page 58)
6 cups packed watercress leaves, washed
1 cup heavy cream
4 eggs
2 Tbs. lemon juice
1 Tbs. sugar
salt to taste
pepper to taste

Melt the butter in a large pot and sauté the onions in it until they just begin to turn golden. Stir in the flour and lower the heat. Cook the roux, stirring constantly, for a few minutes. Continue stirring as you gradually add the hot broth. If you detect any lumps forming, stir briskly with a whisk.

Add the cleaned watercress leaves and simmer the soup for about 10 minutes. Taking the soup in batches of several cups, purée it in a blender until it is perfectly smooth. Return the soup to the pot.

Beat together the cream and the eggs, and continue beating as you pour in about 2 cups of the hot soup. Stir this mixture back into the soup, off the heat. Season the soup with the lemon juice, sugar, salt, and pepper.

Over a moderate flame, stir the soup for about 3 to 4 minutes, or until it is quite hot through but not simmering. Serve immediately.

Serves 8 to 10.

crema de verduras *(puréed vegetable soup)*

1½ cups chopped leeks (white parts)
1½ cups sliced carrots
4 cups diced potatoes (with or without peel, according to preference)
1⅓ cups cut green beans
several large sprigs parsley
1 or 2 cloves garlic, minced
4 tsp. salt
2½ qts. water
1 cup cooked artichoke hearts
½ cup peeled, seeded, diced pimiento pepper
fresh-ground black pepper to taste
½ cup heavy cream
3 Tbs. butter

In a large pot, combine the leeks, carrots, potatoes, green beans, parsley, garlic, salt, and water. Simmer the vegetables for about 40 minutes, then add the artichoke hearts (reserving 2 or 3 for the garnish) and the diced pimiento (reserving about 2 tablespoons for the garnish). Simmer the soup for another 5 or 10 minutes.

Purée the soup in a blender in small batches, or press it through a sieve, and return it to the pot. Grind in a generous amount of black pepper, add the cream and butter, and reheat the soup, stirring occasionally, until the butter is melted. Taste, and correct seasoning if necessary.

Chop the reserved artichoke hearts and pimiento rather finely and sprinkle a little of both on each serving.

Serves 6 to 8.

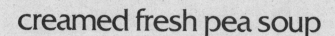

creamed fresh pea soup

3½ lbs. fresh peas (about 4 cups shelled)
1½ qts. water
½ medium-sized onion, chopped
3 to 4 good-sized sprigs parsley
1 tsp. salt.
½ tsp. sugar
1 small head butter or Boston lettuce (5 to 6 oz.)
4 Tbs. butter
½ cup dry white wine
¼ cup heavy cream
dash of white pepper

garnish

Small Dumplings for Soup (page 60)

Shell the peas and put them in a large pot with the water, onions, parsley, salt, and sugar. Bring to a boil, lower the heat, and simmer the soup for about 40 minutes.

Wash and coarsely chop the lettuce. Melt 3 tablespoons of the butter in a skillet and sauté the lettuce in it until the lettuce is completely soft and most of the excess liquid has evaporated. Add the lettuce and butter to the soup and continue simmering it for another 10 minutes.

Purée the soup in a blender, about 2 cups at a time, and return it to the pot. Add the wine and the cream, adjust the seasoning with more salt and a dash of white pepper, and stir in the remaining 1 tablespoon butter. Heat to the simmering point and serve with small dumplings.

Serves 6 to 8.

chilled tomato soup with cantaloupe

6 to 8 medium-sized tomatoes
1   large cucumber, peeled, seeded, and
        chopped
½   cup finely chopped onion
1   cup sour cream
2½ tsp. salt
½   tsp. ginger
pepper to taste
4   tsp. lemon juice
1   Tbs. fresh-grated lemon rind
1   large cantaloupe
1   Tbs. dried basil, crushed, or 2 Tbs.
        chopped fresh

Put the tomatoes in boiling water for a few minutes, until the skins start to crack and peel. Remove the tomatoes and peel them. Purée them in a blender or food processor at high speed. You should have 5 cups of the fresh tomato purée.

Purée the cucumber and onions in a blender or food processor and add this to the tomatoes. If you are using a blender, you could "prime" it with a bit of the puréed tomatoes. Stir in the sour cream and season the soup with salt, ginger, pepper, lemon juice, and lemon rind.

Halve the cantaloupe, remove all the seeds, and either cut it into small balls with a melon scoop or peel and cut it into chunks. Toss the melon with the chopped basil and chill both soup and melon for several hours.

To serve, pour the soup into chilled bowls and put a few spoonfuls of the melon into each one.

Serves 6.

cold cucumber and spinach soup

2½ Tbs. butter
1 large onion
1 lb. fresh spinach
4½ cups Potato Peel Broth (page 58)
3 long, slender cucumbers (about 1½ lbs.)
8 oz. cream cheese
pinch of nutmeg
pinch of hot paprika
2 Tbs. lemon juice
salt and pepper
½ cup light cream

garnish

sweet paprika
sour cream (optional)
fresh snipped dill (optional)

Melt the butter in a large skillet. Chop the onion and sauté in the butter until golden. Meanwhile, carefully wash and remove coarse stems from the spinach.

Add the spinach to the onions and butter and stir until wilted. Combine the cooked vegetables with the broth in a large pot. Peel, seed, and dice the cucumbers and add them to the broth. Simmer the soup for about 20 minutes, then purée it in a blender, in batches, and return it to the pot.

Slice the cream cheese and stir it into the hot soup. Continue stirring, over low heat, until all the cheese is completely melted and thoroughly incorporated into the soup.

Season the soup with a tiny bit of nutmeg, a tiny bit of hot paprika, the lemon juice, and the salt and pepper to taste. Remove the soup from the heat, stir in ½ cup light cream, and chill the soup for several hours.

When the soup is completely cold, taste it again and correct the seasoning if necessary.

Sprinkle a little sweet paprika on the soup after it is ladled into bowls to add a bit of color. This soup may also be garnished with a spoonful of sour cream in the center of each bowl, and a sprinkle of fresh snipped dill.

Serves 6.

gazpacho toledano

7 to 8 medium-sized ripe tomatoes
2   medium-sized cucumbers
1   green bell pepper
1   small onion
2 to 3 cloves garlic
1½ slices French bread
1½ cups cold water
6   Tbs. olive oil
4 to 5 Tbs. wine vinegar, or to taste
3   tsp. salt, or to taste
2   tsp. paprika
pinch of ground cumin
fresh-ground black pepper to taste

garnish

croutons
chopped onions
chopped red and green bell peppers
chopped cucumbers
chopped tomatoes

Cut the tomatoes into quarters. Peel and seed the cucumbers and cut into approximately 1-inch pieces. Seed the bell pepper and cut into approximately 1-inch pieces. Peel and coarsely dice the onion. Put the garlic cloves through a press. Cube the bread.

Now put the prepared ingredients, 2 or 3 cups at a time, into a blender, adding a little of the water each time. Blend at medium or high speed until the vegetables and bread are puréed. Pour the purée into a large bowl.

Add the oil and vinegar, the remaining water, and the seasonings and whisk vigorously until all is very well blended. Taste and correct seasoning. If the soup is too thick, it may be thinned with a little more cold water.

Chill the soup in the refrigerator for several hours before serving. Arrange the garnishes attractively on a large platter and pass them around the table as you serve the soup.

Serves 6 to 8.

my gazpacho

5 to 6 large ripe tomatoes (vine ripened if
   possible!)
1   large cucumber
½   onion
1   clove garlic
½   cup coarsely chopped watercress
3   Tbs. olive oil
3   Tbs. red wine vinegar
2   tsp. salt
2½ cups ice water

garnish

chopped cucumbers
chopped red and green bell peppers
chopped onions
sliced hard-boiled eggs
croutons
chopped tomatoes

Cut the tomatoes into wedges. Peel and seed
the cucumber and cut it into chunks. Chop the
onion and garlic.

Purée the tomatoes, cucumber, onions, and
garlic in a blender, about 2 or 3 cups at a time.
Add the watercress to the last batch, and blend
until smooth.

Pour the puréed vegetables into a large bowl
and add the oil, vinegar, and salt. Blend these
seasonings in with a whisk until the soup is
smooth. Taste and correct seasoning. Now
whisk in the ice water, and perhaps add an ice
cube or two. Chill in the refrigerator until it is
time to serve, and then give it another quick stir
with the whisk just before ladling into bowls.

Pass around the tray of garnishes as the soup is
being served.

Serves 6.

cold avocado soup

2   medium-sized ripe avocados (about 1 lb.)
4   medium-sized tomatoes
½   medium-sized onion
1   clove garlic
1   cucumber
4   Tbs. chopped green chilis
¾   tsp. salt
3½ Tbs. lemon juice
1   Tbs. red wine vinegar
1   Tbs. vegetable oil
1   tsp. sugar
⅛   tsp. ground cumin
1   cup yogurt
½   cup light cream
1½ cups Vegetable Broth I (page 57)

garnish

chopped green onions
chopped fresh cilantro (coriander leaves)
fried tortilla strips

Peel, remove pits from, and coarsely chop the avocados. Cut the tomatoes in thin wedges. Chop the onion and mince the garlic. Peel, seed, and cut up the cucumber. Combine all the vegetables and the chilis and purée them in a blender until no large chunks are left.

Add the salt, lemon juice, vinegar, oil, sugar, and cumin. Run the blender again until the mixture is smooth.

Pour the avocado mixture into a bowl, add the yogurt, cream, and vegetable broth, and beat it lightly with a whisk until it is smooth once more. Taste the soup, and correct the seasoning if necessary. Chill the soup thoroughly.

Chop up a few green onions and about ¼ cup of fresh cilantro and put them aside in small bowls. Cut several corn tortillas into short strips and fry them in oil until they are crisp. Drain them on a paper towel, salt them lightly, and put them in a napkin-lined bowl or basket.

Serve the soup ice-cold, in chilled bowls if possible, and pass the onions, cilantro, and tortilla strips separately.

Serves 4 to 6.

chłodnik *(cold beet soup)*

approximately 2 bunches fresh, young beets
   with leaves
2   qts. water
1   Tbs. salt
1½ to 2 Tbs. cider vinegar
1   Tbs. sugar
3   Tbs. chopped fresh dill
1½ cups sour cream
5   hard-boiled eggs
1   medium-sized cucumber
1½ cups beer

Peel and cut in julienne strips enough beets to fill 3 cups. Wash the stems and tender leaves carefully and chop up enough to solidly fill 2 cups. Put the beets, stems, and leaves in a large enameled pot along with 2 quarts water, the salt, the vinegar, and the sugar. Bring the water to a boil, lower the heat, and simmer until all the beets are completely tender, about 1 hour.

Taste the soup and add a little more vinegar or sugar as needed. Chill.

In a medium-sized bowl, combine the chopped dill with a little salt and pound it with a wooden pestle until it is moist and very fragrant. Add the sour cream and mix thoroughly. Pour in about 1 cup of the beet broth and stir it in with a whisk until the mixture is smooth. Pour the sour cream mixture into the soup and mix everything together completely.

Peel and seed the cucumber and chop it coarsely. Peel the eggs and chop them rather coarsely as well. Add the cucumber and 3 or 4 of the chopped eggs to the soup. Reserve the remaining eggs for a garnish.

Finally, stir in the beer. Taste the soup and correct the seasoning to your own taste, adding more vinegar or sugar to get the right sweet-sour balance—but go easy! A little bit of vinegar or sugar will go a long way.

Serve the soup very cold, in chilled bowls if possible, and put a little ice cube in each bowl. Pass the reserved chopped eggs separately, to be sprinkled on top.

Serves 6 to 8.

cold cherry-lemon soup

grated rind of 3 lemons
juice of 4 large lemons (about 1 cup)
⅔ cup sugar, or more to taste
1 cup water
1 cup light white wine
1 lb. fresh, sweet dark cherries
5 egg yolks
10 to 12 ice cubes
1 cup sour cream sweetened with 2 to 3
   Tbs. sugar

Combine the lemon rind, lemon juice, sugar, water, and white wine in a large enameled saucepan. Heat the mixture until the sugar is dissolved completely, stirring constantly.

Wash the cherries, remove their stems, and pit them. Set aside 18 of the cherries, and add the rest to the soup. Simmer them gently until they are soft, then put them through a fine sieve or purée them in a blender. Return the purée to the soup. Add the egg yolks and beat them in with a whisk. Continue whisking gently for several minutes, over very low heat, as the soup thickens.

Allow the soup to cool somewhat, giving it an occasional stir. Taste, and add more sugar if you like. When the soup is no longer steaming hot,

put in 10 or 12 ice cubes and stir. Then put the soup in the refrigerator and chill it until it is time to serve, at least an hour.

To prepare the sweetened sour cream, just add 2 or 3 tablespoons of sugar to 1 cup fresh sour cream and beat it in thoroughly.

To serve, put 3 of the reserved cherries into each bowl, ladle in the well-chilled soup, and put a nice round dollop of the sweetened sour cream on top.

Serves 6.

chilled buttermilk soup

1½ lbs. potatoes (about 2 large)
5½ cups buttermilk
⅔ cup chopped green onions
2 to 3 Tbs. chopped fresh dill weed, or 1 tsp.
    dried
3   cloves garlic, minced
1   large cucumber, peeled, seeded, and
    chopped
1   Tbs. finely chopped fresh cilantro (cori-
    ander leaves)
¾ to 1 tsp. salt, to taste
pinch of ground cumin

Peel the potatoes and cut them in ½-inch dice. Boil them in salted water until they are just tender, then drain them.

Combine in a blender 2 cups of the butter-milk, ½ the cooked potatoes, ½ the chopped green onions, the dill weed, and the minced garlic. Blend at high speed until vegetables are puréed.

In a large bowl or tureen, stir together the purée, the remaining buttermilk, potatoes, and onions, the cucumber, the cilantro, the salt, and the cumin. Chill well before serving.

Serves 6.

cold cherry soup

A perfect first course for a summer supper.

2½ lbs. fresh, sweet dark cherries
5   cups water
4   Tbs. sugar, or more to taste
⅓ cup white wine, or to taste
juice of 1 or 2 lemons, or to taste
1   cup heavy cream

Wash the cherries, remove their stems, pit them, and put them in a large enameled pot along with the sugar and the water. Bring to a boil and simmer for about 15 to 20 minutes. Drain the cherries, but do not discard the liquid. Remove 24 cherries and put them aside.

Rub the remaining cherries through a fine sieve and return the purée to the cherry liquid. Add a little white wine and fresh-squeezed lemon juice. If the soup is too sour, add a little more sugar.

Chill the soup. When it is quite cold, whip the cream, without sweetening it. Put 4 of the reserved cherries into each of 6 bowls, and divide the soup equally among them. Finish each serving with a generous spoonful of the whipped cream.

Serves 6.

sauces and salad dressings

To be a good cook, you will absolutely need some basic sauces, for they are often the very base of a dish. Soufflés, for instance, and croquettes and many desserts begin with a sauce, which is then added to and altered in various ways. Many other dishes take on their entire character with the addition of a sauce: Where would we be without all those delicious pasta dishes, and good things like asparagus hollandaise, pizza, and applesauce crêpes?

You will have to make these sauces carefully to make them well. As a rule, sauces take a little more skill and concentration than other preparations. You can't stroll away to answer the phone while you are stirring the hollandaise, or turn around to do something else while the roux for the Béchamel scorches. Nevertheless, they are not so mysterious as some cooks like to suggest. If you're a beginner and all this makes you nervous, here's the good news: There really are only a few sauces. All the hundreds of others that can be imagined and concocted are actually variations of those few. When you know how to make a Béchamel sauce, you know essentially everything you need to know about flour-thickened sauces; when you can make one custard sauce, you can make any of them—and so on.

Once you understand the basics, you can unleash all your creativity. Herbs and spices can be used to great advantage; fresh herbs, as always, are best, and if you keep an herb garden, you have a real gold mine of flavor with which to enliven your sauces. I also like to use strong-flavored broths or vegetable purées, reduced to a concentrated richness, and grated cheeses of all kinds. And don't forget the liquor cabinet: Judicious amounts of the right wines or liqueurs can make all the difference for some foods, giving them an irresistible taste and perfume.

To make your sauces, you will want good heavy saucepans, some wooden spoons, a whisk, a little presence of mind, and a little practice. For hollandaise, you will need a double boiler. The quickest and tastiest mayonnaise can be made in a blender or food processor.

Once you know how to make sauces, it's important to learn how to use them properly. The Spanish have a saying: The sauce is worth more than what's under it. It's a clever saying, but the idea can too often be carried to extremes. Diamond Jim Brady once said to his cook, "George . . . if you poured some of that sauce over a Turkish towel, I believe I could eat all of it," and in that case the proverb would undoubtedly hold true. But as a rule, while I eat sauces enthusiastically, I apply them discreetly. Even when the sauce is the most important element of a dish, there's no excuse for drowning a food in it. The flavor of the eggs, or the spaghetti, or the vegetable is important, and a sauce should be used to enhance it, never to mask it. A good lesson can be taken from the Italians and the Mexicans too, who use delicious and sometimes potent sauces sparingly and to great advantage. You'll find that a good sauce, properly used, does not merely add to the savor of a dish, it multiplies it.

Ultimately, the real value of sauces lies in the way that even just a fundamental knowledge of them can increase your culinary repertoire. Quite ordinary foods can be turned into pleasing new dishes. A simple cheese and chili omelet, for instance, took on a whole new aspect one night when I spooned a little Cucumber-Avocado Sauce over it. A dish of ice cream or a plain pudding becomes a distinctive dessert with the addition of some Raspberry Sauce. A Hot Paprika Sauce like the one I use for Stuffed Potato Pancakes, Hungarian Style, could also be added, in small amounts, to hot, buttered noodles or steamed cauliflower or drizzled over poached eggs on dark bread or served with any of several soufflés. In this way, with a little imagination, the mastery of sauces can vastly improve and expand your cuisine.

MAKING SAUCES

One of the most important things to remember in making sauces is timing: A sauce cooked too long or too fast can curdle or separate, scorch or become pasty. On the other hand, an undercooked sauce can have a raw taste or be too thin. But good timing is not difficult to achieve once you realize that keeping your eye on the clock is not as important as keeping your eye on the sauce. You will soon learn to recognize how a sauce should taste and feel.

The other thing to remember is the basic rule for all good cooking, and that is to use good ingredients. If you start with fresh butter, eggs, and milk, rich cream, good fruity olive oil, tasty wine vinegar, fragrant herbs, good aged cheeses, and highest-quality produce of all types, you are already well on the way to being a good cook. For fine sauces, just keep these things in mind, follow directions carefully, and don't spare the whisk.

flour-thickened sauces

The basic white sauce and its most popular refinement, Béchamel, are simplicity itself if the easy rules are followed. The thickening agent for this type of sauce is the *roux*, which is nothing more than a mixture of melted butter and flour. The butter is melted in a heavy-bottomed saucepan over a very small flame. This is important. A flimsy saucepan will not distribute heat evenly or keep it low and steady, and an even, gentle heating is what the roux needs. When the butter is melted, the flour (usually an amount equal to the butter) is stirred in. I use a wooden spoon for this, and throughout the making of hot sauces. Wooden spoons do not scratch up saucepans, nor do they conduct heat, during prolonged stirring, to the hand that holds them. I keep a large crock of them, in every size, near my stove, and find this a very satisfactory arrangement for both convenience and aesthetics.

When the flour is stirred into the butter, you have a pale roux. Continue stirring it, over very low heat, and keep a sharp eye on it. In a moment it will start to foam slightly. Two or three minutes' stirring over the low flame is all it needs: less, and the flour will taste raw; more, and it will scorch. It should not turn brown, but stay a pleasant golden yellow.

At this point, you must remove the saucepan from the heat and stir in the previously heated milk or cream, then beat energetically with a wire whisk. Here some beginners are plagued by lumps, but if you make sure the milk or cream is hot before adding it, and if you beat it in well enough, your sauce will be smooth. Run a spoon around the side of the saucepan, and across the bottom, to get out any bits of roux that are sticking there, and whisk again. I have not yet seen the lump that could not be beaten into submission with a good wire whisk.

Return the sauce to the fire, a little hotter this time, and stir gently with the whisk as the sauce comes to a boil. Continue stirring for about two minutes, then just season with salt and pepper, and you have a white sauce, nicely thickened and perfectly smooth.

This sauce is the basis for many others, as well as for soufflés, croquettes, and many fillings. It can be enriched with the addition of egg yolks, cream, or butter—or all three.

Béchamel sauce is made by the same basic method, with the additional flavoring of a bit of onion and some herbs. Mornay sauce is essentially just a white sauce or Béchamel to which some cheese has been added, though it may also be enriched.

If egg yolks are added to a hot sauce, it is a good idea to beat them with a bit of cream or some other cold liquid first. Then a little bit of the hot sauce should be beaten into them before they are added, away from direct heat, to the rest of the sauce and beaten in with a whisk. This method will prevent curdling by allowing the egg yolks to heat up gradually. Once egg yolks have been incorporated into a flour-based sauce, the sauce may be brought to a boil once more without fear of curdling; however, the same is not true of a custard sauce, made without flour, so don't get them confused.

emulsion sauces

Emulsion sauces depend on the ability of egg yolks to absorb butter or oil. When they are correctly handled, the yolks will thicken the fats and obligingly turn them into the creamiest, richest sauces possible. There are two main categories of emulsion sauces. They are the mayonnaise type, which is made without heat, and the hollandaise type, made with warmed egg yolks and hot melted butter. Mayonnaise, made in a blender or a food processor, is one of the fastest, easiest sauces to make—a stunned monkey could do it. Hollandaise is trickier, but again, if the timing and the proportions are right, you needn't have any problems.

The only things you need to know about making mayonnaise are that it is better to have the ingredients at room temperature, and that the egg yolks, or whole egg, must be beaten to a creamy consistency before the oil is added. In a blender, this takes a few seconds. The oil is then added gradually, while the blender is on, and in moments you have a perfect, thick mayonnaise.

For hollandaise, or any variation of it, the process is more involved. First the egg yolks must be heated very gradually, and *only* until they start to thicken. While it is possible to do this in a heavy saucepan over direct, low heat, it is far safer to use a double boiler.

If the egg yolks are heated too quickly or too long, they will curdle. Secondly, the yolks must be beaten constantly with a wire whisk as they are heated, to ensure that they heat up evenly and stay smooth. Thirdly, the butter should be added very gradually, also with continuous whisking, or the sauce will not emulsify. If you are patient and add the butter in very small quantities, beating conscientiously with your whisk until it starts to look thick and creamy, and watch the temperature carefully, your sauce will be a success. Finally, it is important not to add any more butter than the recipe indicates, and not to overcook the sauce, as either of these errors will curdle the sauce.

In general, the common pitfalls in making a hollandaise are easily avoided if you just familiarize yourself with the whole process before beginning, follow directions, and do not allow yourself to be interrupted—in other words, if the phone rings, ignore it. But if it happens that the sauce does curdle for some reason, chances are that it can still be saved. The best method to reemulsify a curdled hollandaise is to beat a spoonful of it in a warm bowl with a teaspoon of lemon juice until it thickens. Then add small amounts of the sauce, beating in each addition until it is thick. The whole sauce can be reconstituted this way.

If you want to reheat a hollandaise that has been refrigerated, put a small amount of the cold sauce into a double boiler and whisk it over hot water until it is creamy, then very gradually whisk in the remaining sauce. Under no circumstances can the sauce be allowed to simmer or boil.

Mayonnaise and hollandaise both lend themselves to a number of variations, and once you have mastered the basic techniques, you will be able to make any of them with ease.

reduction sauces, salad dressings

Certain sauces, for instance tomato sauces, are thickened by simmering slowly until enough moisture has evaporated from them. These are the most foolproof of all, as it is only necessary to stir them occasionally and keep an eye on them to see that they don't reduce too much and scorch. They take time, sometimes as much as an hour or two of gentle simmering, but it is time during which your attention can mainly be given to other things, so don't let that put you off.

Vinaigrette sauces and any kind of salad dressing likewise do not require the mastering of any special technique. About salad dressings I only want to say that they stand or fall on the quality of the ingredients used and on their freshness. Since they are so easy to make, there is no reason why they should be prepared any earlier than a few hours before they are to be served and in general can be mixed just before being added to the salad or even directly on the salad.

béchamel sauce

This milk-based, roux-thickened sauce is so basic and has so many tasty and useful variations that it cannot be left out of this book. Here is essentially the same recipe that is given in the first *Vegetarian Epicure*, with a few additional comments and a sampler of variations.

3 Tbs. butter
½ medium-sized onion, minced
3 Tbs. flour
2½ cups hot milk
several peppercorns
large pinch of whole thyme
1 small bay leaf
salt to taste
dash of nutmeg

Melt the butter either in the top of a large double boiler or in a medium-sized, *heavy-bottomed* enameled saucepan. (If you are not using a double boiler, keep a very sharp eye on the flame and on the sauce to avoid scorching.) Add the minced onions and cook it over low heat, stirring frequently, until it is soft but not brown.

Stir in the flour and continue cooking what is now a roux for a few minutes more, stirring often. Add the hot milk, beating it in with a whisk until the sauce is perfectly smooth and is beginning to thicken.

Add a few peppercorns, a good pinch of whole thyme, a tiny bay leaf, a little salt, and a little nutmeg. Cook the sauce over very gentle heat, stirring often, for at least 10 to 15 minutes or for as long as 1 hour. The longer the cooking time, of course, the thicker and stronger flavored the sauce.

Strain the sauce through a sieve and dot it with small shavings of butter, which will melt and keep a skin from forming on top. Voilà—you have about 2½ to 3 cups of basic Bechamel, and now you can spoon it over eggs, omelets, vegetables, croquettes, or pasta; or, you can put it aside for a while, then gently reheat it, stirring it up with a whisk; or, you can even refrigerate it for a day or two in a tightly covered container, and no harm done. Furthermore, you can make other good sauces with it, such as these—

VARIATIONS

rich béchamel

½   cup heavy cream
2   egg yolks
hot Béchamel Sauce
salt to taste
½   tsp. lemon juice
2   Tbs. butter (optional)

Beat together the cream and the egg yolks in a bowl and gradually beat in about 1 cup of the hot Béchamel Sauce. Add this mixture to the remaining Béchamel Sauce in the pan, beating it in with a whisk. Heat the sauce very gently, stirring constantly with a whisk, until it comes to a simmer, then continue simmering and stirring for a couple of minutes. Be sure to run a spoon around the bottom and edges of the pan occasionally to prevent lumping there.

Remove the pan from the heat, taste the sauce, and add more salt as needed. Stir in the lemon juice and beat lightly with the whisk again.

Béchamel can also be enriched with butter. To do this, simply beat in about 2 tablespoons butter, a little at a time, just before the sauce is to be served. Butter-enriched Béchamel is delicious, but this method should not be used if the sauce is going into a dish that will be gratinéed in the oven, as excessive heat will make butter separate and float up to the top.

mornay sauce

4   Tbs. grated Swiss cheese
3   Tbs. grated Parmesan cheese
hot Béchamel Sauce (page 98)
dash of cayenne pepper (optional)

Add the grated cheeses to the hot Béchamel and beat them in with a whisk until they have melted and the sauce is perfectly smooth. A dash of cayenne can be added to this sauce with very nice results.

rich mornay sauce

Proceed exactly as for ordinary Mornay Sauce, only use Béchamel that has been enriched with the cream and egg yolk mixture described above.

mild paprika sauce

Add about 2 teaspoons of paprika to either basic Béchamel (page 98) or Béchamel that has been enriched with cream and egg yolks or with butter (see above). Whisk the sauce lightly until the paprika is thoroughly blended.

hollandaise sauce

Hollandaise is tricky. If you haven't had a lot of experience with it, do go back and reread the general information and specific hints on page 96.

3 large egg yolks
1 to 1½ Tbs. lemon juice
pinch of white pepper
1 Tbs. butter
7 Tbs. butter, melted
salt

Put the yolks into the top of a double boiler* and beat them, cold, until they are creamy. Beat in 1 tablespoon of the lemon juice and a pinch of white pepper.

Put the top of the boiler over hot, but not boiling water. Add the tablespoon of unmelted butter and beat the egg yolk–lemon juice mixture steadily with a whisk until the butter has melted and the egg yolks have thickened. Be sure to scrape the egg yolks down from the sides of the saucepan and out from the corners frequently. The yolks should stay perfectly smooth and creamy as they thicken. At any indication of curdling or lumping up, immediately remove the saucepan from above the hot water and stand it in a shallow bowl of cool water for a moment as you continue to beat.

When the egg yolks have thickened, add a tiny bit of the melted butter and continue beating with the whisk, over hot water, until the butter is absorbed. Add another tiny bit, and beat again.

When the sauce thickens and becomes glossy-smooth in texture, the emulsion has formed. Overheating at any point will undo it, however, and so will adding the butter too quickly. Keep beating in the butter gradually, until it is all incorporated. Season to taste with salt and additional lemon juice if desired.

If the sauce does not want to thicken, or if it separates, put 1 tablespoon of it into a smaller bowl with 1 teaspoon of lemon juice, beat till thick and glossy, then gradually beat in the rest of the sauce, a spoonful at a time.

Serve the sauce warm with eggs or vegetables.

Makes about ¾ cup.

*If you don't have a double boiler, you can rig one up by fitting a stainless steel bowl snugly into the top of a pot, so that the bottom of the bowl clears the bottom of the pot by several inches, leaving room for the water.

sour cream horseradish sauce

A good sauce for Broccoli-Walnut Soufflé.

2　Tbs. butter
2　Tbs. flour
1　cup hot milk
2　egg yolks
½　cup grated Wensleydale or other mild cheese
1　cup sour cream
1　Tbs. prepared horseradish
½　tsp. Dijon mustard
salt
pepper

Melt the butter in a heavy skillet and stir in the flour. Lower the flame and cook the roux for a few minutes, stirring constantly. Gradually add the hot milk, stirring with a whisk as the sauce thickens. Then whisk in the 2 egg yolks, one at a time, and stir in the grated cheese.

Continue stirring with the whisk until all the cheese is melted. Do not let the sauce boil.

Add the sour cream, horseradish, mustard, and salt and pepper to taste. Cook over a very low flame for about 5 minutes more, still gently stirring. Serve hot.

Makes about 2¾ cups.

spicy mousseline sauce

Serve the sauce warm with vegetables or eggs. It is great with Wild Mushroom and Dill Soufflé (page 118).

1　recipe hot Hollandaise Sauce (page 100)
½　cup heavy cream
¼ to ½ tsp. hot paprika, or ½ tsp. sweet paprika plus ¼ tsp. cayenne pepper, to taste

Make the Hollandaise Sauce according to instructions. When it is finished, but before it has time to cool, beat the cream in a bowl until it holds firm peaks. Stir it into the warm hollandaise until they are completely blended.

Add the hot paprika, or the sweet paprika and the cayenne, stir it in, and taste. Add more paprika, or cayenne, to taste.

Makes about 1¼ cups.

simple tomato sauce

Serve this sauce hot with soufflés, pasta, omelets, or plain cooked vegetables.

3   lbs. fresh, ripe tomatoes (about 5 cups chopped, with juice)
3   Tbs. butter
1   large clove garlic, minced
1   large pinch thyme
½   tsp. salt, or more to taste
3   Tbs. dry red wine
fresh-ground black pepper to taste
1   tsp. flour
¼   cup heavy cream (optional)

Scald the tomatoes in boiling water and peel them. Chop them finely or purée them.

Melt the butter in a medium-large saucepan and sauté the minced garlic in it for 2 minutes. Add the thyme, the puréed tomatoes with their juice, and the salt. Simmer the mixture for 1 hour over medium heat, or until it is reduced by half.

Stir in the wine, a little pepper, and more salt if necessary. Sprinkle 1 teaspoon of flour over the sauce, whisk it in until the sauce is perfectly smooth, and simmer another 5 minutes or so.

For a milder and richer sauce, add some heavy cream and cook a few minutes longer.

Makes about 2½ cups.

hot paprika sauce

Ladle this over mushroom-filled crêpes, or Stuffed Potato Pancakes, Hungarian Style (page 187).

4   Tbs. butter
4   Tbs. flour
2½ cups heated Vegetable Broth II (page 57)

¼ to ½ tsp. hot paprika or cayenne pepper, to taste
2   tsp. sweet paprika
salt to taste
¼   cup heavy cream

Melt the butter in a medium-sized, heavy-bottomed saucepan and stir in the flour. Cook the roux for several minutes over very low heat, then stir in the vegetable broth and continue to stir with a whisk until the sauce has thickened. Add the hot and sweet paprikas, some salt, and the cream and simmer the sauce gently, stirring often, for about 20 minutes; it should be slightly reduced and thickened.

Makes about 2¾ cups.

cucumber-avocado sauce

Good on filled crêpes, omelets, or vegetables.

2   large cucumbers (about 1¼ lbs.)
5   Tbs. butter
2   Tbs. flour
1   cup milk, heated
½   tsp. salt, or more to taste
white pepper to taste
1   small ripe avocado (about 6 oz.)
1   tsp. finely grated lemon rind
3½ Tbs. lemon juice
1½ Tbs. minced onion

Peel and seed the cucumbers and cut them up in fine dice. Sauté them in 3 tablespoons of the butter, stirring often, for about 20 minutes—all the excess moisture should be evaporated.

Melt the remaining 2 tablespoons butter in a medium-sized, heavy-bottomed saucepan and stir in the flour. Cook the roux for 2 to 3 minutes over low heat, stirring constantly, and then whisk in the milk. Continue stirring over medium heat until the sauce is thick. Season with the salt and some white pepper.

Remove the sauce from the heat. Scoop the avocado out of its shell and mash or chop it. Add the avocado, cucumber, lemon rind, and lemon juice to the sauce and purée.

Return the sauce to the pot, add the minced onion, and heat it up just short of simmering—do not let it boil, or the flavor of the avocado will be affected. Serve immediately.

Makes about 3 cups.

dill sauce

2   Tbs. butter
2   Tbs. flour
2   tsp. dried dill weed or 2 Tbs. minced fresh
1   cup warm milk
¾   cup sour cream
¼   cup dry white wine
2   Tbs. lemon juice
½   tsp. sugar
pinch of nutmeg
pinch of cayenne pepper
salt and pepper

Melt the butter in a heavy-bottomed saucepan and stir in the flour and the dill weed. Stir the roux over very low heat for a few minutes, then whisk in the milk and sour cream. Continue stirring with a whisk over low heat until the sauce is thick and smooth.

Add the wine, lemon juice, sugar, nutmeg, cayenne, and salt and pepper to taste, and simmer the sauce for about 10 minutes more, stirring often.

Serve with soufflés, omelets, or vegetables.

Makes about 2¼ cups.

fresh tomato hot sauce

2   large, ripe tomatoes (about 1¼ cups chopped)
4   Tbs. chopped fresh cilantro (coriander leaves)
1   jalapeño chili pepper (see page 287)
5   Tbs. minced onion
1   Tbs. vinegar
salt to taste (about ½ tsp.)
minced garlic (optional)

Chop the tomatoes rather finely and add the chopped cilantro. Peel and seed the chili pepper and mince it. Stir it well into the tomatoes, add the onions, vinegar, and a generous amount of salt. Add minced garlic and more salt to taste. Serve cold.

Makes 1½ cups.

taratour sauce
(tangy sesame seed sauce)

Serve this with hot, quartered pita bread or use in preparing Hommos bi Tahini (page 151) and Baba Ghanouj (page 152).

1   cup *tahini* (sesame seed paste)
3   large cloves garlic, crushed or finely minced
½   cup fresh lemon juice
1   tsp. salt
½   cup cold water

Stir the *tahini* and the garlic together in a deep bowl. Beat in the lemon juice, salt, and water. If the sauce is much thicker in consistency than mayonnaise, beat in a little more water, 1 tablespoon at a time, until it does resemble a rather solid mayonnaise. Add more salt or garlic if desired.

Makes about 2 cups.

french dressing
(vinaigrette)

3   Tbs. white wine vinegar
¼   tsp. dry mustard
½   tsp. salt
⅛   tsp. pepper
pinch of cayenne pepper
½   cup plus 2 Tbs. olive oil

Whisk together the vinegar, mustard, salt, pepper, and cayenne; then gradually add the olive oil, beating it in as you add it. If you prefer the taste of lemon juice, it can be used instead of the vinegar, and if you want a milder dressing, omit the mustard or use just a pinch.

Makes about 1 cup.

herb dressing

Herb dressing is best on a salad of mixed greens, or a spinach salad, but can be used, in general, much as you would use a regular vinaigrette.

3   Tbs. white wine vinegar
¼   tsp. dry mustard
½   tsp. salt
⅛   tsp. pepper
pinch of cayenne pepper
⅔   cup olive oil
1   Tbs. minced fresh chives
1   Tbs. minced fresh parsley
1   small clove garlic, minced
½   tsp. basil, crushed
¼   tsp. oregano, crushed
¼   tsp. tarragon, crushed

Whisk together the vinegar, mustard, salt, pepper, and cayenne. Pour the olive oil in gradually, beating it in as you do, and then stir in the herbs. If you can get fresh basil, oregano, and tarragon, or if you grow them in your garden, then by all means use them, just doubling the quantities.

Makes about 1 cup.

chiffonade dressing

Try this dressing on a salad of romaine, butter lettuce, and watercress.

¼   cup white wine vinegar
¼   tsp. dry mustard
½   tsp. salt
fresh-ground black pepper to taste
¾   cup olive oil
2   hard-boiled eggs, finely chopped
2   Tbs. finely chopped fresh parsley
2   Tbs. minced pickled beets
1   Tbs. minced onion
1   Tbs. minced green olives

Whisk together the vinegar, mustard, salt, and pepper. Very gradually beat in the olive oil. When the dressing has a creamy consistency, stir in the eggs, parsley, beets, onions, and olives.

Makes about 1¼ cup.

mayonnaise

Along with the basic mayonnaise recipe, here's the way to do it in a blender or food processor, as well as a nearly basic variation—green mayonnaise, which is delicious on sandwiches, hard-cooked eggs, or cold cooked vegetables.

1   egg
½   tsp. salt
½   tsp. dry mustard
2   tsp. cider vinegar
1½ Tbs. lemon juice
⅛   tsp. Tabasco or dash of cayenne pepper
½   cup olive oil
½   cup vegetable oil
if needed: 1 Tbs. hot water

BLENDER METHOD

Put the egg, salt, mustard, vinegar, lemon juice, and Tabasco or cayenne into a blender and blend until smooth. With the blender still on, gradually pour in all the oil in a smooth, steady stream. If the mayonnaise starts becoming very thick immediately, push it down the sides of the container with a spatula. Continue blending at high speed until all the oil is emulsified.

A tablespoon of hot water may be blended in to stabilize the sauce if it shows any sign of separating. Store in the refrigerator, covered.

FOOD PROCESSOR METHOD

Flawless mayonnaise can also be made in a food processor. Using the steel blade, put the egg, salt, mustard, vinegar, lemon juice, and Tabasco or cayenne in the container and process for a few seconds. Combine the oils and, with the processor on, pour them gradually into the feed tube. The oil should be completely emulsified within several seconds.

Makes about 1¼ to 1½ cups.

GREEN MAYONNAISE
1   recipe basic Mayonnaise (above)
2   Tbs. minced watercress
2   Tbs. minced parsley
1 to 2 Tbs. minced chives

Proceed exactly as for regular mayonnaise, adding the minced herbs to the egg mixture in the blender. Give it a good spin before starting to pour in the oil, to make sure that the herbs are really minced and not just finely chopped.

Other herbs can be used and quantities increased for subtly different flavors—basil, tarragon, chervil, small amounts of spinach leaves. Use *only* fresh herbs.

Makes about 1¼ to 1½ cups.

sour cream dressing I

1 cup sour cream
¼ cup fresh-squeezed lemon juice
3 Tbs. sugar
1 tsp. cider vinegar
¼ tsp. salt
1 tsp. dried dill weed or 2 to 3 tsp. snipped fresh
fresh-ground pepper to taste

Stir all the ingredients together in a bowl until they are completely blended. Do not beat with a whisk, as this will cause the sour cream to become quite foamy.

Be sure that your salad greens are patted dry and have no moisture clinging to them before putting on this dressing. Use the Sour Cream Dressing by itself, or, for another delicious salad, toss the salad with a few tablespoons of olive oil first, then add some Sour Cream Dressing and toss again.

Makes about 1½ cups.

sour cream dressing II

Serve this dressing with Cold Omelet Salad (page 161), with cold cooked vegetables, or combine it with more mayonnaise and serve it on tossed salads.

1 cup minced radish
¾ cup minced or grated cucumber
¾ cup sour cream
¼ cup homemade mayonnaise (page 107)
½ tsp. salt, or more to taste
2 Tbs. yogurt
fresh-ground pepper to taste
¼ tsp. hot paprika
1 clove garlic, minced
1 Tbs. lemon juice

Trim, wash, and mince enough radishes to fill 1 cup. Peel and seed a large cucumber and mince or grate it. You should have about ¾ cup of cucumber. Drain the vegetables well in sieves for about 15 to 20 minutes before using.

When the radishes and cucumber are drained, combine all the ingredients in a large bowl and whisk together. Taste, and correct seasoning if necessary. Chill.

Makes about 2½ cups.

avocado
salad dressing

Don't make this dressing more than a couple of
hours in advance, and use it on a fairly simple
tossed green salad: for instance, romaine and
butter lettuce with some thin-sliced bell pepper and a bit of sliced red onion.

1   medium-sized ripe avocado (about ½ lb.)
¼   cup fresh lemon juice
¼   cup olive oil
¼   cup vegetable oil
½   tsp. salt
½   tsp. fresh-ground black pepper
1   clove garlic, minced or crushed
2   Tbs. minced onion
2   Tbs. white wine vinegar
½   tsp. sugar
dash of Tabasco

Cut the avocado in half, remove the pit, and
scoop the fleshy part out of its shell into a bowl.
Immediately add the lemon juice and mash
with a wooden spoon until you have a soft,
smooth mixture. Whisk in the olive and the
vegetable oils, then add all the remaining
ingredients and stir well. Taste, and correct the
seasoning if necessary.

Makes about 1½ cups.

eggs, soufflés, omelets

The marvelous thing about eggs is that they are never out of place, no matter what the time of day, no matter how elegant or simple the meal. But there are two meals for which it seems that nothing else will do but a plate of eggs in one of their simplest forms, and both of them are breakfast. One is the breakfast that good, hard-working, and sober citizens enjoy at an early hour in the morning before launching into another day. The other is that body-and-soul satisfying breakfast that a less temperate group enjoy at an even earlier hour, following a night of revelry. I don't know why eggs and toast should be so indispensable after a bright night on the town, full of eating, drinking, singing, dancing, howling, and laughing, or any combination of those happy employments, but it's so.

At times like those, the less an egg is tampered with, the better. Scrambled, poached, soft-cooked, and—to borrow the Waldorf-Astoria's euphemism for fried—"country-style" are the simplest ways of preparing eggs; uncomplicated by sauce and flavorings, they are ideal for the hours between two and eight in the morning, when reasonable people are asleep.

At more wide-awake and elaborate meals, eggs can reach the heights of sophistication. What is higher and more sophisticated, after all, than a towering soufflé? Nor are they without their humorous moments, as Baked Alaska (known in Spain as soufflé Alaska) has shown us. Between these extremes, we relish eggs in a near-infinity of styles and combinations.

The omelet, which has been called "the egg in its sublime state," is in itself sufficient claim to an egg's fame. I've served them for breakfast, brunch, lunch, and at dinner and supper, and I've dressed those omelets with so many cheeses, vegetables, herbs, spices, creams, sauces, jams, fruits, and liqueurs, that I'm hard put to think of any edible that will not somehow harmonize with the flavor of an egg.

MAKING SOUFFLÉS

Not long after Christopher Columbus made his historic discovery of the New World (believing it to be the East Indies), he was being fêted by Ferdinand and Isabella of Spain. A nobleman seated next to the hero was not inclined to allow him his share of glory and commented that he didn't think it was such a great thing to have reached the East Indies by sailing west. It struck him as a rather simple task, once one knew that the world was round, to reach a place from another direction.

Columbus, so the story goes, picked up a hard-boiled egg, handed it to his aristocratic companion, and asked him if he could make it stand on end. The nobleman tried very hard but couldn't do it. At last he declared it impossible. Columbus took the egg from him, wrapped his hand firmly around it, and brought it down hard on the table, thereby crushing its blunt end—and leaving it standing solidly in place. "You see," he said, "it's easy. It's quite simple, when you know how."

Almost as easily as Columbus made an egg stand on its end (and more easily, I hope, than the way he discovered America), you can turn a few of your eggs into a soufflé—when you know how. For in spite of its awe-inspiring mystique, a soufflé is something that can be easily produced by an ordinary mortal like you or me. No conjuring or witchery is involved. As long as you follow the rules and use the right equipment, you can produce beautiful soufflés every time. And once you know the principles at work, the rules will be easy to understand and follow because soufflés only look like all magic, while they are really all logic.

Every hot soufflé consists of two parts which are put together at the last moment before baking. One part is a sauce, which is made of butter, flour, a liquid, and egg yolks and is usually flavored with something. The second part consists of two indispensable ingredients—egg whites and air. The egg whites, when they are beaten, form thousands of tiny cells or bubbles, each one of which contains some trapped air.

When the beaten egg whites are folded into the sauce and the soufflé is put into a hot oven, the air bubbles in the egg whites expand with the heat, and the soufflé rises. It's just that simple. Of course, the soufflé must be removed from the oven at the right moment, or the bubbles of hot air will expand so much that they burst, and then—it falls. But there's no need for that ever to happen.

Now that you understand soufflés, you can fearlessly set about making them, and here's how:

First, get some things ready. Preheat your oven to the correct temperature and prepare the soufflé dish. If your oven is temperamental, get an oven thermometer so you can be sure that the temperature is right. And be sure that the racks in your oven are adjusted so that the soufflé has plenty of room to rise without hitting the roof!

The choice of soufflé dish is important. A dish that is too wide means that a larger area must be held up by the air bubbles, and thus it will not give you the attractive height you're after. The soufflé dish should be a little wider than it is deep and have straight, smooth sides. It should be just large enough so that the uncooked soufflé mixture fills between ¾ and ⅞ of its capacity.

To prepare the soufflé dish, butter it generously and make a "collar" for it. Tear off a sheet of aluminum foil long enough to wrap around the soufflé dish and overlap by a few inches. Fold it in half lengthwise. Butter a 3-inch strip on one side of the foil, from the edge approximately to the middle. Wrap the foil around the soufflé dish with the buttered strip extending 3 inches up over the top of the dish and facing in. Tie a piece of heavy string around the wrapped dish to hold the foil in place. Straighten the foil if necessary. This collar will keep the soufflé in place as it rises. When you remove the soufflé from the oven, you will take off the collar—by that time, the soufflé will be firm enough to keep its shape and will be beautifully high.

making the soufflé base

The soufflé base is a rather thick sauce, sometimes with solid chunks of food in it. The important thing to keep in mind about this sauce is that its consistency must be right. The proper consistency for this base is somewhere between a thick sauce and a thin pudding. It should not be stiff, but neither should it be runny. I have given exact proportions for each soufflé so just follow them carefully.

To make the sauce, first melt the specified amount of butter in a heavy-bottomed saucepan, then stir in the flour. Cook this butter-flour mixture, or roux, for two or three minutes over very low heat, stirring constantly. Stir in the heated milk or cream, raise the heat to medium, and continue stirring with a whisk until the sauce has simmered for a minute or two. The sauce should be very thick and perfectly smooth.

Remove it from the heat and whisk in the egg yolks, one by one. At this point, you will add the cheese, the chopped or puréed vegetables, the seasonings or liqueurs—in short, whatever you are going to use to flavor the soufflé. If, after you have stirred everything in, the sauce is smooth (allowing for the bits of solid food if the recipe calls for them) and about as thick as a good mayonnaise, all is well.

If you like, you can prepare this much of the soufflé ahead of time and keep the sauce in the refrigerator for several hours or a day, in which case you should brush a film of melted butter over the top to keep a skin from forming. However, if you do store it for a while, don't try to proceed with a cold, stiff sauce. Heat it up very gently, stirring with a whisk, until it is just lukewarm and smooth— then go on.

the egg whites

And now the all-important beating of the egg whites. A pinch of cream of tartar is added to them because this helps to stabilize them and prevents them from "tearing," or separating, when beaten. The number of egg whites in a soufflé is usually one or two more than the number of yolks. This ensures the lightness of the finished product and compensates for the few bubbles that are burst in combining the whites with the sauce.

Be sure that the egg whites have no specks of yolk in them, as any extraneous matter in the whites will inhibit their ability to beat up stiffly. If a bit of egg yolk sneaks into the whites, just scoop it out with a piece of egg shell. Furthermore, the egg whites should be at room temperature before being beaten. If they are cold, you may have trouble whipping them up into the big, shiny pouf you need. Cold egg whites can be safely warmed up a bit by putting them in a bowl and setting it in hot water. Stir them for a minute or two and test. As soon as they are room temperature, take the bowl out of the water and beat them.

Beat the egg whites with a wire whisk, bringing it down into the bowl with a firm, circular motion. Or you can use an electric beater—just move it around in the bowl. The whites will foam up, then they will form soft peaks, and then stiff peaks. As soon as the egg whites form stiff peaks, stop beating. At this point, they have a shiny surface and velvety texture. If you overbeat them, they will become dry, start to break up into clumps, and, finally, revert to liquid, at which time you may as well dump them out and start over because no amount of persuasion will ever puff them up again.

Once the egg whites have been beaten until they are stiff but not dry, stir about a quarter of them into the sauce. This step will lighten the texture of the sauce sufficiently so that the remaining whites can be easily folded in. Put the lightened sauce into a large bowl and pile the remaining egg whites on top of it. Using a small spatula, gently fold the whites into the sauce until they are just blended. Don't overmix, as this breaks the bubbles and deflates the egg whites. Just keep your eyes open and stop folding in the whites when the soufflé mixture appears reasonably homogeneous.

Pile the mixture into the prepared soufflé dish, smooth the top a little, and put it into the center of your preheated oven. Gently close the door, wait for the minimum amount of time given in the recipe, then take a peek. If you have faithfully followed instructions, made sure of your oven temperature, and there was no earthquake in the course of the baking, the soufflé will be high, puffy, and golden. It is done when the top is browned, stiff, and wobbles just slightly when the dish is gently shaken. Some people like their soufflés runnier than others, so the exact moment at which you want to call it done may vary by about five minutes.

And when it's done, serve it immediately.

In its moment of glory, a soufflé is a breathtaking sight, but it takes away your breath only as long as it holds its own, which is a mere few minutes. It is the very brevity of its life that is one of its charms. One moment it is there, proud, lofty, and delicately trembling, the next moment it is served, tasted—vanished. And so it must be. Making a hot soufflé wait is certain disaster. One French chef who was forced to wait with a soufflé because of some unforeseen delay in the course of the meal and watched his creation sink into an irreparable mess was so undone by the incident that he plunged a knife into his belly and died as a result of it. No lost soufflé, however splendid, could be worth such a reaction, but why risk frustration and ill humor? Keep your guests waiting for a few minutes. No one will mind, for they will all be flattered that you went to the trouble to make them that airy, magical thing.

broccoli-walnut soufflé

4   Tbs. butter
4   Tbs. flour
1½ cups hot milk
5   egg yolks
1½ cups chopped cooked broccoli
½   cup finely chopped or sliced walnuts
3   Tbs. minced onion
2   Tbs. grated Parmesan cheese
½   tsp. salt
fresh-ground pepper to taste
7   egg whites
pinch of cream of tartar

garnish

Sour Cream Horseradish Sauce (page 101)

Butter a 2-quart soufflé dish and tie a buttered "collar" around it.

Melt the butter in a heavy saucepan and stir in the flour. Cook the roux over medium heat for a minute or two, stirring constantly. Then add the hot milk and stir with a whisk as the sauce thickens.

When the sauce is perfectly smooth, remove it from the heat and whisk in the egg yolks, one by one. Then add the cooked broccoli, the walnuts, the onions, and the cheese. Stir well and season with salt and pepper.

In another bowl add a pinch of cream of tartar to the egg whites and beat them with a clean whisk or beater until they are stiff enough to form peaks. Do not overbeat them, as they will be too dry.

Stir about 1 cup of the beaten egg whites into the warm sauce. Now add the remaining egg whites and gently fold them in. Do this carefully, as you want to lose as little air as possible.

Pile the soufflé into the prepared soufflé dish, place it in the middle of a preheated 375 degree oven, and bake it for 40 to 45 minutes.

Serve immediately, with hot Sour Cream Horseradish Sauce.

Serves 5 to 6.

onion and cheese soufflé

6 medium-sized onions (about 1½ lbs.)
4 Tbs. butter
4 Tbs. flour
scant ½ cup heavy cream
½ tsp. salt
white pepper to taste
dash of nutmeg
dash of cayenne pepper
2 Tbs. grated Parmesan cheese
4 egg yolks
5 egg whites
pinch of cream of tartar

garnish

any good light tomato sauce

Peel the onions, and cut 5 of them in quarters. Boil the quartered onions in enough lightly salted water to cover them, until they are completely tender. Drain them and reserve the water. Mince the cooked onions.

Finely chop the last raw onion and, in a medium-sized, heavy-bottomed saucepan, sauté onions in the butter until they begin to color. Lower the heat and stir in the flour. Cook the roux for a few minutes, stirring constantly, then add ⅓ cup of the reserved onion water and all of the cream. Stir the mixture over low heat until it is perfectly smooth and very thick.

Remove the sauce from the heat and stir in the minced cooked onions, salt, a little white pepper, nutmeg, cayenne, the grated Parmesan cheese, and beat in the egg yolks.

Beat the egg whites with the cream of tartar until they form stiff, shiny peaks. Stir about 1 cup of the beaten egg whites into the onion sauce, then gently fold in the remaining whites.

Pile the mixture carefully into a buttered 2-quart soufflé dish (see page 113) and bake in a preheated 350 degree oven for 35 to 40 minutes. Serve immediately, with a simple, light tomato sauce.

Serves 4 to 6.

wild mushroom and dill soufflé

2 oz. dried black mushrooms
5½ Tbs. butter
4 Tbs. flour
1 cup hot milk
½ cup sour cream
salt to taste
pepper to taste
pinch of cayenne pepper
6 egg yolks
2 Tbs. chopped fresh dill weed
1 small onion, finely chopped
¼ cup chopped shallots
8 egg whites
pinch of cream of tartar
1 to 2 Tbs. grated Parmesan cheese

garnish: Hollandaise Sauce (page 100) *or*
Spicy Mousseline Sauce (page 101)

Pour about 1½ cups of boiling water over the dried mushrooms and let them soak in it for several hours or overnight. When they are rehydrated, drain them and reserve the liquid in which they were soaked. Wash the mushrooms very carefully to remove every last bit of sand, and chop them coarsely.

Melt 3½ tablespoons of the butter in a sauce-pan and stir in the flour. Cook this roux over low heat for several minutes, stirring constantly. Mix together the hot milk and the sour cream, blend them quickly with a whisk, and pour the mixture into the roux. Continue stirring with a whisk over low heat until the sauce is very thick and smooth.

Season the sauce with a little salt and pepper and a pinch of cayenne. Remove it from the heat and beat in the egg yolks, one at a time. Stir in the chopped fresh dill weed and put the sauce aside.

Melt the remaining 2 tablespoons butter in a medium-sized skillet and add the chopped onions and shallots to it. Sauté them until the onions are golden, then add the chopped mushrooms and salt and pepper. Pour the reserved liquid from the mushrooms through a filter or through muslin to remove the grit and add 1 cup of it to the mushroom mixture. Cook this mixture, stirring often, until all the liquid is absorbed or evaporated. Add the hot mushrooms to the white sauce, mixing it thoroughly.

Prepare a 2-quart soufflé dish by buttering it and sprinkling the Parmesan cheese over the butter. Tie a tall, buttered, stiff-paper or aluminum-foil collar around the dish.

In a large, clean bowl, beat the egg whites with a

little salt and a pinch of cream of tartar until they hold stiff peaks.

Preheat the oven to 400 degrees.

Add a few spoonfuls of the stiffly beaten whites to the sauce and blend them in gently. Now pour the sauce over the remaining egg whites and fold them in, using a spatula or a large spoon. Pour the mixture into the prepared soufflé dish, place it carefully in the middle of the oven, and lower the temperature to 375 degrees.

Bake the soufflé for about 35 to 40 minutes, and serve it immediately with Hollandaise Sauce or Spicy Mousseline Sauce.

Serves 6.

artichoke and cheese puff

Serve the puff hot or cool, cut in wedges or squares. It makes a very nice hors d'oeuvre or can be combined with a rather hearty salad for a perfectly tasty little supper.

12 oz. marinated artichoke hearts
1 medium-sized onion, coarsely chopped
5 eggs
¾ tsp. salt
fresh-ground black pepper to taste
2 Tbs. flour
6 oz. Cheddar cheese, grated
1 oz. Parmesan cheese, grated

Drain off ¼ cup of oil from the artichoke hearts and heat it in a large skillet or shallow, fireproof casserole. Sauté the onions in it until they are beginning to color.

Thickly slice the artichoke hearts or quarter them. Beat the eggs with the salt, some fresh-ground black pepper, and the flour until the mixture is perfectly smooth. Stir in the grated cheeses.

Add the artichoke hearts to the onions and stir them around a little, then distribute the artichokes and onions evenly over the area of the skillet or casserole. Spoon the egg and cheese mixture over the vegetables, spread it around gently, and bake the puff in a preheated 350 degree oven for 20 to 25 minutes, or until it is completely set, golden brown, and slightly crusty on top.

Serves 8 to 10 as an appetizer, 4 to 6 otherwise.

cottage cheese soufflé

This is not really sweet enough for a dessert, but a good dish for brunch or lunch.

1   cup small-curd cottage cheese
½   cup sour cream
5   Tbs. flour
5   tsp. sugar
½   tsp. salt
¼   tsp. cinnamon
crushed seeds from 2 cardamom pods
1   Tbs. butter, melted
5   egg yolks
5   egg whites
pinch of cream of tartar

garnish

cranberry relish *or*
applesauce *or*
fresh fruit

Combine the cottage cheese and the sour cream in a medium-sized, heavy-bottomed saucepan. Add the flour gradually, stirring it in thoroughly after each addition. Add the sugar, salt, cinnamon, cardamom, melted butter, and egg yolks. Beat the mixture with a whisk to make sure that everything is well blended and there are no lumps of flour.

Heat the mixture over very low heat, stirring constantly, until it begins to thicken. Continue stirring, without letting it come to a boil, for about 3 minutes. The sauce should have a custardlike consistency. Remove it from the heat and let it cool to lukewarm, stirring occasionally.

Beat the egg whites with the cream of tartar until they hold stiff peaks. Stir about ⅓ of the beaten whites into the cottage cheese sauce, then gently fold in the rest.

Pile the mixture into a buttered 2-quart soufflé dish (see page 113) and bake it in a preheated 350 degree oven for 35 to 40 minutes. Serve immediately, garnished with cranberry relish, applesauce, or fresh fruit.

Serves 4 to 5.

spicy cheese and potato soufflé

5   Tbs. butter
3   Tbs. flour
1⅓ cups hot milk
6   egg yolks
6   oz. Munster cheese, grated
1   medium-sized potato (about ½ lb.)
1   medium-sized yellow onion, peeled,
        quartered, and thinly sliced
4 to 5 tsp. crushed dried red peppers (depend-
        ing on how hot they are)
1   tsp. salt
8   egg whites
pinch of cream of tartar

garnish: Dill Sauce (page 104)

Melt 3 tablespoons of the butter, stir in the flour, and cook the roux for a few minutes over low heat, stirring constantly. Whisk in the hot milk and continue beating with a whisk until the sauce is thick and smooth.

Remove the sauce from the heat and beat in the egg yolks, one by one, then stir in the grated cheese. Stir the sauce over low heat until the cheese is just melted, then put it aside.

Peel the potato, cut it in ¼-inch dice, and boil it in salted water for a few minutes, then drain immediately. Melt the remaining 2 tablespoons butter in a medium-sized skillet and sauté the onions in it on fairly high heat until they start to color. Add the potatoes and continue sautéing, stirring constantly, until the potatoes are golden brown and tender. Add the crushed red peppers and stir for 2 to 3 minutes more.

Stir the vegetable mixture into the cheese sauce, along with the salt.

Beat the egg whites with the cream of tartar until they hold stiff peaks. Stir about ⅓ of the egg whites into the cheese and vegetable mixture, then fold in the rest. Pile the mixture into a prepared 2-quart soufflé dish (see page 113) and put it in the middle of a preheated 375 degree oven. Lower the heat to 350 degrees and bake the soufflé for about 40 minutes.

Serve the soufflé with Dill Sauce.

Serves 4 to 6.

zucchini soufflé

1 lb. fresh zucchini
1 small yellow onion
5 Tbs. butter
¾ tsp. salt, and more to taste
¼ to ½ tsp. dried basil, crushed
fresh-ground black pepper to taste
3 Tbs. flour
1⅓ cups warm milk
6 egg yolks
2 Tbs. grated Parmesan cheese
7 egg whites
pinch of cream and tartar

garnish

Hollandaise Sauce (page 100) *or*
a cheese sauce

Trim, wash, and grate the zucchini. Peel and chop the onion. Melt 2 tablespoons of the butter in a medium-sized skillet and sauté the onions in it until they are just soft. Add the grated zucchini and toss and stir over fairly high heat until zucchini is tender and the excess moisture has evaporated. Add the salt, basil, and some fresh-ground black pepper, stir for a few minutes more, and remove from the heat.

Melt the remaining 3 tablespoons butter in a medium-sized, heavy-bottomed saucepan and stir in the flour. Cook the roux over very low heat for a few minutes and then stir in the warm milk. Beat the sauce lightly with a whisk over medium heat until it is thick and smooth.

Remove the sauce from the heat and beat in the egg yolks, one at a time, then stir in the Parmesan cheese and the cooked zucchini. Season to taste with more salt and pepper.

Beat the egg whites with a pinch of cream of tartar until they hold stiff peaks. Stir about ¼ of the beaten egg whites into the sauce, then gently fold in the rest. Pile the mixture into a prepared 2-quart soufflé dish (see page 113) and bake in a preheated 350 degree oven for 35 to 40 minutes. The top should be golden brown.

Serve the soufflé immediately, with Hollandaise Sauce or a cheese sauce.

Serves 4 to 6.

spinach soufflé

2 lbs. fresh spinach
2 tsp. salt
⅓ cup chopped green onions
1 Tbs. olive oil
½ tsp. cider vinegar
¼ tsp. dried dill weed
3 Tbs. butter
4 Tbs. flour
1 cup hot milk
pinch of nutmeg
pinch of cayenne pepper
6 egg yolks
3 Tbs. grated Parmesan cheese
black pepper to taste
7 egg whites
pinch of cream of tartar

garnish

Hollandaise Sauce (page 100) *or*
Mornay Sauce (page 99)

Wash and trim the spinach and toss the leaves with 1½ teapoons of the salt. Cook the spinach leaves in just the water that clings to them, tossing constantly over medium heat, until they are wilted and tender. Drain the spinach thoroughly and chop it finely.

Sauté the green onions in the olive oil until they are soft, then stir in the chopped spinach, cider vinegar, and dill weed.

Melt the butter in a heavy-bottomed saucepan and stir in the flour. Cook the roux over very low heat for several minutes, stirring often, then whisk in the hot milk. Cook the sauce until it thickens, season it with a little nutmeg and cayenne, then remove it from the heat and beat in the egg yolks, one by one. Return the sauce to very low heat, add the Parmesan cheese, and stir for about 2 to 3 minutes. Remove it from the heat and stir in the spinach mixture, seasoning it with the remaining ½ teaspoon salt and a little black pepper.

Beat the egg whites with a pinch of cream of tartar until they hold stiff peaks. Stir ¼ of the beaten egg whites into the spinach sauce, then fold in the remaining egg whites.

Pile the mixture into a buttered 2-quart soufflé dish or a 1½-quart soufflé dish prepared with a collar (see page 113). Bake in a preheated 350 degree oven for 35 to 40 minutes and serve with Hollandaise Sauce or Mornay Sauce.

Serves 4 to 6.

MAKING OMELETS

A good omelet is a wonderful thing and can play a fine role at breakfast, lunch, or even dinner. Unfortunately, it is difficult to get good omelets in most American restaurants, which is all the more reason to perfect your skill at preparing them.

Among the simplest of all foods in their composition, omelets require a certain amount of practice and a light touch in their preparation. If you are ready to invest a little time, though, and to eat scrambled eggs when those first efforts don't result in perfection, there is no reason why you shouldn't soon master the art and turn out tender, golden omelets every time, as pretty to look at as they are good to eat.

The first requirement for making a good omelet is to use good ingredients, and that means fresh eggs and plenty of real butter. (There was a dieters' fad, which seems to be passing off, I'm grateful to notice, for cooking eggs with little or no butter in a "nonstick" skillet, a thoroughly barbaric idea.) In addition to the eggs and butter, you will only want some salt and pepper, and perhaps just a bit of milk or cream, but that is strictly a matter of preference. Those are the ingredients of a plain omelet, and you can make that plain omelet as elaborate as you like with any of a great variety of fillings and sauces.

The equipment is simple as well. Every kitchen has mixing bowls and a whisk or eggbeater, but pay attention to the pan. An omelet pan should have a heavy bottom and gently sloping or curved sides—a properly seasoned cast-iron or a Teflon pan. One more thing is needed to make the whole operation much easier, and that is a long, narrow, and flexible spatula.

To make an individual omelet, two eggs are generally sufficient, but three can be used if the appetite warrants it. Beat the eggs briefly in a bowl with a pinch of salt and a smaller pinch of pepper, as well as a dash of milk or cream if you like. Heat an 8- or 9-inch omelet pan and melt about 1 tablespoon butter in it, swirling the butter all over the bottom of the pan. When the butter has melted and foamed and the foam has begun to subside, set a medium flame, pour in the beaten eggs, and tilt the pan around gently so that the eggs spread evenly over the bottom. In a moment, the eggs will begin to set. When they do, run the spatula once around the edge of the omelet to loosen it, and shake the pan a bit. Then start carefully lifting the edges with your spatula and tilting the pan to let the uncooked eggs on top run to the bottom.

In less than a minute, the omelet will be nearly done. Give the pan another quick shake to keep the eggs from sticking. The top of the omelet, at this point, should be moist but not runny. If you are filling your omelet, spoon in some of the prepared filling now. Then slip a spatula under one side and fold it over the other. Leave the omelet in the pan just a few seconds more before sliding it out onto a warm plate. The omelet should be golden in color and tender and creamy inside. And it must be served immediately!

The commonest pitfall in making an omelet is overcooking the eggs, so do move quickly when they are starting to set. Overcooked eggs are tough and rubbery, even less acceptable than overcooked vegetables.

An omelet large enough for two can be made the same way, just by doubling the ingredients and using a slightly larger pan. Smaller omelets, however, are a great deal easier to handle, if you're just beginning, and so I advise starting with the individual sizes and moving on to larger ones when you're an experienced hand.

Because omelets take so very little time to prepare, they are an ideal dish for impromptu meals, and because eggs are so democratic in the way they successfully associate with nearly every other kind of edible, you can make an omelet to fit practically any taste or mood. Omelets with cheese, with vegetables, with hollandaise sauce or tomato sauce are all justly popular, but don't ignore the possibilties of sweet omelets either. A delicious dessert or elegant brunch omelet can be made by using marmalade or sautéed apple slices as a filling, for example.

mushroom omelets

filling

1   oz. dried wild mushrooms
3   Tbs. butter
2   Tbs. minced onion
1   cup sour cream
5 to 6 large, fresh mushrooms, sliced
pinch of thyme
½   tsp. salt
pepper to taste
½   tsp. dried dill or 1 tsp. fresh
chopped fresh parsley

omelets

8   eggs
salt and pepper to taste
¼   cup milk or cream
butter for frying

garnish

chopped fresh parsley

Soak the dried mushrooms in about 2 cups of hot water for several hours, then wash them very carefully, and reserve the water in which they have been soaked. Strain the liquid through several layers of cheesecloth or through a filter and reserve. Coarsely chop the mushrooms.

Melt 2 tablespoons of the butter in a skillet and sauté the minced onions in it until they begin to color. Add the chopped mushrooms, the sour cream, and 1 cup of the strained mushroom liquid. Lower the heat and simmer the mixture, stirring occasionally, until the mushrooms are very tender and the liquid reduced to a thick sauce.

Melt the remaining 1 tablespoon butter in a small skillet and sauté the fresh mushrooms in it for 5 to 6 minutes. Sprinkle them with a little thyme, toss briefly over high heat, then add them to the sour cream mixture.

Season the sauce with the salt, pepper, and dill, and continue cooking it until the sauce is no longer runny.

Make 2 medium-sized omelets, or 4 small, individual omelets according to the directions on page 124. Divide the mushroom mixture evenly between them, rolling the omelets up over it. Sprinkle the omelets with parsley and serve immediately.

Serves 4.

potato and zucchini omelets

This is one of my favorite omelets. It's quick to prepare and makes a hearty, satisfying meal for any time of day. Try it for one of those 4:00 A.M. breakfasts, after a night of serious partying, or else for the 1:00 P.M. brunch the next day.

½   lb. potato (about 1¼ cups diced)
½   lb. zucchini (about 1½ cups diced)
⅔   cup chopped onion (1 small)
1   Tbs. butter
2   Tbs. olive oil
¼   tsp. dried dill weed
¼   tsp. dried basil, crushed
½   tsp. crushed dried red pepper
salt to taste
fresh-ground black pepper to taste
5 to 6 eggs
butter for frying

garnish

sour cream

Peel or scrub the potato and cut it in ½-inch dice. Wash, trim, and finely dice the zucchini. Drop the diced potato into boiling salted water and cook for 5 minutes, then drain it and set it aside. Cook the diced zucchini in boiling water for 3 to 4 minutes, drain, and set aside.

Heat the butter and the olive oil in a medium-sized skillet and sauté the onions in it until they start to color. Add the partially cooked potato and zucchini, the dill weed, basil, crushed red pepper, and salt. Cook this mixture over medium heat, stirring often, until the potatoes are just tender. Grind in some black pepper and add more salt if needed.

Make either 2 medium-sized or 3 small omelets according to the directions on page 124. When the eggs are almost set, spoon some of the hot vegetables onto one side and fold the other side of the omelet over the filling. Slide the omelets out onto warm plates and serve immediately with sour cream.

Serves 2 to 3.

cheese and chutney omelet

¼ lb. fresh white farmer cheese
4 Tbs. preserved chutney
4 to 5 eggs
salt to taste
fresh-ground black pepper to taste
butter

Crumble the cheese coarsely. Spoon out the chutney (you can use a little more or less, depending on how spicy it is), and if it has particularly large pieces of fruit in it, cut them into smaller bits.

Make a plain omelet according to the directions on page 124. When the eggs are nearly set, but still moist on top, sprinkle the crumbled cheese over one side of the omelet, and spoon the chutney on top of the cheese.

Fold the other side of the omelet over the filling and leave it in the pan over low heat for another minute as the cheese and chutney warm up.

Serve immediately on warmed plates.

This omelet serves 2—or you could make 2 individual-sized omelets with the same ingredients.

tomato omelets provençale

2¼ lbs. tomatoes (about 8 medium sized)
1 tsp. salt, and more to taste
1 medium-sized yellow onion
2 cloves garlic
3 Tbs. olive oil
2 bay leaves
½ tsp. dried basil, crushed
½ tsp. dried tarragon, crushed

2 Tbs. chopped fresh parsley
5 cured black olives, pitted and sliced
coarse-ground black pepper to taste
8 to 10 eggs
milk
butter for frying

Blanch the tomatoes in boiling water for about 2 minutes and then peel them. Chop the tomatoes very coarsely and put them aside in a bowl with the salt.

Chop the onion, mince the garlic, and sauté them in the olive oil in a large skillet until they begin to show color. Add the bay leaves and sauté a few minutes more. Add the tomatoes, the basil, tarragon, parsley, and sliced olives, and cook over medium heat, stirring occasionally, until the sauce is thick. It should take about 40 to 45 minutes.

Make individual omelets according to the directions on page 124. Spoon on some of the hot Provençale sauce just when the eggs are nearly set, and fold the omelets over the sauce. Serve immediately.

Serves 4 to 5.

avocado omelets

1   medium-sized ripe avocado (about ½ lb.)
1½ Tbs. mayonnaise
1   Tbs. fresh lemon juice
1   Tbs. finely chopped red onion
salt
fresh-ground black pepper
4 to 5 eggs
2 to 3 Tbs. butter

optional garnish

sour cream and Mexican hot sauce

Halve the avocado, remove the pit, peel off the skin, and trim away any hard or brown spots. Chop the avocado in small bits and combine it in a bowl with the mayonnaise, lemon juice, and chopped onions. Mash slightly and stir everything together thoroughly. Season to taste with salt and pepper.

Make 2 individual omelets according to the directions on page 124. When the eggs are nearly set, but still moist on top, spoon half the avocado filling onto each omelet.

Fold one side of each omelet over the other and leave them in their pans over low heat for another minute or so, then serve immediately on warmed plates. Sour cream and any Mexican hot sauce can be passed separately.

Serves 2.

onion and mozzarella omelets

1 very large red onion (about 1 lb.)
3 Tbs. olive oil
½ tsp. salt
½ tsp. crushed dried red chilis
¼ tsp. oregano, crushed
black pepper to taste
3 oz. mozzarella cheese, grated
4 eggs
salt and pepper to taste
butter for frying

Peel the onion, quarter it, and slice it thickly. Cook in the olive oil over medium-low heat, stirring often, until completely soft and beginning to color. Add ½ teaspoon salt, crushed red chilis, oregano, and black pepper and stir over medium heat for a few minutes more.

Make 2 individual omelets, or 1 large one, according to the directions on page 124. When the eggs are set but still moist on top, spoon the hot onions over one side of the omelet (divide them evenly between the 2 omelets if making individual omelets). Sprinkle the grated mozzarella over the onions and fold the other side of the omelet over the filling. Leave the omelet over medium-low heat another minute until the cheese is melted, then serve immediately.

Serves 2.

cheese and chili omelet

for each individual omelet

2 or 3 eggs
salt and pepper to taste
1 to 2 Tbs. butter
2 oz. Monterey Jack cheese, grated
1 large green onion, chopped
2 Tbs. chopped California green chilis*

optional garnish

sour cream

Make an individual omelet according to instructions on page 124. When the eggs are nearly set, and just moist on top, quickly spread the grated cheese over one side of the omelet. Sprinkle the chopped green onions and green chilis evenly over the cheese and fold the other side of the omelet over the filling. Leave the omelet in the pan, on medium-low heat, for another minute or so, just long enough for the cheese to melt.

Slide the omelet onto a warmed plate and serve immediately, garnished with sour cream if desired.

*A fairly hot variety. If they aren't available fresh, buy canned Ortega chili peppers, whole or chopped.

bell pepper and cream cheese omelets

1½ lbs. bell peppers (about 4 medium sized)
1   large onion
3   Tbs. olive oil
1   large tomato, coarsely chopped
¾   tsp. salt
fresh-ground black pepper to taste
4   oz. cream cheese
8 to 10 eggs
salt and pepper to taste
butter for frying

To make the filling, first roast the bell peppers —either green or red—in the broiler, turning them often, until they are evenly charred and blistered all over. Hold them under cool running water as you slip off their skins, then remove the cores, seeds, and ribs. Cut the peppers into short strips, about 1 inch by ½ inch.

Peel the onion, quarter it, and thickly slice it. Sauté in the olive oil, in a fairly large skillet, until soft and translucent and barely starting to show color. Add the chopped tomato, the bell pepper strips, ¾ teaspoon salt, and fresh-ground pepper and stir over medium heat until the tomato is soft. Cut the cream cheese into small chunks, add it to the vegetable mixture,

and continue stirring over medium heat until the cheese has melted and formed a smooth sauce around the vegetables. Keep the filling hot while making the omelets.

Make 4 or 5 individual omelets, according to directions on page 124. When the eggs are nearly set, but still moist on top, spoon some of the hot filling over one side of each omelet and fold the other side over it. Leave the omelet in the pan for another 30 seconds or so, then serve immediately.

Serves 4 to 5.

See Italian Pastas, Vegetables, and Frittatas for Frittata of Zucchini and Onion and Herb Frittata. See Spanish specialties for Tortilla Española, Eggplant Tortilla, Tortilla a la Paisana, and Asparagus Tortilla.

salads and cold vegetables

Freshness is the essential ingredient of a salad. The simpler the salad, the more essential its freshness becomes, and this holds for the dressing as well, which should be custom-made for the salad, not poured out from a bottle. Beyond that, it is pointless to quibble about what a salad should or shouldn't be.

At many European tables, the most familiar salad consists of lettuce and other greens, tossed with a vinaigrette dressing. In the Middle East, on the other hand, salads are made of sesame seed paste, eggplant, tomatoes, cucumber, oil, spices—many things, but never a leaf of lettuce. I've had warm salads as well as cold; sweet salads; and hearty, filling entrée salads. In this country, we've drawn on many traditions for our dining style, and we use salads of all kinds, and in every imaginable way.

My taste in salads is broad but never indifferent. There are times when a leafy salad of crisp romaine or Boston butter lettuce with an uncomplicated dressing of fruity olive oil and wine vinegar has a place in the menu that no other dish could fill as well. At other times, I prefer salads that are elaborate and filling enough to make a meal in themselves, and I am really inordinately fond of the various marinated, cooked, and pickled dishes that enliven a good antipasto or buffet.

But under no circumstances will I allow that the essential freshness can be dispensed with just because a salad is cooked or marinated. I like flavors that still remember their origins. Even a salad that improves from marinating for a day or so, for instance, one of lima or garbanzo beans, cannot be successfully concocted from tired ingredients. But soaked and newly cooked dried beans can make an admirable salad when they are combined with fresh chopped parsley, slivers of sharp onion, and an excellent oil and vinegar.

I firmly draw the line, however, at bottled dressings, at soggy coleslaws, and at those molds of sweet, artificially flavored gelatins that pop up with dreadful frequency at certain kinds of affairs. And though I admit that through the years I have swallowed many things in the name of courtesy, I really just bail out completely when faced with a sticky, syrupy fruit salad obviously from a can.

If you are lucky enough to have room for a kitchen garden, and industrious enough to grow one, then a rare treat of a salad is at your fingertips. My parents live in the country, and every spring my mother plants a bountiful assortment of vegetables. Like any reasonable being, she grouses at the constant watering and weeding that her garden demands, and she thinks uncharitable thoughts about the deer who will come and nibble away a tender harvest if measures aren't taken to prevent them access. Nor does she subscribe to the popular notion that vegetables come much cheaper when you grow your own, because when she allows for the value of her time and labor, there is ultimately no great savings in it. But year after year, the garden flourishes under her care because, quite simply, she delights in the garden-fresh flavors and the otherwise unobtainable crisp and tender textures.

The salads we eat there are designed in the garden, not too long before mealtime. Late in the afternoon, when the sun is already dipping down behind the hills and the air begins to cool, is my favorite time to pick the salad. We pluck off crisp young lettuces and pull up carrots as thin as my little finger and radishes that are tiny, hard, and stingingly sharp. The littlest spinach leaves are chosen and sometimes the tops of infant beets. The vegetables that make such impressive displays in supermarkets are often urged to a mature, large size before being picked, but in my mother's vegetable garden we can indulge ourselves by picking them while they are still young and delicate and exploding with the flavor that only vine or bush ripening can produce.

We find bell peppers the size of eggs, so thin and crisp that they are almost brittle, and with a pungent taste that makes the bigger ones pale by comparison. We dig up new potatoes, no larger than walnuts, pull up some green onions, and snip off fragrant chives, flat-leaf parsley, and feathery stems of dill weed. The string beans and yellow wax beans are slender, and we hunt through the jungle of zucchini vines carefully, so that we can harvest the bright green squashes while they are still so small that they hardly need slicing. Tomatoes that have ripened in the hot sun until they are ruby-red are added to the baskets, as well as sweet cucumbers, young enough not to require seeding. Invariably hauling in twice as much as we can possibly consume, we take our cornucopia to the house and hose it off in colanders outside the kitchen door, thus losing three or four pounds of mud. Then we rinse, trim, dry, and slice, and the big wooden salad bowl begins to fill up.

Sometimes, after a day of scorching heat, the salad becomes our main course. A particularly memorable one was composed of green beans, zucchini, and new potatoes, all boiled till they were just tender and then cooled under running water, combined with hearts of butter lettuce and thin-sliced cucumbers, mushrooms, and red onions. The salad was tossed first with just a hint of olive oil, wine vinegar, and fresh herbs, then finished with a bit of light sour cream dressing and garnished with quartered hard-boiled eggs. Everyone devoured heroic portions, accompanied with fresh, buttered rolls, and though it was over a year ago, I can recall with clarity the distinct, vivid flavors we relished that night.

The recipes here don't necessarily depend on the abundance of a garden such as my mother's. If you find a good market for greens—and fortunately the increasing demand for fresh produce has encouraged more small green grocers and farmers' markets—you can enjoy lovely salads the year round. Here I've collected samples of the many salads I've enjoyed at home and abroad. Any of them will bolster appetites on a warm day (or even a cool one), but some are perfectly suited to be the heart of a meal. There is also an assortment of salads which are especially good for grouping in an antipasto, but each of them could also stand alone as a nice first course. Between the big, leafy tossed salads and the meticulously arranged, elegant ones there is ample choice, and if only everything that is so good for you could also be so tasty and attractive, what a happy world it would be.

TOSSED SALADS

The making of a good, simple salad is a straightforward operation, but it requires strictest attention to quality and seasoning.

First, choose the greens—and there is usually a wealth to choose from: romaine, butterhead, chicory, curly endive, red-leaf lettuce, salad bowl lettuce, mustard greens, and watercress, to name a few of the best known. Personally, I like my simple salads really simple. One of the nicest I ever tasted consisted of nothing but the inner, tender leaves of butter lettuce, a few thin slices of raw mushroom, and a delicate oil and vinegar dressing. It was ambrosial. But any number of combinations can be equally pleasing if you only remember that the zestier, more assertive ingredients, such as watercress or chicory, are best used sparingly with a larger proportion of one or two mild-flavored lettuces.

If you can pick your greens fresh from the garden, all the better. If you're picking them at the market, just do your choosing with a sharp eye for the youngest, crispest, freshest-looking of the lot, avoid the plastic-wrapped ones, and don't keep them in your refrigerator longer than a few days. When it comes time to clean and tear the greens, take another good look: tough leaves? or wilted? Throw them out instantly! Use only the best or suffer the consequences, for they will not be disguised.

Wash the greens in cool water, handling them gently, and either shake or spin them dry in a salad basket, or very lightly pat them dry on tea towels. Wet lettuce in a salad will make you a fine, soggy mess. Once clean, very large pieces should be torn apart with your fingers, the smaller left whole.

If you want to accent your salad with some slices of raw mushroom or radish, a little cucumber, celery, or tomato, prepare these ahead of time. Test the vegetables for firmness; clean and trim them; cut them in thin, tossable slices; and use them in moderation.

As far as onion and garlic are concerned, there is generally no middle road. If you like them, you probably love them and will relish their flavor in salad more than anywhere. If you don't like them, no amount of talk can convert you, and that's fine too. For those who do, I recommend red onion, cut in paper-thin slices. Green onions are also delightful in a salad, but go easy; they are more potent than they look. For a subtle hint of garlic, rub a wooden bowl with a cut clove before tossing the salad in it. For the true garlic lover, minced fresh garlic should be added to the olive oil.

Fresh herbs are, along with good olive oil, the best thing that can happen to a salad. If you have parsley, dill, basil, chervil, or tarragon growing somewhere in your garden or in pots on the windowsill, this is their big moment. Mince small quantities with a sharp knife and toss them in with the prepared greens, but exercise some discretion because too many kinds mixed together can drown out the flavors of all.

Finally, the all-important dressing of the salad. You may prefer to make a dressing in advance (but not too much in advance), in which case you will now pour a little of it over your salad, toss, taste, add a bit more, and so on, until precisely the right balance of flavor is obtained. Each leaf and sliver should glisten, but no soupy excess must be found lurking in the bottom of the bowl.

I prefer to dress a salad by combing the oil and vinegar directly on the salad. Begin with pure, fruity olive oil; a first-pressing oil, called "virgin olive oil" on the bottle or can, will have the most olivey taste. Pour it on carefully and toss the salad with the oil before adding anything else. When all the lettuce leaves are shiny, add just a bit of wine vinegar, and a very niggardly amount of salt, then toss again, and taste. Adjust your quantities of oil and vinegar (or lemon juice), give it a few grinds of black pepper, add your herbs and fresh-toasted croutons if you like them, and serve at once.

salad torcoloti

One of the best salads I ever ate was served to me in a restaurant called Torcoloti, in Verona. I took careful notes and enjoyed it again at home.

1½ lbs. small white potatoes
1   cup plus 3 Tbs. fruity olive oil
¼ to ⅓ cup fresh-minced parsley
salt
fresh-ground black pepper
1   lb. slender young zucchini
1   lb. thin green beans
1   cup paper-thin carrot slices
2   large heads salad bowl lettuce
¾   cup wine vinegar
½   tsp. basil, crushed
2   cloves garlic, minced

Boil the potatoes, in their jackets, in salted water until they are just tender. Drain the potatoes and chill them. When they are cold, peel and thickly slice them. Put them in a bowl with 3 tablespoons of the olive oil, the parsley, and some salt and pepper. Toss and put aside until you are ready to serve the salad.

Slice the zucchini ¼ inch thick, cutting on a slant if they are particularly slender, and drop the slices into boiling salted water. Cook the zucchini for 5 minutes exactly, drain, and run cold water over them. Chill the zucchini.

Trim and wash the green beans and cut them in 1-inch lengths. Boil them in salted water until tender but still crunchy. Drain the beans, run cold water over them, and chill them.

Wash the lettuce, dry the leaves by patting them gently with a tea towel, and tear them into manageable pieces.

Combine the remaining 1 cup olive oil, the vinegar, basil, garlic, and some salt and pepper, and beat it all together with a whisk or blend in a blender.

Just before serving, combine all the vegetables in a bowl, pour the dressing over them, and toss lightly until everything is evenly coated. Add salt and fresh-ground pepper to taste.

Serves 6 to 8.

paprikasalat

Served cold with pumpernickel bread and Liptauer Cheese (page 203), it makes a great first course.

3   large red bell peppers (pimientos)
½   medium-sized yellow onion
2   Tbs. olive oil
2   Tbs. white wine vinegar
1   tsp. sugar
salt and pepper to taste

Quarter, seed, and derib the peppers. Using a very sharp knife or a vegetable slicer with a good blade, slice the peppers very, very thinly. Peel and quarter the onion, and slice it thinly.

Toss together the pimiento slices, the onion slices, and the remaining ingredients. Taste, and correct for seasoning. Put the salad aside for a few hours before serving.

Serves 4 to 6.

watercress and green bean salad

Serve with rye or pumpernickel bread.

1   medium-small potato
1   lb. string beans
1   large bunch watercress (about ¼ lb. trimmed)
½   medium-sized red onion
4   eggs, hard-boiled
1   medium-small cucumber
8 to 9 large, firm mushrooms (about 1 cup sliced)
¾   cup Sour Cream Dressing I (page 108)
½   cup mayonnaise

Peel and dice the potato, cook it in boiling salted water until it is tender, drain, and run cold water over it until it is cool. Put it in the refrigerator.

Wash and trim the string beans, cut them in 1-inch pieces, and boil them in salted water until they are just tender—not a minute longer. Run cold water over them until they are cool and put them in the refrigerator. Wash the watercress, trim off the heavy stems, and cut in half any very large pieces.

Quarter and thinly slice the red onion. Peel and coarsely chop the hard-boiled eggs. Peel the cucumber, halve it lengthwise, and slice it.

Clean the mushrooms, trim off the stems, and slice them thinly.

Toss all the vegetable ingredients together in a bowl. Blend Sour Cream Dressing I with the mayonnaise; pour the dressing over the salad and toss again until everything is evenly coated.

Serves 4 to 6.

spinach salad

1¼ lbs. fresh spinach
½   lb. mushrooms
½   lb. farmer cheese
1   red onion
⅔   cup olive oil
⅓   cup red wine vinegar
oregano to taste
salt to taste
fresh-ground black pepper to taste

garnish

Guacamole (page 296)

Wash the spinach carefully, trim off the stems, and pat the leaves dry in a tea towel. Tear the larger leaves into pieces.

Clean, trim, and thickly slice the mushrooms. Crumble the farmer cheese and peel, quarter, and thinly slice the red onion.

Combine the spinach, mushrooms, cheese, and onions in a large mixing bowl. Whisk together the olive oil, vinegar, oregano, and a little salt. Pour the dressing over the salad and toss gently until every leaf is evenly coated. Grind some black pepper over the salad and toss again lightly.

Divide the salad among 6 shallow bowls and top each one with 2 or 3 rounded tablespoons of Guacamole.

Serves 6.

florentine bread salad

This green salad, the Tuscan brainstorm for using up yesterday's bread, is unlike most others in that it can be made several hours ahead of time and will still be perfectly wonderful. Just toss it again shortly before serving. Serve it as a first course on its own or as part of an antipasto.

1   lb. romaine lettuce (1 large head or 2 smaller ones)
1   large cucumber
2 to 3 stalks celery, thinly sliced
1   large tomato, cut in thin wedges
1   cup sliced radishes
½   lb. slightly stale French bread, cut in 1-inch cubes (about 4 cups)
½   red onion, thinly sliced
1   cup olive oil
½   cup wine vinegar
1   tsp. basil
2 to 3 cloves garlic, minced or crushed
½   tsp. salt
fresh-ground black pepper to taste
½   cup fresh-grated Parmesan cheese

Wash the lettuce, pat the leaves dry, and tear them into bite-sized pieces. Peel the cucumber, cut it in half lengthwise, seed it by scooping out center with a small spoon, and slice thinly.

Put the lettuce and cucumber in a large bowl along with the celery, tomato, radishes, bread cubes, and onions.

Put the oil, vinegar, basil, garlic, salt, and some pepper in the container of a blender and blend at high speed for about 1 minute. Pour the dressing over the salad, sprinkle on the Parmesan cheese, and toss the salad gently for several minutes. The bread will soak up a lot of the dressing. Taste and correct the seasoning with more salt and pepper if desired.

Chill the salad for at least ½ hour before serving it. Serves 6 to 8.

caesar salad

There are now many versions of this famous salad being prepared all over the world. Quite a few are very good, but this recipe, according to reliable sources, is very much like the original Caesar salad—and, of course, that must be the best.

6 oz. French bread (about 15 to 18 slices from a thin *baguette*)
4 Tbs. olive oil for frying
2 cloves garlic, crushed
2 eggs
3 large heads of fresh, crisp romaine lettuce
¾ to 1 cup fruity olive oil, to taste
juice of 2 large lemons (about ⅓ cup)
salt to taste
fresh-ground black pepper to taste
dash of Worcestershire sauce, or more to taste
½ cup fresh-grated Parmesan cheese

Slice the bread and cut each slice in half or in thirds. Dry the bread out in a medium-hot oven for about 20 minutes. Heat the 4 tablespoons olive oil in a large pan and add the garlic to it. Toss the dried bread in the olive oil, over low heat, for 5 to 10 minutes. Set aside.

Boil 2 eggs for exactly 1 minute, run cool water over them for an instant, and put them aside.

Remove the large outer leaves from the heads of romaine and save them for some other salad. Take apart the hearts, wash the leaves and dry them on tea towels. Chill the romaine leaves.

To prepare the salad at the table, assemble all the ingredients in attractive bowls on a tray. Put the romaine leaves in the largest salad bowl you have. If you want to keep the leaves whole (as in the original), arrange them all in one direction so that you can roll them over and over each other without breaking them. Have two large wooden spoons ready for this operation.

Pour about ½ the fruity olive oil over the lettuce and toss or lift from one side, rolling the leaves over to the other side several times. Break the eggs over the lettuce and flip all the lettuce over several times more. Continue in this fashion, adding some more olive oil, then the lemon juice, then some salt and fresh-ground black pepper, a dash of Worcestershire sauce, and the Parmesan cheese, tossing or rolling over the leaves between each addition. Finally, add the croutons and toss again. Taste one of the smaller leaves. Correct the seasoning with a little more oil, salt, pepper, or Worcestershire sauce if needed.

Serve immediately.

Serves 4 to 6.

paprika-cucumber salad

4 to 5 cucumbers
salt to taste
⅓   cup white wine vinegar
½   large onion, sliced paper-thin
2   tsp. sweet paprika
1   Tbs. minced fresh dill weed or 1 tsp. dried
1½ tsp. sugar
fresh-ground pepper to taste
pinch of hot paprika (optional)

Peel the cucumbers, cut them in half length-wise, and seed them. Slice the cucumber halves thinly, toss them with a generous amount of salt, and leave them to drain in a colander for ½ hour.

Prepare the dressing by combining the vinegar, onion slices, paprika, dill weed, sugar, and pepper. Stir it up well and put it aside for ½ hour.

Give the cucumbers a quick rinse and pat them dry with a tea towel. Combine the cucumbers and the dressing in a medium-sized bowl and toss until all the cucumber slices are evenly coated. Taste and correct the seasoning if necessary. Chill the salad for at least 20 minutes and stir up again before serving.

Serves 6 to 8.

pressed cucumber-sour cream salad

3½ lbs. cucumbers
1   Tbs. salt, and more to taste
½   cup sour cream
2   Tbs. lemon juice
1   tsp. sugar

Peel the cucumbers, cut them in half length-wise, remove any large seeds, and slice the cucumbers as thinly as possible. Toss the slices with the salt and leave them in a colander to drain for at least ½ hour.

Taking the slices a handful at a time, squeeze out the excess moisture between the palms of your hands. Combine the slices in a bowl with the sour cream, lemon juice, sugar, and a tiny bit more salt if it is needed. Toss together until all the slices are evenly coated, chill briefly, and serve.

Serves 6 to 8.

marinated leeks

8 to 10 slender leeks (about ¾ lb. trimmed)
⅓ cup olive oil
½ cup white wine or champagne vinegar
½ cup white wine
2 small (inner) stalks celery
2 bay leaves
10 to 12 peppercorns
10 to 12 whole coriander seeds
½ tsp. salt
3 sprigs parsley

Carefully trim off all the dark green parts and wash the leeks. If they are very long, cut them in 3-inch lengths.

Arrange the leeks in a shallow enameled fireproof casserole. Pour the olive oil, wine vinegar, and wine over them. Add enough water to cover the leeks.

Cut the celery stalks in 3-inch lengths, then slice them lengthwise into strips the size of green beans. Add them to the leeks, along with all the remaining ingredients. Simmer, covered on a medium heat for about 20 minutes, then chill them overnight.

Serves 4 to 6 as an hors d'oeuvre.

garbanzo bean salad

1 cup olive oil
½ cup red wine vinegar
4 cloves garlic, minced
1 tsp. sugar
salt to taste
fresh-ground black pepper to taste
3 Tbs. liquid from cooking beans
6 cups cooked and drained garbanzo beans*
1½ small red onions, peeled, quartered, and thinly sliced

Make a dressing from the oil, vinegar, garlic, sugar, salt, pepper, and bean liquid. While the beans are still quite warm, combine them with the onions and pour the dressing over them. Toss until all the beans are evenly coated, then put aside for several hours before serving.

Serve cool or at room temperature.

Serves 8 to 10.

*To cook dried garbanzo beans: Soak the beans overnight in enough water to keep them covered, with a pinch of baking soda in it. The next day, add more water if needed, salt it well, and bring it to a boil. Reduce the heat and simmer the beans until they are tender, about 1 to 1½ hours. Garbanzos can also be cooked without presoaking, but the cooking time will be longer by ½ to 1 hour. When the beans are tender, drain and use as directed.

peperonata

This makes a very good addition to an anti-pasto, or it can be served as a separate course.

2   large green bell peppers
2   large red bell peppers
1   Tbs. olive oil
1   tsp. white wine vinegar
1   tsp. fresh lemon juice
salt to taste
fresh-ground black pepper to taste

Roast the peppers under the broiler, turning them frequently, until the skins are blistered and brown. Remove the peppers and let them cool until you can handle them easily.

Peel the charred, papery skin from the peppers carefully, then cut them open and remove the seeds and ribs. Slice the peppers evenly into pieces about 2 inches long and ½ inch wide and put them in a bowl.

Add the oil, vinegar, lemon juice, salt, and black pepper to the pepper slices, mix it all up very well, and chill before serving.

Serves 2 to 4 as a first course.

lima bean salad

2   cups large dry lima beans
1½ qts. water
salt
⅓   cup olive oil
¼   cup white wine vinegar
plenty of fresh-ground black pepper

Put the beans in a large pot with the water and 1 teaspoon salt, bring to a boil, then reduce the flame. Simmer the beans gently for about 1 hour, or until they are just tender. Drain them while they are still hot, reserving the liquid.

In a skillet, boil the bean liquid vigorously for a few minutes until it is substantially thickened. Measure out ⅔ cup of the thickened liquid into a bowl.

Add 1 tablespoon salt plus all of the other ingredients to the warm liquid and whisk until well blended and you have a smooth sauce.

Pour the sauce over the beans while they are still warm and mix them up gently with a wooden spoon, being careful not to mash them. Refrigerate for several hours.

Before serving, stir the salad again so that all the beans are well coated with the dressing.

Serves 8.

marinated mushrooms

1   lb. fresh white mushrooms
1½ cups water
1½ cups cider or white vinegar
1   Tbs. pickling spice, or:
    4 cloves, 4 peppercorns, ¼ tsp. mustard
    seeds, ½-inch stick cinnamon, pinch of
    dried rosemary, 1 bay leaf
2½ Tbs. olive oil
¼   tsp. basil, crushed
¼   tsp. oregano, crushed
1   clove garlic, minced
pinch of thyme
¼   cup chopped fresh parsley
salt and pepper to taste

Wash the mushrooms and trim stems. If the mushrooms are very large, cut them in half. Put them in an enameled pot and cover them with equal parts of water and vinegar. Add the pickling spices in a muslin or cheesecloth bag.

Cover the pot and bring the mixture to a boil. Let it boil for about 5 minutes, then turn off the heat and leave the mushrooms covered in the hot liquid for an hour or two.

Drain the mushrooms thoroughly, rinse them, and pat them dry with a paper towel. Put them in a bowl and toss them with the olive oil, herbs, and salt and pepper until each mushroom is well coated. Put them aside for several hours before serving.

The mushrooms can be served chilled or at room temperature. They are excellent as part of an antipasto.

Serves 6.

rice salad vinaigrette

Serve with an antipasto or as a separate course.

⅓   cup finely diced carrots
¾   cup green beans, cut in ¼-inch bits
¼   cup diced celery
¼   cup diced green bell pepper
½   cup chopped red onion
3   Tbs. minced fresh parsley
2½ cups cooked rice, warm or cold
4   Tbs. grated Parmesan cheese
4   Tbs. olive oil
3   Tbs. white wine vinegar
salt to taste
fresh-ground black pepper to taste
pinch of thyme
pinch of basil
pinch of oregano

Cook the carrots and green beans in a minimum of salted water until they are barely tender and drain immediately.

Combine the first 7 ingredients in a large bowl and toss together.

Combine the cheese, olive oil, vinegar, and seasonings and whisk until smooth. Pour the dressing over the salad, toss until everything is thoroughly combined, and put in the refrigerator to chill for several hours.

Serves 4 to 6.

white bean salad

1   lb. small dried white beans (about 2 cups)
2   medium-sized tomatoes, coarsely chopped
⅓   cup finely chopped red onion
⅓ to ½ cup cured black olives, sliced
6   Tbs. olive oil
6   Tbs. white wine vinegar
1 to 2 cloves garlic, minced
½   cup chopped fresh parsley (slightly packed)
¼   tsp. dried basil—or fresh
¾   tsp. salt, or more to taste
fresh-ground black pepper to taste

Rinse the beans and combine in a large pot with several quarts salted water, bring to a boil, then lower the heat and simmer until the beans are quite tender, about 1 hour. Drain the beans and allow them to cool slightly.

Combine the beans in a bowl with all the other ingredients and toss gently until everything is thoroughly combined. Taste, and correct the seasoning with more salt and pepper if necessary. Chill the salad and serve it cold as a first course or as part of an antipasto.

Serves 8 to 10.

gnocchi salad

¾ cup fresh peas
1 lb. chilled cooked gnocchi*
1½ cup red, yellow, and green peppers, cut in thin, short strips
3 Tbs. finely chopped red onion
2 Tbs. olive oil
2 Tbs. thick tomato purée or 1½ Tbs. tomato paste
1 Tbs. red wine vinegar
salt and pepper to taste
basil, crushed, to taste

*For this salad you can use cold Potato Gnocchi (page 252), or buy some good frozen gnocchi from an Italian delicatessen or market, cook them, and chill them awhile.

Drop the peas into boiling salted water and cook them until they are barely tender and not yet soft. Drain them and run cold water over them to cool them.

Combine the cold gnocchi, the peas, the peppers, and the chopped onions in a bowl. Make a dressing of the olive oil, tomato purée, wine vinegar, salt and pepper, and basil, and pour it over the gnocchi and vegetables. Toss everything together until the dressing is very evenly distributed, then put in refrigerator to chill for several hours.

Serve cold as part of an antipasto.

Serves 6 to 8.

insalatone

Insalatone is one of the Italian salads I had in Bologna, a sort of marinade of cooked and raw vegetables. It's a good dish to include in a varied antipasto—but wonderful enough to serve all by itself as a first course.

1½ lbs. potatoes
½ lb. zucchini (about 3 medium-small)
1½ cups sliced celery hearts and inner stalks
2 red tomatoes
2 green tomatoes
7 Tbs. olive oil
4 Tbs. white wine vinegar
3 Tbs. minced fresh parsley
½ tsp. salt
½ tsp. basil, crushed
½ tsp. oregano, crushed
fresh-ground black pepper to taste

marinade

⅔ cup red wine vinegar
2 to 3 Tbs. olive oil
salt to taste
about 1½ cups water

Boil the potatoes in their jackets until they are just tender; do not overcook. Allow them to cool completely before peeling.

Trim and slice the zucchini ¼ inch thick. Put the slices in an enameled pot with the marinade, using just enough water to completely cover the zucchini. Bring the marinade to a boil, then lower the heat slightly. Boil the zucchini slices for exactly 5 minutes, remove them with a slotted spoon (reserving the marinade), and run cold water over them. Chill in the refrigerator until needed.

Put the sliced celery hearts and stalks in the marinade, bring it to a boil again, and cook the celery for 8 to 10 minutes. Drain the slices, run cold water over them, then put them in the refrigerator until needed.

Peel the potatoes, quarter them lengthwise, and thickly slice them. Quarter and slice the tomatoes. Combine all the vegetables in a large bowl, add all the remaining ingredients, and toss gently until the dressing is evenly distributed. Taste, and correct the seasoning.

Chill the salad for at least an hour or two and toss it once more before serving.

Serves 6 to 8.

eggplant caviar

Serve as a salad, on crackers, or as part of an antipasto.

2½ lbs. firm eggplant
1   large, firm tomato
½   cup minced onion
2   cloves garlic, minced
½   cucumber, peeled, seeded, and grated
12 to 15 pitted cured black olives, sliced off the
       pits
1½ Tbs. olive oil
1   Tbs. wine vinegar
1   Tbs. lemon juice, or more to taste
salt to taste
fresh-ground black pepper to taste

Prick the eggplants a few times with a fork and bake them at 400 degrees for 50 to 60 minutes. Allow them to cool until you can easily handle them.

Split the eggplants lengthwise with a sharp knife and scrape out all the pulp. If the seeds are dark brown and starting to separate from the rest of the eggplant, they will be bitter—discard them. Discard the skins. Chop the eggplant pulp coarsely and drain off the excess moisture.

Chop the tomato coarsely. Combine all the ingredients and mix thoroughly. Taste, and correct seasoning. Chill before serving.

Serves 6 to 8 as a first course.

celery root salad

1   lb. celery root
1½ qts. water
½   cup milk
2   Tbs. lemon juice
1½ Tbs. white wine vinegar
2½ Tbs. mayonnaise
2   tsp. Dijon mustard
1   Tbs. heavy cream
salt and pepper to taste

Peel the celery root and cut it in julienne strips. Combine the water, milk, and lemon juice in a large saucepan and bring to a boil. Add the celery root strips to the boiling liquid and leave them submerged until the liquid boils again. Then drain them and run cold water over them. Squeeze out any excess moisture.

In a bowl, toss the celery root strips with the vinegar. Mix together the mayonnaise, mustard, cream, and some salt and pepper. Pour the mayonnaise sauce over the celery root and toss again until strips are evenly coated. Taste, and correct the seasoning.

Chill the salad for an hour or two before serving.

Serves 4 to 6.

gingered eggplant salad

2   lbs. firm young eggplant
1   Tbs. peanut oil
2   Tbs. cider vinegar
2½ Tbs. brown sugar
2   small cloves garlic, minced
2   Tbs. finely minced onion
2   generous tsp. grated fresh ginger
2   tsp. fresh lemon juice

Prick the eggplants in several places with a fork and roast them in a 400 degree oven until they are quite soft.

When the eggplants are cool enough to handle, cut them in half and scrape the pulp carefully out of the skin. If the seeds are dark brown and starting to separate from the eggplant, they will be bitter and must be removed (meaning it wasn't quite young or fresh enough). If the seeds are pale and small, leave them.

Drain the eggplant pulp thoroughly in a large sieve and mince it. Combine the minced eggplant in a bowl with all the remaining ingredients, mix well, and chill several hours.

Serve small portions of the chilled eggplant on lettuce leaves as a first course, or with unsalted crackers as a dip.

Serves 4 to 6.

hommos bi tahini (salad of garbanzos and sesame paste)

This salad has the consistency of a dip or a spread and is served cool or at room temperature with crackers or pita bread on the side.

3   cups cooked garbanzo beans (reserve a little bit of the cooking liquid, as it may be needed)
2   large cloves garlic, finely minced
5   Tbs. fresh lemon juice
1½ tsp. salt, or more to taste
¾   cup Taratour Sauce (page 105)
1   Tbs. olive oil
approximately 2 Tbs. chopped fresh cilantro (coriander leaves)

In a large bowl, mash the cooked garbanzo beans with a pestle until they are puréed, or force them through a coarse sieve. Stir in the crushed garlic and beat in the lemon juice, salt, and Taratour Sauce.

The *hommos* should have a consistency similar to that of mayonnaise; it should be easily spreadable. If it is too thick, add a few tablespoons of the cooking liquid from the garbanzo beans, beating it in a little at a time until the consistency is right.

Spread the *hommos* in a shallow dish, gently spread the olive oil over, and sprinkle with chopped cilantro.

Serves 4 to 6 as a first course.

baba ghanouj
(a salad of eggplant and sesame paste)

Serve with crackers or with hot pita bread as a first course.

1   lb. eggplant
¼   cup Taratour Sauce (page 105)
¼   cup fresh lemon juice
1   tsp. salt, or more to taste
¼   tsp. pepper
1   Tbs. plus 1 tsp. olive oil
2   Tbs. chopped fresh cilantro (coriander
      leaves), or more to taste

Prick the eggplant with a fork in several places and roast it in a preheated 400 degree oven for 45 to 55 minutes, or until it is soft throughout. When the eggplant is cool enough to handle, cut it in half and scrape out all the pulp.

Mince the eggplant pulp and add to it the Taratour Sauce, lemon juice, salt, pepper, and 1 tablespoon of the olive oil. Stir the mixture thoroughly, taste it, and correct the seasonings.

Spread the eggplant mixture evenly in a shallow serving dish, drizzle the remaining olive oil on top of it, sprinkle with chopped cilantro, and chill for several hours before serving.

Serves 4 to 6.

fresh mozzarella salad

This antipasto salad is made from fresh, new mozzarella cheese, which is very white, much lighter in texture than a mature mozzarella, and is stored in water. It is available at well-stocked Italian delicatessens.

1   lb. fresh mozzarella cheese
3   small tomatoes (about ¾ lb.)
¾   lb. zucchini
½   cup very thinly sliced red onion
6   Tbs. olive oil
3   Tbs. wine vinegar
1   tsp. salt
approximately ¼ cup chopped fresh parsley
¼   tsp. oregano
black pepper to taste

Cut the mozzarella into strips or small, ¼-inch-thick slices. Slice the tomatoes in thin wedges. Cut the zucchini in ¼-inch slices and drop in boiling salted water. Cook 2 minutes, then drain and cool briefly under running water.

Combine all the ingredients in a bowl and toss gently until well combined.

Serve immediately or marinate for several hours—toss again before serving.

Serves 6.

lima beans in tomato and garlic sauce

1   lb. large dried lima beans
3   Tbs. olive oil
5 to 6 cloves garlic, crushed or minced
½ to 1 tsp. rosemary, crushed
2   cups thick tomato purée
3   peeled tomatoes, coarsely chopped
⅓   cup dry red wine
1   tsp. salt
¼   cup lemon juice
1   tsp. sugar
fresh-ground black pepper to taste
3   Tbs. minced onion

Put the lima beans in a large pot with about 2 quarts of water and some salt. Bring the water to a boil, then reduce the heat, and simmer the beans until they are tender, but don't let them get mushy. Drain them, and save the broth to use in a soup—it's delicious.

Heat the olive oil in a very large skillet and sauté the garlic and rosemary in it for a few minutes. Add the tomato purée, chopped tomatoes, red wine, salt, lemon juice, sugar, and a generous amount of black pepper. Simmer the sauce, stirring often, for about 15 minutes.

Add the drained lima beans and continue simmering, stirring now and then with a wooden spoon, for another 5 to 10 minutes. The sauce should be quite thick.

If you want to serve the lima beans hot, stir in the minced onions shortly before serving. If you want to serve them cold, as a salad, allow them to cool before stirring in the minced onions and chill them for a few hours or overnight—the flavor improves.

Serves 8 to 10.

tomatoes stuffed with hearts of palm

2½ cups hearts of palm, cut in ¼-inch slices
¼ cup fruity olive oil
3 Tbs. white wine vinegar
fresh-ground black pepper to taste
⅓ cup chopped fresh parsley
salt to taste
10 medium-sized tomatoes

Drain and rinse the hearts of palm and slice them. Combine them in a bowl with the olive oil, vinegar, pepper, parsley, and salt. Toss the mixture gently until all the hearts of palm are evenly coated, then cover the bowl and chill the mixture for several hours.

Slice the tomatoes in half crosswise. With a small, sharp knife, scoop out a shallow bowl in each tomato half. Save the scooped-out tomato pulp for another use. Lightly salt and pepper the tomato shells. Dividing the marinated hearts of palm evenly among the 20 tomato shells, mound a couple of spoonfuls evenly in each one.

Serves 6 to 10 as a salad.

potato salad with caraway seeds

3 large white-skinned potatoes
½ onion
7 Tbs. white wine vinegar
¼ tsp. caraway seeds
7 Tbs. olive oil
salt
pepper
3 Tbs. chopped fresh chives

Boil the potatoes in their jackets until they are tender, then drain and cool them until you can handle them. Peel them while they are still warm and cut them in medium-sized dice. Mince the onion.

Combine the diced potatoes and minced onions in a large bowl. Heat the vinegar with the caraway seeds and pour it over the potatoes. Gently toss the mixture until well combined.

Pour the olive oil over the potatoes, add salt and pepper to taste, and the chopped chives. Toss again, always carefully, and taste. Correct the seasoning.

Chill the salad for several hours and stir it up once more before serving.

Serves 6.

german potato salad

4   lbs. potatoes
1   large yellow onion, finely chopped
1   cup white wine vinegar
½   cup mayonnaise
¼   cup olive oil
1½ tsp. dried dill weed
salt
pepper

Boil the potatoes in their jackets until they are just tender. Drain them and let them cool slightly. When they are just cool enough to handle, peel them and cut them into ½-inch cubes. Spread them evenly in a large, shallow bowl and pour the vinegar over them while they are still warm. Sprinkle the onions over them. Set them aside for a while to absorb the vinegar, turning them gently with a spatula now and then.

After about ½ hour, drain off any excess vinegar. Toss the potatoes carefully with the mayonnaise, olive oil, and dill weed. Season to taste with salt and pepper.

Serve warm or chilled.

Serves 8 to 10.

potato salad tzapanos

I came across this salad at the Taverna Tzapanos, in Athens, and hence the name.

3   lbs. white-skinned potatoes
1½ lbs. carrots
¼   cup olive oil
⅓   cup white wine vinegar
2   tsp. salt
4   tsp. dried dill weed, or 3 Tbs. minced fresh
2   cloves garlic, minced or pressed

Boil the potatoes in their jackets until they are just tender. Drain them immediately and allow them to cool.

Scrape the carrots, cut them into large pieces, and boil them until they are tender; drain them and let them cool.

Cut the potatoes into ½-inch dice and coarsely chop the carrots. Combine them in a large bowl with all the remaining ingredients and toss the mixture until everything is thoroughly blended. Chill the salad for several hours and toss it once more before serving.

Serves 8 to 10.

avocado-stuffed zucchini

6 plump, evenly shaped zucchini (about 1¾ lbs.)
2 medium-sized ripe avocados (about ¾ lb.)
1 Tbs. fresh lemon juice
1 Tbs. olive oil
1 Tbs. wine vinegar
2 Tbs. chopped fresh cilantro (coriander leaves)
½ small onion, finely chopped
1 tsp. salt

garnish

paprika and cilantro sprigs

Trim the stem ends of the zucchini and cut them in half lengthwise. Put them in a pot of boiling salted water for 4 minutes, then drain them and run cold water over them for a minute. Working carefully with a dessert spoon, scoop out the pulp, leaving a shell about ¼ inch thick. Put the pulp in a sieve to drain and turn the shells upside down on a rack for about 10 minutes.

Chop the well-drained zucchini pulp. Peel the avocados, remove the pits, and chop them or mash them with a fork. Add the avocado to the zucchini pulp. Stir in all the remaining ingredients and mix thoroughly.

Fill the zucchini shells with the avocado mixture and sprinkle a line of paprika down the center of each one. "Plant" a small sprig of fresh cilantro in the stuffing of each zucchini, arrange them on a platter, and chill for an hour or two before serving.

Serves 6 as a first course.

asparagus mousse

A rather rich salad that works best as a first course.

2 cups puréed cooked asparagus (about 1½ lbs. fresh asparagus, trimmed)
2 packages (2 Tbs.) unflavored gelatin
½ cup cold water
1½ cups hot milk
½ cup water from cooking asparagus
2 Tbs. butter
3 eggs
1 cup mayonnaise
½ cup sour cream
2 Tbs. lemon juice
1 tsp. sugar
½ tsp. salt
large pinch of cayenne pepper
pinch of nutmeg
pepper to taste

optional garnish

pimiento strips
thinly sliced cucumber
sliced black olives

Soften the gelatin in the cold water. Stir the gelatin into the hot milk along with the asparagus water and the butter. Stir the mixture over very low heat until both the gelatin and the butter are completely dissolved. Remove the liquid from the heat and beat in the eggs. Beat the mixture with a whisk for about 2 minutes. Chill the mixture until it just begins to thicken but can still be easily stirred.

Combine the puréed asparagus, the mayonnaise, sour cream, lemon juice, sugar, salt, and other seasonings and stir until all is thoroughly smooth. Stir in the gelatin mixture.

Pour the entire mixture into an oiled, 2-quart mold and chill it for 3 hours, or until it is firm.

Turn the mousse out onto a well-chilled platter and, if you like, decorate it with strips of pimiento, thin slices of cucumber, and sliced black olives.

Serves 8.

cold broccoli mousse

Serve the mousse with hot Cheese Pastries (page 47).

2   lbs. broccoli
½   lb. mushrooms
2   Tbs. butter
1½ tsp. salt, and more to taste
fresh-ground pepper to taste
2   packages (2 Tbs.) unflavored gelatin)
¼   cup cold water
1   cup light cream
¾   cup Vegetable Broth II (page 57)
2   eggs, beaten
1   tsp. prepared horseradish
¼   cup lemon juice
1   cup mayonnaise

garnish

cherry tomatoes
parsley sprigs

Trim the broccoli, cut the tops into flowerets, and peel and slice the stems. Boil it in salted water until it is tender, then drain it immediately. Divide it in two, chop ½ of it finely, and purée the other half in a blender or food processor.

Wash the mushrooms and mince them or put them through a food mill. Sauté the mushrooms in butter, stirring constantly, until they are completely tender and all the moisture has evaporated. Season them with salt and pepper.

Soften the gelatin in the water. Heat together the cream and the vegetable broth and add the gelatin, stirring over low heat until it is completely dissolved. Remove the liquid from the heat and beat in the eggs.

Combine the mushrooms, the chopped and puréed broccoli, 1½ teaspoons salt, the horseradish, pepper, lemon juice, and mayonnaise, and mix everything together thoroughly.

Allow the gelatin mixture to cool, stirring it occasionally, until it just begins to thicken. Then stir in the broccoli mixture, taste, and correct the seasoning if necessary. Spoon the mousse into 6 to 8 individual oiled molds or cups and chill them for several hours, or until the mousse is completely set.

Unmold each mousse onto a medium-sized plate and garnish with cherry tomatoes and parsley sprigs.

Serves 6 to 8.

beet and pineapple salad

4   large beets (about 1½ lbs. or 3½ cups when
          cooked and diced)
1½ cups chopped, drained fresh pineapple
1   cup thinly sliced inner celery stalks
¼   cup minced onion
2   Tbs. olive oil
6   Tbs. red wine vinegar
salt to taste

Boil the beets, unpeeled, until they are tender
(anywhere from 45 minutes to 1 hour). Cool
them, peel them, and cut them in ¼-inch dice.
Combine the beets with the pineapple, celery,
and onions. Pour the oil and vinegar over them
and toss until everything is evenly coated with
dressing. Taste, and add salt as needed. Toss
again.

Chill the salad for several hours, then stir it up
again and take it out of the refrigerator at least
½ hour before serving, so that it is cool but not
ice-cold.

Serve in small bowls or on lettuce leaves.

Serves 8.

filled cantaloupe salad

Serve as a first course with thin, buttered slices of bread or crisp Cheese Pastries (page 47).

1   large cucumber
1   medium-sized avocado
2   cups sliced fresh strawberries
½   cup lemon juice
2   Tbs. vegetable oil
4   tsp. sugar
¼   tsp. salt
2   medium-sized cantaloupes

Peel the cucumber, quarter it lengthwise, remove the seeds with a small spoon and discard, and slice the cucumber quarters thinly. Cut the avocado in half and remove the pit. Peel it and cut it in medium dice. Combine the cucumber, avocado, and strawberries in a bowl and sprinkle them with the lemon juice, oil, sugar, and salt. Toss gently until everything is evenly coated with the dressing and refrigerate for an hour or so.

Cut the cantaloupes in half crosswise with a zigzag pattern: Using a sharp, pointed knife, push the point of the knife into the center of the cantaloupe, making an angled cut slightly less than 1 inch long. Pull the knife out and make another cut next to it at about a 90 degree angle. Continue around the center of the cantaloupe this way, making the cuts as even as possible, until you come all the way around. Pull the two halves apart and scoop out the seeds.

Fill the cantaloupe halves with the marinated fruit-and-vegetable mixture and chill them briefly before serving.

Serves 4.

cold omelet salad

6   eggs
3   Tbs. butter
salt and pepper to taste
4   Tbs. minced fresh parsley
3   Tbs. minced fresh chives
3   Tbs. minced fresh dill weed
½   Tbs. minced fresh cilantro (coriander
       leaves)
2   Tbs. homemade mayonnaise (page 107)
1   recipe Sour Cream Dressing II (page 108)
red leaf or salad bowl lettuce
3   fresh, ripe tomatoes
1¼ cups sliced pickled beets

garnish

parsley sprigs
radish rosettes

Make 3 thin, plain 9-inch omelets, using 2 eggs and 1 tablespoon butter for each, according to the directions on page 124. Turn them out of the pan without folding, stack them on a plate, and set them aside.

Combine the minced parsley, chives, dill, and cilantro with the mayonnaise and a little salt and pepper. Spread ⅓ of this mixture evenly over 1 of the omelets and roll it up tightly. Place it seam side down on a plate so that it will not unroll. Spread and roll the other 2 omelets the same way. Put the omelets in the refrigerator to chill for an hour or two.

The salad can be arranged on individual plates or on a serving platter. First arrange the lettuce leaves on the platter, then slice the tomatoes and put a layer of tomato slices over the lettuce in a pretty pattern. Put a slice of pickled beet on top of each tomato slice.

Cut the chilled omelet rolls in slices about ¾ inch thick. Arrange the omelet slices over the tomato and beet slices. Garnish the platter with parsley twigs and radish rosettes and pass the chilled dressing separately as you serve.

Serves 4 to 6.

See Spanish Specialties for Ensaladilla Russa.

stews, casseroles, hot vegetable dishes

In the heart of the town of Verona is the beautiful Piazza delle Erbe. It is described at one end by the medieval civic buildings and at the other end by a palazzo from a later period. Stretching across the piazza, from one elegant side to the other, are the dozens of white, umbrella-topped stalls of the vegetable market, and everywhere the happy commotion that always accompanies the choosing of shiny, purple eggplants; earth-colored mushrooms; plum-shaped tomatoes; ruffled lettuces; juicy, sweetly perfumed berries; and cut flowers for the table.

In a sunny, open spot near the middle of the square is a graceful, thirteenth-century fountain. A slender medieval lady gazes serenely across the piazza from above the trickling water, and at her feet several little plastic hoses have been slipped into the pool from which to siphon water into buckets and sprinkling cans to keep all the bright-colored flowers, fruits, and vegetables fresh.

The Piazza delle Erbe is one of my favorite open-air markets, not only because it is filled with such an opulent array of beautiful foods and flowers in an exquisite setting, but also because it expresses something fundamental to the Italian spirit, their unerring aesthetic sense, which built the lovely town, piazza, and the fountain, and their ease and practicality, which allows them to siphon water casually from the priceless fountain in order to keep their vegetables sprinkled.

I always find the atmosphere of open-air produce markets captivating and seek them out wherever I go. Each one is like a crazy salad, with its own special flavor, but all express the same ebullient spirit, as the seasonal abundance of vegetables and fruits is brought to town.

Covent Garden, one of the best-known and surely best-loved markets I have ever visited, has felt the pinch of urban crowding and moved to more spacious quarters outside of town. That once bustling little square of London had an unnaturally still and haunted feeling the last time I saw it. No doubt it will soon be all aroar with new enterprise, but I'll never forget stepping off the tube in Covent Garden Station and into the big elevator, where, several stories underground, the mingled fragrances of a hundred kinds of fruit and vegetable were already present with intoxicating intensity. At the top, one emerged into a land of cabbages and apples and oranges, in the heart of the city.

Other city markets are surviving and even thriving. In Warsaw, the market is everywhere. In every square and on every street, alone or grouped in cozy pairs or trios, the little wooden stalls offer whatever the season dictates in the way of food and flowers. It isn't possible to walk more than a few blocks without passing something very inviting—maybe just a small cart, entirely filled with dark red cherries or maybe a large stall, already aspiring to be a shop, with a dozen fresh vegetables arrayed in front and long ropes of dried black mushrooms hanging from the little roof.

In Cairo, a sprawling street market stays open all night, and the turbaned and caftaned stall keepers sit calmly by their treasuries of vegetables, spices, herbs, and fruits, and by great hills of the reddest, juiciest, absolutely best watermelons in the world. And in Barcelona, the big San Juan Market spills out of its great halls and trails along part of the wide, flowery Ramblas, a beautiful avenue so ideally suited for strolling that it is gradually metamorphosing into a park.

Walking through markets like that was frustrating for me sometimes. I wanted to buy everything and take it right home to a kitchen. Instead, I imagined, translated, took notes in hotel rooms, and carried the notebacks back home. But more than once I've devised dishes and whole meals while rambling through the Los Angeles Farmers Market and watching the good cooks pinch their cucumbers and sniff their melons. That was the way I thought of the Giant Mushrooms Stuffed with Eggplant: On one of those forays, I spotted enormous fresh mushrooms—at least three inches across—huge, firm, and round. I couldn't keep from buying them, so I then proceeded to scout other stalls for something that could do them justice as a stuffing. At the same time, I was already mulling over how to work out a menu around them and deciding that we should ask someone over to help us eat them. A nice party developed that evening.

Like the mushrooms, most of the hot vegetables here are not side dishes but are rather suited to central importance in a meal. Many of them are hearty winter foods, the kind you long for when it starts to rain and blow and turns dark at five o'clock. Then you want a stew and dark homemade bread to go with it, and a fireplace to sit by while you eat them. But even among such plain, straightforward kettlefuls from humble origins are a few combinations made with a light touch. Sweet and Sour Stuffed Cabbage Balls, from my friend Flora Mock's old, unwritten recipe, have an unexpectedly delicate flavor, piquant but subtle.

A dish like that, or like the Squash and Tomato Stew, with its soft, golden corn meal dumplings, makes a fine dinner, needing only the addition of an interesting salad and, the easiest of desserts, fruit and cheese. And because stews and casseroles are generally so uncomplicated to prepare and serve, they lend themselves well to large dinner parties or buffets. A festive but easy-to-handle menu can be designed by making the first course one of the more elegant cold dishes, like Broccoli Mousse, and finishing with a party dessert—a torte or the sinfully rich Crème à la Irena.

In the summertime, when a lighter hot dish is required to set off a cold soup or big salad, try French Fried Mushrooms. Serve them hot from the oil, crisp on the outside and juicy inside, with a fresh tartar sauce—and wash them down with a chilled white wine. Then bring on the peaches or the fresh raspberries sprinkled with kirsch, to complete a perfect alfresco luncheon or supper.

mushroom stew

5   Tbs. butter
1   Tbs. olive oil
2   bay leaves
2   cloves garlic, minced
1   large yellow onion, chopped
2   Tbs. flour
1   cup vegetable broth
1   cup tomato juice
2   cups peeled, quartered tomatoes
1   tsp. thyme
1½ lbs. mushrooms, washed
1   lb. boiling onions
red wine to taste
chopped fresh parsley to taste
salt and pepper
1   cup pitted ripe green olives

In a medium-sized saucepan, melt 2 table-spoons of the butter with 1 tablespoon olive oil and add to it the bay leaves, garlic, and onions. Sauté until the onions are golden and then stir in the flour and lower the heat.

Cook this roux for several minutes, stirring constantly, and then add the vegetable broth and tomato juice. Stir with a whisk to remove all lumps, and add the peeled tomatoes.

In another, larger pot, melt the remaining 3 tablespoons butter and add the thyme and the washed mushrooms. Sauté the mushrooms over a high flame for several minutes, turning them over often, and then adding the boiling onions and the tomato sauce. Turn down the heat and simmer the stew for about 20 minutes. Add a little red wine, some chopped parsley, and salt and pepper to taste. Last, but not least, toss in the green olives. Cook only a few more minutes, and serve hot, with a good bread and some red wine.

Serves 6.

winter vegetable stew

9   Tbs. butter
4   medium-sized leeks
1   lb. boiling onions
3½ oz. parsley root
3 to 4 cloves garlic, minced
¼   tsp. thyme
2   bay leaves
rosemary to taste
1   lb. mushrooms
2   medium-sized turnips
2½ cups dry white wine
3   Tbs. Worcestershire sauce
1   lb. russet potatoes
½   lb. small brussels sprouts
3   Tbs. flour
2   cups hot vegetable broth
2   Tbs. wine vinegar
3   Tbs. molasses
3   tsp. paprika
dash of Tabasco
salt and pepper

Melt 6 tablespoons of the butter in a large, heavy pot. Trim off the green parts, and wash and slice the remaining part of the leeks. Peel the onions. Scrape and thinly slice the parsley root.

Sauté the leeks, onions, and parsley roots in the butter, together with the garlic, thyme, bay leaves, and rosemary until the leeks begin to turn golden.

Wash the mushrooms and, if they are particularly large, cut them in half. Peel the turnips and cut them in ½-inch dice. Add the mushrooms and turnips to the pot, as well as the wine and the Worcestershire sauce. Stir and lower the flame.

Peel and dice the potatoes and wash and trim the brussels sprouts. Add them to the stew, stir again, and cover.

In a small, heavy saucepan, melt the remaining 3 tablespoons butter and stir in the flour. Cook this roux for a few minutes, then add the hot vegetable broth and stir quickly with a whisk. Add the vinegar, molasses, paprika, and a little Tabasco. Stir with the whisk again until the sauce is smooth and pour it over the stew.

Simmer the stew gently, covered, for about 1 hour, or until all the vegetables are tender. Season to taste with salt and pepper, and serve very hot.

Serves 8 to 10.

stewed eggplant

2   large eggplants
olive oil to taste
salt to taste
2   large onions
3   cloves garlic, minced
⅓   cup olive oil
3   large tomatoes
1   cup cooked, chopped spinach
¼   cup chopped chives
½   cup chopped celery leaves
1½ tsp. oregano
plenty of pepper to taste
2   Tbs. lemon juice
¼   cup sesame seeds

Peel and slice the eggplants lengthwise, ⅓ inch thick. Cut each slice again into 2 or 3 lengthwise strips. Arrange the slices on baking sheets, brush them with olive oil, and salt them lightly. Put them in a preheated medium broiler for about 7 to 10 minutes, or until the eggplant starts to turn golden brown. Turn the slices over, brush the other side with olive oil, salt the slices, and put them back in the broiler till the other side is colored as well.

Meanwhile, peel and chop the onions, mince the garlic, and sauté them in the olive oil until the onions are translucent. Cut the tomatoes in thin wedges and add them to the onions, along with the spinach, chives, and celery leaves. Simmer the mixture for about another 10 minutes, then stir in the oregano, salt and pepper, and the lemon juice.

Put a few tablespoons of this sauce in the bottom of a fairly large, fireproof casserole and arrange ⅓ of the broiled eggplant slices over it. Spoon some more sauce over the eggplant and continue layering until all the eggplant is used up. Cover the last eggplant layer with the remaining sauce.

Put a close-fitting lid on the casserole and simmer the vegetables together over a medium flame for 10 minutes.

Toast the sesame seeds by spreading them on a cookie sheet and putting them in a 350 degree oven. Give them an occasional stir and remove them when golden brown.

Sprinkle the toasted sesame seeds over the eggplant just before serving.

Serves 5 to 6.

squash and tomato stew

1½ large yellow onions
4½ Tbs. olive oil
5 to 6 cloves garlic, minced
¾ tsp. ground cumin
¾ tsp. cinnamon
¾ cup diced hot green chilis
1½ qts. cooked tomatoes, with liquid
1¼ lbs. yellow winter squash, peeled and cut
     in ½-inch cubes
1½ tsp. salt
1½ cups water
1   recipe Corn Meal Dumplings (below)
1¼ lbs. zucchini, cut in ¼-inch slices
3 to 4 Tbs. fresh-chopped cilantro (coriander
     leaves)
1½ tsp. sugar

Peel, quarter, and slice the onions. In a very large pot, sauté them in the olive oil until they are clear, then add the garlic, cumin, cinnamon, and diced chilis. Sauté for a few minutes more, stirring constantly, then add the tomatoes and their liquid, the cubed squash, the salt, and the water.

Lower the heat, cover the pot, and simmer the mixture gently for about 1 hour.

Meanwhile make dumpling batter.

Add the zucchini, cilantro, and sugar to the stew. Stir, and cook for another 5 to 6 minutes.

Now drop dumpling batter on the stew by teaspoonfuls, cover the pot tightly, and leave the stew simmering over very low heat for 20 minutes.

Serves 6 to 8.

corn meal dumplings

1   cup yellow corn meal
⅓   cup white flour
1   tsp. baking powder
¾   tsp. salt
1   tsp. sugar
1   egg
½   cup light cream
1½ Tbs. butter, melted

Sift together the corn meal, flour, baking powder, salt, and sugar. Beat together the egg and the cream and stir into the dry mixture. Add the melted butter and continue stirring until the batter is smooth.

Drop the batter by teaspoonfuls into simmering soup, stew, or heavily salted water. Cover and simmer for 14 to 15 minutes.

Makes about 2 dozen dumplings.

ukrainian stewed eggplant

1   cup chopped onions
4   Tbs. olive oil
½   lb. carrots (4 medium sized)
2   medium-sized green bell peppers
2   lbs. eggplant
1½ lbs. tomatoes, peeled and quartered
2   cloves garlic, minced
2½ tsp. salt
pinch of cayenne pepper
⅔   cup lemon juice
2   tsp. sugar
fresh-ground black pepper to taste

garnish

½   cup thin-sliced green onions

Sauté the onions in the olive oil for 5 minutes.

Scrape and thinly slice the carrots. Trim and seed the bell peppers and cut them in thin 1-inch strips. Peel the eggplant and slice it lengthwise ½ inch thick. Cut the slices, again lengthwise, into strips ½ inch wide and 1½ inches long.

Add the carrots to the onions and sauté another 5 minutes. Then add the peppers, eggplant, tomatoes, garlic, salt, cayenne, lemon juice, sugar, and pepper. Simmer the mixture, covered, for about ½ hour, then uncovered for around 15 minutes, stirring occasionally. The liquid from the tomatoes should be greatly reduced.

Serve the eggplant hot or cool, sprinkled with the green onions.

Serves 8.

stewed vegetables with anise and lemon sauce

1 lb. dried lima beans (about 2 cups)
9 cups cold water
2½ tsp. salt, and more to taste
3 medium-sized heads anise (about 2 to 2½
    lbs. untrimmed), or fennel
2 large onions
¾ lb. green beans
½ lb. carrots
½ lb. mushrooms
½ cup butter
3 eggs
juice of 2 large lemons (about ⅓ cup)
pepper to taste

Put the dried lima beans in a pot with 7 cups of the cold water and 1 teaspoon of the salt, bring the water to a boil, then lower the heat and simmer the beans gently for 1 hour. Skim off the foam from the top.

Trim the long stalks and tops off of the heads of anise and peel off the outer leaves if they are blemished. Wash the anise carefully, getting out any dirt that may be trapped between the leaves. Cut the anise into chunks no more than 1 inch across and 2 inches long.

Peel the onions and cut them into 1-inch chunks. Trim the green beans and cut them into 1-inch pieces. Scrape the carrots and slice them thickly or, if they are slender, cut them in ¾-inch lengths. Wash and trim the mushrooms.

Melt the butter in a large pot and sauté the anise and onions in it for about 10 to 12 minutes, stirring frequently. Add the beans, carrots, and mushrooms and stir for a few minutes more. Add the partially cooked lima beans, together with their liquid, 2 more cups of water, and another 1½ tsp. salt. Stir everything together gently, cover the pot, and simmer over low heat for about 45 minutes or a little longer if necessary. All the vegetables should be tender.

Beat the eggs with the lemon juice. Ladle out about 1 cup of the hot broth from the vegetables and beat it into the egg mixture. Add the sauce to the vegetables and stir over lowest possible heat for a few minutes, until the liquid has thickened. Season with more salt and pepper, and serve.

Serves 6 to 8.

mushrooms and potatoes in wine sauce

1½ oz. dried wild mushrooms
5 Tbs. butter
⅔ cup chopped onion
1 clove garlic, minced
2½ lbs. russet potatoes
1¾ cups dry white wine
1 tsp. salt, and more to taste
½ lb. fresh mushrooms
¼ tsp. dried dill weed
¼ tsp. dried whole thyme
4 Tbs. chopped fresh parsley
fresh-ground black pepper

Put the dried mushrooms in a bowl and pour over them enough hot water to amply cover them. Let them soak for about 1 hour, or longer if you have the time, then drain them, reserving the liquid. Wash the mushrooms very carefully, cut them in wide strips, and put them aside. Strain the liquid through several layers of cheesecloth or through a paper filter, and simmer it in a small pot until it is reduced to 1 cup.

Melt 3 tablespoons of the butter in a large pot and sauté the chopped onions and minced garlic in it until they begin to show color. Peel the potatoes, cut them in 1-inch cubes, and add them to the onions and garlic. Pour in the white wine, add the salt, stir, and cover the pot.

Simmer on medium-low heat for 10 minutes, then add the soaked mushrooms and the reduced mushroom liquid, stir, and cover again. Continue simmering, stirring occasionally, for another 20 minutes. The potatoes should be completely tender.

Meanwhile, wash and slice the fresh mushrooms. Melt the remaining 2 tablespoons butter in a skillet, add the dill weed, thyme, chopped parsley, and the sliced mushrooms, and sauté them, stirring constantly, until the mushrooms are tender.

When the potatoes are cooked, add the sautéed, herbed mushrooms to the pot and simmer, uncovered, for a few more minutes, stirring often. Add fresh-ground black pepper to taste, and more salt if needed. The liquid should be reduced to a thick, gravylike sauce. Serve hot.

Makes 6 servings.

italian potato and cheese casserole

2   lbs. russet potatoes
6   Tbs. butter
½   tsp. salt, and more to taste
1½ lbs. ripe tomatoes
pepper to taste
1½ tsp. basil, crushed
⅔   lb. mozzarella cheese
6   hard-boiled eggs
⅔   cup chopped fresh parsley
½   cup fresh-grated Parmesan cheese

Boil the potatoes until they are just barely tender, drain them, peel them, and cut them crosswise in fairly thick slices.

Melt the butter and pour 2 tablespoons of it over the bottom of a large, shallow casserole. Arrange the potato slices in the casserole in one layer and salt them.

Slice the tomatoes and arrange the tomato slices on top of the potatoes. Sprinkle the tomatoes with salt and pepper and the 1½ tsp. basil.

Slice the mozzarella, cut the slices into wide strips, and arrange the strips on top of the tomatoes.

Peel and coarsely chop the eggs, combine them in a bowl with the remaining 4 tablespoons melted butter, the chopped parsley, ½ tsp. salt, and some pepper. Toss the mixture together until it is thoroughly mixed. Spread the egg mixture evenly over the cheese.

Sprinkle the casserole with the Parmesan cheese and bake it in a preheated oven at 350 degrees for 25 to 30 minutes.

Serves 5 to 6.

red cabbage with apples

2   lbs. red cabbage, cored and shredded
1   medium-sized yellow onion, chopped
1½ lbs. tart green apples (about 3 large),
       peeled, cored, quartered, and sliced
½   cup butter
1   tsp. salt
2   Tbs. brown sugar
2   Tbs. cider vinegar
¼   tsp. ground cloves
pinch of cinnamon
pinch of nutmeg
fresh-ground black pepper
¾   cup beer

Sauté the cabbage, onions, and apples in the butter for about 10 minutes, stirring often. Add the salt, brown sugar, cider vinegar, cloves, cinnamon, nutmeg, black pepper to taste, and the beer. Stir the mixture up well, cover it, lower the heat, and let it simmer for 1 hour, stirring only occasionally.

The cabbage can be served at this point but improves if it is allowed to cool and reheated several hours later or the following day.

Serves 6 to 8.

potato kugel

A kugel is a puddinglike dish, best eaten hot or warm. Potato Kugel is generally a side dish, but it could be used as the basis of a light meal, with the addition of a soup or salad, and some fruit.

4   medium-sized potatoes (about 2 lbs.)
1   large yellow onion
2   eggs
1   tsp. salt
pepper to taste
3   Tbs. vegetable oil

garnish

sour cream

Peel the potatoes and grate them as quickly as possible. Peel and grate the onion, beat the eggs lightly, and stir together the potatoes, onions, eggs, salt, and pepper. If you are using a blender or food processor, cut the peeled potatoes and onions into chunks and process them, ½ batch at a time, together with the eggs, until no large pieces are left.

Preheat the oven to 350 degrees, pour the oil into a shallow, medium-sized casserole, and heat it for a few minutes. Pour the kugel mixture into the hot oil in the casserole and bake it for 1 hour. The kugel should be puffed up and browned. Serve hot with sour cream.

Serves 6 to 8.

mushrooms on toast

Use only fresh, firm, rather small mushrooms for this recipe, and don't try to substitute dried herbs for fresh. The flavor of this dish is wonderful, but it depends on just the right balance in seasonings.

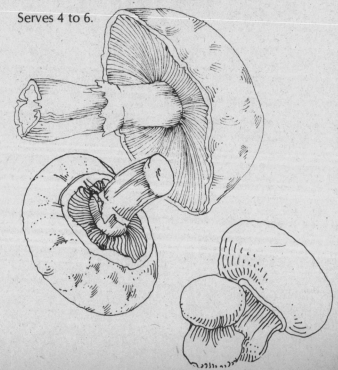

1½ lbs. fresh mushrooms
4   Tbs. olive oil
4   Tbs. finely chopped fresh parsley
2   medium cloves garlic, minced
salt to taste
fresh-ground black pepper to taste
2½ Tbs. butter
2   Tbs. fresh lemon juice
1½ Tbs. cider vinegar or wine vinegar
2   Tbs. chopped fresh cilantro (coriander leaves)
4 to 6 large slices of French or pumpernickel bread, toasted

Wash the mushrooms, trim off the stems, and cut them in half unless they are very small. Toss the mushrooms in a bowl with the olive oil, parsley, garlic, and some salt and pepper. The mushrooms can be prepared ahead of time to this point and kept in the refrigerator, covered, for up to 1 day.

Melt the butter in a large skillet and when it is sizzling, add the mushrooms. Sauté the mushrooms over high heat for 5 or 6 minutes, stirring constantly. They should be just tender and beginning to release water.

Add the lemon juice, vinegar, and cilantro. Cook the mushrooms for about 5 minutes more, still over high heat and still stirring constantly. Mound the mushrooms on top of the toast, dividing them equally among the 4 to 6 slices, and drizzle the liquid that is left in the pan over them. Serve immediately!

Serves 4 to 6.

french fried mushrooms

The mushrooms can be fried ahead of time and then reheated for about 10 minutes in a very hot oven, but the crusts will lose just a bit of their crispy pizzazz that way.

1½ lbs. fresh, firm mushrooms
1 cup dry bread or cracker crumbs
⅓ cup minced fresh parsley
2 eggs
1 clove garlic, minced or crushed
salt to taste
fresh-ground pepper to taste
½ cup flour
vegetable oil for deep frying

garnish

tartar sauce *or*
Hot Paprika Sauce (page 102) *or*
Simple Tomato Sauce (page 102)
grated Parmesan cheese

Choose the mushrooms carefully for uniformity of size, picking medium-small mushrooms rather than very large ones. Wash them quickly, trim off the stems even with the bottoms of the mushrooms, and pat them dry in tea towels.

Combine the bread crumbs and minced pars-ley in a shallow bowl. Beat the eggs and add to them the minced garlic, a generous amount of salt, and some pepper. Put the beaten eggs in another small, shallow bowl.

Add some salt and pepper to the flour as well and put it in a third shallow bowl.

Roll all the mushrooms in the flour first, tapping them lightly after you do to be sure there aren't pockets of flour around the stems. Then dip each mushroom into the beaten egg and immediately afterward roll it in the crumbs and parsley.

Fry the mushrooms in deep, hot vegetable oil until they are golden brown, drain them on paper towels, and serve them hot with tartar sauce, Hot Paprika Sauce, or Simple Tomato Sauce, and grated Parmesan cheese.

Serves 6.

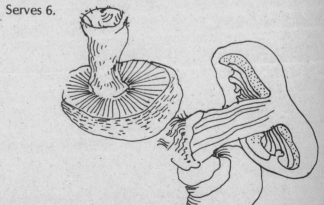

mushroom stroganoff

This dish is made with both dried and fresh mushrooms. The dried mushrooms can be the wild black of dark brown ones that are imported from Italy or Eastern Europe, but I've also had success using the Japanese forest mushrooms—a wonderful, pungent flavor.

2   oz. dried dark mushrooms
1   qt. hot water
1   lb. fresh, firm mushrooms
½   medium-sized onion, minced
4   Tbs. butter
pinch of thyme
salt
fresh-ground black pepper
1   generous cup sour cream
2   Tbs. brandy
2   Tbs. dry sherry
1   lb. wide egg noodles
3 to 4 Tbs. butter, melted
2 to 3 tsp. poppy seeds

Soak the dried mushrooms in a quart of hot water for several hours. Drain them, reserving the liquid. Wash the mushrooms thoroughly under running water, one by one, and trim off the hard stems. Cut the mushrooms in wide strips. Strain the liquid through several layers of cheesecloth or through a paper coffee filter; there should be about 2 cups of it now. Transfer the liquid to a saucepan and simmer it until it is reduced by slightly more than half.

Meanwhile, wash, trim, and thickly slice the fresh mushrooms. Sauté the minced onions in the butter until they are transparent, then add the sliced fresh mushrooms and toss over high heat until they have released their excess water and it is starting to evaporate. Season with a pinch of thyme and salt and pepper to taste. Add the soaked mushroom strips and reduce the heat to medium-low.

Gradually whisk the reduced mushroom liquid into the sour cream, and add this mixture to the mushrooms. Simmer gently, stirring often, for 15 to 20 minutes, or until the sour cream sauce is slightly thickened and the mushrooms are tender. Stir in the brandy and sherry, taste, and correct the seasoning if necessary.

Boil the noodles in a large amount of vigorously boiling salted water until they are just tender but not yet soft. Drain them immediately and toss them with the melted butter and poppy seeds in a heated bowl.

Serve with the poppy seed noodles, and follow it with a tart, crisp salad.

Serves 6.

zucchini and eggplant roulade

Crazy as it may sound, a roulade is really like a big, flat soufflé that has been rolled up around a filling, jelly-roll style. It's served hot, cut into pretty spiral-patterned slices, with a sauce poured over them.

1¼ lbs. zucchini
approximately 1 tsp. salt, and more to taste
1   medium-sized eggplant (about 1 lb.)
2   Tbs. olive oil
2   cups peeled, cooked tomatoes (with liquid)
2   tsp. sugar
2   tsp. lemon juice
⅓   cup cream
salt and pepper to taste
½   cup butter
⅓   cup chopped onions
⅔   cup flour
1   cup warm milk
4   eggs, separated
½   cup grated Parmesan cheese
fine, dry bread crumbs
⅓   cup pine nuts

garnish: Mornay Sauce (page 99)

Wash and grate the zucchini and toss with the 1 teaspoon salt. Put the zucchini in a colander to drain for 20 minutes. Then squeeze out the excess moisture from the grated zucchini, rinsing first only if too salty.

To make the eggplant filling: Peel the eggplant, grate it, and sauté it for 10 to 15 minutes in the olive oil, stirring often. Add the tomatoes, sugar, and lemon juice and cook over medium-high heat, stirring almost constantly until the sauce is thick. Add the cream and the salt and pepper and continue cooking until the consistency is not at all runny.

Melt the butter in a medium saucepan and sauté the onions in it until they are completely transparent. Stir in the flour and continue stirring, over low heat, until the flour is golden, about 5 or 6 minutes. Add the warm milk and stir vigorously until the mixture is smooth and thick. Remove it from the heat and let it cool for 5 minutes. Beat in 4 egg yolks, then stir in the zucchini and the Parmesan cheese.

Beat the 4 egg whites until they hold fairly stiff peaks. Stir ½ the egg whites thoroughly into the egg-zucchini-cheese mixture, then fold in the other ½.

Butter a 10-by-14-inch jelly-roll pan and sprinkle it with fine, dry bread crumbs. Spread the egg-zucchini-cheese mixture evenly over the entire surface of the pan.

zucchini and eggplant roulade (continued)

Bake in a preheated 375 degree oven for about 15 minutes, or until it is puffed and coming away from the sides.

Turn the roulade out on a tea towel and spread it with the eggplant filling, leaving a 1½-inch border along one side. Sprinkle the pine nuts over the filling and, starting with the end where the border has been left, roll it up lengthwise. Use the towel to help roll it evenly.

Put the roulade back in the oven for 5 minutes and serve it with Mornay Sauce.

Serves 6 to 8.

mushroom and barley stuffed cabbage rolls

1   large head green cabbage
Mushroom-Barley Stuffing (page 179)
2½ lbs. fresh, ripe tomatoes
4   Tbs. olive oil
1   large onion, chopped
3 to 4 cloves garlic, minced
1½ tsp. paprika
red wine
salt
pepper

Place the whole head of cabbage in a large kettle and pour boiling water over it. In a few moments, the outer leaves will soften. Lift the cabbage out and very gently peel off the soft leaves. Repeat this procedure until all the leaves large enough to wrap around a spoonful of stuffing have been removed. If the cabbage leaves are not pliable enough to wrap and fold without tearing, douse them with boiling water again and leave them in it until they are soft.

Cut off the very stiff core ends and trim the largest leaves just a little. Place a rounded tablespoonful of stuffing near the thick end of a leaf. Fold the end over the stuffing, then fold over the sides, as if making an envelope. When the sides are neatly tucked over, roll up the cabbage leaf as tightly as possible without squeezing out the stuffing. Continue in this manner until all the stuffing is used. You should have enough for 12 to 15 cabbage rolls.

Blanch the tomatoes in boiling water and peel them. Purée them in a blender at low speed for a very short time—the resulting sauce should be thick and have bits of tomato in it.

Heat the olive oil in a large skillet and sauté the onions, garlic, and paprika in it until the garlic is golden. Add the tomato purée, a little red wine, and salt and pepper to taste. Simmer the sauce gently until it is thickened, at least ½ hour.

Lightly butter or oil a big, shallow (about 2 inches deep) baking dish. Put a few spoonfuls of the tomato sauce in the bottom. Arrange the cabbage rolls in one neat layer in the dish. Pour the remaining tomato sauce over them.

Bake the cabbage rolls in a preheated 350 degree oven for about 40 minutes and serve piping hot.

Serves 6 to 8.

mushroom-barley stuffing for cabbage rolls

2   oz. dried black mushrooms
⅓   cup barley
½   lb. fresh mushrooms
1   large yellow onion
4   Tbs. butter
salt
fresh-ground black pepper

Put the dried mushrooms in a bowl with 2 cups hot water and allow them to rehydrate for about 1 hour. Put the barley in a small saucepan with 1 cup water and let simmer gently for 1½ to 2 hours, until tender.

When the mushrooms have plumped up, take them out of the bowl, one or two at a time, and wash them carefully under running water to get rid of all the gritty dirt that they conceal in such abundance. Set them aside.

Take the liquid in which the mushrooms were soaked and strain through muslin or through a good paper coffee filter. Measure out 1 cup of the filtered liquid and add it to the simmering barley.

Put the soaked dark mushrooms through the medium blade of a food mill.

rice-stuffed cabbage rolls

mushroom barley stuffing (continued)

Wash the fresh mushrooms and halve them, then slice the halves thinly.

Peel and coarsely chop the onion.

Melt the butter in a large skillet and add the onions and fresh mushrooms. Sauté them until the onions are transparent, then add the dark mushrooms and season with salt and fresh-ground black pepper to taste. Sauté this mixture for another 10 or 15 minutes, stirring often.

When the barley is quite tender, add it, along with the remaining liquid, to the mushroom mixture. Stir it all up well and simmer gently, covered, for another ½ hour or so, stirring occasionally.

filling

2 oz. dried dark mushrooms
1½ cups brown rice
3 cups water
1 tsp. salt, and more to taste
2 Tbs. butter
2 cups chopped onions
2 cloves garlic, minced
1 tsp. sweet paprika
⅛ to ¼ tsp. hot paprika
1 tsp. dill seeds
½ cup raisins
⅔ cup finely chopped walnuts
2 eggs, lightly beaten
½ cup dry bread crumbs
pepper to taste

sauce

4 Tbs. butter
1 cup chopped onions
1 qt. cooked tomatoes (with liquid)
½ cup medium-sweet vermouth
2½ Tbs. lemon juice
3 oz. tomato paste
salt to taste
pepper to taste

1 large head cabbage (about 2½ lbs.)

Soak the mushrooms in about a quart of hot water for 1 hour.

Bring the rice to a boil in 3 cups of water with 1 tsp. salt, then lower the heat and simmer it for 25 minutes. Drain the rice.

Melt 2 tablespoons butter in a skillet and sauté the 2 cups chopped onions and the minced garlic in it until the onions are transparent.

Drain the mushrooms, reserving the liquid. Wash the mushrooms carefully, one by one, to remove every speck of sand, and mince them. Add them to the onions and garlic and sauté the mixture for another few minutes.

Strain the liquid from the mushrooms through 5 or 6 layers of cheesecloth or through a paper filter and add 3 cups of it to the mushroom mixture, along with the cooked rice, the two paprikas, the dill seeds, and the raisins. Simmer this mixture gently for about ½ hour, or until most of the liquid is absorbed. Then add the walnuts, eggs, bread crumbs, and salt and pepper. Continue cooking this filling, stirring often, until it is quite thick.

Core the cabbage and blanch it in boiling salted water for 5 minutes. Carefully peel off 14 or 15 leaves. If the inner leaves are still too stiff, put them back in the boiling water for 1 or 2 minutes. Trim 1½ inches off the bottom of each leaf and a little of the sides of the largest ones.

Put 2 or 3 tablespoons of filling in the center of each cabbage leaf and roll it up, folding the sides in as you do.

Chop the remaining cabbage coarsely, and sauté it in 4 tablespoons butter with 1 cup chopped onions. When the onions are translucent, add the tomatoes, coarsely chopped, together with their liquid, the vermouth, the lemon juice, tomato paste, and salt and pepper. Stir this sauce up thoroughly and heat it through.

Put several large spoonfuls of this sauce in the bottom of a large, fireproof casserole. Arrange a layer of the stuffed cabbage leaves in it, seam side down and close together. Cover them with more of the sauce and arrange another layer of cabbage rolls the same way on top of the others. Continue until all the cabbage rolls are used up and finish by pouring the remaining sauce on top. Cover the casserole tightly and simmer over a very low flame for about 1½ hours.

Makes about 8 servings.

baked stuffed tomatoes

¾ lb. green bell peppers (about 2 large)
¾ lb. zucchini
½ lb. small Japanese eggplants (about 3
  eggplants)
1 small yellow onion
¼ cup olive oil
1½ tsp. salt, or more to taste
2 Tbs. chopped fresh cilantro (coriander
  leaves)
1 tsp. crushed dried red peppers
dash of oregano
1½ Tbs. lemon juice
black pepper to taste
6 to 8 large ripe tomatoes
½ lb. Munster cheese, grated
2 Tbs. dry bread crumbs

Roast the bell peppers under the broiler, turning them often, until they are blistered and charred. Hold them under cold running water and peel off the skins. Remove the stems, seeds, and ribs, and cut them in short, thin strips.

Trim and finely dice the zucchini and eggplants. Peel and chop the onion.

Heat the olive oil in a large skillet and sauté the chopped onions in it over very high heat, stirring constantly, just until they begin to color. Add the diced zucchini and eggplant and toss, still over high heat, for about 5 or 6 minutes. Add the salt, cilantro, red pepper, oregano, lemon juice, and black pepper. Stir well and turn off the heat.

Cut out a 2-inch circle from the top of each tomato and scoop out the pulp, leaving a ¼-inch shell. Chop the tomato pulp coarsely, add it to the vegetables in the skillet, and stir again over high heat just until the liquid is reduced to a thick paste.

Remove the vegetables from the heat and quickly stir in about ¾ of the grated cheese.

Spoon the mixture into the tomato shells. Toss the remaining cheese with the bread crumbs and put a little mound of it on top of each tomato.

Bake the tomatoes in a preheated oven at 350 degrees for 15 to 20 minutes and serve immediately.

Serves 6 to 8.

giant mushrooms stuffed with eggplant

8 very large, firm mushrooms (about 3 inches across)
2 to 3 Tbs. butter
1 medium-sized eggplant
1 tsp. salt, and more to taste
1 medium-sized red bell pepper
2 Tbs. olive oil
½ tsp. ground cumin
1 tsp. paprika
3 large cloves garlic, minced
3 Tbs. white wine vinegar
3 Tbs. tomato paste
2½ Tbs. minced red onion
½ cup chopped walnuts
pinch of oregano
fresh-ground black pepper
1 cup grated Monterey Jack cheese

Clean the mushrooms carefully and take out the stems. Then, using a grapefruit spoon, melon baller, or very carefully with a knife, hollow out the centers a little, leaving a thick shell. Sauté the mushrooms in butter for a few minutes only, first on one side, then the other. Remove them from the heat and set aside.

Peel the eggplant and slice lengthwise into ¼-inch-thick slices. Cut these lengthwise into strips ½-inch wide, then cut the strips to 1-inch lengths. Toss the strips with 1 teaspoon salt and leave in a colander for ½ hour.

Seed the red pepper and cut out the white ribs. Cut it into julienne strips.

Heat the olive oil in a large skillet and add the cumin, paprika, and minced garlic.

Rinse the eggplant and press out all excess moisture. Sauté the eggplant and red pepper strips in the olive oil until they are just tender.

Stir in the vinegar, tomato paste, minced onions, and walnuts. Season to taste with oregano, salt, and fresh-ground black pepper. Sauté for a couple more minutes, then stir in ½ the grated cheese.

Spoon the filling into the hollowed-out mushrooms, shaping it into nice, even mounds. Sprinkle the remaining cheese on top.

Bake the mushrooms in a lightly buttered, covered baking dish in a preheated oven at 350 degrees for about 25 to 30 minutes.

Serve hot, if you like with Spinach and Dill Rice (page 188).

Serves 4.

sweet and sour stuffed cabbage balls

1   large head cabbage
¾   cup white rice
¾   cup barley
3½ cups water
1   Tbs. vegetable oil
salt
¾   cup coarsely chopped pine nuts or
      pistachio nuts
2   eggs
½   tsp. dried dill weed or 1 tsp. fresh
black pepper to taste
1   medium-sized onion, finely chopped
½   cup raisins
2   lbs. peeled tomatoes, sliced or coarsely
      chopped
⅓   cup sugar
⅓   cup lemon juice

Bring a large pot of salted water to a boil. Core the cabbage, put it in the boiling water, cover, and let it simmer for about 20 minutes, or just until the leaves are tender enough to peel away easily. Drain the cabbage and allow it to cool enough so that it can be easily handled.

Meanwhile, combine the rice and barley in a medium-sized saucepan and add the 3½ cups water. Stir in 1 teaspoon of salt and 1 table-spoon of vegetable oil, and bring the water to a boil. Lower the heat and simmer, covered, for about 40 minutes. Turn off the heat and let the rice and barley stand, covered, for ½ hour; all the water should be absorbed. Stir in the nuts, eggs, dill weed, black pepper, chopped onions, and raisins, as well as more salt if it is needed.

Scoop out about 2 heaping tablespoons of the mixture and form it into a ball between the palms of your hands, the way you would form a snowball. Peel off one of the soft cabbage leaves and wrap it around the ball of filling, smoothing the cabbage against the rice ball with your hands and overlapping all the edges as securely as you can. The soft cabbage will cling to the rice ball as it is smoothed around. The rice ball must be completely wrapped in the cabbage, but as you continue and the cabbage leaves get smaller, you can use two of them to wrap around one ball of filling. It's all easier than it sounds.

Combine the tomatoes and all their juice with the sugar, lemon juice, and salt to taste; stir well.

Spoon ⅓ of this mixture into a large, heavy-bottomed enameled pot or fireproof casserole.

eggplant with cheese and walnuts

Arrange a layer of cabbage balls on top of the tomatoes, fitting them snugly next to each other but not squeezing them. Spoon another ⅓ of the tomato mixture over them and make a second layer of cabbage balls. Pour the remaining tomatoes over the top, together with any leftover cabbage, coarsely chopped.

Cover the pot or casserole tightly and simmer over lowest heat for 25 minutes. Put the stuffed cabbage away in the refrigerator for 12 to 24 hours, then simmer it for another 25 minutes on low heat or heat it in a preheated 350 degree oven for 45 to 50 minutes.

Serves 6 to 8.

2½ lbs. firm eggplant
salt
3 or 4 cloves garlic, sliced
½ cup olive oil
2 red onions, peeled, halved, and sliced
3 cups peeled plum tomatoes (with all their juice)
⅓ cup dry white wine
fresh-ground black pepper
1⅓ cup walnut pieces
½ lb. Fontina cheese
¼ lb. mozzarella cheese

Trim off the stem ends and slice the eggplants lengthwise, ½ inch thick. Salt the slices liberally on both sides and put them aside for about ½ hour to drain.

In a large skillet, sauté the garlic in the olive oil for several minutes, then remove and discard the garlic. Rinse the eggplant slices and press out the excess moisture between the palms of your hands. Brush the eggplant slices on both sides with the olive oil, and broil them for several minutes on each side until they show dark spots.

When all the slices have been broiled, add to the remaining oil the sliced onions and stir

eggplant with cheese and walnuts (continued)

over high heat until they are limp and beginning to brown. Cut the plum tomatoes in very thick slices and add them, with all their juice, to the onions. Stir in the wine. Cook for several minutes over high heat, stirring often, and add about ½ teaspoon of salt and pepper to taste.

Pour the tomato sauce into a large, shallow casserole. Arrange the sautéed eggplant slices over it in one even, overlapping layer. Sprinkle the slices with a little salt and pepper, then spread the walnut pieces evenly over the eggplant.

Cut the Fontina cheese in slices or strips and arrange it evenly over the walnuts. Grate the mozzarella and sprinkle it over the Fontina.

Bake the casserole in a preheated oven at 350 degrees for 20 to 30 minutes: It should be bubbling hot, and the cheeses should be melted and beginning to brown. Serve immediately.

Serves 8.

lecas *(Basque-style green beans)*

1   lb. fresh green beans
¼   cup olive oil
2   cloves garlic, minced
1   large onion, chopped
1   lb. peeled tomatoes, coarsely chopped
½ to ¾ tsp. salt
fresh-ground black pepper to taste
large pinch of oregano

Wash and trim the green beans and cut them in 1-inch lengths. Bring a medium-sized pot of heavily salted water to a boil.

Heat the olive oil in a fairly large saucepan or skillet and sauté the garlic and onions in it until they begin to color. Add the chopped tomatoes, with all their juice, and simmer.

Plunge the cut green beans into the boiling water and boil them for 5 minutes. Drain the beans and add them to the tomato sauce. A very small amount of water can be added if the tomato sauce seems too thick; it should just barely cover the beans. Add salt and pepper, and simmer covered, for about ½ hour.

Stir in the oregano, taste, and add more salt and pepper if needed. Cook the beans a few minutes more, uncovered, and serve.

Serves 4 to 6.

stuffed potato pancakes, hungarian style

4   lbs. potatoes
4   eggs, beaten
1   cup flour
⅔   cup light cream
½   cup chopped fresh parsley
1   tsp. salt
fresh-ground pepper to taste
butter

To make the pancakes: Peel the potatoes and soak them in cold water for 10 minutes, then grate them. Beat together the eggs, flour, and cream and stir in the grated potatoes, chopped parsley, salt, and pepper.

Melt about 2 teaspoons butter in a 10- or 11-inch pan and pour in about ½ cup of batter. Spread it evenly over the pan and cook for several minutes, flip, and cook a minute or two more. The pancake should be golden brown on both sides. Prepare all the pancakes in this way, adding a little butter to the pan each time, and stack on a plate, keeping them covered with a light cloth to prevent drying out.

Makes 6 to 8 pancakes.

mushroom filling

1½ to 2 oz. dried wild mushrooms
2   cups hot water
¾   lb. boiling onions
2   Tbs. butter
1⅔ cups sliced celery
½   cup chopped walnuts
salt and pepper
approximately 1½ cups Hot Paprika Sauce
      (page 102)

Soak the mushrooms in the hot water for an hour or so. Drain them, reserving the liquid, and wash them very carefully, one by one. Slice the mushrooms in thick strips. Strain the liquid through a filter or through 2 layers of muslin.

Peel the onions and cut in half if large. Sauté the onions and celery in the butter in a large skillet for about 5 minutes. Add walnuts, the mushrooms, their liquid, and the Hot Paprika Sauce. Simmer the mixture, stirring occasionally, until the vegetables are tender and the sauce is thick and glazed, and then season.

To serve the pancakes: Have additional sauce and the filling ready and heated. Reheat each pancake quickly on both sides in a very hot pan. Put one pancake on each plate, spoon some filling down the middle of it, and fold over. Top with several tablespoons of Hot Paprika Sauce and serve immediately.

spinach and dill rice

1 lb. fresh spinach
3 Tbs. olive oil
2 cloves garlic, minced
2 tsp. salt
1 tsp. dried dill weed
2 tsp. white wine vinegar
fresh-ground black pepper to taste
4 cups water
1½ cups long-grain white rice
½ cup finely crumbled feta cheese
½ cup fresh-grated Parmesan cheese

Wash and trim the spinach and mince it. Heat the olive oil in a small skillet and add the minced spinach and minced garlic to it. Season the spinach with ½ teaspoon of the salt, the dill weed, vinegar, and some black pepper.

Cook the mixture over medium heat for about 10 minutes, stirring often. All the excess liquid should have evaporated, leaving a thick purée.

Bring the water to a boil in a medium-large saucepan and stir in the remaining 1½ teaspoons salt. Add the rice and lower the heat to a simmer. Cover the pot and leave the rice to cook over very low heat for 25 minutes. The rice will absorb all the water.

Add the spinach mixture and toss lightly with two spoons until the rice and spinach are well blended. Cover once more and leave over low heat for another 3 to 4 minutes.

Toss together the 2 cheeses. Spoon the green rice onto a warmed platter, sprinkle it with the cheeses, and serve immediately.

Makes 8 servings.

glazed carrots

1½ lbs. slender carrots
3 Tbs. butter
¾ cup water
2 Tbs. lemon juice

salt to taste
1 Tbs. cider vinegar
⅓ cup brown sugar
dash of nutmeg

Scrape and trim the carrots and cut them in 1-

inch lengths. Melt 2 tablespoons of the butter in a medium-sized skillet and add the carrots, water, lemon juice, and a little salt. Simmer, covered, for 20 minutes. Remove the cover and raise the heat. Cook over high heat, stirring often, until nearly all the liquid has evaporated—about 6 to 8 minutes.

Add another tablespoon of butter, the cider vinegar, the brown sugar, and a tiny bit of nutmeg. Lower the heat to medium and stir constantly until all the sugar is melted and the glaze is thick enough to coat the carrots.

Taste, add more salt if needed, and serve.

Serves 4 to 6.

corn and cheese pudding

2   eggs
3   Tbs. flour
½   cup cream
1   cup milk
½   tsp. salt
¼   tsp. white pepper
1   Tbs. sugar
1½ cups fresh-scraped corn (about 3 ears)
3   Tbs. butter, melted
3   oz. sharp Cheddar cheese, grated
¼   cup finely chopped California green chilis

Beat the eggs and flour together to make a smooth paste, then beat in the cream, milk, salt, pepper, and sugar. Add the corn, melted butter, grated cheese, and chopped chilis, and stir the mixture together thoroughly.

Pour the mixture into a buttered medium-sized casserole, and place the casserole in a pan or larger casserole which is about ½ full of water. Bake the pudding for 50 to 55 minutes in a preheated oven at 350 degrees. It should be slightly puffed and golden on top. Serve hot.

Serves 4 to 6.

See Spanish Specialties for Cocido, Stewed Garbanzo Beans, Menestra de Verduras, Champiñónes a la Plancha. See Italian Pastas, Vegetables, and Frittatas for Pomodoro al Gratine and Melanzana al Forno.

croquettes, pâtés, cheeses

Croquettes, pâtés, and the interesting hot and cold concoctions made from cheeses are among the most memorable treats that these past years of traveling, tasting, and experimenting have yielded. They're hard to classify, but only because they're so well suited to so many purposes.

There are hors d'oeuvres and first courses aplenty here, but also some dishes around which a substantial meal can be arranged. The Italian Fondue is a garlicky, pungent variation of the classic Swiss dish and can be served with an antipasto and lots of bread and wine for some superb eating. Croquettes of all types are most often a winning first course, but it's really a question of how hungry you are and how elaborate a meal you want because they also work perfectly well as a light supper, gently sauced and accompanied by a salad.

The pâtés and all the different spiced or potted cheeses, on the other hand, are among the ideal foods to gather together on a groaning board for a festive and opulent cold buffet. When I was planning a gala Christmas party once and wanted to enjoy myself with my guests rather than lurk in the kitchen, I devised a menu for a rich and varied supper that could be entirely prepared ahead of time, most of it *days* ahead of time. The only hot dishes were a selection of soups; for the rest, there were a couple of pâtés, sliced and prettily garnished, some filled Edam cheeses, and a wide assortment of cold vegetable dishes and salads. To this I added baskets of dark and light breads and plenty of butter, cases of champagne, music, and an abundance of mistletoe in every room, as well as one gloriously lighted Christmas tree, of course.

For a small and simple family meal or a hot, comforting lunch on a cold day, the little Russian *vareniki* or the Noodle Kugel, richly veined with fresh hoop or farmer cheese (see page 192), are unsurpassed. Only a clear soup (borscht is nice) or very simple salad and dark bread are required to turn either one into a satisfying meal.

But for that even simpler supper or snack when you have no time or inclination to cook at all I have to recommend again the pâtés and spiced cheeses that serve so well on elaborate occasions. It is at those busiest times that we get hungriest (part of the natural cussedness of life), and even scrambled eggs or omelets seem like too much trouble. That is when it's a real joy to open the refrigerator, pull out a few things that have been hiding there, and sup both deliciously and instantly. The pâtés keep well, if tightly wrapped and chilled, for at least a week or two (I've never been able to keep one around any longer than that). The spiced cheeses, especially those with any beer or wine included in the mixture, only improve with age for a good, long time. Both are a most welcome sight in those desperate "I want it now" moments: Add some bread and butter, a pickle or chutney from the shelf, an appropriate beverage, and sit down. Since all this type of thing is as easy to make in large quantity as small, a few extra hours in the kitchen once a month or so can take care of quite a few hungry moments later, and why shouldn't your midnight snacks be as delicious as any other repast?

For more on cheeses, see the Italian section and the following section, Savory Pastries: Quiches, Pizzas, Pierogi.

A note about hoop cheese: Hoop cheese is very common in Southern California but not in other parts of the country. It is a fresh white cheese, firm enough to slice in blocks, but not hard or dry. It can easily be crumbled into moist (not soggy) bits. The nearest thing to it is farmer cheese, but that, of course, varies from one part of the country to another. If you can find a light, moist farmer cheese, use it. If you can get only a hard one, simply moisten that with a few spoonfuls of cream.

mushroom pâté I

This makes a nice first course with pumper-nickel bread and can also be used as a spread for canapés.

1   lb. fresh mushrooms, chopped
⅓   cup celery, chopped
¼   cup minced parsley
⅓   cup minced shallots
4   Tbs. butter, melted
2   eggs, lightly beaten
½   cup sieved hoop or farmer cheese (see page 192)
¾   cup fine, dry bread crumbs
¼   tsp. basil, crushed
¼   tsp. oregano, crushed
¼   tsp. rosemary, crushed
1   tsp. salt
pinch of cayenne pepper
fresh-ground black pepper to taste

garnish

parsley
thin radish slices *or*
thin carrot slices

Combine the mushrooms, celery, and parsley and put them through the fine blade of a food mill.

Sauté the minced shallots in 1 tablespoon of the butter until they are soft.

In a large mixing bowl, combine the mushroom mixture and the shallots. Add the rest of the butter and all the remaining ingredients. Stir until everything is thoroughly blended.

Butter a medium-sized loaf pan. Line the pan with waxed paper, leaving a large enough edge to fold over the top. Butter the waxed paper.

Spoon the mushroom mixture evenly into the pan and fold the ends of the buttered waxed paper over the top.

Bake the pâté for 1½ hours in a preheated oven at 400 degrees. Allow it to cool in the pan until it is easy to handle.

Carefully take it out of the pan and peel away the paper. Chill for a few hours before serving.

Serve on a board, garnished with parsley and decorated with thin radish or carrot slices.

mushroom pâté II

1   oz. dried black mushrooms
1   lb. fresh mushrooms
¼ to ⅓ cup chopped fresh parsley
⅓   cup chopped celery
⅔   cup chopped walnuts
⅔   cup sieved hoop or farmer cheese (see page 192)
1   cup dry bread crumbs
⅓   cup minced shallots
4   Tbs. butter
2   eggs, beaten
3   Tbs. sweet vermouth
¼   tsp. basil, crushed
¼   tsp. oregano, crushed
¼   rosemary, crushed
1¼ tsp. salt
pinch of cayenne pepper
fresh-ground black pepper to taste

Soak the dried mushrooms in hot water for several hours. Drain them and wash them carefully. Wash the fresh mushrooms. Combine all the mushrooms, the parsley, celery, walnuts, cheese, and bread crumbs and put it all through the finest blade of a food mill or blend in a food processor.

Sauté the shallots in the butter until they are golden and add them to the mushroom mixture, along with all the remaining ingredients. Stir everything together thoroughly.

Butter a medium-sized loaf pan, line it with waxed paper, leaving a large edge of paper around the top, and butter the paper. Spoon the mushroom mixture into the pan and fold the buttered paper loosely over the top. Bake the pâté for 1½ hours in a preheated 400 degree oven. Allow it to cool until it is easy to handle.

Carefully remove the pâté from the pan and peel away the paper. Chill the pâté for several hours before serving.

white bean pâté

3   cups cooked Great Northern white beans
2 to 3 green onions, chopped
4   Tbs. butter
1½ cups finely grated carrots
½   cup minced onion
3   cloves garlic, minced or pressed
¼   cup chopped parsley
2   eggs, lightly beaten
½   cup dry bread crumbs
½   cup cream
1½ tsp. salt
¼   tsp. ground coriander
¼   tsp. basil
¼   tsp. thyme
3   Tbs. beer
fresh-ground black pepper to taste

Put the beans and green onions through the fine blade of a food mill.

Melt the butter in a large skillet and sauté the carrots, onions, and garlic until soft.

Combine everything in a large bowl and stir thoroughly. The mixture should be quite thick.

Butter a round baking dish, about 8 to 10 inches across, and spoon the mixture in evenly. Butter a round of waxed paper and place it, buttered side down, on top of the pâté. Cover the dish with a lid and bake it in a preheated 400 degree oven for 50 to 55 minutes.

This pâté may be served warm or cold—from its dish or turned out on a plate.

egg and olive mold

This is nice for a cold buffet and can also be used as a spread for canapés or sandwiches.

6   hard-boiled eggs
5   Tbs. chopped green, pimiento-stuffed
       olives
3   Tbs. chopped celery
3   Tbs. chopped onion
2   Tbs. chopped parsley
4   Tbs. soft butter
¾   tsp. salt, or more to taste
fresh-ground black pepper to taste
cayenne pepper to taste

garnish

parsley
sliced pickles or radishes
paprika
thin-sliced red bell pepper
sliced olives

Combine all the ingredients. Put the mixture through a food mill, using the fine blade. It may be necessary to put it through more than once to obtain a nice, homogeneous mixture.

Taste, and correct the seasoning.

If you are serving it in a buffet, mound it on a plate or board and, using a butter knife, mold it into a smooth dome. Garnish with parsley, sliced pickles or radishes, and decorate with paprika, thin slices of red bell pepper, and and sliced olives. If you are using it as a spread, just serve it in a little bowl or crock.

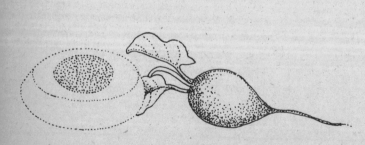

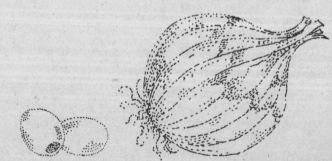

egg croquettes

5   Tbs. butter
¾   cup flour
2   cups warm milk
1   raw egg
6   hard-boiled eggs, sieved or finely chopped
5   Tbs. grated Parmesan cheese
5   Tbs. chopped parsley
1½ tsp. salt
fresh-ground black pepper to taste
dash of nutmeg
dash of cayenne pepper
⅔   cup fine, dry bread crumbs
flour (about ½ cup)
2   eggs, beaten
bread crumbs (about 1½ cups)
vegetable oil for deep frying

Melt the butter in a medium-sized, heavy-bottomed saucepan. Stir the flour in gradually until the mixture forms a soft ball and cook it for 3 or 4 minutes more, stirring constantly over very low heat. Add the warm milk, beating it in energetically with a whisk until the sauce is very thick and smooth.

Remove it from the heat and beat in the raw egg. Then add the sieved or chopped hard-boiled eggs, the Parmesan cheese, parsley, salt, pepper, nutmeg, cayenne, and enough of the bread crumbs to make a stiff mixture.

Form the croquettes by scooping out 1 rounded teaspoonful of the mixture and sliding it off with a second teaspoon into a small bowl of flour. Roll each croquette in flour, dip it in the beaten eggs, then roll it in bread crumbs. Dip it into the beaten egg again and roll it in the crumbs a second time.

Chill the croquettes for about ½ hour, then fry them in deep, hot vegetable oil (without crowding them) until they are golden brown. Drain them on paper towels. The croquettes can be fried ahead of time and reheated in a hot oven for about 10 minutes.

Serve the croquettes hot with a thick chutney or on a bed of rice or creamed vegetables.

Serves 6 to 8.

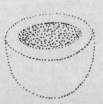

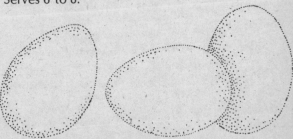

brie croquettes

1½ cups milk
½ cup flour
3 Tbs. butter
2 egg yolks
8 oz. Brie, without rind (about 9 or 10 oz. with the rind)
4 oz. hoop or farmer cheese (see page 192)
⅛ to ¼ tsp. cayenne pepper
¼ tsp. paprika
dash of nutmeg
¼ tsp. salt
fresh-ground black pepper to taste
flour (about ½ cup)
3 eggs, beaten
1½ to 2 cups fine, dry bread crumbs
vegetable oil for deep frying

Beat together the flour and milk until the mixture is smooth. Heat it in a medium-sized, heavy-bottomed saucepan, stirring all the while with a whisk until it thickens. As the mixture thickens, beat vigorously to work out lumps.

Remove from the heat and whisk in the butter and the egg yolks.

Mash the Brie with a wooden spoon until it is a smooth paste, put the hoop cheese through a sieve, and stir the cheeses into the white sauce.

Heat the sauce gently, stirring constantly, until the cheeses are melted. Stir in the cayenne, paprika, nutmeg, salt, and pepper.

Spread the mixture out evenly on a large plate and chill it until it is firm.

Scoop up about 1 tablespoonful of the mixture at a time and drop it into a bowl of flour. Shape it into a round or oval croquette, dip it in the beaten egg, then roll it in the bread crumbs until it is evenly coated. Continue until the cheese mixture is entirely used up, then start over and dip each croquette again into the beaten eggs and roll it again in the bread crumbs. It is important to have a solid and even coating of bread crumbs, or the croquettes will leak when fried.

Fry the croquettes in hot oil for only a few minutes. Do as many at one time as will fit in the pot without crowding. They should be golden brown in color. Drain them on paper towels and serve immediately with seasoned rice, on a bed of cooked vegetables, or with a light sauce.

The croquettes can be reheated in the oven if desired.

Makes about 26 to 30 croquettes, or enough for 6.

garbanzo croquettes

Loosely based on the flavor combination found in *felafel*, these croquettes have the same attractive spiciness but less of a tendency to absorb oil, so the effect is not quite so heavy.

⅓ cup dried bulgur wheat
⅔ cup water
2 cups cooked garbanzo beans (see page 143)
¼ cup fresh lemon juice
3 Tbs. chopped fresh cilantro (coriander leaves)
1½ tsp. crushed dried red chilis
½ tsp. ground cumin
1 tsp. salt
3 Tbs. butter
⅛ tsp. cinnamon
1½ tsp. fresh-minced garlic
3 Tbs. flour
¾ cup hot vegetable broth
2 cups fine, dry bread crumbs
2 eggs, lightly beaten
flour (about ⅔ cup)
vegetable oil for deep frying

Soak the bulgur wheat in the water for 20 minutes, then drain it in a fine sieve, pressing out all the excess moisture.

Mash the garbanzo beans with a potato masher and stir in the lemon juice, cilantro, chilis, cumin, and salt.

Melt the butter in a small saucepan and add the cinnamon and garlic to it. Sauté for about 2 minutes, then stir in the 3 tablespoons flour.

Cook the roux over low heat for several minutes, stirring often, then stir in the vegetable broth. Continue cooking and stirring the sauce until it is thick and smooth. Add it to the garbanzo bean mixture, along with the soaked bulgur and ½ of the bread crumbs. Stir the mixture thoroughly, taste, and correct the seasoning if necessary. Chill the mixture for about 2 hours.

Put the beaten eggs in a small, shallow bowl, the flour in another one, and the remaining 1 cup bread crumbs in a third. Scoop up the croquette mixture by rounded tablespoonfuls and roll each one into a ball—they should be about the size of large walnuts. Roll each ball in flour until it is well coated. When all the balls have been floured, take one at a time and dip it first in the beaten eggs, then roll it quickly in the bread crumbs until it is completely encrusted.

garbanzo croquettes (continued)

Cook the croquettes in deep, hot vegetable oil, about 7 or 8 at a time, for 6 to 8 minutes, or until they are crisp and golden brown all over. Drain them on paper towels and keep them warm in the oven while cooking the rest.

Serve the croquettes hot with a salad or with Chilled Buttermilk Soup (page 89).

Makes about 30 croquettes, enough for 6 to 8 people.

vareniki

Russian *vareniki* are like Italian ravioli: little pockets of pastry are filled with cheese.

dough

1½ cups flour
½ tsp. salt
1 egg
4 Tbs. water
1 Tbs. butter, melted

filling

12 oz. hoop or farmer cheese (see page 192)
½ cup sour cream
1 egg
pinch of salt
2½ Tbs. sugar
2 Tbs. butter, melted
additional melted butter

To make the dough, mix the flour and salt in a bowl and make a well in the center. Beat together the egg and the water, put it in the center of the flour, and stir the flour into it gradually; the dough will be a hard, sticky mass. Add a little more water if necessary to incorporate all the flour, then add the melted butter and knead the dough in the bowl until it is fairly smooth. Turn it out onto a lightly floured board and continue kneading for 5 to 10 minutes, or until the dough is perfectly smooth and starting to feel elastic.

Prepare the filling by putting the hoop cheese (or farmer cheese) through a sieve, beating together the sour cream, egg, salt, sugar, and 2 tablespoons melted butter, and mixing everything together thoroughly. Adjust seasoning.

Roll the dough out as thinly as possible on a lightly floured board and cut out 2-inch circles. Place a small spoonful of filling in the center of each circle, brush the edge of the dough with a little water, and fold the dough over the filling, pressing the moistened edges together firmly to seal it in a half-moon shape.

To cook the *vareniki*, drop them into 2 or 3 quarts of boiling, salted water and boil them for 12 to 15 minutes. Drain them thoroughly and serve them with melted butter.

Serves 6.

italian fondue

Fine with just a good tossed salad, for a really special meal, try this: Prepare an antipasto assortment of, for example, Marinated Mushrooms (page 145), Peperonata (page 144), Garbanzo Bean Salad (page 143), and Insalatone (page 148). Add some hot *peperoncini* and a few cured olives and serve everything at once, with a good Italian white wine. For dessert, fresh strawberries with cream—then expresso and a liqueur.

2 to 3 cloves garlic
2   Tbs. olive oil
½   lb. Fontina cheese, coarsely grated
½   lb. provolone cheese, coarsely grated
3   Tbs. flour
1½ cups dry Italian white wine
pepper to taste
large loaf Italian or French bread, cubed

About 2 or 3 hours before you want to make the fondue, mince the garlic until it is almost a paste and stir it into the olive oil. Toss the grated cheeses together with the flour.

Half an hour before you want to eat, heat the wine in a fondue pot, or a medium-sized enameled saucepan. Be careful to keep the heat *below* a simmer.

Add the cheese mixture, a handful at a time, and stir slowly with a wooden spoon until it is melted. When all the cheese is melted, stir in the olive oil and garlic and some pepper. Continue stirring slowly over low heat for about 15 minutes, or until the fondue is perfectly smooth; it should have a velvety texture.

Place the fondue pot over a candle or other food warmer. Spear bread cubes with long forks and dip them, stirring fondue each time.

The fondue serves 5 to 6.

noodle kugel

A kugel is a puddinglike dish, best eaten hot. Noodle kugel is slightly sweet, but not a dessert. Try it for lunch, with a salad or some fruit.

¾ lb. flat egg noddles
3   eggs
¼   cup sugar
⅔   lb. hoop or farmer cheese, crumbled (see page 192)
½   tsp. salt
½   tsp. cinnamon, and more for garnish
¼   tsp. nutmeg
¼   cup butter
sour cream (optional)

Dump the noodles into heavily salted boiling water and boil them for 8 to 10 minutes, or until they are tender but still firm. Drain them immediately.

Beat together lightly the eggs, sugar, crumbled hoop cheese (or farmer cheese), salt, cinnamon, and nutmeg. Cut ½ the butter into small bits. Stir together the noodles, the egg and cheese mixture, and the cut-up butter.

Preheat the oven to 350 degrees. Put 1 tablespoon butter in a medium-sized casserole and heat it in the oven until the butter is melted. Tilt the casserole around so that the sides are coated with butter and spoon in the kugel mixture. Sprinkle a little more cinnamon on top and dot it with the remaining butter.

Bake the kugel for 25 to 30 minutes, or until the top is golden brown.

Serves 6.

bibbelkäse *(spiced white cheese)*

2   cups small-curd cottage cheese
6   Tbs. sour cream
3   cloves garlic, minced or mashed to a pulp
2½ Tbs. minced fresh parsley
minced chives (optional)
fresh-ground pepper to taste
salt to taste

Press the cottage cheese through a sieve and stir in the sour cream, garlic, and parsley. If you have fresh chives, a spoonful of minced chives could be added to the mixture. Stir the mixture well. Grind in some pepper, add salt, stir again, and put away, in a covered container, to chill for several hours in the refrigerator.

Serve the cheese with black bread and warn all people who are afraid of garlic.

Makes a little more than 2 cups.

liptauer cheese I

½   lb. pot cheese
3   oz. cream cheese
3   Tbs. butter
1 to 1½ tsp. French mustard, to taste
2   Tbs. beer
1   Tbs. minced capers
5   Tbs. finely minced onion
1½ tsp. paprika
cayenne pepper to taste
¼ to ½ tsp. ground cumin or caraway seeds, to
    taste

garnish: paprika and sprigs of parsley

Put the pot cheese through a sieve. Work in the cream cheese and butter until you have a smooth, homogenous mixture.

Add all the remaining ingredients and combine thoroughly. Put the cheese into the refrigerator, in a tightly covered container, and let ripen for at least 24 hours.

To serve, mound the cheese on a plate, shaping it with the side of a knife until it is smooth. Sprinkle with a little paprika, garnish with parsley, and serve with pumpernickel bread.

Serves 8 to 10.

liptauer cheese II

Here is yet another version of Liptauer Cheese, for which so many variations have been devised. The rich flavor of this one is owed largely to the Camembert—but don't use a Camembert that is too ripe, or the mixture will be runny.

8   oz. Camembert cheese (medium ripe)
10   oz. hoop or farmer cheese (see page 192)
4   Tbs. soft butter
2 to 3 Tbs. dark beer
1   tsp. paprika
1   tsp. dry mustard
1½ Tbs. minced capers
2   Tbs. minced onion
salt
black pepper
½   caraway seeds, crushed

garnish

paprika

Scrape or slice the crust off the Camembert cheese and put the cheese in a bowl. Crumble the farmer or hoop cheese and add it to the Camembert, along with the soft butter. Mash the cheeses and butter together with a fork until the mixture is fairly smooth, then add a little beer, more or less depending on the consistency of the cheeses. With the addition of the beer, the mixture should be soft enough to spread, but stiff enough to hold a shape. Add the paprika, mustard, capers, onions, a little salt and pepper to taste, and the caraway seeds. Mix thoroughly and mound the cheese on a plate, smoothing it with a wide, blunt knife to a nice round or oval shape. Cover and chill for several hours, or until the next day.

Sprinkle the cheese with a little more paprika to decorate it and serve it with thin buttered slices of black bread.

Serves 10 to 12.

spiced cheddar and edam cheese

½ lb. Cheddar cheese
½ lb. Edam cheese
½ cup soft butter
½ cup plus 2 Tbs. beer
1½ tsp. caraway seeds
½ tsp. dry mustard
¼ tsp. ground cumin
½ tsp. celery seeds, crushed
1   clove garlic, finely minced
dash of Tabasco sauce

Finely grate or grind the cheeses. Cream together the cheeses, butter, and beer until the mixture is a smooth paste.

Dry roast the caraway seeds by spreading them in a frying pan and gently stirring or shaking them over a medium flame for a few minutes. Add the warm caraway seeds and all the rest of the spices to the cheese mixture and stir (or spin in a food processor) until everything is well blended. Pack into small crocks and store in the refrigerator.

For a milder version, leave out the garlic, Tabasco, and caraway seeds.

Makes about 1¾ pounds.

another way

To make cheese balls, either small ones for hors d'oeuvres or 1 large one, first chill the mixture well and shape into a ball (or balls). Then roll in a half-and-half mixture of finely chopped walnuts and parsley and chill again.

filled edam

1½ lb. round Edam cheese
1   cup soft butter
½   cup brandy
2   tsp. sweet paprika
pinch of hot paprika
½   tsp. dry mustard
½   tsp. celery seeds, finely ground in a mortar
salt to taste
3   Tbs. sweet sherry
1   tsp. sugar

garnish: strips of pimiento

Cut off the top third of a large, round Edam and carefully scoop out the cheese, leaving a ¼-inch shell. Grind or grate the cheese.

In a large bowl, work the butter into the grated cheese. Add the remaining ingredients and stir the mixture vigorously or work it by hand until everything is thoroughly combined. The cheese mixture should be quite smooth and light.

Spoon the cheese back into the large shell, piling it high on top and forming a smooth dome. Cover it with plastic or foil and put it away in the refrigerator for about 1 week.

Remove the cheese from the refrigerator several hours before serving and decorate it with strips of pimiento.

Serve at room temperature with pumpernickel or rye bread.

mamalyga *(a cold dish of cooked corn meal, white cheese, and sour cream)*

This is one of those refreshing cold dishes so welcome during the summer heat: pleasant and filling but not overpowering. A Russian peasant dish, it goes very nicely with a light, cool borscht or a fruit soup.

¾ cup yellow corn meal
5½ to 6 cups water
1 to 1¼ tsp. salt, and more to taste
½ tsp. sugar
4 Tbs. butter
¾ lb. fresh hoop or farmer cheese, crumbled
    (see page 192)
1 cup sour cream
black pepper to taste

Stir together in a pot the corn meal and 5½ cups water. Heat the mixture slowly, stirring often, until it is simmering. Add about 1 teaspoon of the salt, the sugar, and the butter, and continue simmering the mixture gently, still stirring frequently, for 35 to 40 minutes. The corn meal mush should have the consistency of a thin pudding. If it feels stiff or very grainy, stir in a little more water.

Pour the mush into a smooth-surfaced bowl or casserole and allow it to cool completely. It will jell into a solid mold. Chill the corn meal if desired.

When it is quite cool and firm, turn the corn meal mold out onto a plate and slice it thickly. For each serving, cover 1 thick slice of corn meal with a few spoonfuls of crumbled hoop cheese and a large dollop of sour cream.

Serves 8 to 10.

spiced farmer cheese

¾ lb. hoop or farmer cheese (see page 192)
1 cup sour cream
1 Tbs. minced fresh dill weed
⅓ cup chopped chives
1 tsp. lemon juice
¼ tsp. hot paprika
salt to taste
fresh-ground black pepper to taste

Combine the cheese and the sour cream and mash them together thoroughly with a fork until all the large lumps of cheese are broken up. Add the remaining ingredients and stir vigorously until the mixture is smooth and thoroughly blended. Chill the cheese lightly before serving it.

This makes a delicious spread for any kind of rye or pumpernickel bread and keeps for a couple of weeks if covered and refrigerated.

cocktail profiteroles

If there is a good bakery nearby which can supply you with cocktail-sized puffs, by all means buy them and save yourself the trouble. Your time will be better spent making the delicious filling. However, if you insist, here is a reasonably easy way of making puff paste with the help of a food processor.

profiterole puff dough

1 cup water
½ cup butter
½ tsp. salt
1½ tsp. sugar
1 cup plus 2 Tbs. flour
4 eggs

Put the water, butter, salt, and sugar into a medium-sized saucepan and bring to a boil. As soon as the butter is melted, reduce the heat to a simmer and dump in the flour, all at once. Stir quickly with a wooden spoon until the mixture forms a smooth, homogeneous ball. Continue stirring and pressing the dough against the sides of the saucepan for about 3 to 4 minutes. Turn off the heat and let the dough rest for about 5 minutes.

Put the steel blade into the food processor and transfer the dough to the container. Process it for about 20 seconds. Add the eggs and process for about 50 seconds. The dough is now ready to use.

To make puffs for profiteroles, butter several large cookie sheets and preheat the oven at 375 degrees. Using a pastry bag or 2 teaspoons, form balls of dough about the size of very small walnuts. If you are not using a pastry bag and have trouble forming smooth balls, butter your hands and roll the balls lightly and quickly between the palms of your hands until their shape is right.

Arrange the balls about 1½ inches apart on the buttered sheets and bake them for 20 to 30 minutes; they should be puffed and a light golden brown in color. With the point of a sharp knife, make a little slit in the side of each puff and leave them in a warm, turned-off oven for another 15 to 20 minutes to dry out inside.

Slice off the top halves of the puffs, leaving them barely connected at one side so that they can be opened up and stuffed.

This recipe makes about 3½ dozen puffs.

filling

6   hard-boiled eggs, peeled and chopped
½   cup finely chopped fresh parsley
⅓   cut finely chopped marinated mushrooms
⅔   cup chopped cooked asparagus
¼   cup butter, melted
¾   tsp. salt
1   Tbs. white wine vinegar
fresh-ground black pepper to taste

Combine the chopped eggs, chopped parsley, chopped marinated mushrooms, and chopped asparagus in a large bowl. Pour the melted butter over this mixture and toss it lightly.

Add the salt and white wine vinegar, grate plenty of black pepper over it, and toss again or stir carefully until everything is well combined. Taste and add more salt or vinegar if desired.

Place a slightly rounded teaspoonful of this filling inside each puff and press the top of the puff down just a bit into the filling so that it stays where it belongs.

Serve the cold Cocktail Profiteroles with cocktails (what else?), or with chilled white wine as a first course.

Makes about 3½ dozen filled puffs.

savory pastries: quiches, pizzas, pierogi

To make a quiche, you need only some rudimentary baking skills. As long as you have a decent oven, know how to make a pastry crust, and see to it that the shell is large enough to hold the filling, the basic quiche is easily within your powers. All in all, when you consider how good a quiche can taste, what a pretty picture it makes when served, and how altogether versatile and convenient it is, you will see that it doesn't cost much in effort for all those rewards. Besides making lovely lunches, hors d'oeuvres, and dinner or supper dishes, quiches are also many people's favorite picnic food, as they are nearly always just as tempting cold as they are hot.

And while you should stick to the rules in preparing the crust and the custard, you can be as innovative as you like in dressing up the filling. A simple and mouth-watering quiche can be made with a filling of nothing but eggs, cream, cheese, and a touch of flour, seasoned with a bit of salt and pepper. On the other hand, practically anything you happen to have in the larder can probably be successfully incorporated into the egg and cream mixture, so long as you use common sense.

I've used many different cheeses and vegetables, and combinations of both, and have never yet made a quiche that wasn't happily eaten down to the last crumb. I'm not sure why it's so, but there is something nearly irresistible about that combination of a baked dough or crust with a savory filling or topping. It's an idea that is universally popular, and a hot, tender-crusted quiche is but one example. In Greece, very flaky pastry is layered around feta cheese or spinach fillings and baked in the form of large pies or small turnovers. Polish and Russian cooking is full of *pierogi*, or *piroshki*, which are made by wrapping a yeast dough or short crust around any of a variety of stuffings. In Hong Kong and Singapore, *dim-sum*—filled dumplings that are usually steamed—are eaten with midmorning tea.

The Italian pizza is one of the glories of the genre. I've heard that pizza first came into existence when bread was baked in large batches in a communal village bread oven. On bread-making day, the busy housewife wouldn't have much time left to cook dinner, so she would take a piece of the bread dough, flatten it out, moisten it with a sauce, and heap on it whatever leftovers she might have. Then it would be baked in the hot oven, together with the loaves, and supper was ready. It's one of those stories that makes so much sense that one can only say that if it isn't true, it should be.

The pizza has become as firmly entrenched in American eating habits as the sandwich, and, of course, it thrives in every part of its native Italy. When we were in Verona, in the elegant north and far from Naples, the world capital of pizza making, we saw an amusing picture of the popularity that pizza enjoys. We went to see the Scaligeri family tombs, which have been marked for seven centuries by the famous and beautiful equestrian statue of Mastino della Scalla, founder of the Scaligeri dynasty.* Depicted in his medieval armor, with a tall, pointed helmet dropped back off his head, Mastino is a stern-looking man. His armored and hooded horse, however, looks down on passers-by with a droll, sleepy-eyed expression. The statue, one of Verona's major tourist attractions, is well loved by the Veronese people.

Nearby there is a popular pizzeria, and one of the large walls in this restaurant is painted with a mural of people from all over Italy happily eating their pizza. In the center of the mural is an affectionate, larger-than-life portrayal of Mastino, who has dismounted and is smilingly feeding his droopy-eyed horse a large slice of pizza. The mural is an appealing expression of the Italians' fondness for pizza— and of their wit.

*The original statue is now protected in a museum, but an exact replica stands in its traditional place.

basic short-crust pastry

1½ cups flour
½ to ¾ tsp. salt
½ cup butter, well chilled
scant ⅓ cup ice water

Sift together the flour and the salt. Slice the cold butter rapidly and drop the slices into the flour. With a pastry blender or two sharp knives, cut in the butter until the mixture resembles coarse corn meal.

Sprinkle the ice water over the flour-butter mixture and stir it in very quickly with a fork, until the dough gathers together. Form the dough into a ball, wrap it in wax paper or foil, and chill it for about 2 hours.

Makes enough dough for 1 large (11- or 12-inch) quiche shell.

PREPARING A QUICHE OR TART SHELL

On a lightly floured surface, roll the chilled dough out in a circle about 2½ inches larger than your quiche pan. (I like to use an 11- or 12-inch pan.) Roll the circle of dough loosely around your rolling pin and unroll it over the quiche pan, centering it as well as possible. Press the sides in against the rim of the pan, pushing the extra dough down a bit to make an edge that is slightly thicker than the bottom. Trim the dough off with a sharp knife, about ¼ inch above the rim of the pan.

Using a pastry crimper or the blunt end of a kitchen knife, crimp the ridge of dough neatly just above the rim of the pan. Prick the bottom of the shell all over with a fork, and chill the shell for ½ hour.

PREBAKING A QUICHE OR TART SHELL

Line the inside of the pastry shell with a piece of aluminum foil and fill it with dried beans or rice (which can be kept in a jar and reused for this purpose forever). Bake the shell in a preheated 450 degree oven for about 8 minutes, then remove the beans and foil, prick again with a fork, and return to the hot oven for another 4 to 5 minutes, or until the bottom of the shell begins to color. Allow the shell to cool slightly on a rack, then fill and finish baking according to recipe.

roquefort quiche

1 recipe Basic Short-Crust Pastry (page 213)
¼ lb. Roquefort cheese, crumbled
½ lb. dry farmer or dry pot cheese, crumbled
⅔ cup milk
4 large eggs
salt to taste

Prepare the short crust, line an 11-inch quiche pan with it, and prebake according to instructions on page 213.

Combine the crumbled cheeses. Beat together the milk and eggs, with a little pinch of salt. Spread the crumbled cheeses evenly over the bottom of the quiche shell and pour the custard carefully over them.

Bake the quiche in a preheated oven at 375 degrees for 40 to 45 minutes. The filling should be puffed and rather firm, and the top golden brown. Serve either warm or cool as a first course, or with ripe fruit for an unusual dessert.

Serves 6 to 8.

leek and tomato quiche

1 recipe Basic Short-Crust Pastry (page 213)
2 cups sliced leeks (3 or 4 large)
2 Tbs. butter
salt and pepper to taste
½ lb. Swiss cheese
1 oz. Romano or Parmesan cheese
1 Tbs. flour
4 eggs
1¾ cups cream or rich milk
2 tomatoes, thinly sliced

Prepare the short crust, line an 11-inch quiche pan with it, and prebake according to instructions on page 213.

Wash the leeks carefully. Split them lengthwise, trim away the tough green parts, and thinly slice enough to measure 2 cups. Sauté them in the butter until they start to turn golden, seasoning them with salt and pepper.

Grate the cheeses and toss them with the flour. Beat together the eggs, cream, and a little salt.

Spread the sautéed leeks evenly across the bottom of the quiche shell and spread the cheeses evenly over that. Pour the custard over the cheese and leeks and cover the top with a layer of thinly sliced tomatoes. Salt the tomatoes lightly and grind on a little pepper.

Bake the quiche for 15 minutes in a preheated 400 degree oven, reduce the temperature to 325, and bake for another 30 minutes, or until a knife inserted in the center comes out clean. Serve warm or at room temperature.

Serves 6.

pimiento and olive quiche

1   recipe Basic Short-Crust Pastry (page 213)
1   large onion, peeled, halved, and sliced
2   cloves garlic, peeled and thinly sliced
2   Tbs. olive oil
½   lb. Swiss cheese, coarsely grated
2   eggs
1   cup cream
salt and pepper to taste
½   cup sliced (roasted and peeled) pimiento
        pepper
¼   cup sliced, cured Greek olives (black)

Prepare the short crust, line an 11-inch quiche pan with it, and prebake according to instructions on page 213.

Sauté the sliced onions and garlic in the olive oil until they are golden brown. Distribute them evenly over the bottom of the pastry shell. Spread the grated cheese over the onions and garlic.

Beat the eggs and cream together with a little salt and pepper and pour them over the cheese. Arrange the sliced pimientos and ol-

pimiento and olive quiche (continued)

ives on top of the cheese in an attractive pattern and bake the quiche for 15 minutes in a preheated oven at 450 degrees, then reduce the heat to 350 and bake for another 10 to 15 minutes, or until the top of the quiche is lightly browned in spots.

The quiche may be served hot, but I think it's better if it is allowed to cool to room temperature or chilled before serving.

Serves 6 to 8.

cheese and tomato pie

Call it either a quiche or a pizza, it is one of the most delicious pies around.

1   recipe Basic Short-Crust Pastry (page 213)
3   lbs. ripe tomatoes, peeled and seeded
3   Tbs. olive oil
1   clove garlic, crushed or minced
¾   tsp. salt
2   Tbs. chopped fresh parsley
½   tsp. dried basil, crushed
fresh-ground black pepper to taste
1   lb. yellow onions
2   Tbs. butter
⅓   cup grated Parmesan cheese
½   lb. mozzarella cheese
12   cured black olives

Prepare the short crust, line an 11-inch quiche pan with it, and prebake according to instructions on page 213.

Chop the tomatoes coarsely, reserving their juice. Heat the olive oil in a large pan and sauté the garlic in it for a few minutes. Add the tomatoes and their juice, ½ teaspoon of the salt, the parsley, basil, and a little fresh-ground black pepper. Simmer this sauce, stirring occasionally, until it is reduced by about half. It should be quite thick.

Peel, halve, and thickly slice the onions. Sauté them in the butter until they are golden and sprinkle them with the ¼ teaspoon salt.

Sprinkle the Parmesan cheese over the bottom of the quiche shell. Arrange the sautéed onion slices over it in an even layer. Cover the onions with the tomato sauce.

Cut the mozzarella in thin strips and arrange them evenly on top of the tomato sauce. Slice the olives off their pits and sprinkle the olive bits over the mozzarella cheese.

Bake the pie for 35 minutes in a preheated oven at 375 degrees and serve it hot.

Serves 6 to 8.

sweet potato and cranberry quiche

Here is an unusual quiche, somewhat sweet, somewhat savory. Serve it warm or cool, alone or with cream, as an hors d'oeuvre, an accompaniment to soup, with tea, or even as a dessert. This is truly the all-purpose quiche.

1   recipe Basic Short-Crust Pastry (page 213)
½   lb. sweet potatoes (about 2 small)
½   lb. carrots (about 3 medium sized)
½   lb. cranberries
⅔   cup sugar
½   cup milk
4   eggs
½   lb. soft cream cheese
dash of nutmeg
dash of salt

Prepare the short crust, line an 11-inch quiche pan with it, and prebake according to instructions on page 213.

Peel the sweet potatoes and carrots and either grate them or chop them finely. Put the vegetables in a pot, douse them with boiling, salted water, bring to a boil, and cook the vegetables 5 minutes, then drain them.

Wash the cranberries and pick out any that are soft or blemished. Put them in an enameled pot with the sugar and cook them, covered, over low heat for 10 minutes, stirring occasionally. Remove the lid and cook the berries for 5 minutes more, stirring almost constantly.

sweet potato and cranberry quiche (continued)

Add the potatoes and carrots and cook for 3 to 4 minutes more, stirring constantly.

Beat together the milk, eggs, cream cheese, a little nutmeg, and a tiny bit of salt. Stir in the vegetable mixture and pour the filling carefully into the prepared shell.

Bake the quiche in a preheated oven at 375 degrees for 40 minutes, or until the top is golden and the filling firm.

Serves 6 to 8.

pizza

crust

| 1 | package (1 Tbs.) yeast |
1¼ cups warm water
| 2 | tsp. sugar |
| 3 | cups flour |
1½ tsp. salt
| 1 | Tbs. olive oil |
sesame seeds

sauce

| 2 | cups thick puréed tomatoes |
| ½ | cup tomato paste |
1½ cups coarsely chopped, peeled tomatoes
| 1 | tsp. salt |
| 1 | tsp. oregano, crushed |

| 1 | tsp. basil, crushed |
| ¼ | tsp. thyme |
dash of marjoram
dash of cinnamon
2	Tbs. wine vinegar
1	tsp. sugar
2	cloves garlic, crushed or minced
fresh-ground black pepper to taste

topping

| 1 | large eggplant |
plenty of salt
2	Tbs. olive oil
1	medium-sized onion
1	large green bell pepper
¾	lb. mozzarella cheese

To prepare the crust, dissolve the yeast in ½ cup of the warm water, add the sugar, and leave it for 10 minutes. Put the dissolved yeast in a large, warm bowl with the rest of the water. Mix the flour and the salt together and start stirring it into the liquid gradually. Keep adding flour until the mixture is too stiff to stir. Knead it in the bowl briefly, then add the olive oil and continue kneading until the dough is smooth and elastic, adding a little more flour if necessary. Form the dough into a ball, brush it with oil, cover it, and leave it to rise in a warm place for 1 hour, or until it doubles in size.

Punch the dough down and divide it in half. Put the 2 balls of dough on a large, lightly floured board and roll them out into circles. When the dough starts to pull back, cover it with a tea towel and let it rest for 5 or 10 minutes, then roll it again. As the circles of dough start to approach the right size, about 16 inches across, they can be lifted up and gently stretched over the back of your hands.

When the dough is about ¼ inch thick, stop stretching it, adjust the shape as well as you can, and prepare the pans by oiling them with olive oil and sprinkling them with sesame seeds. Put the circles of dough on the pans.

The sauce and the topping can be prepared while the dough for the crust is rising.

To prepare the sauce, simply combine all the ingredients and stir them together very thoroughly. The sauce should be thick, not watery.

To prepare the topping, first peel the eggplant and slice ¼ inch thick. Salt the eggplant slices liberally and let them drain in a colander for ½ hour. Rinse the slices quickly, press out the excess moisture between the palms of your hands, and cut them in ½-inch dice. Heat the olive oil in a large skillet and sauté the eggplant in it, tossing and stirring constantly, for about 5 minutes.

Peel and chop the onion. Core, seed, and dice the green pepper. Grate the mozzarella cheese.

Spread the dough evenly with tomato sauce, eggplant, onions, peppers, and, finally, grated cheese.

Bake the pizzas in a preheated oven at 425 degrees for 15 to 20 minutes, or until the crust is crisp on the edges and bottom and the cheese is bubbling and turning golden brown.

Makes 2 large pizzas.

yeast pierogi

Pierogi are a Polish type of savory pastry, which can be made with almost any kind of filling. Some are boiled in salted water, others fried in butter, but these are made with a yeast dough and baked. They can be served hot, warm, or at room temperature and make a good accompaniment to soup, or they can be served as a course on their own. A selection of *pierogi*, served warm with a salad or a vegetable stew, make a hearty supper.

yeast dough

1	package (1 Tbs.) yeast
¼	cup warm water
2½	Tbs. sugar
¾	cup milk
½	cup butter
1½	tsp. salt
4 to 5	cups flour
2	whole eggs
1	egg yolk

Dissolve the yeast in the warm water with 1 teaspoon of the sugar and leave it for 10 minutes. Heat the milk with the butter, the remaining sugar, and the salt until the butter is melted. Allow the mixture to cool to lukewarm.

Gradually beat about 2 cups of the flour into the milk mixture, and when the dough is smooth, stir in the dissolved yeast. Then beat in the eggs and the egg yolk, and continue beating, either by hand or with a heavy-duty mixer, for several minutes.

Turn the dough out onto a heavily floured board, cover it with more flour, and begin kneading. Knead for about 10 to 15 minutes, working in as much of the remaining flour as needed to make a smooth, satiny, elastic dough.

Form the dough into a ball, brush it lightly with melted butter, put it in a bowl, cover it, and chill it for several hours.

When you are ready to make the *pierogi*, take out the dough, punch it down, and roll it out on a floured board to a thickness of no more than ¼ inch. Cut out rounds about 3½ to 4 inches across. If the dough pulls together too much when the rounds are cut, roll each one a bit more, just before filling it, to make it thin once more.

mushroom filling for *pierogi*

1½	oz. dried wild mushrooms
½	lb. fresh mushrooms
2	slices dark bread
2½	Tbs. butter
1	medium-sized onion, chopped

1   clove garlic, minced
plenty of salt and pepper
dill

Soak the dried mushrooms in hot water for about 1 hour, then rinse them carefully. Wash and trim the fresh mushrooms. Put all the mushrooms through a food mill, using the fine blade, and then put through the dark bread, torn into chunks.

Melt the butter in a large skillet and sauté the onions and garlic in it until the onions are golden. Add the mushroom and bread mixture and season to taste with salt, pepper, and dill weed. Cook the mixture over low heat for 20 to 30 minutes, or until the mushrooms are tender and the mixture is thick. Taste, and correct seasoning.

cabbage filling for *pierogi*

1   large onion
3   Tbs. butter
3   cups finely shredded cabbage, packed
plenty of salt and fresh-ground black pepper
2   hard-boiled eggs
2   Tbs. chopped fresh dill or 2 tsp. dried

Finely chop the onion and sauté it in the butter until it is golden. Add the cabbage and a liberal amount of salt and pepper. Cover the pan and cook the vegetables over a low flame, stirring occasionally, for about ½ hour.

Let the mixture cool slightly. Sieve the hard-boiled eggs and stir them into the cabbage along with the dill. Taste, and correct seasoning.

Note: The feta cheese filling for crêpes (see page 228) can also be used as a filling for *pierogi*.

MAKING THE PIEROGI

Place a heaping tablespoon of filling in the center of each round. Fold the top of the dough over the filling, bring up the sides, and then bring up the bottom, overlapping the edges just slightly. Pinch the dough together where it meets and be sure that the seams are well sealed. When they are, shape the *pierogi* with your hands to make them smooth and rounded.

Place the *pierogi*, seam side down, on a buttered and floured baking sheet. Cover them with a towel and let them rise for about ½ hour.

Make a wash by beating together 1 egg and 1 tablespoonful of milk or cream. Brush the *pierogi* with the egg wash and bake them in a preheated oven at 375 degrees for ½ hour, or until the crusts are golden brown and shiny.

crêpes

Today, everywhere one looks, one sees crêpe restaurants, crêpe cookbooks, crêpe pans for sale. The delectable thin pancake that was too often reserved for dessert in a fancy restaurant, in the form of Crêpes Suzette, is now turning up with frequency at breakfast, lunch, and supper, as well as brunch. I even had a friend phone me recently and say, "Quick, give me some recipes for crêpe fillings. I'm going to a party today where the hostess is going to make crêpes, and all the guests have to bring something good to put in them."

You might think we'd all be sick of them soon, but because crêpes have such a mild, delicate flavor and commendable tenderness, there is hardly a soul who does not like to find a plateful of them served up, the more often the better. And since they combine so agreeably with almost any other food, there are always imaginative new ways of serving them, no two tasting quite alike.

What's more, crêpes are marvelously convenient. They all take a certain amount of preparation time, but most of the work can be done in advance. The crêpes themselves can be made a day or two ahead and kept tightly wrapped in the refrigerator. Since filled crêpes are nearly always heated again with their filling, it is not essential that they be warm, but they should be allowed to reach room temperature for easy folding or rolling. The fillings and sauces, likewise, can generally be prepared hours ahead of time, and usually the crêpes can be stuffed well before mealtime, leaving only the final sautéeing and saucing for the last minute. This flexibility of preparation is a great boon, allowing an elegant and appetizing meal without keeping the cook in the kitchen, sweating and grumbling for hours before the meal and during great parts of it, while the others drink all the wine and enjoy themselves.

As for what can be done with a crêpe, the recipes in this chapter are only a beginning. Any filling that is delicious in an omelet, for example, will be equally tasty in a crêpe; flip through the omelet section and see what appeals. The amount of filling you use for one individual omelet is about what you'll need for one medium-sized crêpe, though the proportions will vary according to your own taste. In general, the mixtures from which you make croquettes will also make excellent stuffed crêpes. Place a few spoonfuls of such a stuffing in the middle of a crêpe, and fold the crêpe around it envelope-style, rolling it up and tucking in the sides. Sauté the filled crêpes slowly on both sides, until they are hot all the way through, and there you are, with a new dish.

Delightful fruit crêpes can be made by cooking fresh fruit with a little butter and sugar, just until it is hot and tender, then folding it in a hot crêpe and serving with a little sour cream on top. These are marvelous for breakfast, but add a little liqueur to the filling and garnish the crêpes with whipped cream instead of sour cream, and you've made an extravagant dessert. Sliced apples, strawberries, cherries, bananas, peaches, and pears are all suitable for this method, and discreet additions of cinnamon or nutmeg can make a pleasant variation in flavor. If that seems too much trouble, you can also spread crêpes with a good jam or marmalade, fold them in quarters, sauté them quickly in butter on both sides, plop a spoonful of sour cream on top, and you have a dessert so easy that it practically makes itself. (For more on dessert crêpes, see the dessert section, where you'll find Hungarian Walnut Crêpes, Fresh Lemon Dessert Crêpes, and Applesauce Crêpes.)

To my mind, the only questionable aspect of this rennaissance of crêperie is some of the gadgetry and gimmickry that propels it. Special equipment, including electric "crêpe kits," has been designed for the upside-down pan method of making crêpes, although an ordinary pan with a decent bottom could be used for this. Touted as easier than the old way, this method consists of putting your crêpe batter in a wide, shallow bowl, then heating the crêpe pan and dipping its convex side into the batter. Enough batter to form a thin crêpe adheres to the hot pan, which you then turn over and place, batter side up, over a burner, until the crêpe finishes cooking. Then you flip the crêpe off the pan and dip again for the next one.

This is an amusing way of making crêpes, but I find it fussier than the traditional way, instead of simpler, and not as foolproof. For one thing, it requires perfect regulation of heat: A pan that is too hot can cause the crêpe it is forming to drop back into the batter as the pan is lifted out, and before there is time enough to turn it over. The batter must then be strained through a sieve to rid it of the lumpy, congealed part before you can begin again. Furthermore, one always reaches that point where there is not enough batter left in the shallow bowl to make successful dipping possible, but still enough for a few more crêpes. Then it's a question of tossing out the rest of the batter or pulling out the good old crêpe pan to finish the job.

All of this, however, would be minor if this method produced a superior crêpe, which it does not. The main fault of the new-fangled crêpe, I think, is the lack of a certain marvelous butteriness which adds so much to the flavor and texture of crêpes. The new crêpes are only cooked on one side, leaving the other side slightly rubbery to the touch. But even the side on which the crêpe is cooked must remain fairly dry; the reason is that if the upside-down pan is well buttered before dipping, the batter will not adhere to it. Instructions on the specially designed pans specify to dip an *unbuttered* pan into the batter, and I've found the results to be dry and dull. However, if these crêpe-making outfits encourage people to try crêpe making, so be it. But after you've played around with yours, go out and treat yourself to a good cast-iron French crêpe pan. With that, a spatula, and very little fuss you'll soon be turning out lovely crêpes, golden, buttery, and tender.

basic crêpes

This batter is slightly different than the one in Book 1, and I've had great success with it. The crêpes are tender and easy to handle and reheat very well. A touch of sugar enhances the delicate flavor but isn't enough to make them actually taste sweet, and so they can be used for entrées or desserts equally well.

3 large eggs
⅔ cup milk
⅓ cup light cream
½ cup water
½ tsp. salt
1 cup flour
1 Tbs. butter, melted
1 Tbs. sugar
2 Tbs. cognac

Beat the eggs, then beat in the milk, cream, water, and salt. When the mixture is well blended, add the flour gradually, whisking it in until the batter is perfectly smooth. Or combine all these things in a blender. Stir in the melted butter, sugar, and cognac and leave the batter to rest for at least 2 hours.

Heat your crêpe pan and melt a piece of butter in it. As soon as the foam subsides, pour a small amount of batter into the pan, then quickly but gently tilt it around so that the batter spreads evenly over the bottom of the pan. (I use about 2½ to 3 tablespoons batter for a 7-inch pan.)

Cook the crêpe over medium heat for about a minute. Loosen the edge by running a knife or thin spatula under it, turn the crêpe over, and

basic crêpes (continued)

cook on the other side for just under a minute. The crêpe should be golden, with golden brown spots here and there.

Brush the pan with a tiny bit of butter between crêpes. If the butter sizzles violently and starts to brown immediately, the pan is too hot; the batter will not want to spread evenly in the pan. If, however, the batter does not start to congeal and coat the pan right away as it is swirled around, the pan is too cool. You may have to make 2 or 3 crêpes before the heat is perfectly adjusted, but after that it all goes quickly and smoothly.

This recipe makes between 15 to 18 7-inch crêpes, which can be used immediately, kept warm in the oven for a while, or refrigerated and reheated later. To keep crêpes warm, stack them on a plate, cover them with a very slightly damp tea towel, and put them in a warm oven. To reheat crêpes, wrap them airtight in foil and put them in a moderate oven for 15 to 20 minutes, or until all of them are hot to the touch, even the ones in the middle of the pile.

parmesan crêpes

Parmesan crêpes are a treat just as they come from the pan and even better when doused with some tomato or mushroom sauce. But they are also delicious when wrapped around almost any of the savory fillings which follow. For this reason I include again here the same recipe for Parmesan Crêpes which I gave in the first *Vegetarian Epicure*, with a few new suggestions for their use.

1 cup flour
1 tsp. salt

6 eggs, beaten
3 cups milk
3 Tbs. butter, melted
½ cup finely grated Parmesan cheese (real, well-aged, imported Parmesan)
butter for the pan

Sift the flour and salt into a bowl and stir in the beaten eggs. Add the milk slowly, beating with a whisk, then beat in the melted butter and the grated Parmesan. The batter should be smooth and have the consistency of thick cream. Let the batter stand for an hour or two before making the crêpes.

Heat your crêpe pan and melt about 2 teaspoons butter in it. When the butter is melted and the foam has subsided, pour in about 3 tablespoons of the batter and swirl it around to the edges of the pan immediately. The crêpe should cook about a minute or so on each side.

Add a bit of butter to the pan between crêpes to avoid sticking. Stack the crêpes on a plate as you make them. The crêpes can be kept warm in the oven until all of them are done if you intend to eat them right away. Or they can be reheated like any other crêpes, wrapped tightly in foil, and put in a moderate oven for about 10 minutes.

Furthermore, they can be wrapped around asparagus, spread with feta cheese filling and folded up, rolled around a stuffing of hearts of artichoke and palm, or of creamed mushrooms, and they can be used in constructing a savory crêpe cake, to be cut in wedges.

This recipe makes about 20 to 24 crêpes.

asparagus crêpes

1½ lbs. fresh asparagus (24 to 30 medium-sized stalks)
½ lb. Swiss cheese
12 crêpes (see page 225)
butter for the pan
hot Cucumber-Avocado Sauce (page 103)

garnish

thin wedges of cantaloupe and ripe strawberries

Trim the asparagus stalks so that they are an even length—about 7 or 8 inches. Peel the lower parts of the stalks thinly. Cook the asparagus in salted boiling water for 8 to 10 minutes (longer if they are thick); they should be tender but firm. Drain the stalks immediately.

asparagus crêpes (continued)

Grate the cheese or cut it in small, very thin slices. Cut the asparagus stalks in half.

Place a small amount of cheese in the center of a crêpe, and arrange 4 or 5 pieces of asparagus on top of it. Fold the crêpe around the cheese and asparagus like an envelope. You should have rectangles about 4 inches long and 2 inches wide.

Just before serving, sauté the filled crêpes in butter, briefly on both sides. They should be golden brown and hot through. Arrange them on a platter or on individual plates and pour hot Cucumber-Avocado Sauce over them. Garnish each plate with thin wedges of cantaloupe and a few ripe strawberries.

Serves 6.

crêpes with feta cheese

12 oz. farmer cheese (about 2 cups, crumbled)
6 oz. feta cheese (about 1 cup, crumbled)
3 Tbs. olive oil
2 eggs, lightly beaten
½ tsp. dried oregano, crushed
½ tsp. dried dill weed, crushed
2 cloves garlic, minced or crushed
fresh-ground black pepper to taste
12 crêpes (see page 225)
butter for the pan

garnish

wedges of cantaloupe or honeydew melon

Mash the cheeses with a fork until there are no large lumps left. Stir in the olive oil, eggs, and seasonings, combining everything thoroughly. Do not add salt, as the feta cheese is already very salty.

Spread a heaping teaspoonful of the filling evenly on ½ of a crêpe and fold the other half over it. Now take a slightly rounded teaspoonful of filling and again spread it on ½ the surface of the folded crêpe. Fold the crêpe over this second layer of filling, so that it is folded in quarters, layered with cheese.

Fill all 12 crêpes in this manner. Just before

serving, sauté the folded crêpes in butter, for several minutes on each side. They should be lightly browned and hot through. Garnish each serving of crêpes with a wedge of cantaloupe or honeydew melon.

Serves 4 to 6.

crêpes with hearts of artichoke and palm

2   cups sliced cooked artichoke hearts (about 1 lb.)
1½ cups sliced hearts of palm (about 14 oz.)
5   Tbs. butter, and more for the pan
2   Tbs. lemon juice
2½ tsp. sugar
1   egg, beaten
salt to taste
12   crêpes (see page 225)
Hollandaise Sauce (page 100)

If you are using canned artichoke hearts, be sure to rinse them in several changes of cool water after draining off the brine, and do the same for the hearts of palm. Cut the artichokes in half, scoop out the chokes, and slice them thinly. Slice the hearts of palm about ¼ inch thick, cutting them in half lengthwise first if they are very thick.

Melt the butter in a large skillet and heat the vegetables in it, stirring constantly, for about 10 minutes. Add the lemon juice and sugar, and some salt if it is needed, and stir again.

Remove the vegetables from the heat and quickly stir in the beaten egg. The heat of the vegetables will cook it slightly. Continue stirring for a minute or two.

Divide the mixture among the crêpes, putting about 2 rounded tablespoonfuls down the center of each one. Roll the crêpes up over the filling and sauté them in butter briefly on both sides before serving—just long enough so that they are hot through and lightly browned. Serve them with warm Hollandaise Sauce and a fresh fruit salad.

Serves 6.

wild mushroom crêpe cake

4   oz. dried black mushrooms
3   Tbs. butter
1   large yellow onion, chopped
¼   cup red wine
salt and pepper
2   large heads butter lettuce
2½ cups Béchamel Sauce (page 98)
1   recipe Parmesan Crêpes (page 226)
¾   lb. Gruyère cheese, grated

tomato-pepper sauce

1½ Tbs. olive oil
4   cloves garlic, minced
3   cups fresh tomato purée
⅔   cup finely chopped roasted pimiento
2   bay leaves
2 to 3 Tbs. red wine
salt and pepper

garnish: paprika

Put the dried mushrooms in a large bowl and cover them completely with hot water. Let them soak while you prepare the tomato sauce.

Heat the olive oil in a large skillet and sauté the garlic in it until it is golden. Add the tomato purée, chopped pimiento, bay leaves, and wine, as well as salt and pepper to taste. Simmer the sauce gently for an hour or two, until it is reduced by half and quite thick. Allow the sauce to cool slightly.

When the mushrooms have soaked for about ½ hour, take them, one by one, from the bowl and wash them each with great care to get rid of all the sand and grit. Strain the water in which they were soaked through muslin or through a coffee filter.

Put the mushrooms through a food mill, using the fine blade, or else mince them finely with a knife. Melt the butter in a large skillet and sauté the onions for a few minutes. Then add the ground mushrooms, a little red wine, some salt and pepper to taste, and at least 2½ cups of the strained mushroom water.

Let this mixture simmer gently, stirring it occasionally, until most of the liquid has been absorbed and it has the consistency of a thick mush.

Blanch the lettuce in a large kettle of boiling water, leaving them in for several minutes. When they are quite wilted, remove the heads, drain them thoroughly, squeezing out all the water, and chop the lettuce. Mix the chopped lettuce with a few spoonfuls of the Béchamel Sauce (just enough to bind it) and salt to taste.

Put a crêpe in the center of an ovenproof serving platter or a shallow baking dish. Spread it with a thin layer of the mushroom mixture, extending it evenly to the edges. Place another crêpe over this and spread it evenly with a thin layer of the tomato sauce. Put down another crêpe, a layer of the chopped lettuce, another crêpe, and an even, thin layer of grated cheese. Repeat this order twice more, just as if making a layer cake. Pour a little Béchamel over the cheese on the very top, and sprinkle it lightly with paprika.

Prepare the second crêpe "cake" in the same manner, using the remaining mushroom filling, tomato sauce, and chopped lettuce. You should have about 1½ cups of Béchamel Sauce and a little grated cheese left over. Stir the cheese into the sauce.

Bake the crêpe cake in a preheated 400 degree oven for about 20 minutes. Heat the remaining sauce. Serve the crêpe cake by cutting it in wedges and passing the sauce separately.

Serves 6 to 8.

crêpes with creamed mushrooms

12 crêpes (see page 225)
1½ lbs. mushrooms
4½ Tbs. butter
¼ cup finely chopped onion
2 Tbs. flour
1 cup heavy cream, heated
salt and pepper
1½ Tbs. dry sherry
1 Tbs. brandy

optional garnish

fresh melon slices

Prepare the crêpes ahead of time and keep them warm, wrapped or covered, in a low oven, or reheat them before filling.

Wash and trim the mushrooms and slice them thickly. Sauté the onions in 2½ tablespoons of the butter for 2 minutes, then add the sliced mushrooms and sauté over high heat, tossing or stirring frequently, until the mushrooms have released their excess liquid and it has evaporated. Season to taste with salt and pepper.

In a small saucepan, melt the remaining 2 tablespoons butter and stir in the flour. Cook this roux over low heat for about 2 minutes, stirring constantly, then stir in the hot cream. Beat lightly with a whisk until the sauce is smooth and simmer, stirring constantly, for several minutes. Stir in the sherry and the brandy.

Pour the sauce over the mushrooms and heat them together, stirring often, for a few minutes.

Spoon a small amount of the creamed mushrooms down the center of each warm crêpe and roll the crêpes up over the filling. Serve hot, garnished with fresh melon slices, or serve with a salad.

Serves 4 to 6.

blintzes

¼ cup raisins
1 lb. fresh hoop or farmer cheese (see page 192)
2 eggs
2 Tbs. sour cream
2 Tbs. butter, melted
3 Tbs. sugar
¼ tsp. salt
10 medium-sized crêpes (see page 225)
butter for the pan

garnish

sour cream and applesauce
or jam

The filling of these blintzes is very simple, and a little bit richer than some with the addition of melted butter and sour cream. Because it has no spices, it depends completely on the quality and freshness of the hoop (or farmer) cheese for its delicate but wonderful flavor.

First, pour some boiling water over the raisins and leave them to plump up in it for a while. Break the cheese up with a fork until it is coarsely crumbled and stir in the eggs, sour cream, melted butter, sugar, and salt. Stir briskly with a fork until the mixture is well blended—the cheese will remain a bit lumpy, and that's as it should be.

Drain the raisins and mix them into the cheese filling. Place a heaping tablespoonful of the filling in the center of a crêpe, fold one side of the crêpe over it, and begin rolling it up. Fold the ends over, envelope-style, and finish rolling up the crêpe. It should have the shape of a short, plump cylinder. Fill all the crêpes this way.

Sauté the blintzes in butter on both sides until they are golden brown and hot through. Serve the blintzes with sour cream and applesauce, or with jam.

Serves 4 or 5 as a light meal, 10 as a dessert.

See Desserts for Applesauce Crêpes, Hungarian Walnut Crêpes, Fresh Lemon Dessert Crêpes.

italian pastas, vegetables, and frittatas

After crossing the Atlantic on an Italian ocean liner, I decided that eating one's self to death on Italian food might not be a bad way to go. We spent nine days on the calm seas, effectively unreachable by phone or mail, surrounded by smiling, attractive Italians and sitting down four or five times a day to delicious, bountiful meals of Italian food, cooked by someone else, with no dismaying check to pay at the end of each repast.

At the beginning of the crossing, everyone had big plans, and all talk was full of activity—tennis, swimming, movies every day, books to be read, and letters to be written. Before long, even the most energetic of us understood the real joy of ocean voyaging. By the third day, no one even thought of shuffleboard or skeet shooting. We did two things: We ate, and we sat in our deck chairs, watching the deck railing slowly dip below the blue horizon line and pause, then inch back up toward the paler blue sky. But mainly, we ate.

It was a bonanza for me. The Italians are awfully good at using interesting fresh vegetables in their cooking, and combining them with cheeses, pastas, and other good things, and there was always much more food than a normal being could consume—so, I always found it easy to choose fine, meatless repasts from the dishes that were offered. There were nine glorious days of pungent olives and peppers, pastas made in innumerable amusing shapes, sauces redolent of herbs and fruity olive oil, soups full of tender vegetables—so luxurious in the middle of the ocean!—fine, aged cheeses, full-bodied wines, eggy frittatas tinted green with spinach, crusty breads, strong, fragrant espresso, and an endless array of delicately flavored, sinfully rich sweets. Early each afternoon and evening a low chime would sound, following by a lovely voice intoning, *"Attenzione, prego . . . ,"* and the announcement of luncheon or dinner. To this day, I can't hear those words without salivating.

We tucked into each meal with an appetite sharpened by sea air, and when we debarked in Genoa, no one's clothes fit very well, but no one minded. The pastas alone were a revelation. Made of hard, golden durum wheat and always served *al dente*, real Italian pasta will never dissolve into a glutinous mess, and it has a sweet, delicious flavor. The Italians like to set it off with a great sauce or cheese, but never disguise it. Sauces are used sparingly, and the effect is brilliant. The sauce can be as sharp and assertive as a peppery Boccalone or as mild and simple as a drenching of melted butter with a sprinkle of aged Parmesan tossed in, but it never overpowers the actual noodle.

Most Italian restaurants in this country favor a softer, saucier dish of pasta, so Americans who go abroad and taste the genuine article are often surprised at the discreet amounts of sauce or cheese they find on their spaghetti. But a bite or two and it all comes clear: When the spaghetti is that good, you want to taste it.

The ocean voyage proved to be but a preview of the culinary treats we'd find in the cities and small towns of Italy. All up and down that rich peninsula we wandered into treasure troves, in museums and restaurants alike. Before long we realized that it was simply hard to miss. In Italy, unlike some places, wonderful food is available in unprepossessing, moderately priced *trattorias* as well as in the most elegant *ristorantes*.

In Florence we discovered the art of antipasto as we had never dreamed it possible. My brother-in-law, who had been living in Florence for two years, said, "I've reserved a table at one of our favorite restaurants—it's terribly popular, but you won't find any tourists there." Well, of course we were ready to love it because, as everyone knows, the one thing every tourist craves is the chance to pretend not to be a tourist. Following him down a maze of narrow streets, we arrived at a place so well hidden and unmarked that an unassisted tourist would never have known it was there, but inside the door everything was bright and full of laughter, and gorgeous aromas surrounded us. A sign above the door said, *"Una Trattoria Tipica . . . i Che' Ce' Ce'"* ("A typical restaurant, and what there is, there is.").

We sat down and took menus from the waiter. "Don't order a main course," instructed my brother-in-law and pointed to the far end of the room where the antipasto tables were arranged. That was when we blew our cover and gaped like the unwashed tourists we really were. A series of ample tables, grouped together and draped in crisp white linen, were laden with such a phantasmagoria of marinated, cooked, raw, pickled, sauced and simple, hot and cold dishes that we literally didn't know where to begin or, alas, where to stop. The gregarious proprietor waved his hand toward the forty-odd platters on display and told us to help ourselves—*"Prezzo per ochio,"* he explained, pointing a finger cheerfully at his eye; it was "price by eye," but no matter how much you took it was always six hundred lire.

We learned about gnocchi salad, an idea that surprised us but shouldn't have. After all, if potatoes can be dressed with olive oil and vinegar and served as a salad, why not potato gnocchi? Tiny bits of roasted pimiento and a light dab of tomato sauce gave it crunch and color. Roasted green and red peppers were bathed in a light, fruity olive oil, and olives of every size and description were gleaming in large bowls. Pickled onions, cucumbers, and *peperoncini* set off milder dishes of subtly flavored lima beans, fava beans, and scrumptious tiny roasted eggplants. Fresh white mozzarella, delicate in texture and flavor, was another discovery, tossed with slices of sweet red onion, wedges of ripe tomato, and the always satisfying vinaigrette. Raw salads, real provolone, and lightly cooked zucchini all tempted us in turn, and we never resisted. Wisely, we decided that there would be plenty of time to worry about our figures when we were visiting places with lesser gastronomic gifts.

Naples was without question the home of the greatest pizza in the world, as well as the most exuberantly flavored tomato sauces, and could one expect less from the people who sing at the slightest whim and throw burning furniture out of second-story windows on New Year's Eve? The personalities of all the different Italian provinces are reflected in their food, and Neapolitans are nothing if not bold and imaginative. Shops on crowded boulevards displayed in their windows thick-crusted pizzas, already cut in squares to be sold piece by piece, with dozens of different toppings in every conceivable combination. We pressed our noses against the glass, trying to decide among them and wondering how many slices we could eat with any pretense at decency.

By the time we arrived in Bologna, we had great expectations, for we had heard that it was called the kitchen of Italy, and every other place we had visited impressed us as a very tough act to follow. Nevertheless, that ancient, arcaded city lived up to its promise. The cooks of Bologna have an aesthetic that is at once generous and refined. Their dishes are rich but never too heavy, and beautifully seasoned. We feasted on incredible pastas, and gnocchi baked with butter, and lots of that very famous cheese from nearby Parma. The most interesting meal I had in Bologna, however, was centered around an excellent risotto, ordered on the enthusiastic recommendation of the waiter. The Lombardy region, not too far from Bologna, produces some of the finest rice in the world, and this particular Bolognese chef simmered it with a bounty of succulent wild mushrooms and tiny slivers of carrot and onion, with memorable results.

All through Italy I filled notebooks with descriptions and ideas. When I was home again, there was a wealth of good things I wanted to make. Often I worked on simply reproducing a dish that I'd tried and enjoyed during my travels. But there are many Italian dishes which use broths or small amounts of meat as a flavoring, and these often lent themselves well to adaptation. Knowledgeable use of fresh herbs, vegetable stocks, wines, and the properly blended and concentrated flavors of vegetables produced from these ideas wonderful new versions of some old favorites. The guiding principle in these experiments was, of course, my memory of the times I spent with the Italians and of their style of doing things.

Everywhere we stopped in Italy we were caught up in the spirit of people who have a talent for enjoying whatever life happens to throw their way, who take everything seriously enough to do it well but nothing so seriously that they get stuffy about it. The trains didn't always get us to the next stop on time, but nobody cared because the opera and the cappuccino were unsurpassed. We finished each evening sated after a leisurely dinner, mellowed with one of the robust red wines or a crisp, dry one, and in an altogether fine humor. In looking back on those travels (and forward to more), I can't remember a bad meal in Italy. Perhaps there were some which I've forgotten, buried as they were in an avalanche of gustatory pleasure, but most likely not. The Italians, from my experience, are people who believe that life is too short to spend a day without music or to eat a bad meal.

COOKING PASTA

Every good pasta recipe eventually comes around to insisting that the pasta must be cooked just until it is *al dente*, a simple Italian phrase which sums up one of the important secrets of those delicious spaghettis, fettucines, and *pennes*. Literally translated, it means "to the tooth." It is a term used to describe pasta that has been cooked until it just tender but still slightly firm; the pasta shouldn't taste raw, but it should have a little bite left.

Overcooked, mushy pasta is a sin: It loses its texture and a lot of flavor, becoming more like a glue than a food. In restaurants, unfortunately, busy cooks and waiters aren't always on the spot at the exact moment the pasta needs to be drained, and then immediately served. But, on the bright side, there is no reason for such a fall from grace at home.

For a marvelous eating experience, try, first of all, to get a good pasta from an Italian grocer, or make your own if you're the lucky owner of a pasta machine. Have your sauce ready and hot. Warm the plates and also the serving dish if you're going to use one.

Bring a large kettle of salted water to a boil and put a few drops of oil in it. Six to eight quarts of water should be sufficient for a pound of pasta. No more than 10 minutes before you want to serve it, put the pasta into the energetically boiling water and stir it around a bit to make sure the noodles are not sticking together. After 8 or 9 minutes (less if the pasta is very thin; or if it's fresh pasta instead of dried, it needs only a few minutes once the water returns to a boil), pull out a strand and taste it. This test must be repeated every minute or so until one strand tells you that it is time to serve: It will be barely tender and will offer a slight, pleasant resistance to the tooth, rather than dissolving quickly into mush. *Al dente!* Drain the pasta immediately in a colander, transfer it to your heated serving dish, and toss it briefly with the hot sauce, grated cheese, or whatever it is that waits in readiness. Then serve and eat, with no further ado.

Aside from overcooking, the most frequent mistake made by overzealous cooks is the drowning of their spaghetti in a veritable pond of sauce. Start with a little less than you think you need. If it's a strong-flavored or very rich sauce, about 1½ cups might be enough for 1 pound of noodles. For a lighter sauce, you could increase the quantity to 2 to 2½ cups per pound of pasta. More can be added to individual servings if desired, but I strongly urge moderation. If the pasta is good to begin with, after all, you will want to taste it.

penne al boccalone

Penne are a type of pasta, similar to *mostaccioli*; they are smooth, hollow tubes about ¼ inch in diameter, cut obliquely in lengths of about 1½ inches. Either *mostaccioli* or ziti could be substituted if you can't get *penne*.

3 Tbs. olive oil
5 medium-sized cloves garlic, minced
1 Tbs. finely minced small hot green chilis
     (2 to 3 small)
1 generous cup fresh tomato pulp
2 Tbs. tomato paste
½ cup chopped fresh parsley
1 Tbs. wine vinegar
½ tsp. dried basil, crushed
½ tsp. salt
fresh-ground black pepper to taste

1 lb. *penne* noodles

Heat the olive oil in a saucepan and add the minced garlic and chilis to it. Sauté the garlic and chilis for 2 or 3 minutes, then add the tomato pulp (made by briefly whirling fresh tomato wedges in a blender), tomato paste, parsley, vinegar, basil, salt, and pepper. Simmer the sauce for 15 to 20 minutes. It should be slightly reduced.

Boil 1 pound of *penne* noodles in a large kettle of salted water until they are *al dente*. Drain the noodles and put them quickly into a heated serving bowl with the sauce. Toss the noodles and sauce together thoroughly, then serve immediately on warm plates.

Serves 4 to 6.

penne al cardinale   *(pasta with creamy tomato sauce)*

6   medium-sized ripe tomatoes
4½ Tbs. butter
2   large cloves garlic, minced or pressed
½   tsp. salt
½   tsp. dried basil, crushed
1½ cups cream
1½ Tbs. flour
1   Tbs. brandy
2   Tbs. tomato paste

1 to 1½ lbs. *penne* noodles

Blanch the tomatoes in boiling water until the skins split and start to curl. Remove them from the water and peel them.

Purée the tomatoes in a blender, a couple at a time. You should have about 3 cups of thin purée.

Melt 2 tablespoons of the butter in a saucepan and sauté the garlic in it until it is just golden. Add the tomato purée, the salt, and the basil. Simmer gently until the purée is reduced by at least ⅓. It should be thick enough to lightly coat a wooden spoon.

In another saucepan, melt another 1½ tablespoons butter, stir in the flour, and cook this roux over a tiny flame, stirring constantly, until it is golden.

Heat the cream until it is hot to the touch but not boiling and add it to the roux, stirring with a whisk. Cook this sauce until it is thickened, whisking it frequently, then stir in the brandy, the tomato paste, and the remaining butter.

Combine the cream sauce and the thickened tomato purée, and cook them together for a while longer, until the desired consistency is reached.

The amount of pasta you can cook will depend on what kind of pasta–sauce ratio you prefer and on how many people you're feeding. About 1¼ pounds will serve 6 people generously.

Boil the noodles until they are *al dente*, or just tender.

Pour the hot sauce into a large, warm serving bowl. Add the drained noodles, toss until well mixed, and serve at once.

Serves about 6 people.

conchiglie tutto giardino

(pasta with fresh vegetables—
"the whole garden")

7   Tbs. butter
1½   cups thinly sliced carrots
1   cup chopped green onions
1   large red onion, coarsely chopped
¾   cup thinly sliced radishes
½   cup coarsely chopped parsley, packed
2   Tbs. fresh chopped basil
3   cloves garlic, crushed or minced
7   medium-sized tomatoes (about 3 cups
        chopped)
3   cups thinly sliced zucchini
1   large green bell pepper, seeded and diced
1½   cups dry white wine, or more to taste
2   tsp. salt
1   tsp. pepper
1   tsp. sugar
1   Tbs. flour
1   cup light cream
6   oz. tomato paste
½   cup grated Parmesan cheese
1½   lbs. shell noodles (*conchiglie*)

garnish: additional Parmesan cheese

Melt 6 Tbs. butter in large saucepan and add the carrots, both the green and the red onions, the radishes, parsley, basil, and garlic. Sauté the vegetables, stirring often, until they begin to color—about 20 minutes. Cover the saucepan and simmer the vegetables for about 15 minutes.

Add the tomatoes, zucchini, bell pepper, wine, salt, pepper, and sugar. Simmer the sauce, uncovered, for about 45 minutes to 1 hour.

In a small pot, melt 1 Tbs. butter and stir in the flour. Cook this roux for a few minutes over very low heat, stirring constantly. Heat the cream and stir it into the roux with a whisk. Add the tomato paste and whisk the mixture again until it is perfectly smooth. Stir it into the vegetables and wine, along with the grated Parmesan cheese.

Continue simmering the sauce over low heat, stirring often, until it is as thick as you want it to be.

Cook the shell noodles (*conchiglie*) in a large kettle of boiling salted water until they are *al dente*, drain them completely, and pour them into a large, heated serving dish. Ladle as much of the sauce over them as you like, toss them, and serve immediately, with more grated Parmesan cheese.

Serves 8 to 10.

penne with sweet and sour onion sauce

2 lbs. red onions
½ cup butter
2 to 3 Tbs. olive oil, to taste
¾ tsp. salt
1 or 2 cloves garlic, minced (optional)
1 quart peeled tomatoes (with liquid)
2 cups dry red wine
½ tsp. dried basil, crushed
½ tsp. dried rosemary, crushed
1 large bay leaf
dash of marjoram
fresh-ground black pepper to taste
1 tsp. sugar
dash of cinnamon
2 tsp. red wine vinegar
¼ cup dried currants
1½ to 2 lbs. *penne* noodles (or other pasta)

Peel the onions, halve them, and slice them. Sauté them in the butter and the olive oil, stirring almost constantly, for ½ hour to 45 minutes—until they are evenly light brown. Add the salt and the garlic and cook for another few minutes.

Add the tomatoes, wine, herbs, pepper, sugar, cinnamon, vinegar, and currants. Lower the heat and simmer the sauce for 1½ to 2 hours, until it is quite thick.

Boil the pasta in several quarts of salted water until it is just *al dente*, then drain it immediately. Toss together the spaghetti and sauce in a heated serving dish and serve immediately.

Serves 8.

spaghetti e cipolle *(spaghetti and onions)*

2½ lbs. red onions
½ cup butter
2 large bay leaves
3 cloves garlic, minced
1 tsp. paprika
½ tsp. salt, and more to taste
1 cup good dry red wine
¼ tsp. thyme
¼ tsp. cayenne pepper
¼ tsp. dried basil, crushed
¼ tsp. dried oregano, crushed
1 tsp. chopped fresh sage, or ½ tsp. dried
2 cups peeled, chopped tomatoes (with liquid)
¼ cup brandy
1 tsp. lemon juice
2 tsp. white wine vinegar
fresh-ground black pepper to taste

1¼ to 1½ lbs. thin spaghetti

Peel the onions, halve them, and slice them rather thickly. Melt the butter in a large pot and add the bay leaves and the garlic and cook them, stirring constantly, for about 1 minute. Add the sliced onions and sauté them over fairly high heat, stirring almost constantly, for at least ½ hour. The onions should be evenly light brown in color. Add the paprika and the salt and stir for another few minutes. Add the wine, herbs, tomatoes, brandy, lemon juice, vinegar, and pepper. Lower the heat and simmer the sauce, stirring occasionally, for about 45 minutes to 1 hour. It should be thick but not pasty.

Taste the sauce and correct the seasoning if necessary.

Boil the spaghetti in 6 or 7 quarts of salted water until it is just *al dente*, and drain it immediately. Pour the hot sauce over the spaghetti, toss them together quickly, and serve.

Serves 6 to 8.

fettucine alfredo

1½ cups heavy cream
1½ cups fresh-grated Parmesan cheese (about
     5½ oz.)
½ cup butter
2 egg yolks
salt
white pepper

1 lb. fettucine noodles

garnish

½ cup chopped fresh parsley

Heat the cream in a medium-sized, heavy-bottomed saucepan. When it is just beginning to simmer, stir the cheese into it, bit by bit. Continue stirring constantly over low heat for about 10 minutes, then start adding the butter, a little at a time. When all the butter is incorporated and the sauce is smooth, remove it from the heat and beat a small amount of it into the egg yolks. Return the egg yolk mixture to the sauce and stir it in thoroughly with a whisk. Season to taste with salt and white pepper.

Bring 3 or 4 quarts of heavily salted water to a rolling boil, add a tiny bit of butter or oil, and cook the noodles in it until they are just *al dente*—barely tender and not yet soft.

Drain the noodles quickly in a colander and transfer them to a large, warm serving dish. Pour the hot cream sauce over the noodles. If the sauce seems too thick, it can be thinned with a tiny bit of cream or milk. Lift the noodles with two wooden spoons until they are all evenly coated. Sprinkle the noodles with the chopped parsley and serve them immediately.

Serves 6.

spaghetti alla carbonara *(spaghetti with egg and cheese sauce)*

6   medium-sized eggs
½   lb. Parmesan cheese, finely grated (about 2 cups)
3   medium-sized onions
6   Tbs. olive oil
salt to taste
fresh-ground black pepper to taste
1   lb. spaghetti

Beat the eggs until they are fairly smooth and stir the grated Parmesan cheese into them. The mixture should have the consistency of a soft paste.

Peel, quarter, and slice the onions, or chop them very coarsely, then sauté them in the olive oil in a very large skillet over medium-high heat until they begin to turn golden brown around the edges.

Meanwhile, cook the spaghetti in 6 to 8 quarts of vigorously boiling salted water until it is just barely *al dente*. If the onions are golden before the spaghetti is cooked, remove them from the heat until about a minute before the spaghetti will be drained, then quickly heat them up again.

As soon as the spaghetti is tender (but not at all soft), drain it thoroughly in a colander. Remove the onions from the heat and add the spaghetti to them in the hot skillet. Pour the egg-cheese paste over the spaghetti and stir it all together quickly, by lifting with two wooden spoons, for about 1 minute. The heat of the skillet and the spaghetti will cook the eggs slightly and melt the cheese, and the result will be a creamy sauce that should coat all the pasta. Direct heat, however, will scramble the eggs, so be sure your skillet is quite hot but off the flame, and pour the paste over the pasta, not directly into the skillet. After about a minute of rapid lifting and stirring, the eggs should be sufficiently thickened, but if they are still runny, just continue the process for another 30 seconds or so.

Season with a little salt if needed, and grate on some black pepper. Serve immediately on heated plates.

Serves 4 to 6.

lasagne

2   lbs. fresh, ripe tomatoes
5   Tbs. olive oil
1½   medium-sized onions, chopped
2   cloves garlic, minced
1   cup peeled, sliced, Italian plum tomatoes
1   tsp. salt, and more to taste
½   tsp. basil
⅓   cup red wine
1½   lbs. eggplant
¾   lb. flat lasagne noodles
1   lb. fresh ricotta cheese
2   oz. fresh-grated Parmesan cheese (about ¾
       cup)
1   lb. mozzarella cheese, sliced

garnish

additional Parmesan cheese and tomato sauce

Plunge the fresh tomatoes into boiling water for 2 to 3 minutes, then hold them under cool running water as you slip off their skins. Chop the tomatoes coarsely.

Heat 3 tablespoons of the olive oil in a medium-sized saucepan and sauté the onions and garlic in it until they begin to color. Add the chopped fresh tomatoes, the sliced Italian tomatoes (fresh ones are preferable, but canned will do), the salt, basil, and wine and simmer, stirring occasionally, for about 25 minutes. The sauce should be somewhat thickened, but still rather juicy.

Peel the eggplant and slice it ½ inch thick, lengthwise. Salt the slices liberally on both sides and let them drain in a colander for about 40 minutes. Rinse them off, squeeze out the excess moisture, and cut them in ½-inch dice. Sauté the eggplant in the remaining 2 tablespoons olive oil over high heat, stirring or tossing constantly, until it is tender.

Boil the lasagne noodles, 6 or 7 at a time, in about 8 quarts of salted water, with a tiny bit of oil, until they are *al dente*. Remove them from the water carefully, with tongs or 2 long forks.

Lightly oil a large, shallow baking dish—about 10 inches by 14 inches. Spoon ⅓ of the tomato sauce across the bottom, and arrange ⅓ of the cooked noodles over it. Spread on ½ the ricotta cheese, and sprinkle it with a few tablespoons of the Parmesan. Evenly distribute ½ the cooked eggplant over the 2 cheeses, cover it with ⅓ of the sliced mozzarella, and spoon on another ⅓ of the sauce.

Make another layer of noodles, cover it with the rest of the ricotta, sprinkle on another few

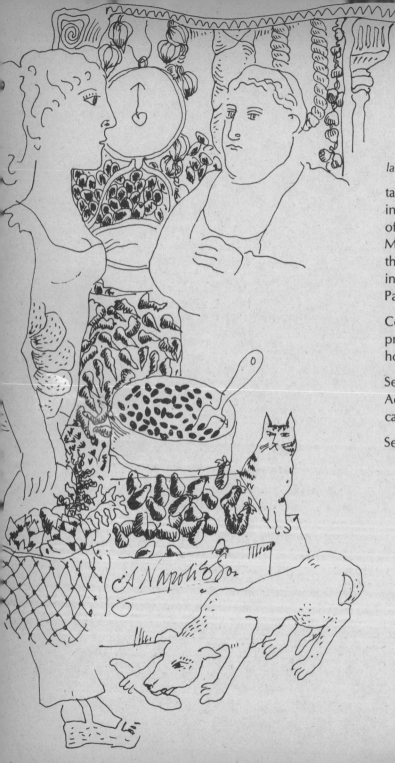

lasagne (continued)

tablespoons of Parmesan, distribute the remaining eggplant over that, and arrange another ⅓ of the mozzarella slices over the eggplant. Make a third layer of noodles, cover them with the remaining mozzarella, spoon on the remaining sauce, and sprinkle on the rest of the Parmesan.

Cover the dish and bake the lasagne in a preheated oven at 350 degrees for about ½ hour.

Serve hot with garlic bread and red wine. Additional Parmesan cheese and tomato sauce can be served separately if desired.

Serves 6 to 8.

melanzana al forno *(baked eggplant)*

This recipe started out as an attempt to re-create a dish I ate in a very good restaurant in Bologna. It took off in a direction of its own, however, emerging as a new version of an old and popular dish—and met with rave reviews.

2½ lbs. firm eggplant (smaller eggplants are preferable)
4   Tbs. olive oil
3   cloves garlic, minced
1   tsp. salt
⅓ to ½ cup pine nuts
2   cups peeled tomatoes (with liquid)
2   Tbs. minced fresh parsley
½   tsp. basil
fresh-ground black pepper to taste
⅓   cup grated Parmesan cheese
½   cup dry bread crumbs, and more if needed
2   eggs, well beaten
½   lb. mozzarella cheese, cut into strips.

For best results, choose eggplants of about ½ to ¾ pound size. Cut them in half lengthwise and cut out all the inside, leaving only a ¼-inch layer inside the skin. Put the scooped-out shells aside and chop the eggplant.

Heat the olive oil in a large pan and add the garlic to it. Stir the garlic in the oil for about a minute, then add the chopped eggplant and the salt. Sauté the eggplant over high heat, stirring almost constantly, for about 10 minutes, or until it is just starting to color.

Add the pine nuts, tomatoes (cut in chunks), parsley, basil, and a generous amount of fresh-ground pepper. Stir the mixture well, turn down the heat, and simmer it for another 10 minutes. Add the cheese and the bread crumbs and stir thoroughly. The mixture should be moist but thick—not at all runny. Add a little more bread crumbs if needed, then stir in the beaten eggs. Taste, and correct the seasoning.

Spoon the mixture into the scooped-out egg-plant shells, filling them to the brim. Arrange strips of mozzarella cheese on top and bake the eggplants in a preheated 350 degree oven for about 35 to 40 minutes. The cheese on top should be golden brown. Serve hot.

Serves 6 to 8.

ravioli with spinach and herb filling

pasta dough

1   lb. flour (about 3 cups)
1½ tsp. salt
3   eggs
3   Tbs. olive oil
approximately ½ cup lukewarm water

spinach and herb filling

1½ lbs. fresh spinach
3   hard-boiled eggs
2   Tbs. butter, melted
2   Tbs. fresh-grated Parmesan cheese
½   cup fresh ricotta cheese
2½ Tbs. minced fresh parsley
½   tsp. dried oregano, crushed
1   tsp. dried basil, crushed
¾   tsp. salt
fresh-ground black pepper to taste

To make the pasta, mix the flour and the salt together in a large bowl and make a well in the center. Break in the eggs and add the oil and the water. Stir the flour into the wet ingredients until you have a moist, firm dough, adding a little more water if necessary. Or, combine all the ingredients in the container of a food processor, equipped with the plastic blade,

and process for a little more than 1 minute, or until a homogenous dough has been formed.

Turn the dough out onto a large, floured board and knead, working in a bit more flour if necessary, until the dough is smooth and satiny, about 8 to 10 minutes. Keep the pasta covered with plastic wrap until it is needed.

To make the filling, wash the spinach, remove the thick stems, and cook it on high heat in a covered pot, in as much water as clings to the leaves, until it is soft and tender, about 8 to 10 minutes. Drain it thoroughly and chop finely or process briefly in a food processor with the steel blade.

Chop the hard-boiled eggs very fine and stir them into the spinach along with the remaining ingredients. Or, in a food processor, add the eggs, quartered, to the spinach and process for about 30 seconds. Then add the remaining ingredients and process again until the mixture is well blended, about 30 to 40 seconds.

This amount of filling makes about 50 to 60 fairly large raviolis, enough for 6 servings.

MAKING THE RAVIOLIS

Divide the pasta dough into 4 equal parts. On a large board or tabletop, lightly dusted with flour, roll 1 part out as thinly as possible; try to keep the shape of it as much like a rectangle as possible, though it will invariably try to make itself into a map of Italy or Africa. Keep the rest of the dough covered until you need it. If the dough sticks, peel it up carefully from the board and dust a little more flour under it.

When it is about 1/16 of an inch thick, put it aside on a flat surface and roll out a second quarter of the dough to the same size and shape (within reason!). It is important to roll the dough out as smoothly and evenly as possible. If it is too thin in some places and too thick in others, parts will overcook and break apart in boiling, while other parts will remain undercooked.

Take one of the sheets of pasta and stretch it out on your lightly floured board. Place tea-spoonfuls of filling on it in neat rows across and from top to bottom, about 2 inches apart from center to center. Using a pastry brush or your finger, moisten with water the pasta in between the mounds of filling, drawing wide lines between the rows.

Carefully lower the second sheet of pasta over the first and press down firmly along the wetted lines to seal the two pasta layers around the filling. If large air bubbles are trapped in the raviolis, prick through the pasta with the tip of a sharp knife, near the edge, then pinch together again securely when all the air has escaped.

Cut the ravioli apart with a pastry wheel, a ravioli cutter, or a sharp knife.

Roll out, fill, and seal the remaining 2 sections of dough in the same way. Be sure that all the seams are securely pressed together: Bad seals will ruin the raviolis in cooking. I've found that letting the ravioli rest for a while before cooking helps prevent breaking seals later. Leave the raviolis on a lightly floured board, in a single layer, for about 20 minutes before putting them in the kettle.

To cook the raviolis, drop them in a vast kettle of fast-boiling salted water and nudge them about very quickly with a wooden spoon for a minute or so to prevent them from sticking to each other. Boil them for 8 to 10 minutes, or until the pasta is tender but not mushy. Drain them thoroughly and serve immediately, with a light tomato sauce, cream sauce, or simply with butter and cheese.

Makes about 50 to 60 fairly large raviolis, enough for 6 servings.

potato gnocchi

2   lbs. russet potatoes
1½ cups flour, and more if needed
2   tsp. salt
1   egg, lightly beaten
approximately ½ cup butter, melted, to taste
Swiss or Parmesan cheese

Boil the potatoes in their jackets until they are tender. Drain them and allow them to cool slightly, then peel them and put them through a ricer or the finest blade of a food mill.

Work the potatoes, flour, salt, and egg into a dough, kneading it with your hand, until smooth. Add a little more flour if necessary. The dough should be manageable but soft.

Take ⅓ of the dough at a time and, on a lightly floured board, shape it into a long, thick cylinder. Roll the cylinder and stretch it gently until you have a rope about 1 inch thick. With a sharp knife, cut it in ½-inch bits. Repeat with the remaining dough.

To cook the gnocchi, drop them into 6 to 8 quarts of boiling salted water and boil them for 8 to 10 minutes, or until they are cooked through. Remove them with a slotted spoon and drain them.

Arrange the gnocchi in one layer in a well-buttered casserole or gratin dish, drizzle melted butter over them, and sprinkle them to your taste with grated Parmesan or Swiss cheese. Bake them in a preheated 350 degree oven for 15 to 20 minutes, or until they are hot through and the cheese is beginning to brown.

The gnocchi can also be served with marinara sauce or cream sauce.

Serves 6 to 8.

spinach and cheese gnocchi

½   lb. spinach leaves
9   Tbs. butter, melted
1   cup well-drained ricotta cheese
⅔   cup grated Parmesan cheese
3   egg yolks, beaten
7   Tbs. flour, and more as needed for rolling
¾   tsp. salt
fresh-ground pepper to taste
pinch of nutmeg (optional)
½   cup grated Parmesan cheese

Wash the spinach leaves carefully and cook them in 3 tablespoons of the melted butter on medium-high heat, stirring often, until they are completely tender and the liquid from them has evaporated completely. They should be just beginning to stick to the pan. This may take 10 to 15 minutes. Purée the cooked spinach in a blender or mince it with a large knife.

In a fairly large bowl, combine the spinach purée with the ricotta cheese, Parmesan cheese, beaten egg yolks, 7 tablespoons flour, salt, pepper, and nutmeg. Stir the mixture vigorously until it is perfectly blended and lump-free. Chill the mixture for at least ½ hour.

Using two teaspoons, form little gnocchi about the size and shape of a pecan: Scoop up a rounded teaspoonful of the mixture in one spoon, then cup the second spoon over it and slide it off to the side. Do this once or twice more to get an even shape and drop the little dumpling into a bowl of flour. Roll it in the flour, dust it off, and put it down on waxed paper. Continue forming the gnocchi until all of the spinach-cheese mixture is used up.

To cook the gnocchi, drop them carefully into about 6 quarts of simmering salted water. Allow them to simmer (not boil) for 10 to 12 minutes, stirring them very gently once or twice with a wooden spoon to make sure they don't stick to each other. Remove them from the water with a slotted spoon and drain them on a clean cloth.

Pour another 3 tablespoons melted butter into a large, shallow casserole or gratin dish. Brush it evenly over the bottom of the dish and arrange the gnocchi in it in one layer. Pour the remaining 3 tablespoons butter over them and sprinkle them with the grated Parmesan cheese. Bake the gnocchi in a preheated 350 degree oven for 15 to 20 minutes, or until they are hot through and the cheese is beginning to color.

Serves 6.

italian spinach and potato roulade

This is like a giant rolled dumpling, with a spinach filling. A potato dough reminiscent of gnocchi is rolled up around the filling, then the whole thing is wrapped in cheesecloth, boiled in salted water, and served hot, in spiral-patterned slices.

filling

2 lbs. fresh spinach
3 Tbs. butter
1 large yellow onion, chopped
1 large clove garlic, minced
1½ Tbs. white wine vinegar
½ tsp. salt
¼ tsp. oregano, crushed
pinch of nutmeg

dough

2 lbs. potatoes
2 whole eggs
1 egg yolk
1½ tsp. salt
⅛ tsp. nutmeg
2 to 2½ cups flour

garnish

½ cup butter, melted
¾ cup fresh-grated Parmesan cheese

To make the filling, wash the spinach carefully and cook it, covered, in the water that clings to the leaves, until it is all completely wilted. Squeeze out the excess moisture and chop the spinach fine.

Melt the 3 tablespoons butter in a medium-sized skillet and sauté the chopped onions and minced garlic in it until they are golden. Stir in the chopped spinach, the vinegar, the ½ tea-spoon salt, the oregano, and the nutmeg. Stir and continue cooking for a few minutes, until the mixture is thick but still moist. Taste, and correct the seasoning if necessary.

To make the dough, boil the potatoes until they are tender, peel them, and press them through a coarse sieve into a large bowl. Beat the 2 whole eggs with the egg yolk and stir the beaten eggs into the potatoes along with the 1½ teaspoons salt and the nutmeg. Stir in about 2 cups flour and begin working the dough with your hand until it is smooth (one hand will do—you don't want to have them both in there at once, or you'll have trouble getting out). Work in as much flour as is necessary to form a dough that is stiff enough to hold its shape in a ball.

Sprinkle a large sheet of waxed paper with a generous amount of flour and roll the dough out on it in an even rectangle, 11 inches by 13 inches. Keep the dough dusted with flour to prevent it from sticking.

Spread the spinach filling over the rectangle of dough, leaving a 1-inch border on both ends and one of the 13-inch sides, and a 2-inch border on the other 13-inch side. Starting with the long side that has the 1-inch border, roll the dough up over the filling, peeling back the waxed paper as you go. Securely pinch together the seam and ends so that none of the filling can squeeze out. Now wrap the entire roulade in cheesecloth, 2 or 3 layers thick and long enough to extend past both ends of the roulade by several inches. Tie the cheesecloth with string at the ends, and tie another strip of cheesecloth, about 3 inches wide, around the middle of the roulade.

Place it in a large, fairly deep pan, such as a roasting pan, and cover it with boiling salted water. Simmer the roulade for 50 minutes, turning it over once, halfway through.

Lift out the roulade and let it rest for a couple of minutes, then carefully remove the cheese-cloth; use a sharp knife to help peel away the cheesecloth if it should stick.

Cut ¾-inch slices and serve them immediately on warm plates, drenched with melted butter and sprinkled liberally with Parmesan cheese.

Serves 6 generously.

fried mozzarella

1½ lbs. mozzarella cheese
1⅓ cups fine, dry bread crumbs
3 to 4 Tbs. finely minced fresh parsley
2   eggs
salt to taste
pepper to taste
approximately 3 to 4 Tbs. flour
approximately ½ to ⅓ cup olive oil

garnish

slices of melon

Cut the mozzarella into evenly sized slices about ¼ inch thick.

Combine the bread crumbs and the parsley in a shallow bowl, mixing them together thoroughly.

Beat the eggs lightly with a little water and some salt and pepper, and pour the beaten eggs into another shallow bowl.

Put a few tablespoons of flour into a third bowl. Dredge the cheese slices in flour on both sides and on the edges. Take one of the floured slices and dip it first in the egg mixture, then in the bread crumb mixture, then once more in the egg mixture and once more in the crumbs.

Bread all the cheese slices this way. Be sure that the slices of cheese are thickly and evenly breaded, including the edges, or else they will come to grief in the frying pan!

Pour a liberal amount of olive oil into each of 2 large skillets and heat it. Put in the cheese slices, regulate the flame to a medium heat, and sauté the cheese for a few minutes on each side. The breading should be crispy and golden brown.

Remove them from the oil and place them on paper towels for an instant, then serve immediately. The cheese should be completely melted inside the crust.

Serve with a salad or garnished with slices of melon.

Serves 6.

pomodoro al gratine *(gratinéed tomatoes)*

Because it's so light and refreshing, this is an ideal hot hors d'oeuvre for a dinner which includes a heavy pasta dish. It's also delightful as an accompaniment to croquettes.

6   medium-sized, firm tomatoes (about 2 lbs.)
2   Tbs. olive oil
3   Tbs. minced fresh parsley
1   tsp. dried basil, crushed
½   tsp. dried oregano, crushed
1 or 2 cloves garlic, minced
½ to ¾ tsp. salt, to taste
fresh-ground black pepper to taste
⅓   cup grated Parmesan cheese
⅔   cup dry bread crumbs

Slice the tomatoes in half crosswise and scoop out the pulp with a spoon, leaving a firm ¼-inch shell. Coarsely chop the pulp and put it in a bowl together with all the liquid, the oil, the herbs, salt and pepper, cheese, and bread crumbs. Stir everything together until it is thoroughly combined.

Lightly salt the inside of the tomato shells and spoon the prepared filling into them, dividing it evenly among the 12 shells.

Bake the tomatoes in a preheated oven at 350 degrees for about 20 to 25 minutes and serve hot.

Serves 6.

frittata of zucchini

1½ lbs. young, firm zucchini (about 4½ cups
    chopped)
1   medium onion
3   Tbs. olive oil
6 . eggs
salt and pepper to taste
basil, crushed, to taste

Cut the zucchini into small dice and chop the onion. Heat the olive oil in a 10-inch skillet and add the onions and zucchini to it. Sauté the vegetables, stirring often, until the onions are golden and the zucchini tender.

Meanwhile, beat the eggs lightly with some salt, pepper, and a little crushed basil. When the zucchini is just tender, spread the vegetables around in the pan evenly and pour the eggs over them. Lower the flame and cover the pan. Cook the *frittata* this way until the eggs are completely set, about 15 to 20 minutes. Check it occasionally to see if it is puffing up in a bubble, in which case pierce it once or twice with a sharp knife.

When the eggs are firm on top, loosen the *frittata* carefully by sliding a spatula around under it. Then place a plate upside down over the top of the pan like a lid and invert it, dropping the *frittata* out onto it. Slide it carefully back into the pan with the top side down and brown it for a few minutes. Then turn it out onto a serving plate.

Serve the *frittata* cut in wedges, as a first course or as part of an antipasto. It can be served hot but is best when served at room temperature. Do not serve it cold.

Serves 6.

onion and herb frittata

1 yellow onion
1 red onion
3 Tbs. olive oil
½ cup chopped fresh parsley
⅓ cup snipped chives
¼ tsp. dried basil or 2 tsp. fresh
6 eggs
salt and pepper to taste

Peel and coarsely chop the onions. Heat the olive oil in a large skillet and sauté the onions in it until they just begin to color. Add the parsley, chives, and basil, and sauté a few minutes more, stirring often.

Beat the eggs lightly with a little salt and pepper.

Give the onions and herbs one more stir, then distribute them more or less evenly in the skillet and carefully pour the eggs over them. Lower the heat as much as possible, cover the pan, and cook until the eggs are barely firm on top; this should take 10 to 15 minutes on very low heat.

Turn a large plate upside down over the skillet like a lid and overturn the skillet quickly, dropping the *frittata* onto the plate. Then slide the *frittata* back into the skillet and brown the other side for a few minutes.

Turn the *frittata* out onto a serving plate and, just before serving, cut it into wedges. It may be eaten hot, cool, or, best of all, at room temperature.

Serves 6 as a first course or as part of an antipasto.

For an antipasto, turn to Salads and Cold Vegetables and see recipes for Lima Bean Salad, Rice Salad Vinaigrette, Florentine Bread Salad, White Bean Salad, Salad Torcoloti, Eggplant Caviar, Garbanzo Bean Salad, Peperonata, Gnocchi Salad, Insalatone, and Fresh Mozzarella Salad. For two versions of Pasta e Fagioli, turn to Soups. In Desserts, see Spumoni Cake and Zuppa Inglese.

spanish specialties, including tapas and tortillas

It's hard to choose favorites, but if you twisted my arm, I'd have to admit that the bars in Spain are the best in the Western world. Vienna, as everyone knows, has the best pastries, Italy brews the best cup of coffee, the German trains run most reliably, and Spain has the greatest bars.

Unlike most American bars, which are designed solely for the consumption of hard liquor by adults, generally in a semidark, slightly decadent atmosphere, many European countries enjoy bars of greater social, and even culinary, importance. So, the competition is keen.

Italian bars, dominated by big, gleaming espresso machines, and full of life from the earliest hours of the morning, are the place to have breakfast—foaming cappuccino and a fresh pastry. Then, they are a place for innumerable coffee breaks through the day, a place to enjoy an occasional game of pinball, to have a snack, and even to have a drink, sometimes. Families run Italian bars, and families patronize them. Often enough, the bar downstairs is the place to make and receive phone calls, as well as to keep up on the local news. English pubs, especially in the country, are the social centers of their neighborhoods. Most of them are very pleasant places to pass an evening, and many serve a perfectly edible lunch. But Spanish bars, which do not lack in any of the recommendations above mentioned, add one more distinction which puts them over the top: Spanish bars serve *tapas*.

Now, while it is true that *tapas* are snacks or small portions of various foods meant to be nibbled with a glass of wine, they cannot be so easily explained. *Tapas* are not so much a food as they are a phenomenon, and snacking, in Spain, is not so much a way of eating as a way of life. To understand *tapas*, it is first necessary to become acquainted with the rhythm of Spanish life and particularly with the custom of the *paseo*. The Spanish day starts early, usually with *café con leche* and crusty rolls (in a bar). By lunchtime, which is around two in the afternoon, appetites are honed, and instead of dashing out in shifts for a sandwich and a cup of coffee, the Spanish close down their shops, offices, banks, and various businesses and settle down at home or in a restaurant for a leisurely and plentiful meal. About two hours later, refreshed and relaxed Spaniards return to their worldly concerns and attend to them until early evening.

The dinner hour, however, particularly on long, warm summer days, does not begin until about ten o'clock. During that very pleasant part of the day when late afternoon is slipping into early evening—

about seven or eight, in the summer—the greater portion of the population of every Spanish town and village streams out into the streets for a walk. But this is no solitary ramble or constitutional: It is the *paseo*, a charming social custom that knocks on ritual. Schoolgirls, linked arm-in-arm, merchants and office clerks, mothers pushing prams, and whole families together come out to take the air.

On all the main streets and avenues they stroll in two strong, lively currents, down one side of the road and back up the other, nodding and greeting each other and stopping to chat. And it is then, during the *paseo*, that the *tapa* bars are at their wonderful best. Oh, you can stop in for a *tapa* almost any time of day. You can have *tapas* for lunch, *tapas* in the afternoon or late into the night, but *tapas* and the *paseo* truly go hand-in-hand. The same bar where you had a quiet cup of coffee in the morning, be it small or large, simple or elegant, is, at this time of day, invariably bright, cheerful, noisy, and tempting.

There are certain districts in Madrid where the *tapa* bars are magnificent in size and justly famous. By four or five in the afternoon, the long, polished surface of the bar in such places is lined with twenty, thirty—sometimes as many as forty—platters and bowls holding a marvelous array of toothsome edibles. There are marinades and salads reminiscent of an Italian antipasto, and stuffed eggs. There are large *tortillas*, those round, golden Spanish omelets that are cut in wedges, still warm and redolent of onions. There are olives in all their variety, *bocadillo* rolls and cheeses, roasted peppers, and even hot dishes—little plates of garlicky cooked mushrooms or brown-crusted croquettes, prepared in moments on request. In the summer, there is always sangría, and icy gazpacho by the cup, and there might be flan, in great pans or in little ceramic cups, and trays of fresh fruit, and more.

It looks like some kind of madly generous buffet, and the bartenders presiding over it dart quickly back and forth, pouring *chatos* of wine and serving up the delicacies to go with it. There are no stools or chairs in most of these establishments; you just find an opening somewhere in the lineup of eager customers, and there you stand, one elbow firmly planted on the counter, as you look over the selection. Then name what you want, or point—a slice of this or a portion of that—and in a twinkling the little plates appear before you, next to your glass. When you've finished one *tapa*, you try another, and another, as the mood strikes you, and when you're ready to go on and favor a different bar for a while, the amazing bartender, who has kept track of your nibbling by some secret, invisible method of his own, tots up a scrap of a bill (it's never very much), and you're off. You join the *paseo* once more and stroll along until some other display of *tapas* lures you in to pause again, enjoy another glass of wine, and have another bite.

In this gratifying manner, you revive your spirits and your strength at that rather peckish time when dinner is still a few hours off and lunch already forgotten. Of course, if the *tapas* are abundant in your part of town, you can all too easily make a meal of several such visits and lose interest in dinner altogether, but what of it? Nor do *tapas* vanish at ten, when restaurants are filling up. It's hard to resist stopping for just a taste of something before going to your table and ordering a serious meal. And finally, after an evening out at the movies, theater, or wherever, how nice if you can contrive to pass a *tapa* bar on the way home and indulge in a last little bite or two with a nightcap.

Real *tapas* don't exist outside of *tapa* bars. There's no such thing, in Spain, as eating *tapas* at home. But I can't think of Spanish food without recalling those delicious evenings in the bars, and because I can't, unfortunately, transport myself to Madrid or Barcelona or Segovia whenever I get the urge, I worked out some recipes for a few of the dishes that are so particular to the *tapa* bars and included them here with my other Spanish favorites. Sometimes on summer days, when nobody especially wants a heavy, hot meal, and when I'm smacking my lips in recollection of sangría, I like to prepare three or four of those *tapas*, put them out buffet-style, together with some pickled peppers, cheeses, breads, and fruits, and call all hungry people.

Spanish cooking does not begin and end with *tapas*, however. It is, in fact, one of the most diverse and delicious European cuisines. In the United States, I've found, there is a rather widespread misconception about Spanish food. Many people have the idea that it resembles Mexican food. Nothing could be further from the truth! The cooking of Mexico derives very strongly from the culinary traditions of the pre-Columbian Indians. It is based on corn and hot chilis, along with an assortment of other New World ingredients, and is popularly accompanied by the excellent Mexican beers. Spain's cuisine, on the other hand, has none of the fiery sting that is so well loved in her erstwhile colony. Furthermore, many of the mild but flavorful Spanish dishes owe a lot to olives and olive oil, all but unknown in Mexican cooking, and wine is always served with Spanish meals.

Two main influences helped shape the character of Spanish cooking, European from the north and Moorish from the south, making an interesting and happy marriage of flavors. Another quality of the cuisine is the great variety that has been preserved by virtue of intense regionalism. It is impossible to find a Spaniard in Spain! Everyone is either a Castillian, a Basque, a Catalonian—in short, a native of his or her own province. The result of this strong regional feeling is a collection of connected but individual cooking styles.

When I was in Spain, I lived most of that time in Madrid and Segovia, so the ideas and recipes I brought back were largely Castillian. One of my immediate and lasting favorites was the Tortilla Española, which needs a bit of introduction. First of all, it has nothing to do with Mexican *tortillas*, which are a bread; this is an omelet. Second, as omelets go, it has very little to do with the French sort, except that both are made mainly of eggs. The Spanish *tortilla* is round, thick, golden brown on both sides, and full of potatoes and onions sautéed in olive oil. It is further recommended by the fact that its delicious flavor is equally compelling when it is hot and when it is quite cool.

Also not to be missed is the experience of drinking a cup of Spanish hot chocolate. This concoction starts appearing in the Segovian bars in late autumn and warms the inhabitants through the bitter cold of a Castillian winter. Not one of those puny, watery liquids that are called cocoa in other parts of the world, this one is almost like a pudding, so rich and thick that it is eaten with a spoon.

Finally, a word about Spanish wine, which is not as well known here as it should be. Everyone drinks wine in Spain, from early childhood onward (though I have yet to be treated to the sight of a Spanish drunkard), so it follows that the wine must be plentiful, cheap, and perfectly drinkable, which it is. This happy generality is punctuated by spectacular moments, though, in the form of certain red wines from the Rioja region. Rather dear by comparison to the 17 peseta (about 29 cent) bottles of Valdepenas that we bought more than once at the local *bodega* and took home for our dinner, these wines are still remarkably affordable by our standards. The best, and best known, of the Rioja wines are Marques de Murrieta and Marques de Riscal. If your wine merchant can supply you with one of them—buy it; drink it. These excellent wines, made by old, traditional methods, have a robust but sophisticated character. Don't drink them with reverence—that's a little uncomfortable—rather, with respect and a happy spirit.

As to sangría and the making of it, I can only say that properly made and served at the appropriate time, it is very, very easy to drink. On a hot summer day it practically drinks itself. But beware: Drink it at lunchtime only if you're planning a siesta.

To make a good sangría, you must start with a decent wine; not a rare or expensive wine, please, but a good, dry, drinkable red wine, and fresh, ripe fruit. It must be prepared shortly before it is to be consumed because it doesn't improve with keeping, and it certainly cannot be bottled. And, like any Spanish potable, it must be drunk with friends so that all can lift their glasses and toast each other with *"Salud, pesetas, y joventud, y tiempo para gastarlos!"*—"Health, money, and youth, and the time to enjoy them!"

ensaladilla russa

3   large, white-skinned potatoes
1   cup cooked peas
1   cup cooked diced carrots
½   cup cooked chopped pimiento peppers
½   cup minced onion
¼   cup olive oil
¼   cup wine vinegar
1½ tsp. salt
pepper to taste
mayonnaise to taste

garnish

parsley sprigs
carrot slices
slivers of pepper
chopped hard-boiled egg, etc.

Boil the potatoes, in their skins, until tender. When they are cool, peel them and cut them into very small dice, about ¼ inch.

Put the diced potatoes in a large bowl. Add a generous cupful of cooked fresh peas, a generous cupful of cooked diced carrots, the pimiento pepper, and the onions.

Toss all the ingredients together thoroughly with the oil, vinegar, salt, and pepper. Taste, and correct seasoning.

Add a few spoons of mayonnaise, according to taste, and toss again until everything is very well combined.

Mound the salad carefully on an oval platter and shape it with the side of a knife until it is smooth and even. Spread mayonnaise over the salad until it has a smooth, even coating over the entire surface. Then decorate it with various garnishes, making pretty patterns, and chill before serving.

Serves 8 to 10.

barcelona white bean salad *(a tapa)*

1   cup dried white beans, washed
1   large onion
1   large green bell pepper
2   ripe tomatoes
2   hard-boiled eggs
10 cured black olives
3   Tbs. olive oil
5   Tbs. wine vinegar
salt to taste
pepper to taste
minced garlic (optional)

Cook the beans in boiling salted water to cover until they are just tender, about 1 to 1½ hours. Drain and cool.

Peel the onion and cut it into 1-inch pieces. Blanch them in boiling water for a few minutes.

Roast the bell pepper under the broiler, turning it frequently, until the skin is blistered and a little charred. Allow the pepper to cool until you can handle it easily, and then peel it and seed it. Cut the pepper into 1-inch squares.

Cut the tomatoes into thin wedges, and halve and slice the eggs. Cut the olives away from their pits in several pieces.

Combine all the ingredients in a bowl and toss with the oil and vinegar and seasonings. Taste, and correct the seasoning.

Serve this salad cold, as a *tapa* in a buffet or as a course on its own.

Serves 6 to 8.

stewed garbanzo beans *(a tapa)*

3   Tbs. olive oil
3   cloves garlic, chopped or thinly sliced
1   Tbs. paprika
2   medium-sized, ripe tomatoes, puréed in blender
1½ cups cooked garbanzo beans (see page 143)
1   Tbs. red wine vinegar
salt
pepper

In a large, deep skillet, heat the olive oil and add the garlic and paprika. Stir constantly for a few minutes, until the garlic begins to turn golden, then add the fresh tomato purée and the beans, along with about 1 cup of the bean liquid.

Stir in the red wine vinegar and add salt and pepper to taste. Continue cooking on a low flame until the sauce is quite thick. Serve hot or warm.

Serves 6 to 8.

roasted eggplant and peppers in oil *(a tapa)*

1   lb. eggplants (5 or 6 small)
2   large green bell peppers
2   large pimiento peppers
2   Tbs. olive oil
2   Tbs. lemon juice
1   clove garlic, minced or pressed
salt to taste
fresh-ground black pepper to taste

Roast the eggplants and peppers in a very hot oven or under the broiler, turning them often, until their skins are blistered and turning brown all over. Remove and allow to cool.

When you can easily handle the vegetables, strip off the skins. Seed the peppers and cut away the white ribs.

Cut both peppers and eggplants into strips about 1 inch long and ½ inch wide.

Toss the vegetables with the oil, lemon juice, garlic, salt, and pepper. Allow to marinate for a few hours before serving. Serve cool or at room temperature.

Serves 4 to 6 (more as a *tapa*).

champiñónes a la plancha

This is one of the most popular hot *tapas* served in the bars in Spain. It is served steaming hot in little individual casseroles, with slices of crusty bread. I've adapted the recipe for six people: Make it in one large casserole and serve it either as part of a "*tapa* dinner" or as a wonderful first course. It would also make a delightful light lunch, preceded by a gazpacho or salad and served with cheese, bread, and wine.

2   lbs. fresh mushrooms
4   Tbs. butter
6 to 7 cloves garlic, chopped
¾   cup chopped parsley
1   cup dry white wine
salt and fresh-ground black pepper to taste

Wash the mushrooms and trim the dry ends off the stems. If the mushrooms are large, halve or quarter them. Melt the butter in a skillet or fireproof casserole and sauté the chopped garlic in it quickly, just until it shows the slightest bit of color. Add the mushrooms and parsley and sauté them over high heat, stirring frequently, until the mushrooms begin to release water—just a few minutes. Add the white wine, some salt and fresh-ground black pepper, and cover the skillet or casserole.

Simmer the mushrooms in the wine until they are quite tender, correct the seasoning, and serve hot in preheated bowls or individual casseroles.

Serves 6.

tortilla española

1   large russet potato
1   large yellow onion
2½ Tbs. olive oil
salt to taste
pepper to taste
5   eggs

Peel the potato and cut it into small dice, about ½ inch. Peel and chop the onion. Heat the olive oil in a large skillet and sauté the potatoes and onions, stirring very often, until the potatoes are just tender. Season the mixture with salt and pepper, stir, and then spread more or less evenly in the skillet.

Beat the eggs lightly, salt them, and pour them over the potato mixture. The eggs should barely cover the vegetables.

Cover and cook over very low heat until the top of the *tortilla* is firm, about 15 minutes. Turn a large plate upside down and place it over the skillet like a lid. Holding the plate in place, overturn the skillet, dropping the *tortilla* on the plate. Slide the *tortilla* carefully back into the skillet and brown the other side for a few minutes.

Employing the same technique, turn the *tortilla* out onto a large, round plate to serve. The *tortilla* may be eaten hot, warm, cool, cold, or at room temperature, and is always delicious.

Serves 4.

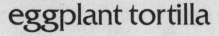

eggplant tortilla

3   Tbs. olive oil
1   large clove garlic, minced
½   large onion, chopped
2½ cups small eggplant, cut in ¼-inch dice
1   tsp. lemon juice
salt to taste
pepper to taste
5   eggs

Heat the olive oil in a large skillet and add the garlic, onions, and eggplant. Sauté the vegetables, stirring often, until the onions are transparent and the eggplant tender. Season with the lemon juice, salt, and pepper.

Beat the eggs lightly, seasoning them with salt and pepper. Pour the beaten eggs over the eggplant mixture in the pan and spread it around evenly. The eggs should barely cover all the eggplant.

Cover the pan and turn down the flame. Cook over very low heat until the *tortilla* is firm on top. Gently slide a spatula around the edges and underneath it to be sure it is not sticking.

Take a large plate and turn it upside down, placing it over the skillet like a lid. Holding the plate in place, overturn the skillet.

Slide the *tortilla* from the plate back into the pan and allow it to brown on the other side for a few minutes.

eggplant tortilla (continued)

Employing the same technique, flip the *tortilla* back onto a large plate for serving.

The *tortilla* may be eaten hot, cold, or at room temperature. One of the more convenient aspects of Spanish *tortillas* is that they really are delicious at any temperature.

Serves 3 to 4.

tortilla a la paisana

1   small potato
½   medium-sized onion
2½ Tbs. olive oil
1   medium-sized carrot
½   cup shelled peas
½   cup diced (roasted and peeled) pimiento
        pepper
1   clove garlic, crushed
salt and pepper
5   eggs

Scrub the potato, peel it if you wish, and cut it into small dice. Coarsely chop the onion. Heat the olive oil in a 9- or 10-inch pan and start sautéing the potatoes and onions, stirring often.

Scrape the carrot, cut it into small dice, and boil or steam it until it is barely tender. In another pot, boil the peas for a few minutes until they are barely tender. Drain the carrots and peas and add them to the potatoes and onions, together with the diced pimiento and the crushed garlic. Continue to sauté all the vegetables for a few minutes more—until the potatoes are nearly soft. Season the mixture to taste with salt and pepper.

Beat the eggs lightly with a little salt and pepper and pour them over the vegetable mixture in the pan. Shake the pan gently to distribute the mixture evenly, reduce the heat to very low, cover the pan, and cook the *tortilla* for about 10 minutes, or until all the eggs are set.

Loosen the edges of the *tortilla* with a knife or spatula and give the pan another shake.

Turn a large plate upside down and place it over the pan like a lid. Holding the plate in place, overturn the pan quickly, dropping the *tortilla* onto the plate. Slide the *tortilla* carefully back into the pan and brown the other side for a few minutes.

Employing the same technique, turn the *tortilla* out onto a serving platter. The *tortilla* may be served at any temperature, from hot to very cool, but I like it best at room temperature. Cut it into wedges to serve.

Serves 3 to 4.

asparagus tortilla

This one is just a little richer than most *tortillas*; it's a bit heavier on egg yolks and uses butter along with the olive oil.

6 to 8 oz. trimmed fresh asparagus
1 medium-sized yellow onion, finely chopped
5 whole eggs
1 egg yolk
½ tsp. salt
pepper to taste
1 Tbs. olive oil
2 Tbs. butter

Thinly peel the thick bottom parts of the asparagus stalks and cut them in ½-inch pieces. Cut the tender tops of the asparagus in 1-inch pieces and keep them aside. Drop the toughest pieces into boiling salted water and boil them for 3 to 4 minutes, then add the tops and boil another 4 to 5 minutes. Drain the asparagus.

Beat the eggs and extra yolk with the salt and a little pepper.

Heat the olive oil and butter in a 10-inch skillet and sauté the chopped onions in it until they begin to color. Add the asparagus and stir gently for about 2 minutes. Pour the beaten egg evenly over the vegetables in the pan, lower the heat, cover and cook 8 to 10 minutes, or just until the eggs are set.

Turn the *tortilla* out onto a plate, then slide it back into the pan to brown the other side for a few minutes. Turn it out onto a serving platter, let it cool to lukewarm if desired, and cut it in wedges to serve.

Serves 3 to 4.

menestra de verduras I *(Spanish-style stewed vegetables)*

This is a dish that I ate innumerable times in Spain. Whatever the restaurant, some version of this *menestra* was almost sure to be on the menu. Although the ingredients and proportions would vary with the cook, artichokes, string beans, and peas appear to be essential and always, always olive oil. Here is a version hearty enough to serve as a main course, preceded by a Spanish *tortilla* or garlic soup and followed by fresh fruit and cheese.

3 to 4 cloves garlic
½ lb. yellow onions (about 2 medium sized)
1 lb. small white-skinned potatoes
¾ lb. carrots
¾ lb. string beans
6 Tbs. olive oil
½ lb. mushrooms
1 tsp. salt
2 Tbs. sweet paprika
fresh-ground black pepper to taste
1 cup vegetable broth
3 cups peeled, chopped tomatoes (with their liquid)
2 bay leaves
pinch of hot paprika
½ lb. fresh asparagus
½ lb. cooked artichoke bottoms
2 cups shelled green peas

garnish

ripe green olives and
quartered hard-boiled eggs

Peel and thinly slice the garlic. Peel, halve, and thickly slice the onions and the potatoes. Scrape the carrots and cut them in ½-inch lengths. Trim the string beans and cut them in 1-inch-long pieces.

Heat the olive oil in a large, heavy-bottomed pot and sauté the garlic and onions in it until the onions are transparent. Add the potatoes, carrots, and string beans and sauté them for 10 minutes, stirring almost constantly.

Wash and trim the mushrooms and add them to the pot along with the salt, sweet paprika, and some fresh-ground pepper. Continue sautéing the vegetables for 5 minutes more, stirring constantly, then add the vegetable broth, tomatoes, bay leaves, and a pinch of hot paprika.

Simmer the mixture, uncovered, over low heat for 45 to 50 minutes. Stir it occasionally.

Peel the bottom ends of the asparagus stalks and cut the stalks in 1- to 2-inch pieces. Thickly slice the artichoke bottoms. Add the peas, asparagus, and artichoke bottoms to the *menestra* and simmer it, covered, stirring often, for 10 to 15 minutes more, or just until all the vegetables are tender. The liquid should be greatly reduced by this time.

Serve the *menestra* hot and garnish each plate with a quartered hard-boiled egg and a few ripe green olives.

Serves 6 to 8.

menestra de verduras II *(a simpler one)*

4 to 5 cloves garlic
1   large red onion
⅓   cup olive oil
1   lb. green beans
1   lb. tomatoes
½   cup dry sherry
1   large green bell pepper
1   large red bell pepper
½   lb. mushrooms
1½ cups shelled peas
¾   cup vegetable broth
3   Tbs. tomato paste
2   tsp. salt
1   tsp. pepper
½   cup sliced stuffed Spanish olives

Slice the garlic cloves very thinly. Quarter the onion and cut it in thick slices. Simmer the garlic and onions in the olive oil in a large, covered skillet until the onions are wilted.

Trim the green beans and cut them in 1-inch pieces. Cut the tomatoes in thin wedges or large chunks. Add the beans and tomatoes to the onions, along with the sherry, and simmer the vegetables, covered, for 15 to 20 minutes.

Cut the bell peppers in quarters or eighths, seed and derib them, and cut the pieces crosswise in ¼-inch strips. Wash, destem, and halve the mushrooms. Add the peppers, mushrooms, green peas, vegetable broth, tomato paste, salt, and pepper to the vegetables in the pot. Cover the mixture and cook for about 10 minutes, then uncover and simmer for about another 15 minutes, stirring often, or until the liquid is somewhat reduced and thickened.

Add the sliced olives, stir up once more, and serve hot.

Makes 4 to 6 large servings.

cocido

Cocido is a peasant dish, variations of which have developed in all the different Spanish provinces. This is my simple version of the Cocido Madrileno that the ever-smiling Delfina used to prepare for us on cold, wet winter days in Segovia. The broths from the garbanzo beans and vegetables combine with *fideos* (vermicelli) to make a light soup for the first course. Then serve the vegetables, beans, and those strange paprika-and-saffron-flavored dumplings. Finish the meal with a very simple, crisp tossed salad. To go with it all, try a red Spanish wine.

1   lb. dried garbanzo beans, rinsed
3   onions
3 to 4 Tbs. olive oil
salt
1½ lbs. potatoes (white-skinned if possible)
1½ lbs. cabbage
1   lb. trimmed leeks (about 2¼ lbs. untrimmed)
¾ lb. carrots
pepper
3   oz. broken *fideo* noodles (vermicelli)

dumplings

1   egg
3 to 4 Tbs. water
1   Tbs. vegetable oil
½ tsp. salt
½ tsp. paprika
¼ tsp. crushed saffron threads
¾ cup whole wheat flour
¾ tsp. baking powder

Soak the garbanzo beans overnight in 4 quarts of water with a pinch of baking soda. Then add 2 peeled onions, 1 tablespoon of the olive oil, and 1 teaspoon salt, and bring the water to a boil. Lower the heat and simmer the beans until they are perfectly tender, probably about an hour and a half.

Meanwhile, prepare the vegetables. Peel the remaining onion and cut it in 1-inch chunks. Peel the potatoes and cut them in large cubes. Trim and core the cabbage and cut it in wedges or large pieces. Cut off the green tops of the leeks, trim the bottoms, and slice them in half lengthwise, almost to the bottom but leaving the two parts connected at the base. Scrape the carrots and cut them in 2-inch lenths.

Put all the vegetables in a large pot with 8 to 10 cups of water—just enough to comfortably

cocido (continued)

cover them—and about 2 teaspoons salt. Bring the water to a boil and cook the vegetables 30 to 40 minutes, or until they are all tender.

To make the batter for the dumplings, beat together the egg, water, vegetable oil, salt, paprika, and saffron. Sift the flour and baking powder together and stir them into the egg mixture.

About ½ hour before you want to serve dinner, drain the garbanzo beans, discarding the 2 onions and reserving the liquid. You should have at least a quart. Leave the garbanzos in just enough broth to keep them moist, cover them tightly, and place in a warm oven. Drain the vegetables, again reserving the broth, and keep warm, moist, and tightly covered, as you have the garbanzos.

Add 4 to 5 cups of the vegetable broth to the garbanzo broth, heat them together, and season to taste with salt and pepper. Toss in the broken *fideos* (vermicelli) and simmer until the noodles are tender—just 6 or 7 minutes. At the same time, bring a pot of salted water to a boil, and drop the dumpling batter into it by scant teaspoonfuls. Cover the pot and leave the dumplings to cook for 20 minutes. They'll be ready when you're finished eating the soup course.

Pile the hot garbanzos in the center of a very large serving platter or shallow casserole and the vegetables in a ring around them. Drizzle the garbanzos and vegetables both with a few tablespoons of the remaining olive oil and sprinkle them with salt and pepper. Lift out the dumplings with a slotted spoon, arrange them at either end of the platter, and serve.

Serves 8.

sangría

½ gallon dry red wine
⅓ cup sugar
⅓ cup brandy
3 large oranges
2 large lemons
¼ cup Triple Sec
ice cubes
1 to 1½ cups club soda, to taste

Pour the wine into a punch bowl and stir in the sugar and the brandy. Cut 2 of the oranges into eighths and 1 of the lemons into quarters. Squeeze the juice from each piece of cut fruit into the wine, then drop the fruit into the punch bowl. Stir again, and chill for an hour or two with the fruit.

At this point, the cut, squashed fruit can be removed if you want a more elegant sangría, or it can be left in if you don't care about looks. Halve and thinly slice the remaining orange and thinly slice the second lemon. Add the sliced fruit to the sangría, floating it on top. Stir in the Triple Sec, add just enough ice to keep the sangría cold, and just before serving, pour in some club soda. Give it one final stir, pour, and drink.

This is a basic sangría recipe. You may want to elaborate by adding some sliced apples, sliced bananas, or other fruit, or by slightly varying some of the proportions. All variations are perfectly acceptable, as long as they taste good.

Makes almost 3 quarts.

Turn to Soups for two kinds of gazpacho, and a garlic soup. In Desserts, see Flan and Castillian Hot Chocolate.

mexican dishes

In the *Popol Vuh*, the book of Mayan tribal legends which has been roughly equated with the Christian bible, the story of the creation of humanity takes some very appealing turns. The Mayan gods seem to have been rather human themselves and did not always succeed at first try when they set out to do something. So, when they decided that it was time to people the world, they did not immediately seize on the perfect raw material for their task. Early prototypes were made from mud and then wood and rushes, but these people didn't quite work, and the gods returned to their drawing board.

In a stroke of divine inspiration, they made people from corn, and these beings took to life with a success far beyond the gods' fondest expectations. In fact, they were rather too good. The corn people saw too far and understood too much. They were dangerously close to being gods themselves; their creators were impelled to "blow a mist" into their eyes and fog their vision so they could only see what was near to them and not know more than they needed to.

This is telling evidence that the native inhabitants of Mesoamerica held a pretty high opinion of corn, and it's easy to understand why when you realize that it was, even more than wheat was to other peoples, the very stuff of life. Corn, in its numerous varieties, was the fundamental and indispensable food of all the Central American Indians, the food on which their cuisines, some of which reached high levels of sophistication, were firmly based.

To a very large degree this is still true today, certainly in Mexico. Corn is an important ingredient of countless Mexican dishes, and corn meal and water are the sole ingredients of the Mexican tortilla, the staple food of the country. The tortilla is an ancient bread that has remained virtually unchanged through the centuries, though it is now cranked out on conveyor belts in tortilla bakeries.

I dare not guess how many millions of these thin, deliciously golden, pancakelike breads are consumed each day in Mexico, but I'm sure the figure is astounding. They are eaten plain and with butter, fried for chips, and used in some of the most popular Mexican dishes. Enchiladas are soft tortillas rolled around a filling and served hot with a sauce. Tacos are tortillas folded over a filling, sometimes left soft and sometimes fried crisp, and eaten like a sandwich. A large tortilla, folded around a filling envelope-style, with the ends tucked in, is called a *burrito*. But most important, no meal is served without a basket of fresh tortillas, still hot, to accompany it, and I've seen good eaters put away a dozen or so at one sitting with some especially searing, chili-laced dish.

This is not an exaggeration, nor is it even an example of unusual overindulgence. Tucking into a basketful of hot tortillas, newly made from fresh *masa* and spread with some melted butter, is a real epicurean experience; it revealed in me, at any rate, a tortilla-eating capacity that I had hitherto little suspected.

Acceptable tortillas are commonly available throughout the American Southwest, but they are really just the poor relations of the tortillas upon which you can feast if luck ever finds you in Mexico. I was no novice at tortilla eating when *my* real moment of revelation came, in the big rustic kitchen of a country house, in the lush Mexican interior. We were staying with the Gonzalez-Madrid family, friends of my husband, in the tiny village of San José de Gracia. On our first morning there, we were hospitably gathered in the kitchen around a big table and treated to one of the heartiest, hottest breakfasts I've ever eaten. There were sweet rolls, and *chilaquiles* with rich, refried beans, fresh fruit, and delicious Mexican hot chocolate, but oh, those tortillas.

The quiet Indian Nacha, who was the family's cook, presided over the stove, patting out perfect little circles of corn *masa* with deft flicks of her hand, snatching them off the griddle the instant they were done, and passing them immediately to the table. They were tiny—a mere four or five inches across—with an irresistibly sweet flavor, and so soft and tender that they really almost melted in our mouths. It was then that I began to suspect that maybe people *were* made of corn, or if they weren't, perhaps they should have been (and might be all the sweeter for it).

The cuisine of Mexico today is still basically an amalgam of several Indian cuisines. The influence of Aztecs, Toltecs, Zapotecs, and Mayans is felt much more strongly that that of their conquerors. Certainly the Spanish conquest made great additions to the indigenous kitchen, but in spite of that, there is little resemblance between the cooking of these two countries today.

Spanish cooking is mild—almost bland—by comparison to the fiery drama of Mexican cooking. In Mexico, the food that is second only to corn in its importance is the chili, which is cultivated and enjoyed in hundreds of varieties, ranging enormously in color, size, and intensity. Even in the *Popol Vuh*, chilis were named as one of the first foods enjoyed by those corn people, and their popularity in Mexico has never waned. The marketplace of every town or village has a generous space devoted to hills of fresh and dried chili peppers, from the tiniest red ones that are like little flames, to the largest, mildest green varieties. They have melodic names like serrano, poblano, jalapeño, pasilla, cascabella, and xcatique—and their power is awesome.

As many sauces as France may have, Mexico has more, and every one of them contains some kind of chili, in some form or another. The chilis are often combined with onion and tomatoes, as well as with some other particularly Mexican ingredients—*tomatillos* and fresh cilantro leaves. *Tomatillos* look like green tomatoes with parchmentlike outer skins covering them and have a fresh, tart flavor. Cilantro (coriander leaves), so much used in Mexico that in California it is sometimes called Mexican parsley, has a distinct, pungent taste and fragrance, unmistakable in any dish.

Some kind of freshly made chili sauce is everpresent on the tables of restaurants and homes alike; it is as essential to Mexican cooking as salt. The flavor of those chilis explodes inside the mouth in a wonderfully exciting way, and the heat that goes with it can be counteracted, not by drinking water or any cold liquid, but by eating tortillas, of course! Mexicans, who have eaten chilis all their lives, can swallow great amounts of them with ease, but foreigners must beware and develop their tolerance gradually. In the recipes I've written down for this book, I've gone very easy with the chilis, in consideration of the fact that most Americans aren't used to them; but feel free to increase them to your taste.

When cooking with chilis, however, always exercise great care. Remember that the seeds are the hottest part of a chili; leave them in for a more intense, fiery effect, and remove them for a more subdued flavor. And always, always, after handling chilis, wash your hands very well with soap and water. Then, even though you've washed carefully, keep your hands away from your eyes for an hour or more, as the tiniest trace of oil from a really hot chili can make your eyes extremely uncomfortable at the least contact.

Another food that is indigenous to Mexico, and to which Europeans took like ducks to water, is chocolate. Bernal Díaz del Castillo, one of Cortez's foot soldiers, wrote an account called *The Conquest of New Spain*, and in it he described how Montezuma, the great Aztec emperor, was served large cupfuls of a strange, dark, foaming hot beverage called *cacao*. It was a substance that was unheard of in Spain at that time, but one that would soon be prized. Mexican hot chocolate is still a foaming drink, beaten with egg whites and almond paste and subtly perfumed with cinnamon and vanilla.

The people of Mexico eat and drink with gusto, and they express their exuberant enjoyment of their food in the way they refer to it. In Spanish, an -ita or -ito added to the end of a word forms an affectionate diminutive. Papas are potatoes, tortas are little cakes, and frijoles are beans, but one rarely hears the words spoken in their ordinary forms. I often remember taking a walk through a park in the lovely colonial town of Guanajuato and hearing the Indian women who were vending freshly cooked snacks calling out in their singsong voices, "Tortitas! Calientitas! Con papitas, frijolitos!"

The foods are savory and delightful, fully worthy of the fondness with which they are named. Although good Mexican food is served in restaurants throughout California, Arizona, and Texas, it is not a fair indication of the gustatory pleasures to be discovered in Mexico itself. In my experience of Mexico's cuisine I found it to be both lighter and hotter by far than its American adaptations. In Guadalajara or Mexico City I was rarely served a dish swimming in its sauce or heavy with too much oil, and I found the lavish use of the chilis, in all their delicious variety, to be quite addictive. One of my husband's friends, a Mexican-American, asked his mother once, "Why do Mexicans eat such hot food?" She summed up the whole issue admirably when she replied, "Because it tastes so good."

corn tortillas

Making your own fresh tortillas needn't be very difficult or time-consuming, and the rewards in flavor are great. Tortillas do suffer with keeping, and if you've never had them freshly made, hot off the griddle, look forward to a real treat.

However, it's only fair to give warning that if you intend to shape your tortillas by hand, you're in for a long stretch of work. Although

I've seen practiced tortilla makers slap out perfect circles, thin and tender, in mere seconds, the first time I tried it, I found myself surrounded by crumbs of dough, holding a shapeless, broken lump. I discovered that a first-timer could turn out decent tortillas, but only by the painstaking process of rolling each one out between two sheets of waxed paper, slowly and carefully.

Fortunately, however, there exists a simple and cheap tool which reduces tortilla-making to a snap. The tortilla press, which can be purchased in most stores that sell ingredients for Mexican food, as well as in some stores which handle ingredients for Indian food (*chapatis* being similar to tortillas), is the miracle worker.

I heartily recommend obtaining one if you are at all fond of tortillas.

As for the ingredients, the *masa harina* from which tortillas are made is nothing more than corn treated with lime water and specially ground to a very fine meal. The Quaker Oats Company packages a perfectly acceptable dry *masa*, which needs only to be mixed with water and salt to taste. Do not attempt to substitute corn meal for *masa harina*—it is much coarser and will not work.

2   cups *masa harina*
1   cup water
¾ to 1 tsp. salt

Combine the *masa*, water, and salt in a bowl and stir until thoroughly combined. Knead gently with your hand for a minute or two, until the dough holds together. A few more drops of water may be added if the dough seems too dry and crumbles away easily. It should be moist but firm.

Divide the dough into 12 pieces of equal size and roll each piece into a ball.

If you are not using a tortilla press, place a ball of dough between two sheets of waxed paper and roll it out carefully into a circle about 6 to 6½ inches across.

If you do have a press, begin by placing the thin plastic sheet (which comes with the press) on the bottom section. Place a ball of dough on it, in the center of the press. Fold the plastic over the dough, leaving enough room for the dough to spread equally in all directions. This is simply a lining, to keep the tortilla from sticking to the press.

Fold the top of the press down, flip the handle over from the other side, and push it down. Open the press up again, and there will be your

corn tortillas (continued)

tortilla, perfectly round and thin, shaped in about 5 seconds.

Peel back the plastic on top, turn the tortilla over onto the flat of your hand, and gently peel back the plastic from the bottom. Keep the uncooked tortillas layered between little sheets of waxed paper.

To cook the tortillas, preheat an ungreased griddle or heavy pan until it is hot enough to make a drop of water jump and sizzle.

Drop a tortilla onto the hot pan and, keeping the flame quite high, cook it for about 30 to 40 seconds. Turn it over with a spatula and cook the other side the same amount of time. The tortilla may start to puff up. This is fine—just press very gently on it with the flat spatula to keep the bubble or bubbles even.

Turn the tortilla twice more, giving it a total of about 2 minutes in the pan. When a tortilla is done, it has a pale golden color, with a few dark brown spots or freckles here and there.

Keep your hot tortillas stacked, wrapped in a tea towel or cloth napkin, inside a close-woven basket or a bowl. They will stay warm for a good ½ hour this way.

Serve as soon as possible, with any kind of Mexican food. Fresh, hot tortillas spread with a little butter are also marvelous just by themselves.

Makes 12 tortillas.

spinach enchiladas suizas

1½ lbs. trimmed spinach
3   Tbs. olive oil
1   Tbs. butter
½   large onion, chopped
2   cloves garlic, minced
salt to taste
¾   lb. Swiss cheese, grated
10 fresh corn tortillas

vegetable oil

sauce

1   Tbs. butter
1   Tbs. flour
1   cup milk, heated
1   cup sour cream, at room temperature
½   cup diced green chilis

optional garnish

sour cream and hot sauce

Wash the spinach leaves carefully, drain them, and chop them. Heat the olive oil and butter in a large skillet; sauté the onions and garlic in it until they are golden. Add the spinach and toss it in the hot oil until all of it is wilted. Salt it to your taste and continue cooking it over medium heat, stirring often, until all the liquid is gone.

Grate the Swiss cheese coarsely. Take a tortilla, brush it very lightly with vegetable oil, and heat it quickly on both sides in a skillet until it is very soft and flexible. Spread a heaping tablespoon of grated cheese in a line down the center of it, then spread a heaping tablespoon of the spinach over the cheese. Fold one end of the tortilla over the filling and roll it up. Continue in this manner until all the tortillas and spinach are used up.

Lightly oil a large, shallow casserole and arrange the enchiladas in it in such a way that they won't unroll.

To make the sauce, melt 1 tablespoon butter in a pot and stir in the flour. Cook this roux over low heat, stirring constantly, until it is golden. Add the heated milk and stir with a whisk until it is slightly thickened. Add the sour cream, diced chilis, and the remaining cheese and cook the sauce over low heat until all the cheese is melted and the sauce is quite smooth. Season it lightly with salt and pepper and pour it over the enchiladas.

Cover the casserole and bake the enchiladas in a preheated oven at 350 degrees for about 20 to 25 minutes. They should be very hot all the way through. If you like, you can uncover the casserole and brown the sauce under the broiler for a few minutes before serving.

Serve the enchiladas hot, and garnish them with extra sour cream and hot sauce if desired.

Serves 5.

egg enchiladas

6 oz. lightly salted, shelled pumpkin seeds
      (*pepitas*)
⅔ cup vegetable broth
3½ Tbs. lemon juice
2 cloves garlic, minced
½ cup plus 2 Tbs. chopped California green
      chilis
¼ tsp. salt, and more to taste
½ tsp. fresh-ground black pepper, and more
      to taste
1 cup heavy cream
10 large eggs
2 Tbs. water or milk
2½ Tbs. butter
2 Tbs. fresh-chopped cilantro (coriander
      leaves)
1 tsp. dried crushed red chili peppers
½ cup chopped green onions or scallions
10 corn tortillas
vegetable oil

Put the pumpkin seeds, vegetable broth, lemon juice, garlic, and green chilis in the container of a blender and whirl at high speed until the mixture is puréed. Add the salt, pepper, and cream and blend again for a very short time.

Beat the eggs in a large bowl with the water or milk, some salt and pepper, and the chopped cilantro. Melt the butter in a large skillet, heat the crushed red chilis in it for a moment, then add the eggs. Cook the eggs, stirring them constantly, until they are set but still moist.

Heat a tortilla by brushing a hot skillet with vegetable oil and placing the tortilla on it for 30 seconds to 1 minute on each side. The tortilla should be completely flexible.

Spread about 2 to 3 tablespoons of the cooked eggs down the center of the tortilla, then pour about 1 tablespoon of the pumpkin seed sauce over the eggs and roll up the tortilla over the filling. Continue until all the eggs are used up.

Arrange the enchiladas, seam side down, in a lightly oiled, shallow baking dish and spoon the remaining sauce over them. Bake the enchiladas in a preheated oven at 350 degrees for about 20 to 25 minutes, then place them under the broiler for a few moments to brown the top.

Sprinkle the enchiladas with chopped green onions or scallions and serve.

Serves 5.

enchiladas salsa verde

2   lbs. *tomatillos**
4   medium-sized jalapeño peppers, peeled, seeded, and minced**
6   Tbs. chopped fresh cilantro or coriander leaves (packed)
1   tsp. salt
1   cup finely chopped onions
vegetable oil for frying
1   lb. panella cheese, cut in thin strips (or fresh mozzarella)
16   corn tortillas
½   lb. farmer cheese, crumbled

optional garnish

hot sauce

Peel the dry skins off the *tomatillos*, wash them, and boil them in lightly salted water for 7 to 10 minutes, or until they are just soft. Drain, purée them in a blender, and put them in a saucepan with the minced jalapeño peppers, 4 table-spoons of the chopped cilantro, the salt, and ½ cup of the chopped onions. Simmer the sauce gently for about 40 minutes.

Heat a very small amount of vegetable oil in a pan and fry a tortilla in it for about 20 seconds on each side. Put 1 ounce of the panella cheese strips on it, spread about 1 teaspoon of the green sauce over the cheese, and sprinkle 1 rounded teaspoon of the remaining onions over the sauce. Roll the tortilla securely around the filling. Continue filling the tortillas in this manner until all the tortillas and cheese are used up. Add a little more oil to the pan whenever necessary.

Arrange the enchiladas seam side down and close together in a lightly oiled baking dish and spoon the remaining sauce over them. Bake the enchiladas in a preheated 350 degree oven for 15 to 20 minutes, then sprinkle the crumbled farmer cheese and the remaining cilantro over them and serve immediately.

Hot sauce can be passed separately for those who really want to clear their heads!

Serves 6 to 8.

*A kind of Mexican green tomato—small, hard, and covered with a dry husk. Do not confuse *tomatillos* with unripe common tomatoes. The *tomatillos* have a distinct, tart flavor and are inedible unless cooked.

**If they are not available fresh, jalapeño peppers can be bought canned. The peppers canned by Ortega have always been very good, in my opinion. Be sure to wash your hands carefully after handling hot peppers, and don't touch your eyes for at least an hour or two afterward.

bean and potato tacos

2 medium-sized potatoes (about 1 lb.)
½ onion
3 Tbs. butter
salt and pepper
14 fresh corn tortillas
vegetable oil for frying
1½ cups refried beans
hot sauce

garnish

chopped cabbage and tomatoes

Peel the potatoes and cut them into small cubes. Boil them in salted water until they are almost tender, then drain. Chop the onion and sauté in the butter for a few minutes and add the potatoes. Continue sautéing this mixture, stirring often, until the potatoes are tender and slightly golden, about 10 minutes. Season to taste with salt and pepper.

Warm the tortillas quickly, one at a time, on a hot griddle or pan. If you like, you may brush them very lightly with oil before warming. Be sure to take them off the heat quickly, or they will become crisp. They should be soft and flexible.

Put a rounded tablespoon of the refried beans on a tortilla and spread it across in a thick line down the center, almost to the ends. Add a heaping tablespoon of the potatoes, and arrange them, the same way, on top of the beans. Fold one side of the tortilla over the filling and roll it up, or if you prefer, simply fold the tortilla in half over the filling.

Just before serving, fry the tacos in a little bit of oil until they are crisp on both sides. Sprinkle them with hot sauce and chopped cabbage and tomatoes, and serve hot.

Serves 4 to 6.

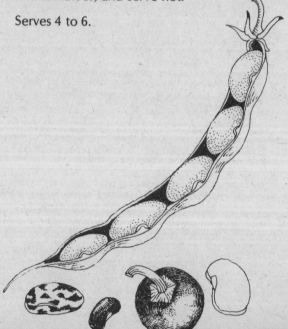

avocado tacos (flautas)

3   medium-sized ripe avocados
juice of 1 large lemon
salt to taste
½   clove garlic, pressed or minced
¼   cup minced onions
12   corn tortillas
vegetable oil for frying
1   cup sour cream
1   onion, chopped
6 to 8 oz. farmer cheese, crumbled

garnish

Fresh Tomato Hot Sauce (page 104)

Peel and mash the avocados, then stir in the lemon juice, a little salt, the garlic, and minced onions. Taste, and add more salt if you like.

Take one of the tortillas and heat it for a moment on each side, either in a lightly greased pan or directly over a gas flame. The instant it is warm enough to roll without cracking, spread a heaping tablespoon of the avocado filling in a slightly off-center line across the tortilla and roll it up around the filling. Continue until all the filling is used up.

Fry the rolled up tortillas in about ⅓ inch of hot vegetable oil, on both sides, until they are just crisp. Drain them quickly on paper towels and arrange them on plates.

Put a dollop of sour cream on each one, sprinkle with the chopped onions and crumbled cheese, and serve warm with Fresh Tomato Hot Sauce on the side.

Serves 5 to 6.

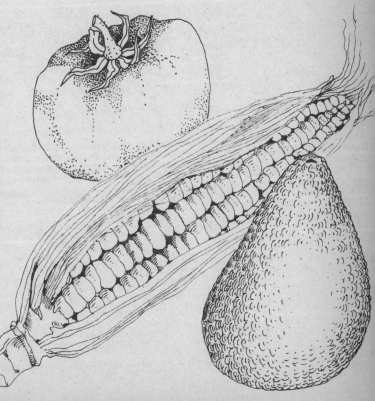

chilaquiles

The first time I ate *chilaquiles*, that thick, porridgelike mixture of fried tortillas, cheese, chilis, and changeable other ingredients, was when we were staying at the house of a friend in the little village of San José de Gracia, in the Mexican countryside. In the big, comfortable kitchen, we were served a breakfast of *chilaquiles*, fresh-made tortillas, hot sauce, *frijolitos* (as our host affectionately called his refried beans), and foamy hot chocolate. It was an eye-opening, sinus-clearing breakfast, and these *chilaquiles* are but a cool, northern shadow of the fiery dish we ate that morning—but what a great meal that was!

Good for breakfast, lunch, or supper, and quite hot enough for most North American palates, is this version of *chilaquiles*.

10 corn tortillas
vegetable oil for frying
salt
1 lb. *tomatillos* (see page 287)
1½ lbs. ripe red tomatoes
2 medium-sized yellow onions
1½ Tbs. olive oil
¾ cup diced green poblano chilis
2 to 3 jalapeño peppers, seeded and minced (see page 287)

2 Tbs. chopped fresh cilantro or coriander leaves (packed)
½ tsp. sugar
1 lb. cheese (Jack, Cheddar, or combination), grated
½ cup milk
½ cup sour cream

garnish

3 hard-boiled eggs, chopped
3 to 4 green onions, chopped
sour cream

Cut the tortillas into eighths and fry them in hot vegetable oil until they are crisp. Drain them on paper towels and sprinkle them lightly with salt.

Peel the dry skins off the *tomatillos*, wash them, and plunge them into boiling water. Boil them for 7 to 8 minutes, or until they start to split. Drain them immediately and purée them in a blender.

Boil the red tomatoes for about 3 minutes, peel them, and purée them as well.

Peel and coarsely chop the onions and sauté them in the olive oil, in a large skillet, until they are golden. Add the puréed *tomatillos* and tomatoes, the diced green chilis, the minced jalapeños, 1¼ teaspoon salt, cilantro, and sugar. Simmer this mixture for about 10 minutes. Taste, and correct the seasoning if necessary with more salt or a tiny bit more sugar.

Spoon a little of this sauce into the bottom of a large casserole. Spread ⅓ of the tortilla chips over the sauce, and arrange ⅓ of the cheese evenly over the chips. Spoon ⅓ of the remaining sauce over the cheese. Make 2 more layers the same way.

Stir together the milk and the sour cream and pour the mixture over the top of the casserole. Slip a knife through the top layer of sauce in a few places to allow some of the milk mixture to seep down.

Cover the casserole tightly and bake in a preheated oven at 375 degrees for 20 to 25 minutes, then remove the lid and bake for 10 minutes more.

Serve hot, and pass little bowls of chopped eggs, chopped green onions, and sour cream.

Serves 6 to 8.

chilaquiles with mushrooms

8 corn tortillas
vegetable oil for frying
salt to taste
1 lb. mushrooms
2 Tbs. olive oil
4 cloves garlic, minced or pressed
pinch of thyme
pinch of oregano
pepper to taste
1 cup sliced green onions

1 lb. tomatoes, peeled and puréed
6 Tbs. chopped green chilis
3 Tbs. chopped fresh cilantro (coriander leaves)
½ lb. Cheddar cheese, grated
3 eggs
1 cup milk

Cut the tortillas into strips about 1 inch wide and 2 inches long, and fry them in vegetable oil until they are crisp and golden. Drain the chips on paper towels and salt them lightly.

chilaquiles with mushrooms (continued)

Wash the mushrooms and slice them. Heat the olive oil in a large skillet and sauté the garlic in it until it begins to color. Add the sliced mushrooms and toss them over medium-high heat until they have released their water and most of it has evaporated. Add the thyme and oregano and some salt and pepper and toss again until the seasonings are evenly distributed. Put the mushrooms aside.

Heat about 1½ tablespoons of vegetable oil in a skillet and sauté the green onions in it for a few minutes. Add the tomatoes, chilis, cilantro, and some salt and pepper, and cook over medium heat for about 5 minutes. Add the mushrooms to the tomato sauce.

Lightly oil a large casserole and cover the bottom with ⅓ of the fried tortilla strips. Sprinkle ⅓ of the grated cheese over them and spoon ⅓ of the tomato-mushroom mixture over the cheese. Make 2 more similar layers.

Beat together the eggs and the milk and pour this custard over the casserole, slipping a knife through the top layer in a few places to allow the liquid to drain through evenly.

Cover the casserole and bake it in a preheated 350 degree oven for about 30 minutes. Serve quickly with a salad and fresh, hot tortillas.

Serves 6.

rajas con queso

(peppers with cheese)

This makes an excellent sauce or filling for omelets.

2¼ lbs. green bell peppers (about 5 large)
1½ lbs. tomatoes or 4 to 5 canned tomatoes
     and 1 cup juice

1   large yellow onion
1   large red onion
3   Tbs. olive oil
1½ tsp. salt
1   small hot green chili, minced
8   oz. cream cheese

Broil the peppers, turning them often, until their skins are evenly charred and blistered over the whole surface. Remove them from the broiler and run a little cool water over them, then quickly peel them. The skins should slip off easily. If you've never done this, have patience—the technique will come to you after 1 or 2 peppers.

Remove the seeds and ribs from the peppers and cut them up in ¼-inch strips.

If you are using fresh tomatoes, plunge them into boiling water for a few moments, then take them out, peel them, and cut them into thin wedges. Reserve all the juice that drains away as you handle the tomatoes.

Peel the onions, cut them in half lengthwise, and slice the halves ¼ inch thick. Heat the olive oil in a large skillet and sauté the onion slices in it until they are golden.

Add the tomatoes, the reserved tomato juice, the salt, the minced green chilis, and the bell pepper strips. Simmer this mixture until the tomatoes are soft (6 or 7 minutes), then slice the cream cheese and add it. Continue simmering the mixture, stirring often, until the cream cheese is melted and the sauce slightly thickened. Serve hot in bowls with warm tortillas.

Serves 6 as a first course or 4 as a main course.

refried kidney beans

6   Tbs. vegetable oil
2   Tbs. butter
1½ yellow onions
1   clove garlic, minced (optional)
4½ cups cooked kidney beans
2   cups cooking liquid from beans
salt to taste

garnish

grated mild cheese such as Jack, mild Cheddar

Heat the oil and the butter together in a large, heavy skillet. Chop the onions and sauté them in the oil and butter until they are golden. If you want to add garlic, sauté it with the onions at this point.

Add the beans and their cooking liquid and lower the flame slightly. Cook the beans, stirring often, until most of the liquid has been absorbed. Mash some of the beans with a wooden spoon—some people prefer to mash all the beans; I like mine about half-mashed,

refried kidney beans (continued)

but this is just a matter of taste. Continue cooking and stirring—for perhaps ½ hour—until the beans have the consistency of a fairly thick paste.

Serve hot as a side dish or use as a filling for tacos, either alone or with cooked potatoes. If served as a side dish, some grated cheese should be sprinkled on top or stirred in.

Serves 4 to 6.

spicy refried beans

1½ cups dried red kidney beans
6 cups water
2 Tbs. corn oil
1½ onions
3 tsp. salt
¼ cup olive oil
3 cloves garlic, minced
1 cup peeled, chopped tomatoes
2 small jalapeño peppers, seeded and
 minced (see page 287)
2 Tbs. lemon juice
¼ tsp. cinnamon
⅛ tsp. cloves
1 Tbs. butter
1 cup grated Jack cheese (optional)

Rinse the beans and put them in a large pot with the water, corn oil, ½ of an onion, chopped, and 2 teaspoons of the salt. Bring the water to a boil, then turn down the heat, cover the pot, and simmer the beans gently for about 1½ hours. Remove the cover and cook the beans a little while longer, until completely tender and the remaining liquid is thick.

In a very large skillet, heat the olive oil and sauté remaining onion, chopped, and the garlic until golden. Add the tomatoes, jalapeño peppers, lemon juice, and spices. Pour the beans, together with their liquid, into the seasonings and stir.

Over a low flame, and stirring often, cook the beans together with the seasonings until the mixture is quite thick, but still moist. Time will vary, but it could take as long as 45 minutes. If the beans become too dry, just add a little water. Stir in the butter and, if desired, the grated cheese. Continue stirring the beans over the low flame until both butter and cheese are melted.

Serves 6.

tortitas con queso

(savory Mexican cheese tarts)

We were having margaritas before dinner one evening in a wonderful restaurant in Mexico City and thought we should have something to nibble with them. The young waiter read our minds—he knew just what we wanted even though we had never heard of it and brought us a plate of fresh, hot *tortitas*. The rest of the dinner has long faded from memory, but ah! those *tortitas*.

They were little pastries, made of *masa*, just like corn tortillas, but fatter—and with edges. I never did find out the name of the cheese but have recaptured its slightly goaty flavor by combining simple dry white farmer cheese with some feta.

2   cups dry *masa harina**
1   cup water
salt
vegetable oil (about 2 Tbs.)
¼ to ⅓ cup medium-hot green chili sauce
4   oz. farmer cheese, crumbled
2   oz. feta cheese, crumbled

*Masa harina is corn treated with lime water and ground to a very fine meal. The Quaker Oats Company sells a good, dry *masa harina*.

Combine the *masa harina* and the water in a bowl, add a little salt, and work it into a dough. Divide the dough into 14 or 15 even bits the size of large walnuts. Shape each one into an even, flat round, about 3 or 4 inches across, and turn up the edges to make a ¼-inch rim. Brush the insides of these shells lightly with vegetable oil.

Bake the *tortita* shells for 20 to 25 minutes in a preheated oven at 450 degrees. They should be slightly darker and almost crisp around the edges.

When they are cool enough to handle, spread each one evenly with a scant teaspoon of the green chili sauce. Combine the two cheeses in a bowl and crumble them together until they are thoroughly integrated. Divide the cheese evenly among the *tortitas*, sprinkling it over the chili sauce.

Serve the *tortitas* with any tequila drink or with beers as an hors d'oeuvre.

Makes 14 to 15 *tortitas*.

mexican rice

2   large onions
3 to 4 cloves garlic, minced
¼   cup olive oil
½   tsp. ginger
½   tsp. ground coriander seeds
¼   tsp. ground cloves
¼   tsp. fresh-ground black pepper
2   cups long-grain white rice
3   cups puréed tomatoes
2   tsp. salt
1½   cups boiling water

Peel and coarsely chop the onions, mince the garlic, and sauté them both in the olive oil until the onions are golden. Add the ginger, coriander, cloves, and pepper, stir, then add the rice. Continue sautéing the mixture, stirring often, until the rice is slightly colored.

Add the puréed tomatoes, the salt, and the boiling water. Stir the mixture once, then cover and simmer the rice over low heat for another 25 minutes. All the liquid should be absorbed.

Serve the rice hot with enchiladas, Rajas con Queso (page 292), or anything at all!

Serves 8.

guacamole

2   lbs. ripe avocados
¼   cup lemon juice
¼   cup minced onion
¼   cup chopped fresh cilantro (coriander
       leaves)
½   lb. tomatoes (about 2 medium sized)
5   Tbs. finely chopped green chilis
1¾   tsp. salt

Cut the avocados in half lengthwise, remove the pits, and scoop out the meat. In a medium-sized bowl, mash the avocado with a silver fork or wooden spoon.

Add the lemon juice, onions, and cilantro. Coarsely chop the tomatoes and add them to the avocado, along with the chilis and the salt. Stir everything together thoroughly and serve chilled with fried tortilla chips.

Serves 6 to 8.

strawberry water

2 lbs. fresh, ripe strawberries
2 cups water
⅓ cup honey
2 Tbs. lemon juice
10 to 12 ice cubes

Hull and wash the strawberries, and purée them in a blender with the water, in 2 or 3 batches. Strain the purée through a fine sieve and discard the seeds.

Stir in the honey and lemon juice thoroughly, and when the honey is completely dissolved, chill the mixture well. Just before serving, add the ice cubes and stir again.

Serves 6.

cantaloupe water

5½ lbs. ripe cataloupe (about 3 medium sized)
1 to 1½ cups cold water
¼ cup honey
10 to 12 large ice cubes

Peel and seed the cantaloupes and cut the fruit into chunks. Purée the fruit in a blender, doing about 2 or 3 cups at a time and adding a little cold water as necessary.

When all the fruit is puréed, stir in the honey and continue stirring until the honey is completely dissolved into the fruit juice. Add the ice cubes, stir, and chill for about ½ hour before serving. If the liquid is too thick for your taste, add a little more cold water.

Delicious with spicy Mexican food.

Serves 6 to 8.

See Soups for Tortilla Soup Tlaxcalteca, Crema de Verduras, Creamed Avocado Soup, and Cold Avocado Soup.

indian foods: curries, raitas, pilaus, etc.

I've never been to India, but I have been to what must be the next best place for sampling and enjoying Indian food—London. The culinary pleasures of that city are vastly enriched by a wealth of Indian restaurants which reflect all the variety of that ancient, sophisticated cuisine, and I've spent many a glad hour pursuing my interest in it at the tables of those fragrant establishments.

Reproducing the more complicated Indian dishes, in all their refinement, is not really possible in a Western kitchen—our tools are different, and many of the necessary ingredients may not be available. Nonetheless, a gratifying range of the simpler and more adaptable dishes can be concocted with relative ease: It only takes a modicum of effort to procure a few unusual but definitely obtainable spices, and you're on your way. The recipes that follow are but a tiny sampling, a few favorites of my own which can be successfully reproduced here without extraordinary measures. The cooking of India is so wonderful and involves such a highly developed meatless cuisine, that it would be a sin to bypass it just because we don't live in a land of buffalo milk, bazaars, itinerant spice grinders and *halvais*, and thus find some of its delicacies elusive. Anyway, I'm hooked on it.

You probably needn't go far to find the spices and herbs you'll need. Perhaps you're familiar with a grocery store that specializes in imported foods; in that case, your problems are over because nothing impossibly exotic is required. If you don't know of such a place, a well-stocked supermarket will provide most of your needs, and the few harder-to-find items can be ordered by mail.* Occasionally, substitutions can be made, but certain ingredients cannot be changed for others without a substantial loss in the texture or flavor that makes a dish what it is. I recommend making the effort to search out what you need or to send for it.

Fresh coriander leaves (cilantro), for example, have a delightfully pungent taste and aroma that no amount of parsley can ever duplicate, although this substitution is suggested in some cookbooks. Fresh ginger is a very different thing from the ground dried ginger you'll find in the spice rack—each has its own uses. Both fresh coriander leaves and fresh ginger can easily be found in Chinese neighborhoods. And there is no substitute for saffron. Turmeric provides a pleasant yellow color at a fraction of the cost, but only saffron tastes like saffron. It is the costliest spice in the world because it

*Write to India Bazaar, 10651 Pico Boulevard, Los Angeles, California 90064; or Sahadi Importing Co., Inc., 187 Atlantic Avenue, Brooklyn, New York 11201. It's a good idea to inquire first to find out what is in stock and what the current prices are.

is made from the stamens of crocus blossoms, and thousands of them are needed to make a single ounce. But the good news is that a little goes a long way.

Dried chilis can be bought anywhere, and fresh chilis are now widely available in many parts of the United States as well. However, if fresh chilis are not to be found, canned chilis do make an acceptable replacement for them. As to the rest, I've never had difficulty buying coriander seeds, cumin, mustard seeds, turmeric, fennel, sesame seeds, or cinnamon in the spice section of any ordinary supermarket, so it's really not so difficult.

I've always found the actual cooking of Indian food a pleasurable experience. The kitchen is filled with the heady aromas of spices from the very start, aromas that conjure up mysterious, distant lands. The colors are beautiful, and the sizzling and popping of mustard seeds or ginger when they are heated in oil keeps one wide awake. Another part of the fun is finding out that curries need not all taste alike, as they do when commercially bottled curry powders are used. As soon as you start using recipes which call for individual mixtures of spices, you'll happily notice that each curry has a distinctive flavor and character of its own. But the nicest surprise is how fast it all goes. A recipe with a list of ingredients as long as your arm shouldn't put you off: It will all find its way into the pot with gratifying speed. Before long, you'll be tasting, and then the real enjoyment starts.

Finally, such dishes always look so exotic and brilliant when they are served. Nothing is easier than serving an Indian meal, for all the dishes are put on the table at once—even the sweet can be brought out with the rest, though we usually succumb to our Western habits in that case and serve it later. The effect is opulent and colorful. In addition to the five or six dishes which make up a well-designed meal, the table is also peppered with an intriguing array of little bowls full of chutneys, pickles, fruits, nuts, raisins, and other condiments—all in all, a dazzling spread.

Everyone proceeds according to his or her own inclination, sampling and combining, to taste, from the rich assortment. Spicy and hot foods are pleasingly contrasted with cooling yogurt *raitas,* or fresh fruit, and dry dishes with moist, rich ones. The quick, hot Indian breads, perfect for scooping up all these things, should be provided in quantity. *Puris* and *chapatis* (see Breads section) are easy to make and delicious. Both are unleavened and made of whole wheat flour. *Puris* are fried in oil, and puffed like little balloons; the griddle-cooked *chapatis* are flat, and a little thicker.

The perfect drink to sip with Indian food is a good pale ale, icy cold, or a gin and tonic with a slice of lime. A hot, sweetly spiced tea can also be very pleasant. I don't recommend wine, as I have not yet discovered the wine which can bring out the best in Indian foods and which is, in turn, enhanced by that well-spiced cuisine.

If you take a fancy to Indian cooking, as I have, you'll see that the strange and bewildering will soon become very manageable and familiar, but with such foods, never ordinary. It is one of the great cuisines of the world, and even the rather elementary level at which it is sampled here does not fall short of gastronomic excitement.

ghee

Ghee is nothing more complicated than clarified butter, and it is one of the staple ingredients used in all types of Indian cooking. Sometimes regular, unclarified butter can be used in a recipe that calls for ghee, but often clarified butter is absolutely necessary. Unclarified butter will quickly burn at high temperatures, whereas ghee will not, and that is a quality that will earn your gratitude when you start to cook Indian food. Clarifying butter is quite a simple procedure, in any case, and well worth the small trouble for the superior results it will yield.

Once clarified, butter will keep for weeks and weeks in the refrigerator, and for quite a while even without refrigeration, so you need to do this job only once in a long while.

To make ghee, melt a pound or more of butter over low heat in a heavy-bottomed saucepan, being careful not to let it brown. When it is entirely melted, skim off all the foam from the top and discard it. Raise the heat until the butter foams up again, then skim off the foam once more. Repeat this procedure another couple of times, or until all the foam is gone and a clear, golden liquid is left.

Remove from the heat and carefully pour the melted butter off into a bowl or other container until only the fine sediment at the bottom of the pan is left. Discard the sediment.

curried vegetables with coconut

¼ cup vegetable oil
3 cloves garlic, minced
1 Tbs. peeled and grated fresh ginger
½ cup chopped onions
1 tsp. mustard seeds
2 Tbs. ground coriander
1 tsp. ground turmeric
¼ tsp. cayenne pepper
1 cup thin-sliced carrots
½ lb. string beans, cut in 1-inch lengths
1 cup sliced green onions
2 green bell peppers, stemmed, seeded, and cut in strips
1 small, hot green chili, minced
1 cup flaked unsweetened coconut
2 cups water
1½ tsp. salt
2 tsp. sugar
½ cup peeled, sliced pimiento pepper
⅔ cup yogurt

Heat the oil in a large, heavy-bottomed pot and sauté the garlic, ginger, and onions in it until the onions begin to show color. Add the mustard seeds, coriander, turmeric, and cayenne, and stir over medium heat for about 2 minutes.

Add the carrots, string beans, green onions, bell peppers, and hot chili and toss with the spices for a few minutes, then add the coconut, water, salt, and sugar. Stir well, cover, and simmer for about 20 minutes. Remove the lid and continue simmering, stirring often, until the liquid is reduced by over half.

Stir in the pimiento strips and yogurt, cook a few minutes more over high heat, and taste. Correct the seasoning if necessary and serve hot with rice and *raitas*.

Serves 6 to 8.

curried cabbage and peas

1   medium-sized head green cabbage
3   Tbs. vegetable oil
1   tsp. crushed dried red chilis
½   tsp. ground ginger
½   tsp. whole mustard seeds
½   tsp. ground cumin
2   bay leaves
1   tsp. ground coriander
½   tsp. ground turmeric
2   tsp. salt
1   cup water
2½ cups fresh peas
1   Tbs. butter
1½ tsp. Garam Masala (page 321)
1   Tbs. lemon juice
½   tsp. sugar
1 to 2 Tbs. yogurt (optional)

Shred the cabbage coarsely. Heat the vegetable oil in a large skillet and stir in the crushed red chilis, ginger, mustard seeds, cumin, bay leaves, coriander, turmeric, and salt. Heat the spices gently for about 2 minutes, stirring often.

Add the shredded cabbage and sauté it, stirring often, until it is all evenly coated with the spices and beginning to wilt, 10 to 15 minutes. Add the water and the peas, cover, and cook over medium heat for 20 minutes.

Remove the cover, stir in the butter, garam masala, lemon juice, and sugar, and simmer, uncovered, for another 10 to 15 minutes. There should be very little or no excess liquid at this point.

Stir in a little yogurt if desired and serve hot with rice and raita.

Serves 6 to 8.

curried garbanzo beans

3   cups cooked garbanzo beans, with
      reserved liquid (see page 143)
1   Tbs. butter or oil
1   tsp. ground coriander
1   tsp. ground cumin
1   tsp. ground turmeric
¼   tsp. cayenne pepper, or to taste
⅜   tsp. ground cloves
⅜   tsp. cinnamon
3   cloves garlic, minced
⅓   tsp. ground ginger
salt to taste
2   Tbs. lemon juice, and more to taste
1   Tbs. chopped fresh cilantro (coriander
      leaves), and more to taste
1   firm tomato, cut in ½-inch dice.

Melt the butter in a saucepan and over low heat stir in the spices. Allow them to heat, stirring often, for a few minutes.

Stir in the garbanzo beans and enough of the reserved liquid to just barely cover them. Stir well, and mash a few of the beans with a fork or potato masher.

Cook the beans over a medium flame for about 20 minutes, or until the sauce is quite thick, stirring often. Remove from heat.

Stir in the lemon juice, the chopped cilantro, and the diced tomato. Taste, and correct the seasoning.

Serves 4 to 6.

cauliflower curry

1   large head cauliflower
1   small potato (6 to 8 oz.)
4   Tbs. vegetable oil
1   tsp. black mustard seeds
1   tsp. ground turmeric
½   tsp. ground cumin
½   tsp. ground coriander
½   tsp. cayenne pepper
1   clove garlic, minced or crushed
½   onion, slivered
1   tsp. salt
1¼ cups water
1   medium-sized tomato, chopped
2   Tbs. lemon juice

Trim and wash the cauliflower and break it up into very small flowerettes. Scrub the potato and boil it in salted water until it is nearly tender, but not quite done.

Heat the oil in a fairly large skillet over medium-low heat and add the mustard seeds, heating until the seeds pop, just a few minutes. When the mustard seeds have finished popping, add the turmeric, cumin, coriander, cayenne, garlic, and onions. Sauté this mixture over medium heat, stirring constantly, for 3 to 4 minutes.

Add the cauliflower and sauté, stirring often, for 4 to 5 minutes, then add the salt and water and cover the pan tightly. Allow the curry to simmer, covered, for 5 minutes, while you cut up the parboiled potato into 1-inch cubes.

Add the potato, stir, cover again, and leave to simmer for 10 minutes. Then add the tomato and the lemon juice and stir, uncovered, over medium heat, for another few minutes before serving.

Serve hot with rice, *raita*, chutneys, and other condiments.

Serves 4.

egg and potato curry

spice paste

1   large onion, grated
2   cloves garlic, minced or crushed
1   tsp. crushed dried red chilis
1   Tbs. peeled and grated fresh ginger
2   tsp. minced green chilis
½   tsp. ground turmeric
½   tsp. ground cumin
2   tsps. ground coriander
2   Tbs. water
½   tsp. salt, and more to taste

2   lbs. potatoes
3   Tbs. vegetable oil
⅔   cup water
3   large tomatoes, cut in thin wedges or
       chopped
2   bay leaves
7   hard-boiled eggs

Combine all the ingredients for the paste and pound them together in a large mortar or blend them for several minutes in a blender or food processor.

Scrub the potatoes and cut them in 1-inch cubes, then sauté them in the vegetable oil, stirring constantly until they start to show some color, about 10 minutes. Add the spice paste and continue stirring over medium heat for another 5 minutes.

Add ⅔ cup water, the tomatoes, and the bay leaves, stir, cover, and simmer over low heat for 20 minutes. Uncover the curry and simmer another 10 minutes, stirring occasionally.

Coarsely chop the hard-boiled eggs, add them to the vegetables, and stir over low heat for several more minutes, just until the eggs are heated through. Add a little more salt if needed, and serve.

Serves 8.

spiced eggplant

2 lbs. eggplant
3 to 4 cups Akni (page 319)
2 Tbs. ground coriander
1½ tsp. salt
½ tsp. ground black pepper
¼ tsp. cayenne pepper
2 tsp. peeled and minced fresh ginger
3 Tbs. fresh lemon juice
3 Tbs. butter or Ghee (page 301)

garnish

chopped chives or fresh cilantro (coriander
    leaves)

Peel the eggplants and cut them in strips
lengthwise, 1 inch wide and about ½ inch
thick. Cut the long strips in 2-inch lengths.

Heat the Akni in a medium-sized enameled
saucepan and simmer the eggplant strips in it
for about 15 minutes, or until they are just
tender. Drain the eggplant well.

Combine the coriander, salt, black pepper,
cayenne, minced ginger, and lemon juice in a
small bowl and mix it all into a smooth paste.

Melt the butter or *ghee* in a fairly large skillet
and sauté the eggplant strips for 5 minutes

only, stirring and tossing them constantly. Add
the spice paste and stir often over medium heat
for about 10 to 15 minutes, or until all the
eggplant strips are evenly coated with spices
and nearly dry. There should be no excess
moisture.

Serve the eggplant hot, sprinkled with chopped
chives or coriander leaves.

Serves 6 to 8.

green curry

So called because of its color, but red-hot from the seasoning point of view. Don't be frightened off because it's truly delcious, but on the other hand, this isn't the curry to start with if you've never made one before and are unaccustomed to spicy foods. (Serve it with plain rice *pilau* and some yogurt or *raita*.)

1	lb. potatoes
1	lb. green beans
¾	lb. zucchini
1	lb. spinach
5	Tbs. butter
1½	lbs. onions
10	medium-sized cloves garlic
2	tsp. ground turmeric
1	Tbs. ground coriander
1	Tbs. ground cumin
½	tsp. hot paprika
½	tsp. cayenne pepper
½	tsp. black pepper
¼	tsp. cinnamon
1½	tsp. salt
1½	Tbs. peeled and grated fresh ginger
4	Tbs. chopped green chilis
2	Tbs. lemon juice
¾	cup water

Scrub or peel the potatoes, quarter them lengthwise, and slice thickly. Boil in salted water for 5 minutes only, drain, and set aside.

Trim the green beans and cut them in 1-inch pieces. Boil them in salted water for 5 minutes, drain, and set aside.

Slice the zucchini rather thickly, boil them in salted water for 3 to 4 minutes only, drain, and set aside.

Wash and coarsely chop the spinach and set it aside.

Melt the butter in a large pot. Halve and thickly slice the onions and crush or mince the garlic, and sauté them in the butter until the onions begin to color. Then add the turmeric, coriander, cumin, hot paprika, cayenne, black pepper, cinnamon, and salt.

Stir this mixture over a medium flame for a few minutes, then add the prepared vegetables, the ginger, green chilis, lemon juice, and water. Stir all the vegetables and spices together thoroughly and simmer, stirring again frequently, until most of the water is gone and the vegetables are just tender.

Serves 6 to 8.

smothered potatoes

2   lbs. potatoes
2   tsp. ground turmeric
1   Tbs. Garam Masala (page 321)
2   tsp. salt
½   tsp. ground cumin
½   tsp. black pepper
⅓   cup yogurt
3   Tbs. butter
2   bay leaves
1   tsp. crushed dried red pepper
1   tsp. sugar

Peel the potatoes and cut them in 1-inch chunks. Boil them in salted water until they are about half done, 8 to 10 minutes. Drain them and prick them a little with a fork.

Make a paste of turmeric, *garam masala*, salt, cumin, black pepper, and yogurt. Roll the hot potatoes in this paste until they are all thoroughly coated.

Melt the butter in a medium-sized, shallow, fireproof casserole and add the bay leaves and red pepper, stir them over low heat for a few minutes, then add the sugar. In a few minutes, when the sugar just begins to caramelize (to turn light brown), add the potatoes, stir and toss them gently for a few minutes, then cover the casserole tightly and bake in a preheated 350 degree oven for about 30 minutes.

Serves 6.

purée of scorched tomatoes

2   lbs. ripe, red tomatoes
2   Tbs. butter
1   tsp. dried basil, crushed
1   tsp. black pepper
½   tsp. crushed saffron threads
¼   tsp. thyme

salt to taste
¼   cup heavy cream

Put the tomatoes under a broiler and turn them often until they are lightly charred all over. Let the tomatoes cool slightly, or hold them under

purée of scorched tomatoes (continued)

cold running water, and slip off the skins. Cut the tomatoes into chunks and purée them in a blender.

Melt the butter in a large skillet and add the basil, pepper, saffron, and thyme. Sauté the herbs and spices, stirring, for 2 minutes, then pour in the tomato purée, and stir in 2 teaspoon of salt, or more to your taste.

Simmer the purée very gently, stirring occasionally, until it is very thick, about 1½ hours. Stir in the cream and stir over high heat, just long enough to regain the right consistency: that of a thin paste.

The purée can be served hot or cool, but I personally prefer it hot. Serve it as a rich, mild accompaniment to spicy Indian dishes.

Serves 6 to 8.

dal

Any purée or souplike dish of spiced lentils, thin or thick, hotly or mildly spiced, is called *dal*. The variations on this theme are endless.

1 cup lentils
1 qt. water
1 tsp. salt
2 Tbs. peeled and grated fresh ginger
¼ tsp. ground turmeric
crushed seeds from 4 cardamom pods
¼ tsp. cayenne pepper
2½ Tbs. butter
½ tsp. crushed dried red pepper
½ tsp. ground cumin
2 Tbs. chopped fresh cilantro (coriander leaves)
lemon juice

Rinse the lentils and combine them in a medium-sized saucepan with the water and salt. Bring the water to a boil, then lower the heat and simmer for 1 hour, skimming off the top as needed. Add the grated ginger, turmeric, crushed cardamom seeds, and cayenne and continue simmering until the lentils are perfectly tender. Add more water if the mixture gets too thick—it should have the consistency of a thick soup or thin gravy.

Melt the butter in a small skillet and sauté the crushed red pepper and cumin in it for a few minutes. Stir the butter and spices into the lentils, along with the fresh coriander leaves and a little lemon juice.

Serve the *dal* hot with curries and rice.

Serves 4 to 6.

plain pilau

This is a fragrant, delicate, slightly sweet rice dish: perfect with a searingly hot curry. It is called plain because some others are very much more complicated, but it is actually not plain at all; rather, quite wonderful.

4 Tbs. butter
2 cups long-grain white rice
¼ tsp. cinnamon
crushed seeds from 8 cardamom pods
¾ cup blanched, slivered almonds*
½ cup raisins
1 cup shelled fresh peas

*To blanch almonds, drop them for a minute in boiling water, then slip off the brown skins as soon as they are loose enough.

4 cups hot water
1½ tsp. salt

Melt the butter in a large, fireproof casserole and fry the rice in it over low heat until it just starts to color. Add the cinnamon and the crushed cardamom seeds. Stir, and continue frying for 1 or 2 minutes.

Add the remaining ingredients and stir briefly. Bring the water to a boil, then lower the heat, cover the casserole, tightly, and let the rice steam for about 20 minutes. All the water should be absorbed and the rice just tender but not mushy.

Serves 6 to 8.

vegetable pilau

This *pilau* is a rather elaborate and satisfying dish and makes a nice meal when served with yogurt or *raita*, an assortment of chutneys, some *chapatis*, and fresh fruit. With the addition of *dal* and a vegetable curry, the meal becomes a feast.

5   Tbs. butter or Ghee (page 301)
2   large onions, chopped
2   bay leaves, crushed
½   tsp. ground cloves
½   tsp. cinnamon
1   tsp. peeled and grated or minced fresh ginger
½   cup potato, cut in small dice
½   cup cauliflower, coarsely chopped
½   cup shelled fresh peas
½   cup carrots, cut in small dice
½   cup green beans, cut in ½-inch pieces
½   cup summer squash, cut in small dice
½   cup green bell pepper, cut in small dice
2½ cups long-grain white rice
½ to ¾ tsp. crushed saffron threads
5   cups water
2   tsp. salt
½ to ⅓ cup coarsely chopped cashews
½ to ⅓ cup raisins

Heat the butter or *ghee* in a large pot and sauté the onions and bay leaves in it until the onions begin to color. Add the cloves, cinnamon, and ginger and stir over medium heat for a minute, then add all the prepared vegetables, the rice, and the saffron. Toss over medium heat for about 5 minutes, then add the water and salt. Bring the water to a boil, turn the heat down to low, cover the pot tightly, and cook for 25 to 30 minutes. All the water should be absorbed.

Add the cashews and raisins and mix everything together by gently lifting and tossing with wooden spoons. Spoon the mixture into a large, well-buttered casserole, cover, and bake in a preheated oven at 350 degrees for about 20 minutes. Serve the *pilau* steaming hot from the casserole.

Serves 6 to 8.

saffron rice

½ tsp. crushed saffron threads
3 Tbs. warm milk
2 Tbs. butter
⅓ cup currants
⅓ cup shelled, chopped pistachio nuts
1½ cups long-grain white rice
3 cups water
1 tsp. salt
1 Tbs. sugar
large pinch of cinnamon

Dissolve the saffron in the warm milk.

Melt the butter in a medium-large saucepan and add the currants, pistachio nuts, and rice to it. Stir over low heat for several minutes, then add the water, salt, sugar, cinnamon, and dissolved saffron.

Stir once, raise the heat, and bring the water to a boil, then lower the heat, cover, and barely simmer for 25 minutes. Serve immediately.

Serves 6 to 8.

tomato raita

1 lb. ripe tomatoes
1 cup shredded coconut
2 Tbs. minced green chilis
½ tsp. salt
2 cups yogurt
1 Tbs. vegetable oil
1½ tsp. whole mustard seeds
½ tsp. crushed dried red pepper

Chop the tomatoes coarsely. If you have fresh-grated or pregrated but unsweetened coconut, combine it with the tomatoes in a bowl. If, as sometimes happens, you are only able to find the sweetened kind, soak it first in several rinses of water, then drain thoroughly and add to the tomatoes. Add the chilis, salt, and yogurt as well and mix it all up.

Heat the oil in a small skillet and fry the mustard seeds and crushed pepper in it until the mustard seeds start to jump and snap. Pour this all into the yogurt mixture and stir it in quickly.

Chill the *raita* for several hours before serving.

Serves 6 to 8.

banana and coconut raita

2   Tbs. butter or Ghee (page 301)
1   tsp. mustard seeds
¼   tsp. cayenne pepper
½   cup flaked unsweetened coconut
2   ripe bananas, mashed
½   tsp. salt
1   tsp. sugar
2   cups yogurt

Heat the butter or *ghee* in a medium-sized, heavy-bottomed saucepan and add the mustard seeds. Stir the seeds over medium heat for a minute or two, then stir in the cayenne. After another minute, add the coconut and bananas, remove from heat, and stir quickly. Add the remaining ingredients, beat together lightly with a fork, and chill for several hours before serving.

Serves 6 to 8.

cucumber raita

1   large cucumber
2 to 3 Tbs. finely chopped onions
2   cups yogurt
¼   tsp. ground cumin
⅛   tsp. cayenne pepper
salt
chopped fresh cilantro (coriander leaves)

Peel the cucumber, seed it, and coarsely grate it. Stir together the cucumber, onions, and yogurt.

Heat the ground cumin for a moment in a small enameled pan, then remove it from the heat and quickly stir in a little of the yogurt mixture. Return the yogurt-cumin mixture to the rest and stir thoroughly.

Stir in the cayenne, salt to taste, and as much chopped cilantro as you like. Serve chilled with curries or other Indian dishes.

Serves 4 to 6.

eggplant raita

1 large eggplant (about 1½ lbs.)
2 Tbs. vegetable oil
⅓ cup chopped onions
1 tsp. peeled and grated fresh ginger
1 tsp. Garam Masala (page 321)
¼ tsp. cayenne pepper
1 small tomato, coarsely chopped
1 tsp. salt, or more to taste
2 cups yogurt
1 Tbs. coarsely chopped fresh cilantro
    (coriander leaves)

Prick the eggplant with a fork in several places and roast it in a preheated 400 degree oven until it is completely soft and collapsed—about 1 hour. Allow it to cool slightly, then split it in half and scoop out all the pulp. Drain off the excess liquid and coarsely chop the pulp.

Heat the vegetable oil in a medium-sized saucepan and sauté the onions in it until they are translucent. Add the grated ginger, *garam masala*, and cayenne. Stir over low heat for about 2 minutes, then add the chopped tomato. As soon as the tomato is starting to get soft, remove from heat and stir in the eggplant pulp, salt, yogurt, and cilantro. Taste, and adjust the seasoning with more salt if necessary.

Chill the *raita* for an hour or two before serving.

Serves 6 to 8.

cachumber *(an Indian salad)*

2   large tomatoes
1   large cucumber
½   cup chopped green onions
½   cup thinly sliced radishes
2   Tbs. coarsely chopped fresh cilantro
       (coriander leaves)
2   Tbs. lemon juice
¾   tsp. salt
1   tsp. finely minced green chilis
black pepper to taste

Cut the tomatoes in ½-inch chunks, Peel and seed the cucumber and cut it in ½-inch dice. Combine the tomatoes, cucumber, green onions, radishes, and cilantro in a bowl.

Mix together the lemon juice, salt, and minced green chilis, and pour over the vegetables. Toss everything together so that it is thoroughly combined and add a little black pepper to taste. Chill for about ½ hour, toss again, and serve.

Serves 4 to 6.

uppama

(farina with vegetables and spices)

¼   cup vegetable oil
1   medium-sized yellow onion, chopped
1½ tsp. whole mustard seeds
1   green chili, minced
1   tsp. crushed dried red chilis
1   cup farina
5   cups hot water
½   cup sliced green onions
⅓   cup finely diced carrots
1   large, ripe tomato, diced
2   tsp. salt

optional garnish

lemon juice and cilantro (coriander leaves)

Heat the vegetable oil in a large saucepan and sauté the onions in it until it is translucent. Add the mustard seeds and both chilis and stir over medium heat for a minute or two. Add the farina and stir for another few minutes.

Still stirring, gradually add the hot water. Beat lightly with a whisk to get rid of any lumps. Add the green onions, diced carrots and tomato, and the salt. Simmer the mixture, stirring often, until it is quite thick, and the vegetables are tender. This may take as long as 45 minutes to 1 hour, over low heat.

Serves 8 to 10.

raisin and tamarind chutney
(a fresh chutney)

1 cup raisins
1 Tbs. tamarind concentrate*
6 to 8 Tbs. water
½ tsp. ground ginger
¼ tsp. cayenne pepper
¼ tsp. salt

Combine all the ingredients in a blender or food processor and purée, scraping down as necessary, until there are no lumps left. Add a bit more water if needed to make a mixture that is thick and not stiff.

This chutney is ready to use immediately, and will keep for a week or two if properly covered and refrigerated.

Makes about 1½ cups.

*Tamarind concentrate is a very thick, dark paste which can be purchased in specialty stores stocking foods imported from India. The thick tamarind juice that is reconstituted from the concentrate has a pungent, tart flavor and combines wonderfully with the sweetness of raisins.

khagina *(Indian spiced omelet)*

5 large eggs
5 Tbs. chick-pea flour
dash of black pepper
¼ tsp. ground coriander
crushed seeds from 4 to 5 cardamom pods
½ tsp. salt
½ cup minced or finely chopped onions
2 Tbs. chopped fresh parsley
3 to 4 Tbs. yogurt
3 Tbs. butter

Beat the eggs, gradually sprinkling in the chick-pea flour, then add all the remaining ingredients except the butter and beat together thoroughly.

Melt the butter in a 9-inch skillet and pour the egg mixture into it. Cook over low heat, covered, until the eggs are set on top. Flip the omelet out onto a plate and slide it back into the pan on the other side. Cook it for a few minutes more, just enough to lightly brown the other side, and then turn it out on a platter.

Serve the omelet in wedges as an accompaniment to a vegetable curry or with a chutney. It can be served warm or at room temperature.

Serves 4 to 5.

pakoras *(hot vegetable fritters)*

Pakoras are spicy fritters, ideal to serve hot as an appetizer or snack, with a tall, cool drink. Try them with a gin and tonic, or a Pimm's and soda with a slice of cucumber in it.

⅔ cup chick-pea flour
¼ tsp. baking soda
5 Tbs. cold water
¼ tsp. ground cumin
¼ tsp. cayenne pepper
1 scant tsp. salt
¼ tsp. ground turmeric
pinch of crushed saffron threads
½ cup finely diced potato
½ cup slivered onions (paper-thin slices, 1 to 1½ inches long)
2 Tbs. finely chopped fresh cilantro (coriander leaves)
2 cups vegetable oil

Mix together the chick-pea flour, baking soda, and cold water, stirring or rubbing the dough between your fingers until it is absolutely smooth and free from lumps. Add the cumin, cayenne, salt, turmeric, and saffron and stir again until well combined. Stir in the potato and the onions.

Heat the vegetable oil in a 10- to 12-inch wok until it is about 350 degrees. Stir up the batter, scoop up a teaspoonful of it and, with a second spoon, slide it off into the hot oil. Fry 6 or 7 *pakoras* at once, for about 8 minutes, or until they are a light golden brown all over. Scoop them out with a slotted spoon, drain on paper towels, and serve hot.

Serves 4 to 6.

akuri *(spiced scrambled eggs)*

6   eggs
¼   cup milk
½   tsp. salt
black pepper to taste
3   Tbs. chopped fresh cilantro (coriander leaves)
3   Tbs. butter or Ghee (page 301)
½   onion, finely chopped
1   small green chili (jalapeño), minced
1   Tbs. minced fresh ginger
½   tsp. crushed dried red pepper
½   tsp. ground turmeric
½   tsp. ground cumin

Beat the eggs lightly with the milk, salt, pepper, and chopped cilantro.

Heat the butter or *ghee* in a large skillet and sauté the chopped onions in it until they begin to color. Add the chilis, ginger, red pepper, turmeric, and cumin. Stir over medium heat for about 2 minutes.

Raise the heat slightly and pour in the beaten eggs. Stir constantly until the eggs are just set but still creamy. Serve immediately with *chapatis* or *puris* and some spiced vegetables.

Serves 3 to 6.

akni

Akni is a delicate, aromatic broth made with a combination of spices. It is used to poach or flavor certain Indian foods, and can be kept for several days in the refrigerator.

1½ Tbs. butter or Ghee (page 301)
1   yellow onion, coarsely chopped
4   cloves garlic, sliced
2   Tbs. coriander seeds, crushed
1   tsp. fennel seeds
1   Tbs. peeled and chopped fresh ginger
1   qt. water

Heat the butter or *ghee* in a medium-sized saucepan and sauté the onions and garlic in it until they are soft. Add the coriander seeds, fennel seeds, and ginger and stir over medium heat for 2 minutes. Add the water and simmer the broth for 30 minutes, then strain.

potato chat puris

18 small Puris (page 49)
⅓ cup slivered onions
2 cups cubed, cooked white-skinned potatoes (waxy)
1½ cups cooked garbanzo beans (see page 143)
1 Tbs. minced hot green chilis
3 Tbs. coarsely chopped fresh cilantro (coriander leaves)
2 Tbs. lemon juice
½ tsp. salt
½ cup Raisin and Tamarind Chutney (page 317)
½ cup mango chutney
1 cup crisp *saveth* noodles*

Punch in the tops of the little *puris* so that they have the shape of rough-edged little bowls.

Combine the slivered onions, cubed potatoes, garbanzo beans, minced chilis, chopped cilantro, lemon juice, and salt, tossing everything together until it is thoroughly combined. The ingredients should be at room temperature.

Thin the Raisin and Tamarind Chutney with a little water, using just enough to give it a "pourable" consistency. Purée any sweet mango chutney and thin it likewise.

Fill the *puris* with the potato–garbanzo bean mixture, mounding a couple of heaping tablespoons in each *puri*. Pour a teaspoonful or so of each of the thinned chutneys over the vegetable mixture in each *puri*. Sprinkle the filled *puris* with the crisp *saveth* noodles and serve.

Serves 6 to 8 as an hors d'oeuvre or snack.

Saveth noodles, also called *sev* noodles, are tiny, thin, crisp noodles made from chick-pea flour and are available in specialty stores which stock Indian foods. They are similar in texture to the dry chow mein noodles that can be purchased in cans, and the chow mein noodles could be substituted if absolutely necessary.

garam masala

A *masala* is a mixture of spices, either dry or in the form of a paste, and there are many *masalas* for many uses. This one is a fragrant blend of spices—not especially hot—which is sometimes added to food during cooking and sometimes sprinkled over a dish just before serving. It is not curry powder. It can be used alone, but more often it is blended with other seasonings.

¼ cup cardamom pods
2 Tbs. peppercorns
2 Tbs. cumin seeds
2 sticks cinnamon, each 2 inches long
2 tsp. whole cloves
1 tsp. ground mace
2 Tbs. ground coriander
1 bay leaf

Spread the spices out on a large metal pan and roast them in a 200 degree oven for about 20 minutes, stirring them often and making sure they don't scorch.

Remove them from the oven and shell the cardamom seeds, discarding the pods. Crush the cinnamon sticks by wrapping them in a towel and pounding them with a wooden mallet or other blunt instrument.

Combine all the spices and grind them, in batches if necessary, in an electric blender or food processor, until they are a powder. If you don't have a blender, you can grind the spices in a stone or ceramic mortar and good luck to you.

Keep the *masala* in an airtight container, at room temperature.

See Preserves for several chutneys. Turn to Breads for Puris and Chapatis, and to Desserts for Carrot Halva.

desserts

From my earliest recollections, the importance of an occasion in our family could be gauged by the opulence of sweets in which we indulged. Each birthday or anniversary was marked by my mother's gloriously rich walnut torte, spread with generous layers of coffee buttercream. More a confection than a cake, this elegant pastry had to be cut in small pieces and nibbled slowly to savor all of its sweetness and sophisticated flavor. For Easter, a very special time, there were tall, light *babas* and delicate almond cakes, as well as sturdier ones that were dense with raisins and nuts.

As preparations for Christmas began, a nearly tangible excitement filled the air, and aromas of honey and spice enveloped us when we came into the kitchen after school, cold and wet with snow. It is a feeling that still haunts me each year, and spicy *pierniki*, like Proust's madeleines, bring it back with greatest clarity. At Christmas there were fruitcakes and marzipan, and *pierniki*, of course, flavored with honey and spices and aged in tins for weeks or even months to ripen, and there was a beautiful thing called *chrust* (hrōōst), which means "frost": These were light, lacy, brittle pastries, fried in hot oil and dusted heavily with confectioners' sugar. With all this, there was still a great quantity of pale, crumbly butter cookies, dried fruits, several kinds of nuts, candied orange peel, the finest chocolates that could be found, and, of course, the traditional poppy-seed-filled *struçla* (strudel). On Christmas Eve, after the gala supper, these things were arrayed in all their splendor and abundance on a prettily decorated buffet by the Christmas tree. Those who still had room could pick and choose from that phantasmagoria for the length of the happy evening (of course, everyone had room because, as we all know, dessert goes to a different stomach).

Rich desserts, along with such things as great wines and rare spices, are certainly among the luxury items in the world of food, so one must dismiss all ideas of practicality in even thinking of them. It is fine to be practical when planting a lawn or cooking soup for the family on a cold day, but that is altogether the wrong attitude for choosing tickets for the opera, buying perfume or diamonds, or making a special dessert. I just attend to quality rather than quantity, and all is well. Pure marzipan and chocolate, pounds of butter, cupfuls of sugar and honey, drenchings of brandy and rum, and high, soft mounds of whipped cream are the wonderful stuff that great desserts are made of. Of course, we cannot lap up such things every day (for we are vain enough to think of slim figures), but now and then, in a party mood, how agreeable it is to forget time, forget expense, forget calories, and treat ourselves and everyone around us to a memorable sweet.

sponge cake

6   eggs, separated
1   cup sugar
¼   cup boiling water
1   Tbs. lemon juice
½   tsp. vanilla extract
1½ cups flour
1½ tsp. baking powder
pinch of salt
4   Tbs. butter, melted and cooled

Beat the egg yolks until they are creamy and light, then gradually add the sugar a bit at a time, while you continue beating. Beat the yolks and sugar together until the mixture is pale colored and fluffy—another 10 minutes or so. Gradually add the boiling water, lemon juice, and vanilla and beat another few minutes.

Sift together the flour and baking powder and fold it into the egg yolk mixture. Beat the egg whites with a pinch of salt until they hold firm peaks and fold them gently into the batter, using as few strokes as necessary. Pour the melted, cooled butter over the batter, leaving out the milky sediment at the bottom of the pan. Again using as few strokes as necessary, in order not to deflate the egg whites, scoop in the butter.

Spoon the batter into a buttered and floured 9- or 10-inch springform cake pan. Smooth the batter lightly in the pan.

Bake in a preheated oven at 325 degrees for 40 to 45 minutes if you're making 1 large cake, slightly less time if you're making 2 layers. The cake is done when it is golden on top and shrinking away from the sides and when a toothpick inserted in the cake comes out clean.

Let the cake cool in the pan for a few minutes, then transfer to a rack until it is completely cool.

Sponge cake, as its name indicates, is ideally suited for all those splendid tortes and desserts in which a quantity of rum or brandy is meant to be soaked up by the cake layers.

Makes 1 large cake.

genoese

One of the very best basic cakes, from which any number of tortes can be made, Genoese is especially good for soaking up rum or brandy, as in a Zuppa Inglese.

8   eggs
1½ cups sugar
grated rind of 1 lemon
1¾ cups sifted flour
½   cup butter, melted and cooled

Break the eggs into a large bowl, and place that bowl inside an even larger one, which is about half full of hot water. Add the sugar and grated lemon rind to the eggs and beat them with an electric mixer for 8 to 10 minutes. They should be puffed up to 3 times their former volume, creamy white in color, and they should fall in a thick ribbon when scooped up with a spoon.

Take the bowl of beaten eggs out of the hot water and put it in a bowl of cold water. Beat the eggs for several more minutes, until they are cool. Sprinkle the sifted flour over them and fold it in with a small spatula or flat wooden spoon, using the minimum number of strokes needed to blend the flour into the eggs.

Pour the melted and cooled butter over the cake batter, leaving out only the milky sediment in the bottom of the saucepan. Again, fold in the butter with light, smooth strokes, stopping as soon as it is incorporated.

Pour the batter into a large (10-inch) buttered and floured springform pan, or into 2 large (9-inch) buttered and floured layer pans. Smooth the batter very gently in the pans, and bake in a preheated oven at 350 degrees for about 45 to 50 minutes, or until the cake is golden brown on top and pulling away from the sides of the pan.

Remove the cake or cakes from the pans and cool on cake racks.

Makes 1 very large cake or 2 large layers.

sweet pastry crust

1⅓ cups flour
1   Tbs. sugar
¼   tsp. salt
½   cup butter
scant ⅓ cup ice water

Sift together the flour, sugar, and salt in a mixing bowl. Slice the cold butter rapidly and drop the slices into the flour mixture. With a pastry blender or two sharp knives, cut in the butter until the mixture resembles coarse corn meal.

Sprinkle the ice water over the flour-butter mixture and stir it in quickly with a fork, until the dough gathers together. Form the dough into a ball, wrap it in waxed paper or foil, and chill it for about 2 hours.

Makes enough for 1 large (11-inch) tart.

lemon torte

1¼ cups egg whites
2   cups confectioners' sugar
2   Tbs. cornstarch
¼   tsp. almond extract
1⅔ cups ground almonds (unblanched)
Lemon Filling (page 327)

garnish:

blanched almond halves

Beat the egg whites with 1 cup of the confectioners' sugar until they hold soft peaks. Sift together the second cup of sugar and the cornstarch, add it to the egg whites along with the almond extract, and continue beating until the egg whites are stiff.

Fold in the ground almonds.

Butter and flour two 10-inch cake pans and divide the beaten egg white mixture between them, spreading it as flat and smooth as possible. Bake the layers in a preheated oven at 275 degrees for 1½ hours. They should be pale gold in color and shrinking away from the sides of the pan.

Allow the layers to cool slightly in the pans, then carefully remove them and let them finish cooling on racks.

Spread a little more than half the lemon filling on one layer and place the second layer on top of it. Spread the remaining filling over the top and sides of the top layer, leaving the sides of the bottom layer exposed. Decorate the torte very simply with a few blanched almond halves or just swirl the lemon topping evenly with a butter knife and leave it plain. Chill the torte for at least an hour.

Serves 10.

lemon filling

4 Tbs. cornstarch
¾ cup cold water
⅓ cup fresh lemon juice
1 cup sugar
1 Tbs. finely grated lemon zest
3 egg yolks
1½ Tbs. butter

Combine the cornstarch, water, lemon juice, sugar, and grated lemon zest in a medium-sized, heavy-bottomed saucepan. Stir over very low heat for 15 to 20 minutes, or until the mixture begins to thicken. Stir with a whisk, if necessary, to keep the mixture smooth.

When it is quite thick, remove it from the heat and beat in the egg yolks, one at a time. Return the mixture to low heat and heat it for 3 minutes only. Remove it from the heat and stir in the butter. Allow the filling to cool, stirring it occasionally.

Makes about 2 cups.

chocolate cheesecake

You only live once, so do it.

1½ cups fine graham cracker crumbs
½   cup butter
2   cups plus 3 Tbs. sugar
1½ lbs. soft cream cheese
3   eggs
½   lb. semisweet chocolate
3   Tbs. heavy cream
2   cups sour cream
¼   cup dark rum
¾   tsp. cinnamon
¾   tsp. almond extract
1   cup confectioners' sugar
approximately 1 cup fresh strawberries

Mix the graham cracker crumbs with the butter and 3 tablespoons of the sugar, working it together with your fingers until it is all well blended. Press the mixture evenly onto the bottom of a 10-inch springform cake pan, using a potato masher to make a flat crust.

Beat the cream cheese with an electric mixer until it is fluffy, then gradually beat in the remaining 2 cups sugar and the eggs. Continue beating until the mixture is perfectly smooth. Or spin these ingredients in a food processor until perfectly smooth.

Melt the chocolate together with the heavy cream in a small saucepan and beat the mixture into the cheese, along with 1 cup of the sour cream. Add the rum, cinnamon, and almond extract and beat for a few minutes more.

Pour the cheese mixture into the prepared springform pan and bake in a preheated 350 degree oven for 55 minutes to 1 hour. The sides will probably be puffed up higher than the center—don't worry, this is easily dealt with. Allow the cake to cool and carefully remove the sides of the pan. With a sharp, long knife, slice the uneven edges off of the top. Because this cheesecake has such a moist, creamy consistency, you can smooth the sides and the trimmed top with a butter knife until it is as lovely and evenly shaped as you wish.

Beat together the remaining 1 cup sour cream and the confectioners' sugar and spread it over the top of the cake, but not down the sides. Wash the strawberries, hull them, and slice each one in half lengthwise. Arrange the strawberries, cut side down and tips pointing in to the center, in a solid ring around the edge of the cake. Chill the cake until serving, at least 1½ hours.

Serves 12 to 14.

kate's cake *(chocolate cream torte)*

So named because it was designed and first made for Katherine Bradley, a very wonderful lady, on the occasion of her eighty-fifth birthday.

⅔ cup butter
1¼ cups sugar
⅔ cup ground walnuts
5 oz. semisweet chocolate, melted and cooled
½ tsp. almond extract
7 eggs, separated
1¼ cups flour
3 to 6 Tbs. brandy
2 cups heavy cream
1 cup confectioners' sugar
chocolate curls or shaved bittersweet chocolate

Cream the butter with ½ cup of the sugar, then beat in the ground walnuts, the melted chocolate, the almond extract, and the egg yolks. Beat the egg whites with the remaining ¾ cups sugar until they hold soft peaks, and fold them into the chocolate mixture. Finally, sift in the flour and mix it in gently until it is completely incorporated.

Pour the batter into a buttered 8- or 9-inch springform cake pan and bake it in a preheated oven at 325 degrees for about 1¼ hours, or until a toothpick inserted near the center comes out clean and dry—it may be a little longer.

Allow the cake to cool slightly in its pan, then remove it and let it finish cooling on a rack.

Cut the cake in 3 thin, even layers and drizzle 1 or 2 tablespoons of brandy over each layer.

Whip the cream with the confectioners' sugar until it is stiff. Spread ⅓ of the whipped cream on top of the first layer and place the second layer carefully over it. Spread another ⅓ of the cream on the second layer, put on the top layer, and spread it as beautifully as you can with the remaining cream, bringing it just out to the edge but not letting any get on the sides of the cake. The three dark layers and the cream filling should make a dramatic striped effect around the sides.

Arrange chocolate curls, or sprinkle bits of shaved chocolate, inside the edge of the whipped cream on top in a 1-inch-wide ring. Chill the cake.

Serves 8 to 10.

spumoni cake

In the restaurant Torcoloti in Verona, we ate one of the most sublime cakes in the world. After the first long moment of silent ecstasy had passed, we asked our extremely friendly waiter if he could tell us a little something about it. Well, we found out that it was made every day by the aged and talented mother of the owner, that it was called Spumoni Cake, and a little something more—but the recipe was not revealed.

On returning to my own kitchen, I experimented with several variations of the obvious basic ingredients and finally came up with a cake which, though it is not exactly the same is a great deal like the Verona one—and *awfully good!*

¾   cup confectioners' sugar
⅓   cup flour
2   eggs
2   egg yolks
2   cups milk
1   Tbs. butter
½   tsp. vanilla extract
½   cup plus 1 Tbs. brandy
½   cup strong, cold espresso
1   1-day-old Genoese layer, 9 inches across and about 2 inches thick (page 325)
sweet powdered cocoa (about 2 to 3 Tbs.)

Mix together the confectioners' sugar and the flour. Beat together the eggs and the yolks, and mix them into the dry ingredients, stirring until you have a thick, smooth paste.

Scald the milk and stir it quickly into the egg paste. Heat the mixture over a low flame, stirring constantly with a whisk, until it begins to simmer. Continue beating it with the whisk, over lowest heat, for 3 more minutes. Remove the custard from the heat, stir in the butter, vanilla, and 1 tablespoon of the brandy and beat it again until it is perfectly smooth.

Allow the custard to cool, stirring it occasionally to prevent a skin from forming.

Combine the cold espresso and the remaining brandy in a measuring cup. Using a long, very sharp knife, cut the Genoese into 2 even layers. Place the bottom layer on the 9-inch false bottom of a cake pan. Spoon ⅓ of the espresso-brandy mixture over it, moistening it evenly but lightly.

Spread the cold custard over the moistened cake layer in an even layer. Place the top of the cake on the custard layer and spoon the remaining espresso-brandy mixture over it. Go slow with this part of the operation: You don't want the liquid to run off the top layer and be soaked up by the bottom one. It is important that the bottom layer be less moist than the top one, or you will have difficulty serving the cake when you cut it.

When all the espresso and brandy have been used up, put several tablespoons of sweet cocoa in a fine sieve and sift it evenly over the top of the cake. The layer of cocoa should be fairly thick, or it will have dark spots where the moisture from the cake seeps through.

Place the cake, false bottom and all, on a serving platter and chill it for several hours before serving. Cut the cake with a thin, sharp knife, and wipe the knife clean with a napkin between slices. Serve fresh, hot espresso with the cold cake.

Serves 8 to 10.

zuppa inglese

It means "English Soup" because its base is English custard, but it's really a marvelous, moist Italian confection—cake soaked with rum, layered with marmalade and custard, and covered with a meringue. The curious name presumably derives from a resemblance to English trifle.

½ cup sugar
½ cup flour
pinch of salt
2 cups hot milk
4 egg yolks, lightly beaten
2 Tbs. Marsala or brandy
¼ tsp. vanilla extract
1 large sponge cake, preferably stale
1 cup dark rum
¾ cup apricot or peach marmalade
4 egg whites
pinch of salt
pinch of cream of tartar
¼ cup sugar

Mix together the sugar, flour, and salt in a medium-sized, heavy-bottomed saucepan. Pour the hot milk over the dry mixture and beat it with a whisk until it is smooth. Heat it gently, stirring all the while with a whisk, until it

zuppa inglese (continued)

begins to thicken, about 4 to 6 minutes. Whisk in the egg yolks and continue stirring over low heat a few minutes more, until the custard is very thick and glossy. Remove it from the heat and stir in the Marsala or brandy and the vanilla. Allow the custard to cool completely, stirring it occasionally to prevent a skin from forming.

Cut a stale sponge cake in ¾-inch strips. Arrange a layer of the sponge cake strips in the bottom of a large, ovenproof serving dish. Sprinkle the cake with ½ the rum, then spread the marmalade over it evenly and, over the marmalade, carefully spread about ⅔ of the custard.

Arrange the remaining cake strips in an even layer on top of the custard and sprinkle the rest of the rum over it. Spread the remaining custard over the second layer of cake. Chill the *zuppa*.

Beat the egg whites with a pinch of salt and a pinch of cream of tartar until they hold stiff, glossy peaks. Gradually beat in the sugar.

Cover the *zuppa* with the meringue and swirl it around with a spoon or small spatula so that it forms peaks in an attractive pattern. Bake the *zuppa* in a preheated 325 degree oven for 10 to 12 minutes, or until the meringue is golden brown on its peaks. Chill for an hour or two before serving.

Serves 10 to 14.

wenia's mazurek (Věnyä's Mäzōōrěk)

This wonderful cake was first made for me by my Aunt Wenia in Poland, and I immediately demanded the recipe. It is the perfect cake for a very special occasion, a baroque, luscious creation that really looks like a celebration.

1   sponge cake, baked in a 10" by 14" pan
        (page 324)

½ to ⅔ cup rum
1   cup plum jam
1   cup raisins
1   cup chopped walnuts
½   cup chopped candied orange peel
1   recipe Chocolate Buttercream, chilled till
        firm but not stiff (page 334)
1   tsp. unsweetened powdered cocoa

With a long, sharp, serrated knife, slice the sponge cake into 2 even layers. Sprinkle the rum evenly over both layers. Spread the plum jam over the entire surface of the bottom layer, right out to the edges. Toss together the raisins, chopped walnuts, and chopped candied orange peel. Sprinkle about ½ of this mixture evenly over the plum jam.

Spoon ⅔ of the buttercream over the fruit and nut layer, and spread it, lightly and smoothly, out to the edges of the cake. Place the top cake layer gently on the buttercream layer.

Spread the remaining buttercream over the top of the cake, bringing it out to the edges but not down the sides. Through a very fine sieve, dust the cocoa over a 3-inch by 6-inch rectangle in the center of the cake. Don't worry if the edges of your rectangle aren't perfect—the next step will fix that.

Take the remainder of the fruit and nut mixture, a little at a time, and sprinkle it over the top of the cake, covering the buttercream *around* the rectangle that has been dusted with cocoa. To make a straight edge around the rectangle, hold a long, wide knife along the line on one side of the rectangle and sprinkle the fruits and nuts along the blade on the buttercream side. Repeat on all sides of the rectangle, then fill in the remaining areas out to the edges of the cake. Press the fruit and nut mixture very gently into the buttercream, just enough to make it stay. If there are creases in the buttercream from holding the knife on it to make the straight edge, press the fruits and nuts immediately next to the cocoa rectangle very lightly toward the middle, just enough to hide the crease.

The finished cake should look like this: On the sides, all layers will be visible—cake, then jam, then buttercream, cake again, and more buttercream. On top, the surface will be covered with fruit mixture, except for a rectangular chocolate "window" in the center.

Chill the cake until just before serving it (at least 1 hour) and slice it with a very sharp, serrated knife, using a tiny, sawing motion.

Serves 10 to 12.

chocolate buttercream

4   egg yolks
1¼ cups sugar
3   Tbs. unsweetened powdered cocoa
⅔   cup milk
½   lb. soft butter

Beat the egg yolks until they are creamy, then beat in ¾ cup of the sugar and continue until pale and fluffy. Beat in the cocoa.

Bring the milk to a boil and add it to the egg yolk mixture, a little at a time, while continually beating. When all the milk has been added, transfer the custard to a heavy-bottomed sauce-pan and stir it with a wooden spoon over very low heat until it thickens enough to heavily coat the spoon. Don't even let it simmer.

When the custard has thickened, return it to the mixing bowl and set inside a larger one ½ full of cold water. Beat the custard until cool.

In another bowl, beat the soft butter with the remaining ½ cup sugar until it is fluffy. Add the chocolate custard and beat the two together until they are one perfectly smooth, creamy mixture. Chill the buttercream for about ½ hour before using it.

Makes about 2½ cups.

rum and chocolate fruitcakes

Make these before Thanksgiving Day if you want to eat them at Christmas—they need aging to develop proper flavor.

1   lb. dried apricots, cut in small pieces
12   oz. pitted prunes, cut in small pieces
8   oz. pitted dates, cut in small pieces
1   lb. currants
12   oz. golden raisins
12   oz. candied citron
4   oz. candied lemon peel
4   oz. candied orange peel
8   oz. shelled pecans or filberts, or a mixture, chopped
1½   cups whole wheat flour
1½   cups white flour
2   tsp. baking soda
2½   cups honey
1   cup butter, melted
½   cup dark rum
2   tsp. ginger
2½   tsp. cinnamon
½   tsp. ground cloves
1   tsp. ground cardamom
¾   cup ground sweet chocolate or powdered cocoa
6   eggs
⅔   cup currant jelly
brandy or rum*

In a large bowl mix all the chopped fruit, currants, raisins, candied peel, and nuts. Sift together the two flours and the baking soda and sprinkle this over the fruit. Toss the mixture until all the bits of fruit are separate and coated with flour.

In another bowl, combine the honey, melted butter, rum, spices, and chocolate. Beat together the eggs and the currant jelly until the mixture is thick and foamy, and then beat it into the honey mixture. Pour this over the floured fruit and stir with a large wooden spoon until the batter is smooth and homogeneous.

Butter 8 medium-small (7½ by 3½ inch) loaf pans or a smaller number of large pans, line them with waxed paper, and butter the paper. Divide the batter among the pans and smooth it down with a wet spoon. Bake the cakes in a preheated oven at 300 degrees for 2 to 2½ hours, depending on their size. The cakes are done when a toothpick inserted near the center comes out clean and dry.

Allow the cakes to cool, remove them from the pans, and peel off the paper. Wrap each cake in several layers of cheesecloth and soak the cloth with brandy or rum, then wrap them securely in plastic wrap or foil to keep the moisture in. Put the cakes away in a cool, dry place to age for about 1 month.

Makes 8 medium-sized fruitcakes.

*The amount will vary—from a pint to a quart or more, depending on your taste and the number of soakings you want to give the cakes as they age.

apple strudel grandma clar

(as passed down to Flora Clar Mock)

Where it came from before Flora's grandmother started calling it her own, nobody knows, but this is not a classic version of apple strudel. It is as unusual as it is tasty.

When Flora makes this strudel, she makes double or more the amount given here, but not everyone has such an immense table on which to stretch the dough, so I've reduced the quantities a bit. You'll still need a table about 5 feet long and 2 or 3 feet wide, covered with a clean sheet or smooth tablecloth, for preparing the pastry, and though you can do it alone, the whole process is more fun if you have a friend or two around to help. Stretching the dough is not as difficult as it sounds, and spreading all the sugar, cinnamon, nuts, coconut, jam, and apples over such a large surface is a complete delight. Flora says "when it starts to look like a Jackson Pollock painting," you know you're getting there.

4 cups flour
1¼ cups water
½ cup corn oil
½ cup sugar
approximately 2 tsp. cinnamon

1 cup shredded sweetened coconut
1 cup strawberry or raspberry jam
¾ cup raisins
½ cup finely chopped walnuts
1¼ lbs. tart pippin apples, peeled, cored, quartered, and thinly sliced
additional sugar and cinnamon to sprinkle on top

Put 3 cups of the flour in an ample bowl and gradually stir in the water until you have a sticky, pasty mass, a little more moist than a normal bread dough. Work it a little with your hands—just enough to get out the lumps but no more. Gather the dough into a ball and dust a little more flour over it, patting it smooth as you do, until it has a nice, even shape, dry and flour coated on the outside but very soft inside.

Spread a clean sheet or smooth tablecloth over a large, preferably oblong table, and dust it evenly with the remaining flour. If the table is oblong, shape the dough gently into a loaf with proportions similar to those of the table top. For a round table, leave it in a ball.

Put the dough down in the center of the table and flatten it slightly with a rolling pin. Turn the dough over and roll it out a little more, rolling always from the center to the edges. Continue turning the dough over and rolling it out, always making sure the area under it is well floured and keeping the shape as even as possible, until it is about ¼ inch thick. Now slide your hands under the dough, palms up, and begin pulling it out very gently and carefully, letting it slide off your hands as you draw them back out to the edge. This process is really nothing but a very light "stroking" of the sheet of pastry from underneath. Begin at the center and work your way around, pulling it out only a little at a time. Continue stretching the pastry this way until it is paper-thin and quite transparent. Try to avoid putting holes in it, but don't panic if a little one appears here or there: They'll disappear in the rolling up.

When the dough is as thin and fine as a piece of silk (it should nearly cover the surface of the table), press out the inevitably bumpy edges with your fingers and then drizzle not quite ½ cup of corn oil over it. Spread the oil over the pastry with your hands until coated all over.

This is where the real fun begins. Sprinkle the pastry sheet evenly with sugar, then sprinkle on about 2 teaspoons of cinnamon, or more if you like. Next sprinkle on the coconut, always covering the surface of the pastry as evenly as you can, and then drizzle or dab on the jam. After the jam, sprinkle on the raisins and the walnuts (it's starting to look like a Jackson Pollock), and finally, the apple slices. You're ready to roll.

Oil 2 or 3 large cookie sheets very generously and have them ready, along with a very sharp knife. Starting at one of the narrow ends, lift up the sheet or cloth and shake it lightly to loosen the pastry so that it starts to roll up. Continue gathering up the cloth and lifting it evenly, rolling the strudel up until it looks about as thick as you want it: about 2 inches is good. Slice off the rolled up part with a sharp knife, cut into manageable lengths and transfer them with spatulas to the cookie sheets.

Now gather up the cloth, lift, and begin rolling again, proceeding the same way until all the pastry is rolled up, cut, and on the cookie sheets. Sprinkle the strudels with a little sugar and cinnamon and bake them in a preheated oven at 375 degrees for 15 to 20 minutes. They are done when the pastry is golden brown on top. Flora recommends cutting off a little slice and tasting the strudel to determine when it is ready, but I find it hard to maintain any objectivity about such matters when the first bite of strudel is actually in my mouth.

If it is allowed to cool and then wrapped well in waxed paper, the strudel will supposedly keep for several days to a week—but I've never been able to keep any that long!

Makes 2 or 3 large strudels.

dark brandied fruitcakes

These also should be aged at least a month to develop their full flavor.

2   cups coarsely chopped dried figs
2   cups chopped dried apricots
½   cup chopped candied lemon peel
1½   cups golden raisins
1½   cups chopped dates
2   cups chopped pecans
⅔   cup green candied cherries, halved
⅔   cup red candied cherries, halved
1½   cups whole wheat flour
1½   cups white flour
1   tsp. baking powder
¾   tsp. nutmeg
½   tsp. cinnamon
½   tsp. ground cloves
½   tsp. ground cardamom
1   cup butter, well chilled
6   eggs
1½   cups sugar
1   cup Sauterne wine
½   tsp. baking soda
2   Tbs. water
approximately a fifth of brandy

In a large bowl, combine the figs, apricots, lemon peel, raisins, dates, pecans, and cherries.

In another bowl, sift together the flours, baking powder, and spices and cut in the chilled butter using two knives or a pastry blender until the mixture has the texture of coarse corn meal. Add the flour mixture to the fruit and toss them together until all the bits of fruit are separate and coated.

Beat the eggs with the sugar until they are light and pale lemon colored. Stir in the Sauterne. Dissolve the baking soda in the water and stir it in, too.

Combine the egg mixture with the flour and fruit mixture and stir them together thoroughly.

Butter 6 medium-small (7½ by 3½ inch) loaf pans or a smaller number of larger ones, line them with waxed paper, and butter the paper. Divide the batter among the pans, smooth down neatly with a moist spoon, and if you like, arrange some pecan halves or cherry halves in a design on the cakes.

Bake the cakes in a preheated oven at 275 degrees for 2 hours or slightly longer, until they are browned and a toothpick inserted near the center comes out clean.

Allow the cakes to cool, remove them from the pans, and peel off the paper. Wrap each cake in several layers of cheesecloth and soak the cloth with as much brandy as it will absorb. Wrap the cake again, securely, in foil or plastic wrap to keep the moisture in.

Put the cakes away in a cool place for 2 weeks, then check them. If the cheesecloth is quite dry, drizzle a little more brandy on it. Replace the foil or plastic wrappings and put the cakes away for another 2 weeks or for as long as you like.

Makes 6 medium-sized fruitcakes.

apple pudding

3 large pippin (tart green) apples
4 Tbs. butter
3 Tbs. sugar
½ tsp. cinnamon
¼ tsp. ground cloves
1 tsp. grated lemon rind

batter

3 eggs
½ cup flour
1½ cups milk
3 Tbs. sugar
2 Tbs. brandy
½ tsp. vanilla extract
dash of nutmeg

garnish

¼ to ½ cup confectioners' sugar

Quarter, peel, and core the apples and cut the quarters in thin slices. In a shallow, fireproof casserole, sauté the apple slices in butter for several minutes. Add the sugar, cinnamon, cloves, and lemon rind and continue to cook the apples, stirring often, for another 5 minutes, or until the apples are just tender.

apple pudding (continued)

Beat together the eggs, flour, milk, sugar, brandy, vanilla, and nutmeg, or blend them in a blender. Pour the batter over the apples and bake the pudding for 25 to 30 minutes in a preheated oven at 400 degrees, or until it is puffed and golden brown on top.

Sift confectioners' sugar over the top of the pudding and serve it warm with coffee or milk.

Serves 6 to 8.

apple tart

crust

1⅓ cups flour
¼ tsp. salt
1 Tbs. sugar
½ cup butter, well chilled
scant ⅓ cup ice water

filling

2 lbs. firm pippin apples
juice of 1 large lemon
½ cup sugar
½ to ⅓ cup apricot glaze (optional, see below)

To make the crust, mix together the flour, salt, and 1 tablespoon of sugar, then cut in the butter with a pastry blender or two sharp knives until the mixture resembles coarse corn meal. Sprinkle the ice water over it and toss together quickly until the flour is evenly moistened and the dough is starting to hold together. Form the dough into a ball and chill it for 1 hour, then roll it out in a 12-inch circle and fit it into a 10½-inch false-bottom quiche tin or flan ring.* Trim off the excess, leaving a ¼-inch

*If you don't have a quiche pan or flan ring, a shallow 10-inch pie pan can be used, but I recommend getting a false-bottom quiche pan—they're inexpensive and very useful.

rim above the pan, and flute the rim with the blunt edge of a butter knife. Chill the shell for ½ hour.

Line the shell with foil and fill it with dried beans or rice.† Bake in a preheated oven at 425 degrees for 8 minutes, then remove the beans and foil, prick the shell in several places with a fork, and put it back in the oven for 4 to 5 minutes, just until the bottom of the crust begins to color.

Meanwhile, peel and core the apples and cut them in even, lengthwise slices, no thicker than ¼ inch at the outside. Put the apple slices in a bowl with the lemon juice and ½ cup of the sugar, toss lightly, and leave them there for 45 minutes. Drain the apples and reserve the liquid.

The partially baked crust can be painted with apricot glaze before the apples are arranged on it. This is one more way to fight the soggy crust problem. Heat up the glaze and brush it on lightly with a pastry brush.

Arrange the apple slices neatly in the crust by

†The dried beans or rice are used as a weight, to keep the crust from slipping down the sides and puffing up in the middle. Keep the beans or rice in a jar—they can be reused for this purpose indefinitely.

very closely overlapping them in concentric circles, starting at the outside edge. Use all the apples. Sprinkle the remaining sugar (about 3 tablespoons) evenly over the apples. Bake the tart for 30 to 35 minutes in a preheated oven at 375 degrees. The apples should just be starting to brown at the edges.

While the tart is baking, boil the reserved liquid from the apples until it is reduced to a medium-thick, glazelike consistency. When the tart is done, brush the apples lightly with this glaze, or drizzle it over them.

Serve the tart warm or cool, with or without the apricot glaze.

optional apricot glaze

½ cup apricot preserves or jam
1   Tbs. sugar

To make an apricot glaze, just rub the apricot preserves or jam through a fine sieve, add the sugar, and boil for a few minutes. The mixture will be thick and sticky. Keep it warm over hot water until you need it, and while using it. If it gets too thick to handle, it can be thinned out with a few drops of water.

Serves 8 to 10.

pumpkin pie I

This is my favorite. I love ginger, and this one is particularly spicy.

pastry for two 9-inch 1-crust pies (page 326 or 340)
¾ cup brown sugar
¼ cup white sugar
1 Tbs. molasses
¼ tsp. salt
½ tsp. cinnamon
¾ tsp. ginger
¼ tsp. nutmeg
¼ tsp. ground cloves
2 cups puréed cooked pumpkin
3 eggs
1⅔ cups undiluted evaporated milk
3 Tbs. sweet dark rum
2 to 3 Tbs. chopped crystallized ginger (optional)

garnish

sweetened whipped cream

Prepare two 9-inch pastry shells with high fluted rims. Chill the shells for about 15 minutes while you preheat the oven to 400 degrees. When the shells are cold and firm, line them with waxed paper or foil and fill them with raw rice or beans.

Bake the shells for 10 minutes, then remove the paper or foil and rice or beans, prick the shells in several places with a fork, and bake them for another 10 minutes.

In a bowl, combine the two sugars, molasses, salt, spices, and puréed pumpkin. In another bowl, beat the eggs with the milk and rum. Combine the two mixtures and mix them thoroughly.

Sprinkle the chopped crystallized ginger evenly across the bottoms of the pastry shells. Ladle the filling carefully over the ginger, dividing it evenly between the two shells.

Bake the pies in the preheated 400 degree oven for 35 to 40 minutes, or until a knife inserted near the center comes out clean.

Cool the pies on a rack and serve with sweetened whipped cream.

Makes two 9-inch pies.

pumpkin pie II

This one is slightly milder in flavor—but delicious!

pastry for two 9-inch 1-crust pies (page 326 or 340)
¾ cup sugar
½ tsp. salt
½ tsp. ginger
¼ tsp. nutmeg
1 tsp. cinnamon
½ tsp. ground cloves
1½ cups puréed cooked pumpkin
3 eggs
1½ cups light cream
2 Tbs. sweet dark rum

garnish

sweetened whipped cream

Prepare two 9-inch pastry shells with fluted rims. Preheat the oven to 400 degrees while chilling the shells for about 15 minutes. Line the shells with waxed paper or foil and fill them with raw rice or beans. Bake the shells for 10 minutes, then remove the paper or foil and rice or beans, prick the shells in several places with a fork, and bake for another 10 minutes.

Combine the sugar, salt, spices, and puréed pumpkin and mix them thoroughly. Beat together the eggs, cream, and rum and then beat together the two mixtures.

Divide the filling evenly between the two pastry shells and bake the pies for 10 minutes in the preheated 400 degree oven, then lower the temperature to 350 and bake them for another 25 to 30 minutes, or until a knife inserted near the center comes out clean.

Cool the pies on racks and serve them with sweetened whipped cream.

Makes two 9-inch pies.

cherry and amaretto soufflé

3   Tbs. butter
4   Tbs. flour
⅔   cup milk
⅓   cup cream
⅔   cup sugar
4   egg yolks
2   Tbs. Amaretto liqueur
1   cup halved, pitted dark cherries (preferably fresh)
5   egg whites
pinch of cream of tartar

garnish

Raspberry Sauce (page 345)

Melt the butter in a medium-sized, heavy-bottomed saucepan and stir in the flour. Stir the roux frequently as it cooks for several minutes over very low heat. Meanwhile, combine the milk and cream, and heat them to just below simmering.

Pour the milk and cream into the roux and stir vigorously until the mixture is smooth and thick. Stir in the sugar, and as soon as it is completely dissolved and incorporated into the sauce, remove the saucepan from the heat.

Beat in the egg yolks, one at a time, then return the sauce to very low heat. Stir constantly for a few minutes, just until the egg yolks begin to thicken. Remove from the heat and stir in the Amaretto and the halved cherries.

Preheat the oven to 400 degrees and prepare a soufflé dish with a buttered collar (see page 113).

Beat the egg whites with the cream of tartar until they hold stiff peaks but are still glossy. Stir ⅓ of the egg whites into the thick sauce, then gently fold in the remaining egg whites.

Pile the soufflé mixture into the prepared dish and place it gently on the middle rack of the preheated oven. Turn the heat down to 375 degrees. Bake the soufflé for 35 to 40 minutes and serve it immediately, alone or with Raspberry Sauce.

Serves 4 to 6.

raspberry sauce

3 to 4 cups fresh raspberries*
sugar
2 to 3 Tbs. kirsch

Press the washed raspberries through a fine sieve. Sweeten the purée to your own taste with sugar and beat it with a whisk or whip it in an electric blender until all the sugar is dissolved. Beat in the kirsch.

Serve the sauce with ice cream, puddings, or a sweet soufflé.

Makes about a pint, but the amount will vary as ingredients are flexible.

*In a pinch, frozen berries can be used.

flan (caramel custard)

3   whole eggs
3   egg yolks
1¾ cups sugar
2   cups milk
1   cup heavy cream
½   tsp. vanilla extract

Beat the eggs and yolks with ¾ cup of the sugar until thick and creamy. In a small saucepan, combine the milk and cream and heat to just below the simmering point. Pour the hot milk and cream gradually into the egg mixture, beating as you do. Stir in the vanilla.

Slowly heat the remaining 1 cup of sugar in a heavy-bottomed saucepan until it starts to melt. Continue heating gently, stirring constantly, until the sugar has been turned into a light-brown syrup, or caramelized. This will probably take about 5 to 8 minutes. Divide the hot caramel between 6 or 8 custard cups, and quickly tilt them around so that it coats the bottoms and part of the sides. The caramel will set almost immediately.

When the caramel has set, pour the custard mixture into the cups. Place the cups in a baking pan half full of hot water, cover the tops of the custards with a sheet of aluminum foil to

flan (continued)

prevent them from browning too much, and bake in a preheated oven at 350 degrees for 45 to 50 minutes.

The custard is done when a sharp knife inserted in the center comes out clean. Cool the custards, then unmold them by running a thin knife around the edges and overturning them above rimmed plates or shallow bowls.

Serve the custard cool, or chilled, as you prefer.

Serves 6 to 8.

coffee mousse

1½   cups confectioners' sugar
1   cup milk
6   Tbs. triple-strength espresso
¼   tsp. cinnamon
2   packages (2 Tbs.) unflavored gelatin
½   cup cold water
2   egg whites
2   cups heavy cream
1   oz. shaved bittersweet chocolate

Combine the sugar and the milk in a medium-sized saucepan and heat it over a medium flame, stirring constantly, until all the sugar is dissolved. Stir in the espresso and the cinnamon.

Dissolve the gelatin in the cold water and then stir it into the milk. Heat the mixture until the gelatin is completely dissolved, then remove it from the heat and allow it to cool, stirring occasionally.

Beat the egg whites until they hold stiff peaks, and in a separate bowl whip the cream until stiff.

As soon as the cooled gelatin mixture begins to thicken, stir in the whipped cream and fold in the beaten egg whites. Pile the mousse into 6 or 8 individual dessert dishes, decorate it with the shaved chocolate, and chill it for about 2 hours before serving.

Serves 6 to 8.

clafouti of cherries

Clafouti is a very simple pudding, best eaten warm. A mixture similar to pancake batter is poured over fruit and baked—that's all there is to it.

4   eggs
1   cup flour
2   cups warm milk
¾   cup sugar
2   Tbs. butter, melted
2   Tbs. kirsch
pinch of salt
1 to 2 Tbs. soft butter
1   lb. sweet, dark cherries, washed, stemmed, and pitted

garnish

sieved confectioners' sugar
heavy cream, well chilled (optional)

Beat the eggs lightly and gradually stir in the flour. When the mixture is smooth, beat in the milk, sugar, melted butter, and kirsch, along with a tiny pinch of salt.

Preheat the oven to 425 degrees. Very generously butter a large, shallow baking dish and pour a very thin layer of the batter across the bottom of it. Put it in the hot oven for 2 to 3 minutes, or just long enough for the batter to begin to set.

Arrange the pitted cherries evenly over the layer of batter and pour the remaining batter carefully over them.

Reduce the heat to 400 degrees and bake the *clafouti* for about 30 to 35 minutes. It should be golden brown and slightly puffed.

It's a good idea to check it once or twice during the baking, and if it is starting to puff unevenly in large bubbles, pierce it with a skewer or fork.

Sprinkle the hot *clafouti* with sieved confectioners' sugar and serve it hot or warm. I've found that it's especially wonderful with some cold heavy cream poured over it.

Serves 6 to 8.

paskha

This rich, sweet, white cheese dessert is a great delicacy and a Russian Easter tradition. It takes two days to make and is worth every moment of it.

5   egg yolks
3   cups sugar
1   cup milk
½   tsp. vanilla extract
¾   cup butter
3   lbs. hoop or farmer cheese (see page 192)
½   cup heavy cream
2   tsp. grated lemon rind
½   cup finely chopped blanched almonds
    (optional)

Beat the egg yolks with 1 cup of the sugar until they are pale and fluffy. Add the milk and vanilla, and heat the mixture very gently, stirring constantly, until it thickens—this may take about 20 minutes. Add the butter and continue stirring until it melts. Cool the mixture, whisking it occasionally to keep it smooth.

Press the hoop or farmer cheese through a sieve to remove any lumps and whip the cream until it is stiff. When the sauce is completely cool, beat in the remaining sugar, the sieved cheese, the lemon rind, and the whipped cream. If you want to add almonds, stir them in at this point.

Paskha is traditionally shaped in a special carved wooden mold, but we must proceed on the assumption that the average American kitchen does not have one. So . . . line a colander with 2 pieces of muslin or 6 to 8 layers of cheesecloth. Pour the paskha mixture into the lined colander, gather up the cloth around it, pull it together as tightly as you can, and tie it firmly with string. Put a plate on top of the paskha and place a weight on the plate (a cast-iron saucepan should be heavy enough). Stand the colander over a bowl or deep dish to catch the drips and put it away in a cool place for 24 to 36 hours. Quite a bit of liquid will drain off. The paskha is ready when it is firm enough to keep its shape and be cut in slices.

Unwrap the paskha and turn it over carefully onto a plate. Slice it or cut it in little wedges and serve it alone or with a yeast cake. The paskha will keep for several days in the refrigerator if it is well covered.

Serves 15 to 18.

carrot halva *(Gajar Halva)*

This Indian dessert is a rich and sweet confection with a hint of exotic flavor. After a dinner of curries, *raitas*, chutneys, and other wonderful things, take a break for an hour or so; then serve halva in small wedges, with cold, unsweetened cream poured over it, and drink a fragrant tea.

1½ lbs. carrots
1½ qts. milk
1   cup sugar
⅓   cup raisins
¼   tsp. crushed saffron threads
pinch of ground cardamom
¼   tsp. rose extract
1   Tbs. butter
⅓   cup ground blanched almonds
⅓   cup slivered blanched almonds
unsweetened cream, well chilled

Trim and scrape the carrots and shred them as finely as possible. Combine the carrots with the milk in a large, heavy saucepan and bring the milk to a boil. Lower the heat and simmer the mixture very gently, stirring often, for about 2 hours, or until it is reduced by more than ½ and is thick enough to lightly coat a spoon.

Stir in the sugar, raisins, saffron, cardamom, and the rose extract and continue simmering until the mixture is thick enough to hold a soft shape. This could take another long while, so relax. Add the butter and ground almonds and stir over low heat for about 10 minutes more, taking care not to let the mixture scorch. It should now be thick enough to form a solid mass.

Remove it from the heat and allow it to cool slightly. Turn the halva out onto a platter and shape it into an even mound. Decorate it with the slivered almonds and serve it either warm or cool, with cream.

Serves 8 to 10.

brandy cream

One of the simplest of all desserts to make, and sensationally rich and flavorful.

1   cup heavy cream, well chilled
⅓   cup confectioners' sugar
⅓   cup honey
⅓   cup brandy

optional garnish

chocolate curls or sliced, glacéed cherries

Whip the chilled cream with the confectioners' sugar in a large, deep mixing bowl until it just begins to hold firm peaks. Stir the honey and brandy together until they are well blended. Pour the liquid into the whipped cream and continue beating it until it is perfectly smooth and thick. It won't get stiff enough to hold peaks, but it will thicken considerably.

Spoon the cream into 6 dessert or shallow wine glasses. If you like, you can decorate each serving with a few chocolate curls or with some sliced, glacéed cherries. Chill the dessert for 2 hours before serving.

Serves 6.

crème à la irena

½   cup raisins
½   cup cognac
2   oz. semisweet chocolate
1   cup chopped fresh pineapple
2   cups heavy cream
½   cup sugar
1   tsp. vanilla extract

garnish: pirouette cookies*

Soak the raisins in the cognac for several hours. Coarsely chop the chocolate.

Divide the fresh pineapple among 6 to 8 shallow dessert glasses.

Beat the cream with the sugar and vanilla just until it holds fairly stiff peaks. Drain the raisins, reserving the cognac, and add them to the cream, along with the chopped chocolate. Stir the mixture thoroughly.

Put a large dollop of the whipped cream on top of the pineapple in each dessert glass. Pour a spoonful of the cognac over the whipped cream, and garnish it with a pirouette cookie. Serve immediately.

Serves 6 to 8.

*A delicate cookie, rolled into the shape of a little cylinder—any cookie of this general type will do.

frozen strawberry mousse

1   qt. fresh strawberries (about 1½ lbs.)
1½ cups sugar
1   package (1 Tbs.) unflavored gelatin
½   cup cold water
1   cup heavy cream
½   cup egg whites
pinch of salt
⅓   cut Triple Sec or curaçao

garnish

additional fresh strawberries

Hull and wash the strawberries and purée them in a blender. Pass the purée through a medium-fine sieve and discard the seeds. Combine the purée with 1 cup of the sugar.

Soften the gelatin in the cold water, then heat it gently until it is completely dissolved. Add the remaining ½ cup sugar and stir over low heat until the liquid is clear. Stir in the strawberry purée and let the mixture cool in the refrigerator until it just begins to thicken—don't forget to check frequently or you'll be sorry! I check it at least every 10 minutes, at first, then every 3 or 4 minutes when the mixture is already cool to the touch.

Beat the cream until it begins to hold fairly stiff peaks. Beat the egg whites with a pinch of salt until they are stiff.

When the purée begins to thicken, first stir in the Triple Sec or curaçao, then fold in the whipped cream and finally the beaten egg whites.

Spoon the mixture into an oiled charlotte mold or into individual serving dishes and freeze without stirring for 4 to 6 hours. Unmold onto a platter if you have used a charlotte mold.

If you must leave the mousse in the freezer for a longer time and it gets too hard, just let it sit at room temperature for 15 to 20 minutes before serving.

Garnish the mousse with fresh strawberries.

Serves 8 to 10.

castillian hot chocolate

This is the thickest hot chocolate you'll ever drink—any thicker, and it would be a pudding. In Segovia, it is one of the most popular winter drinks: A cup of this and some gossip will take the chill off any icy day.

½ cup unsweetened powdered cocoa
1   cup sugar
2   Tbs. plus 1 tsp. cornstarch
½   cup water
1   qt. milk

Rub the cocoa and sugar together. Dissolve the cornstarch in the water and combine it in a medium-sized saucepan with the cocoa and sugar. Stir this mixture until it is a smooth paste.

Begin heating the mixture, stirring it with a whisk, and gradually pour in the milk. Continue stirring with the whisk as you bring the liquid to a simmer.

Simmer the chocolate, stirring often, for about 10 minutes, until it is thick, glossy, and completely smooth. Serve steaming hot.

Serves 6.

applesauce crêpes

2   cups applesauce
12 Basic Crêpes (page 225)
butter for the pan
¼   cup sugar

Spread 1½ tablespoons of the applesauce over half a crêpe and fold the other side over it. Spread another tablespoon of applesauce over half the surface of the folded crêpe, and fold it in half once more. The crêpe will be folded in a triangle, with a layer of applesauce between each layer of crêpe.

Fill all the crêpes in this manner. Shortly before serving, sauté the crêpes in butter for a few minutes on each side, until they are golden brown and hot through. Put two of the folded crêpes on each dessert plate and sprinkle each serving with about 2 teaspoons sugar. Serve hot.

Serves 6.

fresh lemon dessert crêpes

¾   cup white flour
½   tsp. salt
3   eggs
2   cups milk, scalded and cooled
2   Tbs. butter, melted
2   Tbs. cognac
½   tsp. fresh-grated lemon rind
½   tsp. nutmeg
2   tsp. sugar
butter for the pan
3 to 4 whole fresh lemons
sifted confectioners' sugar (about 1 to 2 cups)

Mix together the flour and the salt. Beat in the eggs until you have a smooth paste, then beat in the milk, melted butter, cognac, lemon rind, nutmeg, and sugar. Let the batter rest for an hour or two.

Heat a crêpe pan and brush it with butter. Pour 3 to 4 tablespoons of the batter into the pan and tilt it around to distribute the batter evenly. Cook over medium heat for about a minute, then turn the crêpe over and cook for another minute on the other side.

To keep the crêpes hot, stack them on a warm plate, cover with a slightly damp tea towel, and keep them in a very low oven.

To serve, fold the crêpes in quarters or roll them loosely. Arrange 2 or 3 on each warm plate. Cut the lemons in wedges and pass the lemons and a bowl of confectioners' sugar when you serve the crêpes. Each person should squeeze a generous amount of lemon juice over the crêpes, then sprinkle them with the confectioners' sugar, and eat!

Serves 5 to 6.

hungarian walnut crêpes

filling

½   cup milk
¾   cup sugar
1   Tbs. butter
2   cups coarsely ground walnuts
½   tsp. cinnamon
¼   tsp. almond extract
2   tsp. rum
¾   cup fine dry bread crumbs
grated rind of 1 lemon

sauce

½   cup strong coffee
6   oz. semisweet chocolate
½   cup sugar
3   Tbs. butter
2   Tbs. brandy

16   medium-sized, pale crêpes (page 225)
butter for the pan

garnish: walnut pieces (about ¾ to 1 cup)

Heat the milk to scalding and stir in the sugar and the butter. As soon as the butter is melted, add the liquid to the ground walnuts, along with the remaining ingredients for the filling. Stir well until everything is thoroughly combined. The mixture should be quite thick.

To make the sauce, heat the coffee and chocolate in a small, heavy-bottomed saucepan, until the chocolate is melted. Add the sugar and butter and stir gently over medium-low heat until the sugar is dissolved and the butter is melted. The sauce should be glossy and smooth.

Remove the sauce from the heat and let it cool for a few minutes. Stir in the brandy. The sauce can be kept warm for a short while over very low heat, or it can be reheated just before serving.

Place about 2 level tablespoons of walnut filling on a crêpe and spread it out in a small oblong shape, about 3 inches by 1 inch. Fold the sides of the crêpe over the filling, then fold over the ends to make an envelope, snugly fitted around the filling. When all the crêpes are filled in this manner, sauté them in a little butter for several minutes on each side until they are golden-brown and hot through.

Place 2 of the hot crêpes on each dessert plate and spoon a few tablespoons of the hot chocolate sauce over them. Garnish each serving with a few walnut pieces and serve immediately.

Serves 8.

baked apples

6 to 8 large baking apples
⅔ cup flour
⅔ cup brown sugar
½ cup butter
grated rind of 1 lemon
½ tsp. cinnamon
¼ tsp. nutmeg
½ cup chopped raisins
¼ cup brandy
¼ cup curaçao
¼ cup water
heavy cream, well chilled

Core the apples, cutting out a generous round cavity in each one but not breaking through the bottom.

Mix together the flour and brown sugar and cut in the butter with a pastry blender or work it in with your fingers. Add the lemon rind, cinnamon, nutmeg, and raisins and mix thoroughly. Stuff the apples with this mixture.

Arrange the apples in a medium-sized, shallow casserole. Combine the brandy, curaçao, and water, and pour the liquid over the apples.

Bake the apples in a preheated oven at 400 degrees for 40 to 45 minutes, basting them with the liquid every 6 or 7 minutes.

The filling will puff up and form hard little caps on top where the sugar caramelizes. When you take the apples out of the oven, let them cool for about 15 minutes, then cut the stiff, dark-brown sugar crusts off of the filling, leaving just the soft, tender part. Spoon any remaining liquid over the warm apples. Serve them either warm or cool, with heavy cream.

Serves 6 to 8.

peaches in red wine

2 to 2½ lbs. small, perfect peaches (10 to 12)
4½ cups red wine
¾   cup sugar
1   stick cinnamon, 2 inches long

Wash the peaches, handling them gently to avoid bruising. In a fairly large enameled saucepan, simmer the wine with the sugar and cinnamon until all the sugar is dissolved. Add the peaches and simmer them very gently for 8 minutes. Remove the saucepan from the heat and leave the peaches in the hot wine for about ½ hour.

Spoon out the peaches, allow them to cool slightly, then carefully slip off their skins. Arrange them in an attractive serving dish, pour the wine over them, and chill for at least 1 hour.

Serves 6 to 8.

oranges in wine

6   large navel oranges
¾   cup sugar
8 to 10 whole cloves
1   stick cinnamon, 1 inch long
1¼ cups dry white wine (a good one, please)
2   Tbs. brandy
seeds from 1 pomegranate

Peel the oranges with a sharp knife, cutting away all the white pith and outer membrane. Slice the oranges very thinly, cutting 6 or 7 slices from each one. In an attractive, medium-sized serving bowl, arrange the orange slices in layers, sprinkling each layer with some sugar and adding a few cloves and a bit of the cinnamon stick here and there.

When all the oranges and sugar are used up, slowly pour the wine over the slices, being careful not to wash all the sugar down to the bottom. The wine should just barely cover all the orange slices. Drizzle on the brandy, cover the bowl tightly, and let the oranges marinate in the refrigerator for several hours.

Just before serving, sprinkle the fresh pomegranate seeds over the orange slices.

Serves 6 to 8.

melons in vermouth

Fresh, ripe melons and an excellent vermouth are the requirements for this dessert, but proportions of one melon to another can be altered to your taste, and sliced or cubed melons will do very well if you don't have a melon scoop.

2   cups honeydew melon balls
3   cups cranshaw melon balls
3   cups watermelon balls
1   cup sweet Italian vermouth

Seed and cut the melons and combine them in a deep bowl. Pour the vermouth over them and, using wooden spoons, lift the melon pieces from the bottom several times. Cover and chill for at least 2 hours, carefully stirring the mixture up 2 or 3 times in the course of the chilling.

Serve in an attractive glass or crystal bowl.

Serves 8 to 10.

peaches and cream

Brandy-drenched and not overly sweet, this is marvelous tasting and very refreshing.

4   medium-sized peaches
3   medium-sized bananas
juice of ½ large lemon
½   cup brandy
⅛   tsp. cinnamon
1   cup heavy cream
⅓   cup confectioners' sugar
⅓   cup slivered blanched almonds
1 to 2 tsp. powdered sweet chocolate

Peel the peaches as thinly as possible and slice them in thin wedges. Peel and slice the bananas. Toss the fruit gently in a bowl with the lemon juice, then add the brandy and the cinnamon. Toss again until evenly coated, then refrigerate for ½ to ¾ hours.

Whip the cream with the confectioners' sugar until it holds fairly stiff peaks.

Put the fruit and brandy mixture in an attractive, shallow serving bowl and sprinkle it with the slivered almonds. Spoon the whipped cream over the fruit in swirls and peaks. Through a fine sieve, sprinkle on the powdered chocolate. Serve immediately.

Serves 6.

rum baba

1   package dry yeast
⅔   cup warm milk
½   cup + 1 Tbs. sugar
2¼   cups flour
4   eggs
pinch of salt
½   tsp. vanilla extract
¼   tsp. almond extract
½   cup soft butter
grated rind of 1 lemon
½   cup seedless raisins

rum sauce

¾   cup water
⅔   cup sugar
2   Tbs. lemon juice
½ – ⅔ cup dark rum

garnish

light sweetened whipped cream
several glacéed cherry halves (optional)

Dissolve the yeast in the warm milk, stir in 1 tablespoon of sugar and 1 cup of flour. Put this sponge in a medium-sized bowl, cover it with a light towel, and leave it in a warm place to rise for about half an hour, or until it has puffed up to nearly twice its original size.

Beat the eggs lightly with the remaining sugar. Add the salt, vanilla and almond extracts, and the remaining flour, and beat vigorously until the batter is perfectly smooth. Add the sponge and beat vigorously again, either by hand with a wooden spoon, or with a strong electric mixer, until the batter is smooth and elastic, and beginning to blister.

Cover the bowl with a light towel and leave the batter in a warm place to rise until it has doubled in bulk, about 45 minutes to an hour. Stir the batter down, add the softened butter, and beat vigorously once more until the butter is completely incorporated and the batter is glossy and elastic. It will be quite soft, and should fall away easily from the spoon and the sides of the bowl.

Stir in the grated lemon rind and the raisins. Butter a medium-large ring mold and dust it with very fine dry breadcrumbs. Pour the batter into the mold: the batter should fill about half the mold at this point. Cover it with a light towel and let it rise in a warm place for half an hour.

Put the mold gently into a preheated 400 degree oven. After 5 minutes, lower the heat to 350 degrees and bake 30 to 40 minutes more, or until the cake tests done.

Make the rum sauce: combine the water, sugar, and lemon juice in a medium saucepan and boil for 10 minutes. Let the syrup cool to lukewarm, then add the rum.

When the cake is done, tip it delicately out of the mold onto a cake rack and let it cool to lukewarm, then put it back into its mold. Pierce the top of the baba carefully in about a dozen places, either with a thin skewer or the point of a very sharp knife. Spoon the rum sauce over the cake gradually, letting some of it seep in where the top was pierced, and some of it run down the sides and center. Cover tightly with aluminum foil and leave to ripen for several hours.

Turn the baba out on a platter and let it rest in that position for about half an hour before serving. Decorate it with glacéed cherry halves if desired. Garnish each serving with a large dollop of lightly sweetened whipped cream.

Serves 10 to 12.

preserves and relishes

Having a row of pretty, jewel-like jars of marmalade, chutney, jam, and other such preserved delicacies secreted away, somewhere in the cool, dim recesses of your pantry or kitchen cupboards, is a wonderful feeling and, at the same time, both sensible and opulent. In the summer and fall, when fruits and vegetables are abundant, we delight in eating everything fresh and ripe and hardly open that cupboard, unless it's for a chutney. But in the winter, there are days of little enough light and less warmth, even here in California, and what a pleasure it is then to open one of those jars and spoon out a rich, sweet-flavored concentration of summery goodness. Homemade jams, fruit butters, and chutneys are always more satisfying that way than anything you can buy in a store. It isn't just a matter of the sunny memories that are sealed up with the jam and that drift out with its fruity perfume when you pry off the lid—I think the flavors really are superior.

Putting things up in jars is not as mysterious a process as it is sometimes given out to be. After all, not so long ago it was a perfectly ordinary and frequent activity in nearly every household's kitchen. What your grandmother could do, you can do as well: You only need to put in a small stock of easy-sealing mason jars and have on hand some large kettles and a few other basic pieces of equipment that you probably already have and use for other things. Then, when a neighbor's tree is heavy with ripe fruit and boxes of rosy peaches or apricots are being left on doorsteps, you can cheerfully take advantage, and in the less bountiful months that follow, you can spread your toast with ambrosial fruit butter or garnish a dinner with a piquant relish.

It will take several hours to put up a batch of any one of these things, but how little time that seems when you realize how long and how variously you'll be enjoying the product of your labors. Month after month, I turn quite ordinary fare into something exciting or exotic by dipping into my stores. A bit of spicy Tomato-Apple Chutney added to a mild cheese in an omelet turns that ten-minute meal into something special. A sumptuous breakfast or tea can be arranged by putting out a selection of sweet conserves, jams, or butters to spread on the toast or biscuits. Pickled onions or spiced pickled peaches, served in small quantities to garnish a mild, creamy dish, also multiply the interest and effect of a meal. And a perfectly elegant dessert can be produced on a moment's notice by opening a jar of brandied apricots.

I've collected here a small sampling of my personal favorites. There is a definite emphasis on fruit butters and spicy concoctions of various kinds, which reflects my taste. In general, I prefer butters to jams, for the great latitude possible in the proportion of sugar to fruit and the possibility of creating subtle blends of flavors. I like chutneys and spicy relishes for the incomparable way that they enhance and enliven a multitude of other foods. But most of all, I like preserves that are unusual—unavailable in the supermarket at any price and therefore doubly exciting.

Start now with a little batch of something or other—there's always *something* in season, no matter what time of year it is—and if it's your first try, well, all the more reason to make it something very special. Before long, you'll amass a tidy little collection of gleaming jars, full of gold, red, green, and russet brown riches, and amazing amounts of flavor for such tiny spaces.

MAKING PRESERVES

Before you start making any preserves, be sure you have the following things: an accurate kitchen scale, a couple of very large pots or kettles, sharp knives, long-handled wooden spoons, sieves, and plenty of mason jars with rings and lids. The jars are an investment—they aren't cheap, but you will reuse them many times, only buying new lids, as those are used but once. A funnel for filling jars and tongs for lifting them out of boiling water or while they are hot are both a great help. It's also a good idea to have a supply of labels—ordinary small office labels will do the job—and to label everything with contents and date as soon as the jars are cool. You may think, after a few hours over your stove, that what went into each jar is burned into your memory forever, but when a few months go by and you've made more than one kind of preserve, it can get very confusing.

There are basic steps to be followed in any kind of preserving, and they vary according to the kind of food being used and the type of preserve. Certain rules must be followed, or the preserved food could be susceptible to spoilage and unsafe to eat. The recipes here, however, are all relatively high-acid foods, which are much less susceptible to bacteria. So at least we needn't bother with pressure canners, and only sometimes with a boiling-water bath.

sterilizing jars

If the preserve is not going to be processed in a boiling-water bath, the jars you are using must be sterilized. If a boiling-water bath is used, then the jars will be sterilized along with the contents. To sterilize jars, cover them completely with water and boil them for 20 minutes. I use a tall spaghetti kettle for this job, with a small rack in the bottom to keep the jars from bouncing around. Leave the jars in the hot water until just before you want to use them, then remove them with tongs, drain them, and fill them while they are still hot. Self-sealing lids with rubber strips should not be boiled. Just put them in a bowl, pour boiling water over them, and leave them there until you need them.

sealing jars

Modern mason jars, with two-part metal lids, are essentially self-sealing. To seal the jars, fill them with the hot preserve, leaving the specified amount of headroom. Wipe the rim dry. Put the clean, dry lid on the jar and screw down the ring securely. Allow the jars to cool gradually. As they cool, the hot air in the top (that's why you need headroom) will begin to contract, forming a vacuum. The lid will be sucked in by the vacuum, and you will hear a nice, satisfying "ping" when it seals.

Note: If you are making a jam or preserve with large chunks of whole fruit in it, allow it to cool for about 10 minutes, stirring often, before filling the jars. This will prevent the pieces of fruit from floating to the top.

the boiling-water bath

Some preserves, such as the brandied apricots, are processed in a boiling-water bath. This simply means that the filled and sealed jars are placed in a large kettle, on a rack, with enough boiling water to cover them by 2 inches, and boiled for a specified amount of time. Both the jar and contents are sterilized, while the air trapped in the contents of the jars and in the headroom left in the top is forced out. A vacuum seal is formed almost immediately after the jars are removed from the boiling water.

Some old-fashioned, screw-top mason jars have lids which must be screwed on, then loosened a bit before being placed in the boiling water, in order to allow room for the air to escape. Modern mason jars, however, have enough give in the metal caps to allow air to escape, during the boiling-water bath, when they are screwed tight, and need no further tightening on removal.

cooling, labeling, and storing

The hot jars should be allowed to cool gradually. When they are quite cool, the screw-on rings can be removed. The jars should be wiped perfectly clean, the seals checked, and every jar labeled with contents and date. Store preserves in a cool, dry place.

making jams

Slightly underripe fruit, freshly picked if possible, is best for jam making. Overripe fruit tends to lose some of its natural pectin, the substance in the fruit which makes it set. Without sufficient pectin, what you intend to be jam will, in fact, remain syrup.

The fruit should be sorted carefully, and any soft or blemished pieces discarded. It should then be quickly and gently washed, and, when necessary, peeled, cored, or pitted. Hard fruits should be cut up in small pieces. Soft fruits, such as berries, should be slightly crushed so that some juice is released, and the fruit can be heated without adding water.

The prepared fruit and the sugar should both be carefully weighed. It's not a good idea to double quantities when making jams—a very large quantity will take longer and could easily boil over the top of your kettle, causing you no end of grief.

The prepared fruit is cooked in a big pot until it is tender, with frequent stirring to prevent scorching. Then the premeasured sugar is stirred in. The sugar can be warmed slightly beforehand to keep it from lowering the temperature of the fruit very much and help it dissolve more quickly, but this is not a do-or-die step. When the sugar is dissolved, the mixture must be brought to a rolling boil, and that means it's boiling so hard that it spits. No compromise allowed here. Jam cooked at too low a temperature won't set. The jam will foam up considerably at this point; thus the need for very large pots. The hard boil must be maintained until the jam sets. This could take from 5 to 25 minutes, depending on the type of fruit, its ripeness, et cetera.

The easiest way to test for set is to drop a small amount of jam onto a cold plate and let it cool. If it thickens enough to form a skin and wrinkle when touched, it's time to put it in jars.

Spoon the jam into sterile, hot jars, wipe the rims dry, and screw down the lids tightly. Label when the jars are cool and store in a cool, dry place.

making fruit butters, chutneys, relishes, and catsup

These are the most foolproof of all preserves, as no "setting" is involved. The ingredients are prepared according to a recipe and cooked together until the proper consistency is reached through reduction. When the substance is as thick as you want it, it's done, and that's that. Just fill your hot, sterile jars and seal immediately. Since pectin is not necessary to butters and chutneys, completely ripe fruit can be used, but don't try to save fruit that is really past its prime by turning it into any kind of preserve: The flavor will suffer.

One point to remember about making fruit butters is that it could be dangerous to adjust the seasoning and spicing too early in the cooking. Remember that as the butter thickens, all those flavors will be concentrated, so wait until the consistency is nearly right before adding those final touches.

Do not overcook chutneys, unless you are prepared to have them turn into pulp. I prefer chutneys with whole chunks of fruit or vegetable in them. As soon as a chutney is thick, it is ready to be put into jars.

And remember that, in any recipe involving vinegar or brine, glass, stainless steel, or enameled utensils should be used. Avoid brass, copper, iron, and tin.

One final note: Chutneys, pickles, and relishes of all kinds invariably improve with some aging. Put them away and forget about them for a few months, then taste and see how marvelously the flavors have ripened.

raspberry jam

2   lbs. fresh, clean raspberries
4   tsp. fresh lemon juice
2   lbs. sugar

Wash and sterilize five 8-ounce jars.

Put the clean berries in a large enameled pot along with the lemon juice. Squash some of the berries with a wooden spoon to start releasing the juice. Heat the berries slowly, stirring constantly and gently until they are boiling, then lower the heat and simmer them for 5 minutes, stirring often.

Meanwhile, spread the sugar in a metal baking pan and heat it in a low oven for about 5 minutes.

Add the warmed sugar to the simmering berries and stir over low heat until the sugar has completely dissolved. Turn the heat up as high as possible, bring the jam to a boil, and boil it hard for 5 to 6 minutes. Stir often with a long-handled wooden spoon.

Test the jam for set by dropping a bit of it on a saucer that has been chilled in the freezer. Put the saucer back in the freezer for about 2 minutes. If the jam has thickened by the time it is cool and forms a surface that wrinkles when touched, it has set and is ready to be bottled.

Ladle the jam into sterile, hot jars, leaving about ¼ inch of headroom. Wipe the rims until they are perfectly clean and dry, and seal the jars. Label them and store in a cool, dry place.

Makes about 2½ pints.

strawberry jam

2½ lbs. fresh, firm strawberries
2½ lbs. sugar (about 6 cups)
¼   cup fresh lemon juice

Wash and hull the berries. Cut them in half if they are very large; leave smaller berries whole.

Combine the prepared berries, the sugar, and the lemon juice in a large enameled kettle.

Stir often and carefully with a wooden spoon, over very low heat, until the sugar is completely dissolved and the syrup clear.

Turn the heat up very high and, stirring constantly, bring the jam to a full, spitting boil. Boil hard, and continue stirring gently, until the jam sets—this could take up to 15 or 20 minutes, depending on the pectin content of the fruit.

As soon as the boiling jam starts to make a heavy plopping sound, test for set (see page 364). When it is starting to set, remove the jam from the heat. Let it cool for a few minutes, stirring occasionally. Ladle it into hot, sterile jars, leaving at least ¼ inch of headroom. Wipe the rims until they are perfectly clean and dry, and seal immediately.

Label the jars, and store in a cool, dry place.

Makes 3 pints.

apple butter

3½ lbs. tart green apples
2 cups apple cider
1 cup white sugar
1 cup brown sugar
½ tsp. allspice
½ tsp. cinnamon
¼ tsp. ground cloves
⅛ tsp. salt
2 Tbs. molasses

Quarter, peel, and core the apples. Cook the peels and cores in the cider, covered, for about ½ hour. Strain the cider and discard the solids.

Add the apples and all remaining ingredients to the cider and simmer the mixture, stirring often, until the apples are very soft. Press the mixture through a fine sieve or purée it in a blender.

Continue cooking the apple butter over a low flame, stirring often, until it is very thick and smooth. Spoon it into hot, sterile jars, leaving about ⅓ inch of headroom, and seal.

Makes about 3 pints.

cranberry-fig conserve

1 lb. cranberries
1 lb. fresh figs
2 pippin apples (or other firm, tart green apples)
2 lemons
½ cup water
2 lbs. sugar
2 Tbs. kirsch

Wash the cranberries and pick them over, discarding any that are soft or brown. Trim the stems off the figs, quarter the figs lengthwise, and slice them thinly. Peel and core the apples and coarsely chop them. Slice 1 of the lemons and remove all the seeds, then chop it finely, peel and all, or put it through the coarse blade of a food mill. Squeeze and reserve the juice of the second lemon and discard the rind.

Combine the cranberries, figs, apples, chopped lemon, lemon juice, and water in a large, heavy-bottomed enameled kettle, and heat gently, stirring, until the berries begin popping and releasing their juice. Bring the mixture to a simmer and cook it, stirring often, until all the fruit is tender.

Add the sugar and stir over low heat until it is completely dissolved. Bring this mixture to a hard, spitting boil, and keep it boiling, stirring often with a long-handled wooden spoon, until it sets (see page 364)—about another 8 to 10 minutes. Add the kirsch, stir it in, and cook another minute or so, then ladle into hot, sterile jars, leaving about ¼ inch of headroom, and seal. Allow the jars to cool, then wipe them off, label, and store in a cool, dry place.

Makes about 3½ pints.

apricot or peach butter with brandy

Because a fruit butter does not depend on pectin to set, the proportions of fruit to sugar can be varied. I like mine slightly less sweet than jam (which still leaves plenty of room to be sweet). The spices also can be increased or decreased to taste.

8 cups peeled, pitted, and coarsely chopped apricots or peaches (about 6 lbs. whole)
2 Tbs. lemon juice
3 cups sugar
½ tsp. cinnamon
¼ to ½ tsp. ginger
¼ to ½ tsp. allspice
¼ cup brandy

Combine the prepared fruit and the lemon juice in a large enameled kettle and heat very gently until the fruit starts to release its juice. Simmer, stirring often, until it is tender.

Purée the fruit in a blender, in batches of several cups, and return the purée to the kettle. Add the sugar and spices and simmer again, stirring often, until the mixture is as thick as you want it. This may well take an hour or two, so be patient.

Add the brandy and cook for a few minutes more, just until the proper thickness is regained.

Spoon the hot fruit butter into hot, sterile jars, leaving about ⅓ inch of headroom, and seal immediately.

Makes 3 to 4 pints, depending on how concentrated you like it.

pickled spiced peaches

4 lbs. firm, unblemished peaches
3¼ cups cider vinegar
2 cups sugar
1 stick cinnamon
1 Tbs. allspice
1 Tbs. whole cloves
½ tsp. ginger
zest of 1 lemon, peeled off in thin strips

Put the peaches carefully into a large pot of boiling water and let them simmer for 3 minutes, then remove them with a slotted spoon. Run a little cool water over the peaches and slip off their skins. Halve the peaches, remove the pits, and put them in a bowl of cool, salted water.

In a large enameled pot, heat the vinegar with the sugar and spices.

When the sugar is completely dissolved, add the peach halves and simmer them, turning them occasionally with wooden spoons so that they cook evenly, until they are just tender, about 20 to 25 minutes.

Arrange the peach halves carefully in sterile glass jars. Strain the vinegar and return it to the pot. Boil it for 5 to 10 minutes, or until it has the consistency of thin syrup. Pour the spiced vinegar over the peaches, covering them completely and leaving about ½ inch of headroom. Wipe the rims and seal the jars immediately. Let the peaches ripen for about 3 months.

Makes about 3½ pints.

whole apricots in brandy

4 lbs. firm, ripe apricots
4 cups sugar
4 cups water
1 generous cup brandy

Use only firm, blemish-free apricots for this recipe and follow it carefully.

Wash the apricots. Heat the water and sugar together in a large pot. When the sugar is completely dissolved and the syrup is boiling, add the apricots and simmer them for 4 minutes *only*. Remove them gently with a slotted spoon, being careful not to bruise them or break the skins.

Fit the apricots in clean, hot jars, Don't crush them, but do fit them as closely as you can. Pour in 6 tablespoons of brandy to each quart jar or 3 to a pint jar. Fill the jars with the hot sugar syrup, leaving only ½ inch of headroom, wipe the rims, and screw down the lids. Process in a boiling-water bath for 15 to 20 minutes (see page 363). Remove the jars and allow them to cool gradually.

Makes approximately 3 quarts.

tomato catsup

9 lbs. ripe, red tomatoes
4 medium-sized yellow onions, chopped
1 red bell pepper, seeded and chopped
1 cup cider vinegar plus 2 to 3 Tbs. (optional)
1 tsp. whole allspice
1 tsp. whole cloves
5 sticks cinnamon, broken
1 tsp. celery seeds
½ tsp. dry mustard
⅛ to ¼ tsp. cayenne pepper
4 Tbs. brown sugar
5 Tbs. honey
1 tsp. salt, or more to taste

Cut the tomatoes in quarters and purée them in a blender, in batches, together with the chopped onions and red pepper. Strain the purée through a coarse sieve to eliminate the tomato skins, and pour it into a large, enameled kettle.

Cook the mixture over a low flame, stirring often, until it has thickened considerably, possibly as long as 1 hour.

Wrap the allspice, cloves, cinnamon, and celery seeds in a piece of cheesecloth and put them in a small pot with the vinegar. Heat the

tomato catsup (continued)

vinegar and bag of spices together for about 30 minutes, then remove the bag of spices.

Add about ½ the spiced vinegar to the tomato mixture, stir it in, and taste. For a spicier flavor, add a little more of the spiced vinegar. If it is already sufficiently spicy for you, just add 2 or 3 tablespoons of plain cider vinegar. This seasoning must be done to your taste. Then add the mustard, cayenne, sugar, honey, and salt.

Cook the mixture again, stirring often, until it has reached the consistency that you prefer for catsup. Time will vary, depending on what consistency you want, but it could take another hour. Taste it, and correct the seasoning if necessary. Pour into hot, sterile jars, and seal, leaving at least ½ inch of headroom.

Makes about 3 to 4 pints, depending on consistency of catsup.

peach chutney

4   lbs. peaches
1   lb. brown sugar
10 oz. raisins
2   lbs. onions, minced or ground
2   cups cider vinegar
2   oz. peeled and finely chopped fresh ginger
    (about ⅓ cup)
1   Tbs. chili powder
2   Tbs. whole mustard seeds
1   Tbs. salt
grated rind and juice of 1 lemon
grated rind and juice of 1 orange
¼   tsp. cayenne pepper
½   tsp. cinnamon

Peel and remove the pits from the peaches and cut them into smallish bits—but don't chop them. Combine all the ingredients in a large enameled pot and simmer gently, stirring often, until quite thick. This could take over an hour.

Spoon the boiling hot chutney into hot, sterilized jars, leaving ¼ inch of headroom, and seal.

Makes about 5 pints.

tomato chutney

4   lbs. red tomatoes
¾   lb. onions
6   oz. raisins
4   oz. pitted prunes, sliced
1¼ cups cider vinegar
½   cup brown sugar
1   tsp. ginger
1   tsp. cayenne pepper
2½ Tbs. salt
½   tsp. ground cloves
1½ tsp. ground coriander
1   tsp. whole mustard seeds

Blanch the tomatoes in boiling water and peel them, then half them (or, if very large, quarter them) and cut them in fairly thick slices. Peel and chop the onions. Combine all the ingredients in a large enameled kettle and simmer until the mixture is quite thick—it may take over 1 hour.

Spoon the chutney immediately into hot, sterile jars, leaving at least ¼ inch of headroom, and seal. The flavor will mellow with time.

Makes 2½ to 3 pints.

tomato-apple chutney

4   lbs. ripe tomatoes (about 12 large)
2   lbs. tart green apples (8 to 9)
2½ cups cider vinegar
2½ cups brown sugar
3   large onions, peeled and chopped
1   Tbs. mustard seeds, crushed
¼ to ½ tsp. cayenne pepper
2   Tbs. salt
4   tsp. ginger
1½ cups raisins

Cut the tomatoes into quarters and purée them in the blender in batches. Strain the purée through a coarse sieve to eliminate the skins.

Peel and core the apples and cut them into ½-inch chunks.

Combine all the ingredients in a large enameled kettle and simmer gently, stirring often, until the mixture is very thick. Cooking time will probably be about 1½ hours. Spoon the hot chutney into hot, sterile jars and seal.

Makes about 3 pints.

dill pickles

2¼ lbs. pickling cucumbers
1   pint cider vinegar
1½ cups water
3   Tbs. sugar
2   Tbs. salt
1   bay leaf
5 to 6 whole cloves
¼   tsp. celery seeds
½   tsp. whole peppercorns
½   tsp. mustard seeds
1   tsp. dill seeds or 2 heads fresh dill weed

Wash the cucumbers and quarter them length-wise.

Combine the vinegar, water, sugar, salt, and bay leaf in an enameled pot. Put the cloves, celery seeds, peppercorns, mustard seeds, and ½ teaspoon of the dill seeds in a muslin bag and add it to the vinegar mixture. (If using fresh dill, omit the dill seeds here.) Bring this liquid to a boil, lower the heat, and let it simmer for 15 minutes.

Remove the bay leaf and spice bag from the vinegar. Put ¼ tsp. dill seeds, or 1 head fresh dill weed, into each of 2 clean quart jars. Fit the cucumber spears as compactly as possible into the jars and pour the hot vinegar mixture over them. The cucumbers should be completely covered with the liquid, and there should be at least ½ inch of headroom at the top.

Screw down the lids and process the jars in a boiling-water bath for 20 minutes. Allow the pickles to cool, check the seals, and label the jars.

The pickles will improve in flavor if left to ripen for a few months.

Yields approximately 2 quarts.

william bryan's pickled onions

3   lbs. small white onions
2   qts. water
½   lb. salt
2   cups distilled white vinegar
2   cups cider vinegar
2   sticks cinnamon
½   tsp. whole cloves
1   tsp. mace
1   tsp. allspice
⅔   cup sugar
2 to 2½ tsp. crushed dried red chilis

Peel the onions. Heat the water and dissolve the salt in it. Let the brine cool to room temperature and pour it over the onions in a large glass or ceramic bowl or crock. All the onions should be covered. Leave the onions in the brine for 24 hours.

Put the 2 vinegars in an enameled pot with the cinnamon, cloves, mace, and allspice. Bring it to a boil, then turn off the heat, cover it, and let it steep for at least 2 hours. Strain the vinegar through a cheesecloth-lined sieve and discard the spices. Add the sugar to the vinegar and stir till it is completely dissolved.

Arrange the onions in sterile pint jars, leaving at least ½ inch of headroom. Put ½ teaspoon of crushed red chilis into each jar and cover the onions with the spiced vinegar. Seal the jars and put them aside for 1 month.

Makes 4 to 5 pints.

open-jar dill pickles

A great-tasting pickle to make in small quantities all summer long, these are ready in a few
days, at their prime in a week, and no trouble
to make. But only make as many as you'll want
to eat in a week's time, as they don't keep well.

2½ lbs. pickling cucumbers
2 qts. water
⅓ cup sugar
¼ cup salt
1½ to 2 oz. fresh dill (stalk, seeds, and all)
3 to 4 cloves garlic
8 large grapevine leaves

Scrub the cucumbers clean. Combine the
water, sugar, and salt, stirring until all the sugar
and salt are dissolved. Break or bend the stalks
of dill into pieces about 3 inches long, and peel
and thickly slice the garlic.

Put 2 or 3 grapevine leaves in a gallon-sized
crock, then a few pieces of dill and a few pieces
of garlic, and on top of this arrange a layer of
cucumbers. Put down a couple more grapevine leaves, some more dill and garlic, and
another layer of cucumbers. Continue in this
fashion until the ingredients are used up. Pour
the brine over the layered cucumbers.

Place a small plate or saucer on top of the
cucumbers and put a weight on it (a jar full of
water will do) to keep all the cucumbers
completely submerged in brine. Place the
crock on a deep plate or in a shallow bowl, as
the brine will start to foam over a bit as it
ferments.

Leave the crock at room temperature for 6 to 7
days, skimming off the top of the brine whenever necessary. The pickles are ready to eat,
right out of the crock, as soon as they taste sour
and salty enough to suit you.

Makes about 2½ pounds.

cranberry relish

1½ cups water
2 cups sugar
3 cups clean, picked-over cranberries
1 medium-sized navel orange
1 tsp. ground ginger
dash of cinnamon
dash of cloves
crushed seeds from 4 cardamom pods

Combine 1 cup of the water and the sugar in a medium-sized saucepan and heat until the sugar is dissolved. Add the cranberries and simmer them, covered, for 10 minutes, then uncovered for another 10, stirring occasionally.

Cut the unpeeled orange into chunks and put it through a food grinder or chop it finely. Add ½ cup water to the cranberries along with the ground-up orange, the ginger, cinnamon, and crushed cardamon seeds. Simmer the mixture for about 20 minutes, stirring often. Chill the relish before serving.

Makes about 5 cups.

quick pickled peppers

Serve the peppers as a relish with rich, mild-flavored dishes.

4 large bell peppers
4 cups water
1 cup cider vinegar
½ cup sugar
2 tsp. pickling spice
1½ Tbs. salt
1 clove garlic, peeled

Cut the bell peppers into thick strips or 1-inch squares. Do not discard the tops and seeds.

Heat the water in an enameled or stainless steel saucepan with the vinegar, sugar, pickling spice, salt, and garlic. Add the peppers, including the tops and seeds, and let them simmer gently for about 15 minutes, or until they are just tender. Turn off the heat and let them stand for another 15 minutes, then transfer the peppers to a jar, strain the liquid, and pour in as much as is needed to cover the peppers completely. Cover the jar with waxed paper and let it stand for 24 hours.

Makes about 1 quart.

tiny open-faced sandwiches

Little open-faced sandwiches are popular all through Eastern Europe as an hors d'oeuvre, or as an accompaniment to tea. In Vienna, an astonishing variety of these tiny sandwiches is displayed in windows or glass cases in certain restaurants at lunchtime. Set out in rows on big trays, they are pretty enough to rival the displays of pastries and make a quick but elegant lunch for the busier Viennese.

These are really canapés, much smaller than the famous open-faced sandwiches of Scandinavia. They're perfect as appetizers or for a cocktail party, but I also like to have them for supper sometimes—7 or 8 different little sandwiches with a glass of champagne make a pleasant meal in hot weather.

One of the best things about them is that you can create a marvelous-looking tray in a very short time, out of whatever tidbits you have on hand. The ingredients are all very flexible, and meant to be used as a guideline, so no specific amounts are given. In any case, most people don't like to make more than a few of one kind unless it's for a large affair because an assortment is always more fun. So, I've just written down descriptions of how I put together my favorites, and you take it from there.

cottage cheese and green onion sandwiches

slender sourdough or French bread, or pressed
    pumpernickel bread
butter
small-curd cottage cheese
chopped green onions
salt and pepper to taste

Cut thin slices from a sourdough *baguette*, or cut slices of square, pressed pumpernickel into quarters. Butter the bread, and put a heaping tablespoon of small-curd cottage cheese on each slice. Shape the cottage cheese evenly over the entire slice, then sprinkle about 1 tablespoon of chopped green onions over it and press the onions in very slightly so that they do not fall off quite so easily. Salt the sandwiches lightly and grind a little black pepper on them if you wish.

cream cheese and radish sandwiches

cream cheese
slender sourdough bread
radishes
salt to taste

Spread a thick layer of cream cheese on thin slices cut from a sourdough *baguette*. Wash and trim some radishes, and slice them about ⅛ inch thick. Arrange the radish slices over the cream cheese in rows, overlapping them so that at least 10 to 12 slices fit on each sandwich. Salt the radishes lightly.

smoked cheese and tomato sandwiches

pressed pumpernickel bread
butter
tomato slices
sprigs of fresh parsley
smoked cheese slices
salt to taste

Cut square slices of pressed pumpernickel into quarters and butter them generously. Cut some medium-sized tomato slices in half. Put ½ a tomato slice on each sandwich so that the cut edge goes diagonally from corner to corner. Tuck a few small sprigs of fresh parsley in under the cut edge of the tomato slice so that they peek out in a pretty ruffle.

Cut a few thin slices of a good smoked cheese and, using little aspic cutters,* make cutouts in nice shapes no bigger than 1 inch across. Salt the sandwiches lightly before placing one of the cheese cutouts on top of each tomato slice.

*If you don't have aspic cutters, you can use very tiny cookie cutters; failing that, simple shapes of the appropriate size could be cut out free-form with a sharp-pointed knife.

egg and cucumber sandwiches

pressed pumpernickel bread
butter
cucumber
hard-boiled eggs
stuffed cocktail olives

Cut square slices of pressed pumpernickel into quarters and butter them generously. Score a large, firm cucumber with a fork and slice it about ¼ inch thick. Put a cucumber slice in the center of each piece of bread. Peel some hard-boiled eggs and carefully slice them about ¼ inch thick as well. Using only the slices that have some of the yolk, center 1 slice of egg on each cucumber slice.

Cut several medium-sized pimiento-stuffed cocktail olives into 4 or 5 slices each and put 1 olive slice in the center of each egg slice.

cream cheese and cucumber sandwiches

slender sourdough bread, or pressed
    pumpernickel bread
cream cheese
cucumber
salt to taste
paprika to taste

Cut thin slices from a sourdough *baguette*, or cut slices of square pressed pumpernickel into quarters. Spread each slice rather thickly with cream cheese. Score a large, firm cucumber with a fork to give it a pretty pattern and slice it about ⅛ to ¼ inch thick. Put a slice of cucumber in the center of each sandwich and salt it very lightly, then delicately sprinkle some paprika down the center of the sandwich so as to make a bright red line straight across it.

egg and onion sandwiches with parsley

slender sourdough bread
butter
hard-boiled eggs
salt
sprigs of fresh parsley
pickled cocktail onions

Cut thin slices from a sourdough *baguette* and butter them generously. Peel several hard-boiled eggs and slice them about ¼ inch thick. Use only the larger slices that have part of the yolk in them.

Put 1 slice of egg in the center of each sandwich and salt to taste. Put medium-sized sprigs of fresh parsley at intervals around the edge of each sandwich, tucking the stems under the egg. Put a tiny pickled cocktail onion in the center of the egg slice and attach it to the sandwich with a toothpick.

smoked cheese and pickle sandwiches

pressed pumpernickel bread
butter
smoked cheese
large dill pickle(s)

Cut square slices of pressed pumpernickel into quarters and butter them generously. Slice some good smoked cheese thinly and trim the slices to fit the small pumpernickel squares.

Using aspic cutters (see page 381), make dainty little cutouts from the bits of cheese you have trimmed off, or from additional slices. Slice a large dill pickle, slanting the slices to make them a little larger.

Put a square slice of cheese on each piece of bread, then a large slice of dill pickle, and on top of that 1 of the small cheese cutouts.

monterey cheese and chili sandwiches

slender sourdough French bread
butter
strips of green chilis (canned are fine)
Monterey Jack cheese

Cut medium-thin slices from a long, slender loaf of sourdough French bread and butter them.

Cut some long, peeled and seeded green chilis into ¼-inch strips. Thickly slice some Monterey Jack cheese and cut the slices into bits about 1½ inches long by ½ inch wide.

Wrap 2 or 3 of the green chili strips around each piece of cheese in a coil pattern and put 1 such piece on each slice of bread. If the chili strips are to short or uneven, cut them into shorter pieces and just lay the chilis over the cheese in slanting stripes.

egg and pickled mushroom sandwiches

slender sourdough French bread
butter
hard-boiled eggs
long strips of pimiento pepper
marinated mushrooms
salt and pepper (optional) to taste

Cut thin slices from a long, slender loaf of sourdough French bread, and butter them generously. Peel some hard-boiled eggs and carefully slice them about ¼-inch thick. Cut a large, peeled and seeded pimiento pepper into long ¼-inch strips.

Using only the larger slices that include part of the yolk, put 1 slice of egg in the center of each piece of bread. Wrap a strip of pimiento around the outside of the egg slice. Place a small marinated or pickled mushroom cap on top of the egg slice and secure it with a toothpick if necessary.

Salt the sandwiches lightly and dust them with a little black pepper if desired.

cream cheese and watercress sandwiches

slender sourdough French bread
cream cheese
watercress
cherry tomatoes
salt to taste

Cut thin slices from a long, slender loaf of sourdough French bread and spread them generously with cream cheese.

Wash and trim a bunch of watercress, shake or pat it dry, and break it up into sprigs. Arrange 4 or 5 sprigs of watercress on each sandwich and put ½ a cherry tomato, cut side down, in the center. Salt the sandwiches lightly.

index

akni, 319
akuri, 319
Amaretto and cherry soufflé, 344
anise and lemon sauce, vegetables
    stewed in, 170
antipasto, 9, 191, 201, 236–7
  eggplant caviar, 149
  Florentine bread salad, 140
  fresh mozzarella salad, 152
  garbanzo bean salad, 143, 201
  gnocchi salad, 147
  insalatone, 148, 201
  lima bean salad, 144
  marinated mushrooms, 145
  peperonata, 144
  rice salad vinaigrette, 146
  salad Torcoloti, 137
  serving dishes, 10
  white bean salad, 146–7
apple(s)
  baked, 355
  butter, 367
  pudding, 339–40
  red cabbage with, 173
  strudel Grandma Clar, 336
  tart, 340–1
  -tomato chutney, 373
applesauce crêpes, 352
apricot(s)
  butter, with brandy, 369
  whole, in brandy, 370
artichoke(s)
  -cheese puff, 119
  hearts of, crêpes with hearts of
    palm and, 229

asparagus
  crêpes, 227–8
  mousse, cold, 157
  tortilla, 271
avocado(s)
  -cucumber sauce, 103
  filling for cantaloupe salad, 160
  guacamole, 296
  omelets, 129
  salad dressing, 109
  soup, 80, 88
  tacos, 289
  zucchini stuffed with, 156

baba ghanouj, 105, 152
banana-coconut *raita*, 314
Barcelona white bean salad, 266
barley and mushroom stuffed
    cabbage rolls, 178–80
Basque-style green beans (*lecas*), 186
beans
  garbanzo
    cocido, 275
    croquettes, 199–200
    curried, 304
    hommos bi tahini, 151
    potato *chat puris*, 320
    salad, 143, 201
    stewed, 267
  green, Basque-style (*lecas*), 186
  kidney
    pasta with (*pasta e fagioli*),
     68, 69

beans, kidney (*cont.*)
    potato tacos, 288
    refried, 293–4
  lima
    salad, 144–5
    in tomato and garlic sauce, 153
  white
    pâté, 195
    salad, 146–7, 266
Béchamel sauce, 98, 99,
  about, 93, 95
beer
  bread, 36–7
  onion soup, 55, 72
beet(s)
  -pineapple salad, 159
  soup, 89
    borscht, 56, 65, 191
    chłodnik, 89
beverages
  cantaloupe water, 297
  hot chocolate, 282
  Indian, 301
  sangría, 277
  strawberry water, 297
bibbelkäse, 203
biscuits, 50
blender, 93, 96
  mayonnaise, 107
blintzes, 233
borscht, 191
  with mushrooms, 65
Brie croquettes, 198
brandy
  apricot or peach butter with, 369

brandy (cont.)
  whole apricots in, 371
brandy cream, 350
bread(s), 23–53, 300
  baking, 23–6
  beer, 23, 36–7
  biscuits, 50
  braided whole wheat egg, 27
  brioches, 23, 30–1
  buttermilk dinner rolls, 44
  cheese-filled, 39–40
  cinammon, 38–9
  corn, 23, 45
    pumpkin-, 45
    -rye muffins, 52
  dinner rolls, 42–3, 44
  easy herb, 35–6
  flat, 23
  fried, 23
  muffins, 52–3
    corn and rye, 52
    four-grain, 52
    oatmeal, 53
  oatmeal-raisin, 38
  oatmeal-rye, 32
  puris, 23, 49, 320 .
  raisin-rye, 34–5
  rye, 23
    with fruit, 33
  salads
    in Caesar, 141
    Florentine, 140
  sweet, 45–7
    coffee, 23, 41–2
    cranberry, 23, 46
    Finnish rusks, 51
    orange-date, 46–7
    pumpkin corn, 45
    Vienna, 23, 28

bread(s), sweet (cont.)
  whole wheat anadama, 29
brioches, 30–1
broccoli
  mousse, cold, 158, 165
  -walnut soufflé, 116
  sauce for, 101
broth(s), 93; see also soup(s)
  akni, 319
  garlic, 58, 59
  vegetable, 57–8
brunch, 125, 127
burrito, 279; see also tortillas
butter, see fruitbutter(s); ghee
buttermilk
  dinner rolls, 44
  soup, chilled, 91

cabbage
  balls, sweet and sour stuffed, 184
  and peas, curried, 303
  pierogi filled with, 221
  red, with apples, 173
  rolls
    mushroom and barley stuffed, 178–80
    rice-stuffed, 180–1
cachumber, 316
Caesar salad, 141
cake(s)
  chocolate cheese, 328
  chocolate cream torte, 329
  fruit
    dark brandied, 338–9
    rum and chocolate, 334–5
  Genoese, 325
  Kate's, 329

cake(s) (cont.)
  lemon torte, 326–7
  sponge, 324
  spumoni, 330
  Wenia's mazurek, 332–3
  wild mushroom crepe, 230
cantaloupe
  chilled tomato soup with, 84
  filled, salad, 160
  water, 297
caramel custard (flan), 345–6
carrot(s)
  cream soup, 77
  glazed, 188–9
  halva, 349
  white bean pâté, 195
  -yogurt soup, 79
casserole(s)
  corn and cheese pudding, 189
  eggplant with cheese and walnuts, 185–6
  Italian potato and cheese, 172
  mamalyga, 207
  noodle kugel, 202
  potato, 173
  sweet and sour stuffed cabbage rolls, 184–5
  vegetable pilau, 312
catsup, 365, 371–72
cauliflower curry, 305
celery root salad, 150
champiñónes a la plancha, 268
chapatis, 23, 48, 283, 300
Cheddar cheese
  artichoke and cheese puffs, 119
  cheese pastries, 47
  chilaquiles with mushrooms, 291–2
  corn and cheese pudding, 189
  spiced, 205

cheese, 93, 191; see also names of cheeses
-artichoke puff, 119
asparagus crêpes, 227–8
baked stuffed tomatoes, 182
bibbelkäse, 203
bread filled with, 39–40
Brie croquettes, 198
cake, chocolate, 328
chilaquiles with mushrooms, 291–2
-chili omelets, 130
-chili sandwiches, 383
and chutney omelet, 128
-corn pudding, 189
crêpes with feta, 228–9
eggplant with walnuts and, 185–6
-egg sauce, spaghetti with, 246
enchiladas salsa verde, 287
filled Edam, 206
fried mozzarella, 256
and green chili soup, 75
Italian fondue, 201
lasagne, 247–8
liptauer, 203, 204
Mornay sauce, 99
mozzarella salad, 152
onion and mozzarella omelet, 130
-onion soufflé, 117
Parmesan crêpes, 226–7
pashka (dessert), 348
pastries, 47
pizza, 218–9
-potato casserole, Italian, 172
potato gnocchi, 252
-potato soufflé, spicy, 121
-potato soup, Dutch, 71
quiches, 213–18
    cheese and tomato pie, 216–7
    leek and tomato, 214–15

cheese, quiches (cont.)
• pimiento and olive, 215–16
    Roquefort, 214
    sweet potato and cranberry, 217–18
    smoked
        and pickle sandwiches, 383
        and tomato sandwiches, 381
soup, 55, 67, 71, 75
sour cream horseradish sauce, 101
spiced, 192
    Cheddar and Edam, 205
    farmer, 208
    white, 203
spinach and dill rice, 188
-spinach gnocchi, 253
tarts, savory Mexican, 295
-tomato pie, 216–17
wild mushroom crêpe cake, 230–1
cheesecake, chocolate, 328
cherry(ies)
-Amaretto soufflé, 344
clafouti of, 347
-lemon soup, cold, 90
soup, cold, 91
chiffonade dressing, 106
chilaquiles, 290–1
with mushrooms, 291
chili peppers, 130n, 280–1; see also
        Indian cuisine; Mexican cuisine
-cheese omelets, 130
-cheese sandwiches, 383
chilaquiles, 290–2
dried, 300
egg enchiladas, 286
enchiladas salsa verde, 287
guacamole, 296
sauce, 281
    Mexican cheese tarts, 295
chłodnik, 89

chocolate
    buttercream, 334
    cheesecake, 328
    cream torte, 329
    -rum fruitcakes, 334–5
Christmas, 191, 323
chutney, 361, 362
    -cheese omelet, 128
    peach, 372
    raisin and tamarind, 317
    tomato, 373
    tomato-apple, 373
cilantro (coriander), 281, 299
cinnamon bread, 38–9
clafouti of cherries, 347
cocido, 275
cocktail profiteroles, 208–9
coconut
    -banana raita, 314
    curried vegetables with, 302
    tomato raita, 313
coffee mousse, 346
cold dishes; see also mousses; raitas;
        soups
    mamalyga, 207
    omelet salad, 106
conchiglie tutto giardino, 242
cooking equipment, see kitchen
        equipment
coriander leaves, 281, 299
corn and corn meal
    -cheese pudding, 189
    tortillas, 282–4
    bread, 23, 45
    dumplings, 168–9
    mamalyga, 207
    -rye muffins, 52
cottage cheese
    bibbelkäse, 203

cottage cheese *(cont.)*
  -green onion sandwiches, 380
  soufflé, 120
cranberry
  bread, 23, 46
  -fig conserve, 368
  relish, 377
  -sweet potato quiche, 217–18
cream
  brandy, 350
  peaches and, 357
cream cheese
  -bell pepper omelets, 131
  chocolate cheesecake, 328
  -cucumber sandwiches, 382
  liptauer cheese, 203
  peppers with, 292–3
  -radish sandwiches, 380
  sweet potato and cranberry quiche,
    217
  -watercress sandwiches, 384
creamed soups
  avocado, 56, 80
  carrot, 77
  crema de verduras (puréed
    vegetables), 82
  fresh pea, 83
crème à la Irena, 165, 350
crêpes, 223–33
  about, 223–5
  asparagus, 227–8
  basic, 225–6
  blintzes, 233
  with creamed mushrooms, 232
  dessert
    applesauce, 352
    fresh lemon, 353
    Hungarian walnut, 354
  with feta cheese, 228

crêpes *(cont.)*
  fruit, 224
  with hearts of artichoke and palm,
    229
  "upside-down pans," 224–5
  Parmesan, 226–7
  sauces for, 102–3
  wild mushroom cake, 230–1
croquettes, 93, 191
  Brie, 198
  egg, 197
  garbanzo, 199–200
cucumber
  -avocado sauce, 94, 103
    asparagus crêpes, 227–8
  -cream cheese sandwiches, 382
  -egg sandwiches, 381
  gazpacho, 86, 87
  -paprika salad, 142
  raita, 314
  -sour cream salad, 142
  and spinach soup, cold, 85
curry
  cabbage and peas, 303
  cauliflower, 305
  egg and potato, 306
  garbanzo beans, 304
  green, 308
  vegetables with coconut, 302
custard sauce, 96

dal, 310–11
date-orange bread, 46–7
dessert, 323–57
  apples
    baked, 355
    pudding, 339–40

dessert, apples *(cont.)*
    strudel Grandma Clar, 336–7
    tart, 340–1
  blintzes, 233
  brandy cream, 350
  cake
    cheesecake, chocolate, 328
    chocolate cream torte, 329
    Genoese, 325
    Kate's chocolate cream, 329
    lemon tortes, 326–7
    sponge, 324
    spumoni, 330
    Wenia's *mazurek*, 332–3
    zuppa inglese, 331–2
  caramel custard *(flan)*, 345–6
  carrot *halva*, 349
  Castillian hot chocolate, 352
  cherry
    -Amaretto soufflé, 344
    clafouti of, 347
  chocolate
    buttercream, 334
    cheesecake, 328
    cream torte, 329
  coffee mousse, 346
  crème à la Irena, 350
  crêpes, 224
    applesauce, 352
    fresh lemon, 353
    Hungarian walnut, 354
  flan, 345–6
  fruitcakes
    dark brandied, 338–9
    rum and chocolate, 334–5
  lemon
    crêpes, 353
    filling, 327
    torte, 326–7

dessert *(cont.)*
  melons in Vermouth, 357
  mousse
    coffee, 346
    frozen strawberry, 351
  oranges in wine, 356
  -*paskha*, 348
  pastry crust, sweet, 326
  peaches
    and cream, 357
    in red wine, 356
  pudding
    apple, 339–40
    clafouti of cherries, 347
  pumpkin pie, 342, 343
  raspberry sauce, 345
  rum baba, 358–9
  soufflé, cherry and Amaretto, 344
  tart, apple, 340–1
dill
  pickles, 374
    open-jar, 376
  sauce, 104
  -spinach rice, 188
  -wild mushroom soufflé, 118–19
double boiler, 93, 100
dressing, *see* salad dressing
dumplings, 60, 275
Dutch cheese and potato soup, 55, 71

Edam cheese
  filled, 206
  spiced, 205
eggplant
  baba ghanouj, 152
  baked, 249
  caviar, 149
  with cheese and walnuts, 185–6

eggplant *(cont.)*
  giant mushrooms stuffed with, 183
  gingered, salad, 150–1
  and peppers roasted in oil, 267
  raita, 315
  soup, 78
  spiced, 307
  stewed, 167
    Ukrainian, 169
  tortilla (omelet), 269–70
  -zucchini roulade, 177–8
egg(s), 111–31
  akuri (spiced scrambled), 319
  -cheese sauce, spaghetti with, 246
  croquettes, 197
  -cucumber sandwiches, 381
  enchiladas, 286
  frittata, 258, 259
  -olive mold, 196
  omelets, 124–31
  -onion sandwiches, with parsley, 382
  -pickled mushroom sandwiches, 384
  and potato curry, 306
  sauces for, 100
  soufflés, 93, 111–23
enchiladas, 279; *see also tortillas*
  egg, 286
  salsa verde, 287
  spinach, 284–5
ensaladilla russa, 265
equipment, *see* kitchen equipment

farina with vegetables and spices, 316
farmer cheese, 192
  avocado tacos, 289

farmer cheese *(cont.)*
  blintzes, 233
  Brie croquettes, 198
  cheese and chutney omelet, 128
  crêpes with feta cheese, 228–9
  enchiladas salsa verde, 287
  liptauer cheese, 203, 204
  mamalyga, 207
  Mexican tarts, 295
  mushroom pâté, 193, 194
  noodle kugel, 202
  paskha, 348
  spiced, 208
  vareniki, 200–1
feta cheese
  crêpes with, 228
  Mexican tarts, 295
  spinach and dill rice, 188
fettucine Alfredo, 245
fig-cranberry conserve, 368
flan, 345–6
Florentine bread salad, 140
fondue, Italian, 201
Fontina cheese
  eggplant with cheese and walnuts, 185–6
  Italian fondue, 201
food processor, 93, 96
  brioches, 31
  mayonnaise, 104
  puff paste, 208–9
four-grain muffins, 53
French cuisine, 3; *see also* crêpes; mousses; pâtés; quiches
French dressing, 105
French-fried mushrooms, 165, 175
frittata
  onion and herb, 259
  of zucchini, 258

fritters, hot vegetable, 318
fruit; *see also* names of fruits
  crêpes, 224
  rye bread with, 33
fruit butters, 361, 362
  apple, 367
  apricot or peach, with brandy, 369
  making, 365
fruitcakes
  dark brandied, 338
  rum and chocolate, 334

garam masala, 321
garbanzo beans
  cocido, 275
  croquettes, 199–200
  curry, 304
  hommos bi tahini, 151
  potato *chat puris*, 320
  salad, 143, 201
  stewed, 267
garlic
  broth, 58, 59
  in salad, 136
  soup, 55, 64
  -tomato sauce, lima beans in, 153
  -tomato soup, 64
gazpacho, 86, 87
Genoese cake, 325
German potato salad, 155
ghee, 301
ginger, fresh, 299
gingered eggplant salad, 150–1
gnocchi
  potato, 252
  salad, 147, 236
  spinach and cheese, 253

Gouda cheese
  Dutch cheese and potato soup, 71
Greek cuisine, 4
  crêpes with feta cheese, 228–9
  potato salad *tzapanos*, 155
  pastries, 211
green beans
  Basque-style, 186
  salad Torcoloti, 137
  -watercress salad, 138–9
green chili and cheese soup, 55, 75
green curry, 308
greens, salad, 135
Gruyère cheese; *see also* Swiss cheese
  wild mushroom crêpe cake, 230–1
guacamole, 296

halva, carrot, 349
hearts of palm
  crêpes with artichoke hearts and,
    229
  tomatoes stuffed with, 154
herb(s), 93
  bread, easy, 35–6
  dressing, 106
  -onion *frittata*, 259
  salad, 136
  -spinach filling, for ravioli, 250–1
Hollandaise sauce, 93, 100; *see
    also* mousseline sauce
  technique for, 96–7
hommos bi tahini, 105, 151
hoop cheese, 192; *see also* farmer
    cheese
hors d'oeuvres, 191, 377; *see also*
    antipasto; salads, snacks; *tapas*
horseradish sour cream sauce, 101

hot chocolate, 264, 352
Hungarian cuisine, 4, 16
  stuffed potato pancakes, 187
  walnut crêpes, 354

Indian cuisine, 283, 299–321
  about, 299–301
  akni, 319
  akuri (spiced scrambled eggs), 319
  cachumber, 314
  carrot halva, 321
  chapatis, 23, 48, 283, 300
  chutney, 361, 362
    -cheese omelet, 128
    making, 365
    peach, 372
    raisin and tamarind, 317
    tomato, 373
    tomato-apple, 373
  curry
    cabbage and peas, 303
    cauliflower, 305
    egg and potato, 306
    garbanzo beans, 304
    green, 308
    vegetables with coconut, 302
  dal (spiced lentils), 310–11
  eggplant, spiced, 307
  farina with vegetables and spices,
    316
  garam masala, 321
  ghee (clarified butter), 301
  khagina (spiced omelet), 317
  pakoras (hot vegetable fritters),
    318
  pilau, 311
    vegetable, 312
  potatoes, smothered, 309

Indian cuisine (*cont.*)
puris, 23, 49
  potato *chat*, 320
raitas, 313–15
  banana and coconut, 314
  cucumber, 314
  eggplant, 315
  tomato, 313
  yogurt, 300
saffron rice, 313
saveth noodles, 320*n*
tomatoes, purée of scorched, 309–10
uppama, 316
ingredients
Indian, 299
omelet, 124
quality of, 8
salad, 133
sauce and salad dressing, 94, 97
insalatone, 148, 201
Italian cuisine, 3, 94, 235–59
about, 235–9
antipasto, 9, 10, 191, 201, 236–7
  eggplant caviar, 149
  Florentine bread salad, 140
  fresh mozzarella salad, 152
  garbanzo bean salad, 143, 201
  gnocchi salad, 147
  insalatone, 148
  lima bean salad, 144
  marinated mushrooms, 145
  peperonata, 144
  rice salad vinaigrette, 146
  salad Torcoloti, 137
  serving dishes, 10
  white bean salad, 146–7
conchiglie tutto giardino (pasta with fresh vegetables), 242

Italian cuisine (*cont.*)
desserts
  crème à la Irena, 350
  rum baba, 358–9
  spumoni cake, 330–1
  zuppa inglese, 331–2
eggplant
  baked (*melanzana al forno*), 249
  caviar, 149
fondue, 201
frittata
  onion and herb, 259
  of zucchini, 258
gnocchi
  potato, 252
  salad, 147, 236
  spinach and cheese, 253
melanzana al forno (baked eggplant), 249
menus, 7, 10–11
mozzarella
  fried, 256
  salad, 152
pasta
  e fagioli, 68, 69
  fettucine Alfredo, 245
  with fresh vegetables, 242
  lasagne, 247–8
  penne, 240, 241, 243
  ravioli with spinach and herb filling, 250–1
  spaghetti, 244, 246
pizza, 211–12, 218–19
pomodoro al gratine, 257
potato
  -cheese casserole, 172
  gnocchi, 252
spinach
  -cheese gnocchi, 253

Italian cuisine, spinach (*cont.*)
  -potato roulade, 254–5
  tomatoes, gratinéed, 257

jams, 361, 364–6
  raspberry, 366
  strawberry, 366

Kate's cake, 329
khagina, 317
kidney beans
  refried, 293–4
kitchen equipment
  crêpes
    "kits," 224–5
    pans, 225
  double boiler, 93, 100
  mason jars, 362–3
  omelet pan, 124
  oven, 112
  oven thermometer, 112–13
  for preserving, 361, 362–5
  for sauces, 93, 95, 100*n*
  spatula, 124
  soufflé dish, 113
  Teflon, 124
  tortilla press, 283
  whisk, 93
  wooden spoons, 93, 95

lasagne, 247–8
lecas (Basque-style green beans), 186
leek(s)
  marinated, 143

leeks (*cont.*)
-tomato quiche, 214–15
lemon(s)
-anise sauce, vegetables stewed in, 170
-cherry soup, cold, 90
dessert crêpes, 353
filling, 327
torte, 326–7
lentil(s)
dal, 310–11
soup, spiced, 76
lima bean(s)
salad, 144
in tomato and garlic sauce, 153
liptauer cheese, 138, 203, 204
liqueur, 93, 224
liquor, 93

mamalyga, 207
marinated leeks, 143
marinated mushrooms, 145, 201
mayonnaise, 93, 107
green, 107
technique for, 96, 97
melanzana al forno (baked eggplant), 249
melons in vermouth, 357
menestra de verduras (stewed vegetables), 272–7
menus, 7–21, 164–5, 191, 201
vegetarian vs. traditional, 7
Mexican cuisine, 94, 279–97
about, 279–82
beverages
cantaloupe water, 297

Mexican cuisine, beverages (*cont.*)
hot chocolate, 281–2
strawberry water, 297
cheese tarts, spicy, 295
chilaquiles, 290–2
chili, 280–1
enchiladas, 286
egg, 286
salsa verde, 287
spinach *suizas*, 284–5
guacamole, 296
kidney beans, refried, 293–4
menus, 12–13
peppers with cheese, 292–3
rajas con queso, 292–3
rice, 296
soup
cold avocado, 88
creamed avocado, 80
crema de verduras (cream of vegetable), 82
tortilla tlaxalteco, 66
tacos, 279
avocado, 289
bean and potato, 288
tortillas, 264, 279–80, 282–4
corn, 282–4
soup, 55
tortitas con queso (spicy cheese tarts), 295
Monterey Jack cheese
-chili sandwiches, 383
-green chili soup, 75
Mornay sauce, 95, 99
mousse(s)
asparagus, 157
broccoli, 158
coffee, 346
frozen strawberry, 351

mousseline sauce, spicy, 101
mozzarella cheese
cheese and chili omelets, 130
cheese and tomato pie, 216–17
eggplant with cheese and walnuts, 185–6
fried, 256
lasagne, 247–8
-onion omelet, 130
pizza topping, 218
potato and cheese casserole, Italian, 172
salad, 152
muffins, 52–3
Munster cheese
baked stuffed tomatoes, 182
cheese-filled bread, 39–40
spicy cheese and potato soufflé, 121
mushroom(s)
-barley stuffed cabbage rolls, 178–80
broccoli mousse, cold, 158
champiñónes a la plancha, 268
chilaquiles with, 291
clear beet borscht with, 65
creamed, crêpes with, 232
filling for *pierogi*, 220–1
French-fried, 175
marinated, 145
omelets, 126
pâtés, 193, 194
pickled, and egg sandwiches, 384
and potatoes in wine sauce, 171
stew, 165
winter vegetable, 166
stroganoff, 176
stuffed with eggplant, 183
stuffing for potato pancakes, 187
on toast, 174

mushroom(s) (cont.)
  wild
    crêpe cake, 230–1
    -dill soufflé, 118–19

noodles; see also pasta
  kugel, 191, 202
  simple soup, 60

oatmeal
  muffins, 53
  -raisin bread, 38
  -rye bread, 32
olive(s)
  -egg mold, 196
  -pimiento quiche, 215–16
omelet(s), 124–31
  avocado, 129
  cheese and chili, 130
  cheese and chutney, 128
  cold, salad, 161
  khagina (Indian spiced), 317
  mushroom, 126
  onion and mozzarella, 130
  pan for, 124
  pepper and cream cheese, 131
  plain, 124
  potato and zucchini, 127
  sauces for, 102, 103, 107
  sweet, 125
  tomato provençale, 128–9
  tortillas (Spanish), 264, 268–71
    asparagus, 271
    eggplant, 269–70
    alla paesana, 270–1

omelet(s), tortillas (cont.)
    española, 268–9
onion(s)
  -beer soup, 72
  cheese souffle, 117
  -egg sandwiches, with parsley, 382
  green, and cottage cheese
    sandwiches, 380
  -herb frittata, 259
  -mozzarella omelet, 130
  pickled, William Bryan's, 375
  for salads, 136
  spaghetti and, 244
  sweet and sour sauce, penne with,
    243
orange-date bread, 46–7
oranges in wine, 356
oven, see kitchen equipment

pakoras, 14, 318
pancakes, potato, Hungarian style
    stuffed, 186
paprika
  -cucumber salad, 142
  paprikasalat, 138
  sauce, 94
    hot, 102–3
    mild, 99
Parmesan cheese
  cheese pastries, 47
  cheese and tomato pie, 216–17
  crêpes, 226–7, 230
  fettucine Alfredo, 245
  Mornay sauce, 99
  -onion soufflé, 117
  potato gnocchi, 252
  spaghetti alla carbonara, 246
  spinach and dill rice, 188

Parmesan cheese (cont.)
  -spinach gnocchi, 253
paskha, 348
pasta
  about, 235–6
  balancing meals with, 8
  with beans, 68, 69
  conchiglie tutto giardino, 242
  cooking, 238–9
  with creamy tomato sauce, 241
  e fagioli, 55, 68, 69
  fettucine Alfredo, 245
  with fresh vegetables, 242
  lasagne, 247–8
  penne, 240, 241, 243
  ravioli with spinach and herb
    filling, 250–1
  sauces for, 102
  spaghetti, 244, 246
pastries, 211–21
  basic short-crust, 213
  cheese, 47
  pierogis, 211, 220–1
  pizzas, 211–12, 218–19
  quiches, 211, 213–18
  sweet crust, 326
pâtés, 191
  mushroom, 193, 194
  white bean, 195
peaches
  butter, with brandy, 369
  chutney, 372
  and cream, 357
  pickled spiced, 370
  in red wine, 356
peas
  and cabbage, curried, 303
  split, soup, 70
pectin, 365

penne
  al boccalone, 240
  al cardinale, 241
  with sweet and sour onion sauce,
    243
peperonata, 144, 201
peppers; *see also* chili peppers
  baked stuffed tomatoes, 182
  with cheese, 292–3
  cream cheese omelet, 131
  and eggplant roasted in oil, 267
  gnocchi salad, 147
  jalapeño, 281
  peperonata, 144
  quick pickled, 377
pickled mushrooms and egg
    sandwiches, 384
pickled onions, William Bryan's, 375
pickled peppers, quick, 377
pickled spiced peaches, 370
pickles, 365
  open-jar dill, 376
  -smoked cheese sandwiches, 383
pie; *see also* pastries; quiche
  cheese and tomato, 216–17
  pumpkin, 342, 343
pie crust, 213
pierniki, 323
pierogi, 211, 220–1
  cabbage filling, 221
  mushroom filling, 220–1
pilau
  plain, 311
  vegetable, 312
pimiento and olive quiche, 215–16
pineapple and beet salad, 159
pistou, 55, 74
pizza, 218–19, 237
  cheese and tomato pie, 216–17

Polish cuisine, 4
  menus, 16–17
  pierogis, 211, 220–1
  Wenia's *mazurek,* 332–3
pomodoro al gratine, 257
potato(es)
  -bean tacos, 288
  chat puris, 320
  -cheese casserole, Italian, 172
  -cheese soufflé, spicy, 121
  -cheese soup, Dutch, 71
  -egg curry, 306
  gnocchi, 252
  kugel, 173
  and mushrooms in wine sauce, 171
  pancakes, stuffed Hungarian style,
    187
  peel, broth, 58–9
  salad
    with caraway seed, 155
    ensaladilla russa, 265
    German, 155
    insalatone, 148
    Torcoloti, 137
    tzapanos, 155
  smothered, 309
  -spinach roulade, 254–5
  tortillas
    a la paisana, 270–1
    española, 268
  -zucchini omelets, 127
preserves and relishes, 361–77
  about, 361–65
  apricots, whole, in brandy, 371
  basic steps, 362–4
  catsup, 371–72
  chutney, 361, 362, 365
    peach, 372
    tomato, 373

preserves and relishes *(cont.)*
    tomato-apple, 373
  cranberry-fig conserve, 368
  cranberry relish, 377
  fruit butters, 361, 362, 365
    apple, 367
    apricot, with brandy, 369
    peach, with brandy, 369
  jam, 361, 364–7
    raspberry, 366
    strawberry, 366–7
  pickled onions, William Bryan's,
    375
  pickled peppers, quick, 377
  pickled spiced peaches, 370
  pickles, dill, 374
    open-jar, 376
profiteroles, cocktail, 208–9
provolone cheese
  Italian fondue, 201
pudding
  apple, 339–40
  clafouti of cherries, 347
  corn and cheese, 189
pumpkin
  corn bread, 45
  pie, 342, 343
purées, 93; *see also* creamed soups
  lentil (*dal*), 310–11
  of scorched tomatoes, 309
  vegetable soup (*crema de
    verduras*), 82
puris, 23, 49, 300
  potato *chat,* 320

quiches, 211
  cheese and tomato pie, 216–17
  leek and tomato, 214–15

quiches *(cont.)*
  pimiento and olive, 215–16
  Roquefort, 214
  shell for, 213
  sweet potato and cranberry, 217–18

radish and cream cheese sandwiches
    380
raisin(s)
  -oatmeal bread, 38
  -rye bread, 34–35
  -tamarind chutney, 317
raitas
  banana and coconut, 314
  cucumber, 314
  eggplant, 315
  tomato, 313
  yogurt, 300
rajas con queso, 292–3
raspberry jam, 366
raspberry sauce, 94, 345
ravioli with spinach and herb filling,
    250
red cabbage with apples, 173; *see
    also* cabbage
reduction sauces, 97
relishes, *see* preserves and relishes
rice
  Mexican, 296
  plain *pilau*, 311
  saffron, 313
  salad vinaigrette, 146
  spinach and dill, 188
  -stuffed cabbage rolls, 180–1
  vegetable *pilau*, 312
ricotta cheese
  cheese and spinach gnocchi, 253

ricotta cheese *(cont.)*
  lasagne, 247–8
risotto, 237
rolls, dinner
  buttermilk, 44
  soft, 42–3
Roquefort cheese
  cheese-filled bread, 39–40
  quiche, 214
roux, 95
  for soufflé base, 113
rum baba, 358–9
Russian cuisine
  mamalyga, 207
  paskha, 348
  piroshki, 211
  vareniki, 191, 200–1
rye bread
  with fruit, 33
  with raisins, 34–5

saffron, 299–300
  rice, 313
salad, 133–61
  accents, 136
  asparagus mousse, 157
  avocado-stuffed zucchini, 156
  baba ghanouj, 152
  beet and pineapple, 159
  broccoli mousse, 158
  cachumber, 316
  Caesar, 141
  celery root, 150
  cold omelet, 161
  cucumber
    -paprika, 142
    sour cream and pressed, 142
  dressing, *see* salad dressings

salad *(cont.)*
  eggplant
    caviar, 149
    gingered, 150–1
    and sesame paste, 152
  filled cantaloupe, 160
  Florentine bread, 140
  garbanzo bean, 143
    and sesame paste, 151
  garden-fresh, 133–5
  gnocchi, 147, 236
  greens for, 135
  herbs for, 136
  hommos bi tahini, 151
  insalatone, 148
  leeks, marinated, 143
  lima bean, 144–5
    in tomato and garlic sauce, 153
  as main course, 134
  mozzarella, 152
  paprika-cucumber, 142
  paprikasalat, 138
  peperonata, 144
  potato
    with caraway seed, 154
    ensaladilla russa, 265
    German, 155
    insalatone, 148
    tzapanos, 155
  pressed cucumber-sour cream, 142
  rice vinaigrette, 146
  spinach, 139
  tomatoes stuffed with hearts of
    palm, 154
  Torcoloti, 137
  tossed, 135–6
  watercress and green bean, 138–9
  white bean, 146
    Barcelona, 266

salad dressing(s), 97; *see also* sauce(s)
 avocado, 109
 chiffonade, 106
 French, 105
 herb, 106
 mayonnaise, 107
 sour cream, 108
 technique, 136
sandwiches, 197, 379–84
 cottage cheese and green onion,
  380
 cream cheese
  -cucumber, 382
  -radish, 380
  -watercress, 384
 egg
  -cucumber, 381
  -onion with parsley, 382
  -pickled mushroom, 384
 Monterey cheese and chili, 383
 open-faced, tiny, 379–84
 smoked cheese
  -pickle, 383
  -tomato, 381
sangría, 264–5, 277
saucepans, 93, 95, 100n
sauce(s), 93–109; *see also* salad
  dressing(s)
 about, 93–7
 Béchamel, 98
 chili, 281
 crêpe, 223
 cucumber-avocado, 103
 custard, 96
 dill, 104
 emulsion, 96
 flour-thickened, 95–6
 Hollandaise, 100

sauce(s) *(cont.)*
 hot, for *tortillas*, 284–5
 mayonnaise, 107
 Mornay, 99
 mousseline, spicy, 101
 paprika
  hot, 102–3
  mild, 99
 pasta, 235–6, 239
 pizza, 218
 raspberry, 345
 reduction, 97
 sesame seed, 105
 soufflé base, 113–14
 sour cream horseradish, 101
 Taratour, 105
 tomato, 97
  fresh hot, 104
  simple, 102
 vinaigrette, 97
sauerkraut soup, 55, 73
saveth noodles, 320n
sesame paste
 baba ghanouj, 152
 hommos bi tahini, 151
sesame seed sauce, 105
short-crust pastry, basic, 213
smoked cheese
 -pickle sandwiches, 383
 -tomato sandwiches, 381
snacks, 11, 191; *see also* tapas
soda breads, 23
soufflés, 93, 111–23
 artichoke and cheese puff, 119
 base, 113–14
 broccoli-walnut, 116
 cheese and potato, spicy, 121
 cherry and Amaretto, 344

soufflés *(cont.)*
 cottage cheese, 120
 egg whites, 114–15
 onion and cheese, 117
 sauces for, 101, 102, 107
 spinach, 123
 wild mushroom and dill, 118–19
 zucchini, 122
soups, 55–91
 about, 55–6
 avocado, 80, 88
 beer and onion, 72
 beet
  borscht with mushrooms, 65
  chłodnik, 89
 carrot
  cream of, 77
  -yogurt, 79
 cheese, 67
  -green chili, 75
  -potato, Dutch, 71
 cocido, 275
 cold
  avocado, 88
  beet (chłodnik), 89
  buttermilk, 91
  cherry, 91
  cherry-lemon, 90
  cucumber and spinach, 85
  gazpacho, 86–7
  tomato with cantaloupe, 84
 creamed
  avocado, 80
  carrot, 77
  crema de verduras, 82
  fresh pea, 83
 dumplings for, 60, 275
 eggplant, 78

soups (cont.)
  garlic, 69–70
    broth, 58, 59
    -tomato, 64
  gazpacho
    my, 87
    toledano, 86
  green chili and cheese, 75
  lentil, spiced, 76
  noodle, very simple, 60
  pasta e fagioli, 68, 69
  pea
    fresh creamed, 83
    split, 70
  pistou, 74
  potato peel broth, 58–9
  sauerkraut, 73
  spinach, 63
  sweet potato, 66–7
  tortilla tlaxcalteca, 66
  vegetable, 61, 62
    broth, 57
    cocido, 275
    pureed (crema de verduras), 82
  watercress, 81
sour cream
  dressing, 108
  -horseradish sauce, 101
  mamalyga, 207
  -pressed cucumber salad, 142
spaghetti
  alla carbonara, 246
  e cipolle, 11, 244
  with egg and cheese sauce, 246
  and onions, 244
Spanish cuisine, 3, 261–77
  about, 261–5
  asparagus tortilla, 271

Spanish cuisine (cont.)
  dessert
    Castillian hot chocolate, 264, 352
    flan, 345–6
  eggplant tortilla, 269–70
  ensaladilla russa (salad), 265
  menestra de verduras (stewed
    vegetables), 272–3, 274
  menus, 7, 11–12, 268, 272
  sangría, 264–5, 277
  soup, 55
    cocido, 275–6
    garlic (ajo), 69–70
    gazpacho, 86, 87
  stewed vegetables, 272–3, 274
  tapas, 11, 261–3
    Barcelona white bean salad, 266
    champiñónes a la plancha, 268
    roasted eggplant and peppers in
     oil, 267
    stewed garbanzo beans, 267
  tortillas (omelets), 262
    asparagus, 271
    eggplant, 269–70
    española, 268–9
    a la paisana, 270–1
  wine, 264
spatula, 124
spices
  farina with vegetables and, 316
  garam masala, 321
spinach
  -cheese gnocchi, 253
  -cucumber soup, cold, 85
  -dill rice, 188
  enchiladas suizas, 284
  -herb filling for ravioli, 250–1
  potato roulade, Italian, 254–5

spinach (cont.)
  salad, 139
  soufflé, 123
  soup, 63
  stewed eggplant, 167
split pea soup, 55, 70
sponge cake, 324
spumoni cake, 330
squash and tomato stew, 164, 168;
    see also zucchini
stew
  mushroom, 165
    with potatoes in wine sauce, 171
  squash and tomato, 168
  vegetable
    Spanish style, 272–3, 274
    with anise and lemon juice, 170
    winter, 166
strawberry(ies)
  filled cantaloupe salad, 160
  jam, 366–7
  mousse, frozen, 351
  water, 297
strudel, apple, 336–7
stuffed potato pancakes, 102
sweet coffee bread, 23, 41
sweet Finnish rusks, 51
sweet pastry crust, 326
sweet potato
  -cranberry quiche, 217
  soup, 66–7
sweet and sour stuffed cabbage balls,
    164, 184–5
Swiss cheese
  asparagus crêpes, 227–8
  leek and tomato quiche, 214
  Mornay sauce, 99
  pimiento and olive quiche, 215

Swiss cheese *(cont.)*
    potato gnocchi, 252
    wild mushroom crêpe cake, 230–1

tacos, 279
    avocado, 289
    bean and potato, 288
tamarind and raisin chutney, 317
tapas, 11, 261–3
    Barcelona white bean salad, 266
    champiñónes a la plancha, 268
    roasted eggplant and peppers in
      oil, 267
    stewed garbanzo beans, 267
Taratour sauce, 105
tarts
    apple, 340–1
    savory Mexican cheese, 295
    shell for, 213
Teflon, 124
tomatillos, 281
    chilaquiles, 290–2
    enchiladas salsa verde, 287
tomato(es)
    baked eggplant, 249
    baked stuffed, 182
    catsup, 371–72
    -cheese pie, 216–17
    chilaquiles, 290–2
    chutney, 373
      with apple, 373
    gratinéed, 257
    -leek quiche, 214–15
    Mexican rice, 296
    omelet provençale, 128
    peppers with cheese, 292
    purée of scorched, 309

tomato(es) *(cont.)*
  raita, 313
  sauce, 97
    with garlic, lima beans in, 153
    hot, 104
    pizza, 218
    simple, 102
  -smoked cheese sandwiches, 381
  soup
    chilled, with cantaloupe, 84
    with garlic, 64
    gazpacho, 86, 87
    -squash stew, 168
    stuffed with hearts of palm, 154
  torte(s); *see* cakes
  tortillas; *see also* enchiladas; tacos
    Mexican
      basic recipe, 282–4
      chilaquiles, 290–2
      press, 283
    Spanish (omelets)
      asparagus, 271
      eggplant, 269–70
      española, 246, 268
      a la paisana, 270–1
      soup, 55, 66
  tortitas con queso, 295
  turmeric, 299

Ukrainian cuisine
  stewed eggplant, 169
uppama, 316

vareniki, 191, 200–201
vegetables; *see also* names of
    vegetables

vegetables *(cont.)*
  curry
    with coconut, 302
    green, 308
  dressings for, 106
  farina with spices and, 316
  fritters (*pakoras*), 318
  pasta with, 242
  pilau, 312
  profiterole filling, 209
  sauces for, 100, 102, 103, 107
  soup, 61, 62
    broth, 57–8
    cocido, 275–6
    puréed (*crema de verduras*), 82
  stew
    in anise and lemon sauce, 170
    Spanish style, 272
    winter, 166
    tortilla a la paisana, 270–1
vegetarian cooking, 7–21
  meal planning and service, 7–9
  menus, 10–21
  timing, 9
Vienna bread, 23, 28
vinaigrette sauce, 97

walnut(s)
  -broccoli soufflé, 116
  crêpes, Hungarian, 354
  eggplant with cheese and, 185–6
  mushrooms stuffed with eggplant,
    183
watercress
  -cream cheese sandwiches, 384
  -green bean salad, 138–9
  soup, 81

Wenia's *mazurek*, 332–3
whisk, 93
white bean(s)
    pâté, 195
    salad, 146
        Barcelona, 266
white sauce, 95
whole wheat bread, 23
    anadama, 29
    braided egg, 27
wild mushrooms
    crêpe cake, 230
    and dill, soufflé, 118–19
        sauce for, 101

wine, 93
    oranges in, 356
    peaches in, 356
    sauce, mushrooms and potatoes
        in, 171
wooden spoons, 93, 95
Worcestershire sauce, 67*n*

yeast bread(s), *see* bread
yeast *pierogi*, 220–1
yogurt-carrot soup, 79; *see also*
        raitas

zucchini
    avocado-stuffed, 156
    baked stuffed tomatoes, 182
    -eggplant roulade, 177–8
    frittata of, 258
    -potato omelets, 127
    salad
        insalatone, 148
        Torcoloti, 137
    soufflé, 122
zuppa inglese, 331–2

a note about the author

Born in Stuttgart, Germany, in 1948, Anna Thomas came to this country as a child. After graduating from UCLA she continued to study for several years there in the film department. Her first book, *The Vegetarian Epicure*, was written during that period, both out of the need to support herself as a young film-maker and to provide herself and her friends with a more exciting repertoire of vegetarian recipes than had ever been collected before. The phenomenal success of that book has enabled Anna Thomas to further her career as a writer, producer, and director of films (she has recently finished her first feature film, shot in Scotland), and to expand her culinary horizons through much travel, tasting, and testing of new recipes. In 1975 she married a film producer with whom she has collaborated, and they make their home in Los Angeles.

a note about the type

The text of this book was set in Musica, a film version of Optima, a typeface designed by Hermann Zapf from 1952–55 and issued in 1958. In designing Optima, Zapf created a truly new type form—a cross between the classic roman and a sans-serif face. So delicate are the stresses and balances in Optima that it rivals sans-serif faces in clarity and freshness and old-style faces in variety and interest.

The book was composed by Superior Printing, Champaign, Illinois; printed and bound by American Book–Stratford Press, Saddle Brook, New Jersey; and designed by Carole Lowenstein and Karolina Harris.